Philosophy and Its Epistemic Neuroses

Philosophy and Its Epistemic Neuroses

Michael Hymers

Routledge
Taylor & Francis Group
LONDON AND NEW YORK

First published 2000 by Westview Press

Published 2019 by Routledge
52 Vanderbilt Avenue, New York, NY 10017
2 Park Square, Milton Park, Abingdon, Oxon OX14 4RN

Routledge is an imprint of the Taylor & Francis Group, an informa business

Copyright © 2000 by Taylor & Francis

All rights reserved. No part of this book may be reprinted or reproduced or utilised in any form or by any electronic, mechanical, or other means, now known or hereafter invented, including photocopying and recording, or in any information storage or retrieval system, without permission in writing from the publishers.

Notice:
Product or corporate names may be trademarks or registered trademarks, and are used only for identification and explanation without intent to infringe.

Library of Congress Cataloging-in-Publication Data
Hymers, Michael.
　Philosophy and its epistemic neuroses / Michael Hymers.
　　p. cm.
　Includes bibliographical references and index.
　ISBN 0-8133-9137-7
　1. Skepticism.　2. Knowledge, Theory of.　I. Title.
BD201.H95　1999
149'.73—dc21　　　　　　　　　　　　　　　　　　　　　　　　　　99-37918
　　　　　　　　　　　　　　　　　　　　　　　　　　　　　　　　　　　CIP
ISBN 13: 978-0-367-28285-1 (hbk)
ISBN 13: 978-0-367-29831-9 (pbk)

*In memory of my mother,
Phyllis (Kaiser) Hymers*

Contents

Acknowledgments   xi

Introduction: Philosophy and Neurosis   1
Notes, 11

1   *The "External" World*   12
Two Kinds of Realism Conflated, 13
The Same Conflation Again, 15
Real Possibility, 18
Really Possible Worlds, 20
Brains in a Vat, 21
The Modal Consequences, 23
The Interactive Conception, 24
Epistemic Neurosis, 26
Notes, 33

2   *Internal Relations*   36
Some History, 37
The *Philosophical Remarks*, 38
The *Philosophical Grammar*, 39
Wittgenstein's Later Writings, 41
A New Picture, 42
Quine's Critique, 45
A New Picture of Analyticity, 46
Necessity and Revisability, 49
Notes, 53

3   *Truth and Reference*   57
Correspondence Theories of Truth, 58
The Individuation of Facts, 60

Causal Theories of Reference, 63
Putnam's Argument, 66
Objections, 69
Epistemic Neurosis—Again, 74
Notes, 77

4   *Renouncing All Theory* — 80

Epistemic Privilege, 82
Renouncing Theory, 84
The Uses of *True*, 87
"Experience" and Theory, 92
Theories of Knowledge, 97
Notes, 100

5   *Conceptual Schemes* — 103

So-called Relativists, 104
Other Schemes, 108
Incommensurability, 112
Scheme and Content, 113
Radical Interpretation, 115
Other Concepts, 121
Notes, 124

6   *The Ethical-Political Argument* — 127

Nietzsche, Inc., 128
Realism and Scientism Conflated, 133
Each Without the Other, 137
Analytic Philosophy, 139
Marxism, 143
Notes, 148

7   *Realism and Self-knowledge* — 151

Burge's Anti-individualism, 152
A Problem for Burge, 156
Self-knowledge as "Knowing How," 158
Expressivism, 161
Self-ignorance, 164
Notes, 169

8   *Self-knowledge and Self-unity* — 173

The Decentered Subject, 174

Multiple Selves, 180
Agency and False Unities, 184
Unity: Its Possibility, 186
Unity: Its Desirability, 188
Notes, 190

Conclusion: The Rhetoric of Neurosis — 193

Notes, 199

Credits — 201
Reference List — 202
Index — 213

Acknowledgments

Several people read and commented on earlier drafts of this work. I owe special thanks in this connection to Bruce Hunter, who tried to keep me honest. Thanks also to Diane Chisholm, Wes Cooper, Peter Schouls, and Richard Rorty. The present version of this work was made possible by a visiting postdoctoral fellowship from the Calgary Institute for the Humanities, where I spent the 1995–1996 academic year. There I received helpful criticism from Marc Ereshefsky, Tom Hurka, Janet Sisson, and Robert Ware.

Others have been good enough to comment on portions of the text or to discuss related issues with me. They include Guillermo Barron, Bob Bright, Rich Campbell, Robert Kermode, John King-Farlow, Brendan Leier, Tilman Lichter, Bernie Linsky, Steve Maitzen, Bjørn Ramberg, Roger Shiner, Edrie Sobstyl, Matthew Stephens, Martin Tweedale, Tom Vinci, and Jan Zwicky.

I have presented some of this material, as well as related work, at the annual meetings of the Canadian Philosophical Association, and I thank my commentators on those occasions—Don Ainslie, Paul Bernier, Pierre Boulos, Emily Carson, and Rocky Jacobsen—as well as David Davies. Thanks to many of the above and to David Braybrooke, Sue Campbell, Sue Sherwin, Bob Martin, and Catherine Wilson for publishing advice.

Most of Chapter 2 appeared as "Internal Relations and Analyticity: Wittgenstein and Quine" in the *Canadian Journal of Philosophy* (26, no. 4 [1996]: 591–612) and reappears here with permission. The first two sections of Chapter 7 summarize the argument of my "Realism and Self-knowledge: A Problem for Burge," *Philosophical Studies* (86 [1997]: 303–325). Parts of that paper reappear here with kind permission from Kluwer Academic Publishers. Work on both papers was funded by a postdoctoral fellowship from the Social Sciences and Humanities Research Council of Canada.

My thanks also to Sarah Warner and two reviewers at Westview Press. Most of all, I want to thank Kathryn Harvey, who provided last minute help with the index and without whom philosophy would be for me at most a consolation.

Michael Hymers

Introduction:
Philosophy and Neurosis

The philosopher, John Wisdom once wrote, is like the obsessional neurotic who cannot leave his apartment without checking again and again to see whether he has turned off the lights or locked the door. These doubts of the neurotic seem peculiar in much the way that the "doubts" of the philosopher seem peculiar to the nonphilosopher. I speak here of skeptical doubts: Do we have knowledge of the "external" world? Can we have knowledge of other cultures? Can I even know my own mind?

But the philosopher's "doubts" are of not quite the same sort as the neurotic's. The philosopher "entertains" doubts as if they were occasional dinner guests: Though they seem real enough for the duration of the meal, they are not allowed to linger once the party is over. He keeps them from interfering in his nonphilosophical life. By contrast, the neurotic, says Wisdom, is moved to act. As little as he believes that he has left the lights on, he still feels the need go back and check. "The philosopher doesn't," says Wisdom. "His acts and feelings are even less in accordance with his words than are the acts and feelings of the neurotic" (1957, 174). The philosopher, unlike the neurotic, often "doubts" and "worries" in a way that does not directly touch his life—*or his philosophy*.

Is this diagnosis of "the philosopher" correct? If so, what is the etiology of such psycho-philosophical disorder? And is there some course of therapy that might alleviate or resolve it?

The "philosopher"—and I mean this term neither to include all philosophers nor to exempt myself, necessarily—I shall argue, suffers from forms of "epistemic neurosis": She is tempted by philosophical views that, if they are to be expressed, must "entertain" skeptical "doubts." But the philosopher cannot take those doubts seriously, since so honoring the skeptic would undermine all available justification for the very positions that mandate the validity of those doubts. With such doubts always about, philosophy can get no peace—it is "tormented by questions which bring *itself* in question," questions that may "leave no room for the rational activity of philosophy" (Putnam 1981, 113). The philosopher's difficulty is not simply that, like Hume, he cannot take his views seriously when he leaves the study, but that he cannot quite take them seriously while he is still in the study either.

An important source of the philosopher's temptation in such matters, I shall maintain, is a commitment to the idea that philosophy must provide explanatory theories about its objects of inquiry—theories of truth, theories of reference, theories of knowledge, and so on. Epistemic neurosis is a predictable malady of those who succumb to this assumption, for it induces a compulsion to think of the objectivity of the world as something that is to be defined in relation to the scenarios of the external-world skeptic, and it encourages the application of a similar conception of objectivity to normative notions like truth and reference.

The therapy appropriate to such a disorder consists partly in painting a picture of an alternative, uncolored by the hue of objectivity that characterizes the neurosis, and partly in bringing the philosopher's substantive assumptions about the perceived explanatory tasks of philosophy to consciousness wherever an epistemic neurosis shows its influence. This philosophical compulsion must face the "slow cure" (Wittgenstein 1981, §382) of critique.

In a compelling critique of traditional epistemology (both foundationalist and coherentist varieties), Michael Williams has argued that we must distinguish between two different kinds of diagnostic critique in philosophy: therapeutic and theoretical (1996c, 31–40). A therapeutic diagnosis of skeptical doubts, he argues, tries to silence those doubts by showing that "the skeptic doesn't or can't mean what he seems to mean, perhaps even that he does not succeed in meaning anything at all" (32). Such therapy, he objects, can never be convincing to the skeptic, or to those who have no doubts about the intelligibility of the skeptic's concerns, because it rests on "intuitions about meaningfulness" that are "highly controversial, hence far more open to question . . . than our pre-theoretical sense that we understand the skeptic very well" (36f.). A theoretical diagnosis, by contrast, tries to redistribute the burden of proof onto the shoulders of the skeptic by showing that skeptical doubts are "unnatural doubts"—that is, by showing that these doubts rest on controversial theoretical assumptions about knowledge and are not the inevitable outcome of philosophical reflection on our quotidian epistemic practices. There is nothing unintelligible about skeptical doubt, but it matters only if the skeptic's theoretical baggage need be carried in order to arrive at a clear understanding of our prereflective attitudes toward knowledge.

Williams's distinction should not be thought of as a firm one. For one thing, as I shall argue in Chapter 1, the therapeutic philosopher can concede that the skeptic's doubts are intelligible in the sense that they violate no laws of logic. What are contentious are the claims that the skeptic's scenarios would be explanatory of our experience as of a world beyond our senses and that, if we were deluded in the way that the skeptic suggests, we could say that we were so deluded. If the philosophical therapist is right in saying that meaning and truth are not appropriate objects of any theory, then it does follow (as we shall see in Chapter 1) that what the skeptic is trying to say really cannot be said, unless it is false. The mistake lies in construing this as an attempt to *refute* the skeptic, which it cannot be, given that it relies on empirical premises that the skeptic will call into doubt.

I also think that proponents of traditional epistemology are no less likely to find Williams's alternative theses about knowledge controversial than they are the therapist's "intuitions about meaningfulness." One of Williams's central claims is that our "knowledge of the external world" (1996c, xii) is not a proper object for theoretical explanation. The category "knowledge," we could say, is more like the category "chair" or "letter opener" than it is like the categories "acid" or "beta radiation"—it is not the name of a natural kind, but of an artifact.[1] But this is precisely the kind of claim that the therapist wants to make about categories like "truth" and "reference" as well. And it is the validity of this claim—that truth and reference do not pick out natural kinds—that supports my therapeutic diagnosis of philosophical views that "entertain" skeptical doubts. So, unless Williams can find a way of showing that knowledge requires no explanatory theory and yet truth does, I doubt that he can sustain the firm independence of his theoretical critique from the kind of therapeutic critique about which he has reservations.[2]

The view I present here draws significantly on the later work of Ludwig Wittgenstein. This is most true of the attitudes toward objectivity and meaning central to my arguments. But it also holds of the metaphors of neurosis and therapy, which give thematic unity to the issues I confront. In his *Philosophical Investigations* Wittgenstein makes some difficult remarks about the proper nature and task of philosophy. Among them is the following passage, which I quote at length:

> It is not our aim to refine or complete the system of rules for the use of our words in unheard-of ways.
>
> For the clarity that we are aiming at is indeed *complete* clarity. But this simply means that the philosophical problems should *completely* disappear.
>
> The real discovery is the one that makes me capable of stopping doing philosophy when I want to.—The one that gives philosophy peace, so that it is no longer tormented by questions which bring *itself* in question.—Instead, we now demonstrate a method, by examples; and the series of examples can be broken off.—Problems are solved (difficulties eliminated), not a *single* problem.
>
> There is not *a* philosophical method, though there are indeed methods, like different therapies. (1968, §133)

"The philosopher's treatment of a question," he says later, "is like the treatment of an illness" (§255), and elsewhere he stresses the importance of providing a "*slow* cure" for "a disease of thought" (1981, §382).

In some ways my efforts fall short of the philosophical therapy Wittgenstein recommends. I lack his clarity and simplicity of style (not to mention his insight), and it is not easy for my argument to be "broken off," since it relies less on examples and more on engagement with other philosophical texts. (But this, too, as writers like Richard Rorty and Stanley Cavell have shown, can be therapeutic.) Moreover, there is a sense in which I take myself to be pursuing a "single problem" that manifests itself in different contexts. But what needs to be emphasized about my approach, as it needs to be emphasized about Wittgenstein's, is that thinking of philosophy as a kind of therapy does not comprise what some have termed a therapeutic "farewell to philosophy" (Habermas 1987b, 306). Nothing in the idea of therapy need imply the desirability of abandoning philosophy. Philosophical problems, like the real neuroses to which I compare some of them, have seldom been, and need never be, in short supply, though they may change with historical and cultural circumstances. The philosophical therapist need not claim to have "attained nirvana," as Michael Dummett has disparagingly suggested (1996, 16),[3] though, like most philosophers, he or she does claim to be right, however fallible.

Exactly what I find important about the problems I take up here is the persistent attraction of the views I criticize, the scientistic attraction—which I feel myself—in thinking that truth and knowledge are fit objects of explanatory theories. The "real discovery," the discovery "that gives philosophy peace," is the one that lets us approach philosophical questions without being led into the philosophically neurotic, self-defeating ways that spring, for example, from a metaphysical picture of objectivity or from trying to give "theories" of meaning and truth as though they were the objects of some *science*. Only when thinking does not rely on "doubts" that undermine philosophy itself can we deal properly with the philosophical questions that remain, and only then can we "break off" our list of examples, so that philosophical dispute does not "go on too long" (Wisdom 1957, 178), without worrying that an ultimate ground of warrant might have been found, if only we had world enough and time.

When Wittgenstein tells us that therapeutic philosophy "leaves everything as it is" (1968, §124), he is not proposing an uncritical quietism, as Jürgen Habermas seems to suggest (1987b, 306), or worse, as Herbert Marcuse complained, an "academic sado-masochism, self-humiliation, and self-denunciation of the intellectual whose labor does not issue in scientific, technical or like achievements" (1964, 173).[4] He is simply denying that there is a hidden essence of language awaiting discovery by the scientifically minded philosopher, and that there is any need or possibility of replacing our actual words and expressions with a pure, logical language that could sustain meaning apart from our possible interests and practices. Such complaints do not do justice to the critiques of scientism and essentialism in Wittgenstein's later writings. Indeed, I think it would not be utterly amiss to view that work as a contribution to critical theory in much the sense upheld by thinkers like Marcuse and Max Horkheimer, though it does not wear such credentials on its sleeve.[5]

It is not my chief task to interpret Wittgenstein's philosophy, but to the extent that I draw on his work I want to insist on like *provisos* for my interests in the therapeutic aspect of philosophy. And although the present work is not primarily a work of radical theory either, its undertones will be clear enough. Like Horkheimer's "critical theorist," I doubt that "social reality and its products" are "extrinsic" to philosophical work and that such matters belong solely to the sphere of "political articles, membership in political parties or social service organizations, and participation in elections" (1982, 209). As Alasdair MacIntyre says, "All philosophy, one way or another, is political philosophy" (1987, 398). Part of what I want to achieve, even as I focus on the work of mainstream philosophers influenced by the analytical tradition of the twentieth century, is a clarification of concepts and problems that have an important role to play in radical theory. This aspect of my position is most evident in Chapters 6 and 8.

My investigation will fall roughly into three parts, in which knowledge of the "external" world, knowledge of other cultures, and knowledge of ourselves will, respectively, provide the foci of discussion. Each of these aspects of human knowledge is a site of skeptical "doubt" and, so, a likely locus at which to encounter some form of epistemic neurosis.

In Chapter 1, I examine Hilary Putnam's ostensibly antiskeptical argument against the possibility that we are now and always have been brains in a vat. The argument is best understood not, as most commentators have assumed, as an attempt to refute the skeptic, but as a means of illustrating the differences between two kinds of realism that are often conflated: metaphysical realism and modest realism. The former variety treats the skeptic's scenarios not merely as consistent logical possibilities, but as real possibilities—possibilities whose actuality would explain our experience as of a world beyond our senses. The modest realist rejects this thesis, but she concedes happily that the world is independent of our knowledge of it in the sense that our knowledge claims are sometimes mistaken and that the world could have existed much as it does without there ever having been any epistemic agents to be right or wrong about it. The metaphysical realist's views are prone to epistemic neurosis, because his position is defined by reference to skeptical doubt, but he is epistemically justified in advancing none of the other philosophical theses that he typically wants to advance, unless he can refute the skeptic. Consequently, he is often tempted to dismiss external-world skepticism as a mere logical possibility, even though it is central to his own view that such skepticism be treated as a real possibility. This concurrent need to admit and deny a thesis, especially a skeptical one, is characteristic of what I call "epistemic neurosis."

Putnam's argument also implicitly relies on an important claim about reference—namely, that reference is paradigmatically an *internal* relation between word and object, in the sense that a competent speaker cannot understand the standard use of a referring term without also understanding what its referent is. A failure to recognize that Putnam depends on this "interactive conception" of reference ("interactive" because it places the speaker squarely in the world of spatio-temporal objects and persons) has led many critics to object that Putnam shows only that if we had always been brains in a vat, then we could not knowingly say so. But such a criticism itself turns on a substantive assumption about reference—namely, that it is an *external* relation between word and object such that I might understand the use of a referring term, but not understand what its referent is. A popular version of this assumption is the claim that reference can be reduced to causal relations of some sort. However, the metaphysical realist is not entitled to any such empirical theory of reference until the skeptic has been refuted. So this attempted criticism of Putnam is an additional symptom of epistemic neurosis.

Putnam's reliance on an "interactive" conception of reference—one that treats reference as an internal relation between word and object—draws our attention to a crucial distinction for the philosophical therapist: the distinction between concepts that are appropriate objects for explanatory theories and concepts that are not. But the notion of an internal relation may itself sound suspect to the pragmatically inclined ear that has taken in W. V. Quine's critique of the analytic-synthetic distinction. Thus, in Chapter 2, I consider the idea of an internal relation in greater detail, examining the development of the notion in Wittgenstein's work from the *Tractatus* to his later writings.[6] I argue that in Wittgenstein's transitional and later work there emerges a picture of internal relations that possesses four interesting features: (1) it treats such relations as obtaining between "instruments of language," including words, but also, for example, gestures, facial expressions, and spatio-temporal objects used as paradigms; (2) it does not entail that all propositions expressing internal relations must be analytic; (3) it allows some distinction to be drawn between the analytic and the synthetic; and (4) it does so in a way that is largely compatible with Quine's critique, except where that critique is led off the rails by Quine's scientistic outlook. That scientistic viewpoint, as we shall see, expresses itself precisely in a failure to distinguish between concepts that are appropriate objects for explanatory theories and concepts that are not.

Chapter 3 holds up causal theories of reference and the correspondence theory of truth, which they are invoked to support, for closer examination. Causal theories derive much of their attraction, I argue, from their apparent ability to deal with a number of traditional problems that plagued classical versions of the correspondence theory of truth, especially the latter's inability to provide any clear means of individuating the "facts" or "states of affairs" that are alleged to make true statements true. However, causal theories prove to be epistemically neurotic in themselves, precisely because (1) they treat reference as an external relation, in the sense clarified in Chapter 2, and (2) they treat that external relation as an explanatory relation—explanatory of truth. This, I argue, is the real point of another of Putnam's arguments, his "model-theoretic" argument against the correspondence theory of truth. What this argument shows is just that by treating reference as an explanatory notion, the causal theorist paves the way for skeptical doubts about our knowledge of the reference of our terms. The very activity of theory building undermines itself when an internal relation is treated as an external one.

In supposing that reference and truth are fit objects of explanatory theories, the philosopher is automatically committed to drawing a distinction between the phenomena to be explained by such a theory—phenomena that are taken for granted—and the hypotheses that would serve to explain those phenomena. (Or, in the language of the inductivist, he or she must distinguish between the evidence, which is taken for granted, and the conclusions that such evidence might be taken to support inductively.) Treating reference as an external relation—thinking that I can understand the use of a referring term without knowing what it refers to—is thus an unavoidable methodological commitment of all explanatory theories of reference, and of contemporary correspondence theories of truth that hope to explain truth by recourse to a theory of reference. To treat reference as an internal relation is thus to eschew all explanatory theories of truth and reference and also to abandon the skeptical doubts that they incur.

In Chapter 4, I generalize this principle to include the doubts of the external-world skeptic. To treat some phenomenon as an appropriate object of an explanatory theory is to place that phenomenon in an external relation of epistemic priority over the real possibilities whose actuality would explain it. When internal relations are misconstrued as such external, explanatory relations, skeptical problems quickly ensue. The root of the metaphysical realist's overgrown conception of objectivity, then, is a commitment to the view that the philosopher should be in the business of providing explanatory theories. In particular, by regarding the scenarios of the external-world skeptic as real possibilities, the metaphysical realist expresses a commitment to traditional epistemology's theoretical explanations of knowledge and of experience of the so-called external world in general. And this is to treat mind and world, knower and known, as related only externally. If, on the contrary, we suppose that we are internally related to the world in our experience of it, then we must conclude that we can have no knowledge of our own experience without knowing something of the world around us. This is to join Michael Williams in holding that "knowledge of the external world" is an inappropriate object for theoretical explanation.

In this chapter I also consider why philosophers are so tempted to give explanatory theories of truth and knowledge, taking Putnam's erstwhile obsession with a "substantive" notion of truth as my example. Though such theories can be either metaphysical or naturalistic, in these scientistic days it is the latter variety that bears the mark of respectability. An important source of our desire for such theories is our sense that truth and knowledge are phenomena with hidden natures. But our initial difficulty in answering questions like "What is truth?" arises from the fact, which Wittgenstein emphasized, that we learn to use such concepts in extremely complicated contexts that we do not, however, learn to describe in any satisfying way. This suggests that the proper way of alleviating our puzzlement in the face of such questions is to try to get a better grasp on the contexts in which words like *truth* and *knowledge* and the concepts of experience are taught and learned.

Having diagnosed a recurrent cause of epistemic neurosis in the desire for theoretical explanations of nontheoretical notions, I turn in Chapter 5 to our knowledge of other cultures. Here I focus on critics of metaphysical realism who are often attracted to various forms of relativism. Would-be relativists, such as Barry Barnes, David Bloor, Barbara Herrnstein Smith, and Paul Feyerabend, I argue, are frequently less deeply committed to relativism than their own rhetoric might lead us to believe. Many of their arguments and clarifications suggest a position akin to the modest realism that I counsel. But thinkers can be tempted by relativism for three main reasons: (1) the perceived failure of the strong objectivist's theories of truth and knowledge can be readily taken as a sign that some other theory of truth and knowledge is needed, if one has not joined the philosophical therapist in eschewing traditional epistemology and truth theory; (2) the apparent plausibility of conceptual relativism, the idea of alternative "conceptual schemes," seems to offer a way of making sense of the epistemic relativist's claim that truth is relative to cultures or communities; and (3) a perceived association of objectivist epistemologies and scientism with inter- and intracultural intolerance can make talk of truth, knowledge, and objectivity appear as though it were unavoidably linked with power and oppression.

Considering the second of these motivations, I argue that conceptual relativism, far from being a way of overcoming the disorders of metaphysical realism, itself suffers from much the same problems. The conceptual relativist holds that different cultures possess different, incommensurable "conceptual schemes" that carve up the world into different ontologies and accompanying sets of ontology-relative truths, such that the holders of one scheme may be unable in principle to comprehend the holders of another. Offering a novel reinterpretation of Donald Davidson's arguments against conceptual relativism, I show that the doctrine of conceptual schemes recapitulates the assumptions of strong objectivism and causal theories of reference. First, this doctrine turns on the premise that concepts are only externally related to their empirical "content" so that the same content—whether it be called "experience" or "the world" or "reality"—can be organized by different sets of concepts and identified independently of having applied any particular set of concepts to it. However, if it is the same content that is differently organized, then holders of different concepts would seem to have a basis for mutual interpretation and understanding. Second, the assertion that the holders of one scheme might be incomprehensible to the holders of another turns on the premise that the reference of a referring term is only externally related to its use. We might, that is, be able to trace the linguistic behavior of others well enough to determine that they express their beliefs by making statements that possess truth-values without ever being able to say what things they refer to—what ontology they possess. The conceptual relativist thus proves to be a strong objectivist at heart, for her position simply applies the metaphysical realist's skeptical conception of objectivity to conceptual schemes.

In Chapter 6, I return to the would-be relativist's third source of temptation, the "ethical-political argument." According to this line of reasoning, often recognized by critics of relativism but seldom examined in any detail, realism and terms like *knowledge, truth,* and *objectivity* are bound up with the discourse of power and oppression, and morally or politically progressive thought should eschew such concepts. Although the relativist who endorses this argument may have laudable goals, her reasoning, I argue, conflates metaphysical realism with modest realism, and both of these, in turn, with scientism. These conflations, I suggest, are an understandable reaction to the scientism that is often present both in analytical philosophy and in varieties of Marxist theory. In both cases, however, the links between realism and scientism must be regarded as historically contingent. Indeed, one might be an epistemic relativist and still endorse scientism. So the best response to scientism is to forego the search for explanatory, scientific theories of nonexplanatory, nonscientific concepts like truth and knowledge.

The therapeutic philosopher's claim that mind and world are internally related, so that I cannot understand my own mind without understanding something of the world around me, is a version of what Tyler Burge has called psychological "anti-individualism," the view that the nature and classification of an individual's intentional phenomena depend on certain aspects of her environment. However, in Chapter 7, I show that my anti-individualism is not like the anti-individualism advocated by Burge. Burge's view is premised on construing the relation between mind and world as an external one. He is not only an anti-individualist, but a metaphysical realist, and this makes it difficult for him to account for "first-person authority": the special justification that a person has when making claims about her own intentional attitudes. If I can be completely mistaken about the world that determines the contents of my intentional attitudes, then it seems that I can be completely mistaken about those attitudes too. According to Burge, the difficulty is to be solved by weakening the "Cartesian" account of first-person authority. The Cartesian, he claims, is correct to maintain that I am authoritative about my actual intentional phenomena and that in counterfactual situations I would be authoritative about my intentional phenomena in those situations, but wrong to think that I am *actually* authoritative about my intentional phenomena in counterfactual situations. Relinquishing this third requirement, he argues, lets us reconcile first-person authority with anti-individualism.

I show, on the contrary, that an adequate understanding of external-world skepticism and metaphysical realism presupposes the Cartesian's third requirement. Burge cannot avoid posing a threat to the special justification that attaches to paradigmatic claims of self-knowledge. Making sense of both first-person authority and anti-individualism requires that we be modest realists, eschewing the real possibility of external-world skepticism and treating mind and world as related internally.

First-person authority is then better accounted for by embellishing on Davidson's view that part of being a competent speaker is knowing what intentional attitudes one's own words express. It is my ability to use language that justifies my self-knowledge claims. By contrast, I can be a competent language user and have very little idea concerning what another thinks and feels. However, Davidson overstates the role of interpretation in my understanding of the utterances of another. Some of our knowledge of each other is direct and unmediated, and this shows that the asymmetry of justification between self- and other-knowledge is characterized by an additional dimension: Many first-person utterances of psychological predicates are *expressive*—they serve not as reports about the speaker, but as extensions of nonverbal, expressive behavior like crying, grimacing, smiling, and sighing. To hold such a view, I argue, is not to commit oneself to the claim that *all* first-person uses of psychological words are expressive, nor to the claim that expressive uses cannot be truth-apt.

Such mitigated expressivism is also compatible with acknowledging the possibility and importance of what I call "Socratic" self-knowledge and its opposite, self-ignorance. But some, including Davidson, have thought that such self-ignorance requires some kind of self-division, and literary theorists and radical philosophers have made much of the notion of a "fragmented subject," even to the point of celebrating fragmentation as a potential source of resistance to oppression and ideology. So I conclude with Chapter 8, in which I consider how a therapeutic outlook might affect our understanding of self-unity. Critically examining the views of Louis Althusser, Jacques Lacan, and Maria C. Lugones, I argue that regarding an individual as a competent language user requires attributing to her a certain minimal degree of self-unity—a "grammatical unity of self-description," I call it—which consists in the ability to make judgments about one's prior judgments and expressive utterances. Critics, such as Lugones, who fear that self-unity amounts to identification by the oppressed with the self-descriptions provided them by their oppressors really fear a false unity that depends crucially on self-ignorance, and talk of the value of multiplicity implicitly gestures at a kind of self-knowledge: the *recognition* of one's multiplicity. Asking whether any further unity of the self is desirable reduces to asking whether particular kinds of self-descriptions are desirable for the person to whom they are applied. Although there is no argument to show that self-unity is always a good or that knowledge is always better than ignorance, there is good reason to suppose that its absence can certainly be a harm. Indeed, the prima facie value of self-unity is presupposed in my portrayal of the views of theoretical philosophers as undesirable because epistemically neurotic.

I do not regard the positions I criticize here as simple errors of careless thinkers. I think there is an understandable attraction toward the opposed views I examine, an attraction extending beyond the fuzzy boundaries of philosophy to other academic disciplines, and beyond the fuzzy boundaries of the academy as well. Philosophy, in this instance, as in others, reflects its cultural circumstances

Introduction: Philosophy and Neurosis

at the same time as it contributes to them. I also believe that, as a result of this cultural embeddedness, the debates explored below are ones that, as Putnam says, "we seem doomed to repeat ... (like a neurotic symptom), unless, perhaps, we can step back and offer a better (and deeper) diagnosis of the situation" (1983, 288). To be sure, there is no proxy for practical action in dealing with the contextual features that lead to neuroses—philosophical or genuine—and a better diagnosis is not necessarily a cure. But part of the distinctive character of therapy is that an awareness of the etiology of one's disorder can, under the right description, contribute to a change in one's practice.

Notes

1. Williams (1996c, 106–11) actually thinks that *knowledge of the external world* is best compared to nonreferring theoretical terms like *witch*, but he allows the possibility of the comparison to artifacts that I have chosen here.

2. Williams himself has little sympathy for theoretical treatments of truth. See 1996c, 111–13, 237–47. For related reservations about the therapeutic-theoretical distinction, see Skorupski 1994.

3. Dummett points this epithet at Baker and Hacker, who are not known for the delicacy or charity of their rhetoric, but he adds that Rorty "essentially preaches the same doctrine" (1996, 16). With the interviewer's prompting, he allows that Baker, Hacker, Rorty, and even Hilary Putnam (17) could all be classed as "intruders" on the tradition of analytic philosophy.

4. Crispin Wright complains that the rejection of theoretical treatments of meaning constitutes an embarrassing "quietism" (1992, 202–30). But such quietism has no clear political implications of the sort that I think Habermas has in mind. As John McDowell makes clear, it is no embarrassment to be "quietist" in Wright's sense: "Wittgenstein aims to cast suspicion on an aura of mystery that certain thoughts about meaning acquire in an uncongenial environment.... Wright's mistake is to take it that Wittgenstein means to cast suspicion on such thoughts themselves" (1994, 176).

It has been suggested to me that such views have the effect of "emasculating" philosophy. If philosophy is so gendered that it *can* be emasculated, perhaps this is not such a bad thing—but I would prefer not to analogize the dialectic to the presence or absence of male potency.

5. I spell out a similar claim about Rorty in Hymers 1996b; see Ramberg 1993. Some feminist scholars have tried to forge links with Wittgenstein's work; see, e.g., Lovibond 1983 and Scheman 1983, 1996. Others have drawn connections with pragmatism, broadly construed: Code 1991; Nelson 1990; Heldke 1988; Smith 1988, 1997; and Frye 1983. See also the selections in Alcoff and Potter 1993.

6. The distinction between internal and external relations should not be confused with the distinction between internalism and externalism (or individualism and anti-individualism) with respect to semantic and intentional content. My position is a kind of "externalism" or anti-individualism in the latter sense. See Chapter 7.

1
The "External" World

> *The neurotic may discuss his problems—he may indeed—but he never means business; the discussion is not a means to action, to something other than itself; on the contrary, after a while we get the impression that in spite of his evident unhappiness and desire to come from hesitation to decision he also desires the discussion never to end and dreads its ending. Have you not quite often had this impression with philosophers?—philosophers other than ourselves, for we, of course, are never neurotic.*
>
> —John Wisdom, Philosophy and Psycho-Analysis

What could a diagnosis of the habits of philosophers as "neurotic" amount to, beyond unflattering rhetoric? Wisdom is reluctant to press the comparison with neurosis: "There is a big difference between the philosopher and both the psychotic and the obsessional neurotic," he says, locating that difference in "the flow of justificatory talk, of rationalization, which the philosopher produces when asked why he takes the extraordinary line he does" (1957, 174). Of course, the psychologically disordered sometimes give reasons too—even quite elaborate justifications. But the difference, says Wisdom, is that "we are impressed by the philosopher's talk" (174f.). Even if we are not quite convinced by it, it retains a ring of plausibility that is absent from the reasons we get from the neurotic or the psychotic.

Now, there is a much greater difference than the one Wisdom offers: Neuroses make people miserable, and psychoses destroy people's lives. Philosophy usually does not—though it might on occasion trouble the sleep of the impressionable. Wisdom is well aware of this, describing his encounter with a man who felt compelled to "starve himself and study the Scriptures" (1957, 172). But the point is worth mentioning, so that it will be clear that I do not regard philosophers as people in suffering or as deserving of special sympathy. (Madness is worse than philosophy.) And the only therapy that I recommend—paradoxically—is more philosophy.

We can see better what Wisdom's simile might amount to, I think, if we turn our attention to a real case of "epistemic neurosis"—the attempt to be a metaphysical realist without being a skeptic about the "external" world.

Two Kinds of Realism Conflated

The term *realism* has acquired so many different, at times conflicting, connotations in so many different contexts that it might seem prudent to avoid it altogether. (I shall not exercise such prudence.) *Realism* has at one time or another been used to refer to a view regarding the existence of universals, as a synonym for *materialism* or *physicalism* (in contrast to *idealism*), as a view about the existence of unobservable entities postulated by the sciences (in contrast to *instrumentalism*), as a view in the semantics of natural languages that takes the meaning of a sentence to be given by its truth-conditions, rather than its assertibility-conditions (as is contended by proponents of "antirealism"),[1] and as the related, but distinct, view that the truth-conditions of sentences of natural language in some sense "transcend" our abilities to recognize them.[2]

The sense of realism I have in mind is most closely connected with the realism-idealism contrast. I want to distinguish two kinds of realism that I shall refer to as *metaphysical* realism and *modest* realism, viewing the former with disfavor and the latter with favor. These two kinds of realism diverge precisely over how to interpret the "mind-independence" or "discourse-independence" or "objectivity" of the world, as I explain below. But the approach I shall take here also has consequences for how we should conceive of truth. Part of my contention later (see Chapter 4) will be that truth is an epistemic notion not in the sense that it can be defined or analyzed in terms of epistemic concepts like warrant and justification, but in the sense that its use cannot be understood without an acquaintance with such concepts. There is an internal relation (in a sense to be further specified) between the concept of truth and the concept of justification.

The construal of realism as an epistemic or semantic doctrine has been criticized by Michael Devitt, who has insisted that we "Settle the realism issue before any epistemic or semantic issue" (1997, 4). Realism, in his view, is primarily a metaphysical doctrine, and it should be justified or criticized on those grounds before one turns to any considerations about knowledge or meaning and truth. Michael Dummett, he thinks, is a clear example of someone who has not heeded this advice.

We have Dummett to thank for the "colorless term 'anti-realism'" (1979, 145), though we should not blame him for the reckless abandon with which that term has come to be used. On Dummett's account, antirealism opposes a view called (surprisingly enough) "realism," and realism is, in turn, a view that one can hold of a particular set of statements, for example, statements about theoretical entities, statements about the past or the future, or statements about material objects.

A realist about a class of statements is someone who maintains of those statements that they "possess an objective truth-value, independently of our means of knowing it: they are true or false in virtue of a reality existing independently of us" (146). The antirealist, by contrast, holds of the "disputed" class of statements that their possessing truth-values depends on our "means of knowing" them. Dummett's antirealist "insists . . . that the meanings of these statements are tied directly to what we count as evidence for them, in such a way that a statement of the disputed class, if true at all, can be true only in virtue of something of which we could know and which we should count as evidence for its truth" (146). These descriptions of realism and antirealism run together just the sorts of issues that Devitt thinks ought to be kept quite distinct: epistemic or semantic issues about truth, on the one hand, and metaphysical issues about independently existing reality, on the other.

Devitt, as we have seen, holds that realism is best defined as a doctrine about the "mind-independence" of the world, and that epistemic and semantic questions must be held secondary to a proper account of this independence. But the phrase *mind-independence* is notoriously difficult to make clear. Putnam contends that the sort of independence at issue can be neither causal nor logical, on the ground that no careful opponent of realism is likely to deny either of these modes of independence. "The problem of the inexplicability of metaphysical realism," he proclaims, "simply re-emerges as the problem of the inexplicability of the required notion of 'independence'" (1992b, 355).

However, Devitt is reasonably clear that the sort of independence that he has in mind is, in part, an epistemic independence: "Realism, though largely metaphysical, *is* a little bit epistemic and semantic: the world must be independent of our knowledge of it and of our capacity to refer to it" (1997, 4). Part of what he means by this, I presume, is that what we believe about the world typically neither causes the world to be that way nor entails that the world is that way. Neither does the world's being a certain way usually entail that I believe it to be, though it might often cause me to believe it. Of course, inasmuch as I am part of the world, there are some beliefs that can be causally self-fulfilling. My lack of self-confidence might lead me to believe that I will fail at some task, and this belief might then undermine my chances of success. As well, my believing that I believe something logically guarantees that I do, and the world's being such that I believe that p entails that I believe that p. But my believing that the wolf is at the door neither causes the wolf to be at the door nor entails it.

Such epistemic independence Devitt takes to characterize the notion of objectivity: "To say that an object has objective existence . . . is to say that it is not *constituted by* our knowledge, by our epistemic values, by our capacity to refer to it, by the synthesizing power of the mind, by our imposition of concepts, theories, or languages" (1997, 15). But a commitment to the objectivity of the world, he thinks, is insufficient for realism, because certain forms of idealism share that commitment: "The unsensed sense data of some empiricists, and Kant's pre-conceptualized intuitions, have objective existence in the above sense" (15). Thus, independence for the realist is independence both from our epistemic capacities and from all things "mental," where the latter qualification is intended to be an affirmation of the "material" or "physical" nature of things.[3]

But all this still leaves a difficulty for the idea of "mind-independence." In particular, Devitt's formulation does nothing to distinguish the two ways of interpreting "mind-independence" that I have said separate metaphysical realists from modest realists. They differ in their contrary attitudes toward the vulnerability of our knowledge claims about the world around us to a certain kind of skeptical doubt. Realists of both kinds think that the nature and existence of the world are independent of our epistemic capacities or, better yet, of the *reliability* of those capacities—that is, of the tendency of our cognitive abilities to provide us with true empirical beliefs. But there are two ways in which the world could be so independent.[4]

First, it might simply be that the world could exist much as it does, with trees and shrubs and diatomaceous earth and planetary nebulae, in the absence of human beings and a fortiori in the absence of our epistemic capacities. It is not unusual to believe that it once did so exist, and sober reflection will easily convince many that someday it might so exist once again. Call this view *modest realism*. Modest realism is a view that does not have a great deal of content (hence its "modesty"). The modest realist further believes that we can hold empirical beliefs that are false, but she does not draw the additional conclusion that there is a serious skeptical threat to our knowledge of the world around us. From the mere fact that any given empirical belief might be wrong it does not follow that all our empirical beliefs might be wrong, any more than from the mere fact that some money is counterfeit it follows that all money might be counterfeit.[5]

There is nothing aberrant in referring to the foregoing position as a kind of realism. It is certainly not a variety of idealism. But it is not yet *metaphysical realism*. The metaphysical realist insists that the nature and existence of the world are independent of the reliability of our epistemic capacities in a much stronger sense: Our empirical beliefs might fail quite systematically to represent the world correctly. In other words, the metaphysical realist, but not the modest realist, sees the mind-independence of the world as characterized by our vulnerability to the doubts of the external-world skeptic. (I say "the" external-world skeptic, but there is more than one way to be skeptical about the "external" world, as we shall see shortly.) Of course, as I indicated above, the modest realist allows that we can have false beliefs, but that fact, she insists, does not *entail* that we can be wrong in the encompassing way that the skeptic suggests.

The Same Conflation Again

The link I have suggested between metaphysical realism and skepticism has been made by other philosophers. But in making this link, they have often, like Devitt, run together metaphysical realism (or "strong objectivism," as I shall also sometimes call it) and modest realism. According to Colin McGinn, for example, anyone who adopts a position that "manifestly . . . foreclose[s] the threat of skepticism" is automatically an "anti-realist" (1979, 115).[6] Thomas Nagel writes that "The search for objective knowledge, because of its commitment to a realistic picture, is inescapably subject to skepticism" (1986, 71). Realism, he tells us, can take "two possible forms," namely, "skepticism and objective knowledge," and "The two are intimately bound together" (70f.). There is no distinction here between metaphysical and modest versions of realism, because any deviation from "the realist claims of objectivity" (71) is a lapse into "a form of idealism," which "conflicts with" the idea that "the world is independent of our minds" (90).

David Papineau concurs. Sounding at first like a modest realist, he remarks that "the Cartesian picture of self-intimating 'insides' contrasting with inaccessible 'outsides' shouldn't still be on the philosophical agenda thirty years after Wittgenstein's private language argument and Sellars's attack on givens" (1987, x). Yet he goes on to write:

> Intuitively, realists are philosophers who accept that there is an independent reality which is as it is independently of human judgment. But because they think of reality and judgment as separate in this way, realists think there is always a possibility that our judgments might fail to represent the world as it is. And so realists, unless they are to subside into skepticism . . . will feel that there is a need for us somehow actively to ensure that our beliefs do get the world right. (2)

But subsiding into skepticism is a worry characteristic of metaphysical realism, not modest realism, and the "Cartesian picture of . . . inaccessible 'outsides'" belongs, I suggest, with the former doctrine, not the latter.

Nagel and Papineau are not alone in their treatment of realism. Bernard Williams, in a discussion of Descartes's philosophy, links realism to what he calls the "absolute conception of reality" (1978, 65)—a conception of "the reality which is there 'anyway'" (65): "If knowledge is what it claims to be, then it is knowledge of a reality which exists independently of that knowledge, and indeed . . . independently of any thought or experience. Knowledge is of what is there *anyway*" (64). Reality's "independence" from our knowledge of it—its being there "anyway" —sounds rather like the independence that a modest realist might attribute to the world of spatio-temporal objects. However, Williams glosses it as "the source of the invitation" to skeptical doubt (64), and he insists that it is not Cartesian demands for certainty that issue this invitation (62ff.). It is the very objectivity of the world, in Williams's view, as in Nagel's, that threatens our knowledge of it.

Barry Stroud's excellent book on skepticism offers us a similar picture of objectivity, portraying it as a conception that is already bound up with our everyday practices:

> I think we do have a conception of things being in a certain way quite independently of their being known or believed or said to be that way by anyone. I think the source of the philosophical problem of the external world lies somewhere within just such a conception of an objective world, or in our desire, expressed in terms of that conception, to gain a certain kind of understanding of our relation to the world. But in trying to describe that conception I think I have relied on nothing but platitudes we would all accept. (1984, 82)

In Stroud's view the conception of objectivity that gives rise to skepticism embodies nothing that we are not obliged to accept by our ordinary thinking about our epistemic practices. Nagel agrees: "The possibility of skepticism is built into our ordinary thoughts" (1986, 73). Trying to avoid skepticism and its enabling picture of objectivity would require a massive overhaul of our understanding of ourselves as knowers in an objective world.[7]

There is something to this last claim, insofar as the metaphysical realist's way with objectivity can be linked to what Putnam calls a "God's Eye point of view" (1981, 49). Western culture surely is characterized in part by its openness to such a metaphysical point of view, and maybe that is why skeptical doubts can seem "convincing, or at least exasperating ... to those who come upon them for the first time" (Stroud 1996, 349). But I think that our actual epistemic doings seldom, if ever, rely on deference to such an imagined perspective. All we need in order to draw a distinction between correctness and error is the modest realist's conception of what it means for the nature and existence of the world to be independent of the reliability of our epistemic capacities. If this entails an overhaul in our understanding of ourselves, then perhaps we should consider performing such an overhaul. Perhaps, as Rorty says, citing Sartre, this is merely the sort of thing that happens when "we attempt to draw the full conclusions from a consistently atheist position" (1993, 449).

This allegedly commonplace character of skeptical doubt has recently been isolated by Michael Williams as the starting point for the dialectic between metaphysical realism and skepticism.[8] "As I see it," he writes, "the pre-condition for the success of any response to skepticism is a *shifting of the burden of theory*. We must show that skeptical arguments depend essentially on theoretical commitments that are not forced on us by our ordinary ways of thinking about knowledge, justification and truth" (1996c, 31f.). It seems to me that the metaphysical realist's conception of objectivity and independence is just such a noncompulsory theoretical commitment.[9] Metaphysical realist and skeptic alike are free to argue for it, but it cannot simply be asserted to capture *the* intuitive account of objectivity, when much of that picture can be accounted for by modest realism. I think Stroud's conviction that the skeptic's premises are platitudinous can be sustained only by conflating metaphysical and modest realism. We find Stroud doing so on an earlier page:

> The world around us that we claim to know about exists and is the way it is quite independently of its being known or believed by us to be that way. It is an objective world.... If I do not know what to believe and I ask or wonder whether there any mountains in Africa more than five thousand metres high, my question has an answer which is completely independent of anyone's knowing or believing or being in a position to assert anything. It is quite independent of whether any human or other animate beings have ever existed. (1984, 77)

That the world existed and had certain determinate characteristics before language users existed to describe it constitutes nothing stronger than modest realism. But it is just this picture that Stroud takes to illustrate the "idea of ourselves and of our relation to the world that lies behind the skeptical reasoning" (76)—the conception of an "objective world" that is "the source of the philosophical problem of the external world."

This conflation, I think, plays an influential role in convincing thinkers that they either should or should not be realists. As long as the two kinds of independence on which I have remarked are conflated, metaphysical realism can seem compulsory to the would-be realist. Those with a taste for strong objectivism embrace it; others pull back and turn to varieties of "antirealism" and relativism. It is appropriate, then, that we should consider more carefully the role played by skeptical doubt in distinguishing metaphysical realism from its modest rival. As we shall see, the metaphysical realist cannot help displaying an ambivalent attitude toward the skeptic.

Real Possibility

I said above that metaphysical realism is characterized by its acceptance of a certain vulnerability of our empirical beliefs to the doubts of the external-world skeptic, and, hence, that it can be distinguished from modest realism, which does not allow such vulnerability to skeptical doubt. But there is more than one kind of external-world skeptic and, so, more than one kind of metaphysical realist.

The skeptic about the external world is a philosopher's fiction most closely associated with Descartes.[10] But in Descartes's writings skepticism is inextricably linked with the idea that knowledge is only rightly so called when it meets the demands of certainty. As long as there is a logical possibility that he is massively mistaken about the external world, Descartes, in his role as narrator of the *Meditations*, takes himself to lack the justification that knowledge of the external world requires. "Reason now leads me to think that I should hold back my assent from opinions which are not completely certain and indubitable" (1984, 2:12). Only such radical doubt, he thinks, will enable him to find a firm foundation on which to build "anything at all in the sciences that [is] stable and likely to last" (12).

However, among philosophers in the English-speaking world it is generally held, I think, that certainty is not a necessary condition for knowledge. Most "analytic" philosophers subscribe to some version of *fallibilism*. According to this view, I need not be certain that my belief is true before it can count as knowledge, merely justified in so thinking. It is enough (to know that which I take myself to know) that I have a true belief and that I have a good reason for thinking it to be true.[11] For the fallibilist the mere logical possibility that I might be in the clutches of Descartes's evil demon, or that I might always have been a disembodied brain receiving artificial neuronal stimulation while I float in a vat of nutrient solution, amounts to little more than an intellectual curio. Such possibilities pose no threat to my epistemic justification, because I do not have to rule out every logical possibility whose actuality would be incompatible with my knowing in order to know that which I take myself to know.[12]

How then are we to express the vulnerability to skeptical doubt that I have said typifies metaphysical realism? It is tempting to say that the skeptic is trying to raise an *epistemic* possibility in the following sense: It is logically compatible with everything I know that I am right now a brain in a vat and always have been. However, the skeptic is entitled to treat her challenge as an epistemic possibility of this sort, only if she presupposes that I do not know that I am not a brain in a vat. If the skeptic's hypothesis is meant as an epistemic possibility of this sort, then it begs the question.[13] So, this kind of constraint will not quite do.

Still, the suggestion that epistemic considerations play a role in the sense of "possibility" relevant to the skeptic's scenarios is correct. Those considerations just enter more obliquely than was suggested above. What matters for the skeptic, I think, is, first, that the actualization of skeptical scenarios is logically compatible with my regularly and predictably seeming to say and do the many things that I do seem to say and do in a regular and predictable world and, second, that those scenarios, if true, would be *explanatory* of my seeming interaction with a world beyond my senses.[14]

The external-world skeptic, then, is presenting us with what purports to be an explanatory possibility. She assumes that I have knowledge of my intentional phenomena,[15] and she casts doubt on the hypothesis that the best explanation for my intentional phenomena is that I am in epistemic contact with a world beyond my senses.[16] That I have always been a brain in a vat, she claims, is as good an explanation for my intentional phenomena. And, she continues, if two rival hypotheses provide equally good explanations for a certain class of phenomena, then I am no more justified in believing one than in believing the other. If knowledge of the "external" world requires that the external-world hypothesis have superior justification, then I cannot correctly claim to have knowledge of a world beyond my senses.

The kind of possibility that is relevant to external-world skepticism is an explanatory possibility—more particularly a possibility that is explanatory of some phenomenon or phenomena, knowledge of which is already assumed. I shall call this species of possibility "real possibility."[17] Real possibility imposes a constraint beyond those imposed by logical possibility: All real possibilities are logical possibilities, but not all logical possibilities are real ones. Real possibility is also a relative notion; it is relative to the phenomena that are assumed as known. A real possibility relative to the sublimation of solids to gases need not be a real possibility relative to the "red-shifting" of spectra from distant galaxies. A possibility that would explain one phenomenon need not explain another, though that possibility's actualization could easily be compatible with phenomena that it does not explain.[18]

Really Possible Worlds

It will be useful for my purposes to express some of these features of real possibility by resorting to the figure of possible worlds.[19] That idiom can lend itself to extravagant metaphysical speculation.[20] So it is important for me to make clear that I do not regard such talk with any ontological seriousness, and I certainly do not assume that our commonplace modal talk is given any sort of analysis or explanation by logical formulae that quantify over things called "worlds."[21] I prefer to see possible-worlds talk as a metaphorical extension of our commonplace modal talk, an extension that can be clarificatory if used wisely. My message to my readers, then, is dual. To metaphysical realists: Please do not mistake me for a "modal realist." To modest realists: Please bear with me—this won't take long.[22]

I shall stipulate then that a really possible world is one at which some real possibility obtains, and such a world is characterized by that possibility. Put another way, if a real possibility is a possibility whose actuality would explain some given phenomenon of which we are assumed to have knowledge, then a really possible world is one at which that given phenomenon occurs and is so explained. (Remember that I am not trying to analyze the notion of real possibility—*really possible world* is a mere *façon de parler*, and possibility is a primitive notion.) Because real possibility imposes additional constraints beyond those imposed by logical possibility, the really possible worlds compose a subset of the logically possible worlds. But real possibility is a context-relative kind of modality, and what counts as a really possible world likewise depends on context. A world is really possible only relative to some phenomenon of which knowledge is assumed, and it is really possible only if the given phenomenon occurs at that world and is explained by the possibility that characterizes that world.

The notion of real possibility is neither synonymous nor coextensive with that of physical possibility (compatibility with the laws of physics). Gordon Brittan, in an explication of Kant's category of the synthetic a priori, treats really possible worlds as though they were always physically possible worlds (1978, 20–24). But because the really possible varies from context to context in the picture that I have sketched, I propose that we take the set of really possible worlds to intersect with the set of physically possible worlds. On one hand, there are really possible worlds that are not physically possible, for it is plausible that many phenomena with which we are acquainted could still occur in a world with different physical laws. On the other hand, there are physically possible worlds that are not really possible relative to particular phenomena that stand in need of explanation. It is physically possible that human beings should never have existed, but no world at which such a state of affairs obtains would be explanatory with respect to any human behavior. So, though real possibility and physical possibility can overlap, they are not coextensionally equivalent, and neither encompasses the other.

The skeptic's doubts can thus be rephrased: Relative to the nature and variety of my experience, there is a really possible world at which I have always been a brain in a vat. At some world all the marks of evidence that suggest my embodiment in a varied, but regular, world with which I am in epistemic contact are explained by my always having been a brain in a vat. The problem, from the skeptic's point of view, is that I have no better reason for thinking that I am *not* at such a world than I have for thinking that I *am*. Either possibility, says the skeptic, would explain my experience equally well.

Brains in a Vat

If this portrait of the philosophical doubts of the external-world skeptic as rooted in the availability of what are alleged to be alternative explanatory hypotheses is accurate, then the antiskeptic has several possible ways of responding to those doubts:[23]

1. Argue that the skeptic's account of justification or knowledge is faulty, so that I could be justified in believing in the "external" world, despite the explanatory power of the skeptical hypothesis.
2. Deny that knowledge requires justification at all.
3. Argue that although the skeptical scenario is a real possibility, it does not give as good an explanation of my intentional phenomena as does the external-world hypothesis.
4. Deny that the skeptical scenario is a real possibility at all.

The position of the modest realist is that we should embrace the fourth option—the scenarios raised by the external-world skeptic are not real possibilities. When she says this, she does not mean that the skeptic's scenario is an inferior explanation to the external-world hypothesis. That is the strategy expressed by the third option above and embraced by some metaphysical realists.[24] Rather, she thinks that the skeptic's "hypothesis" is *no explanation at all* of my intentional phenomena—and neither, for that matter, is the external-world "hypothesis." This is because she holds that my seeming to myself to interact in manifold ways with a complex but regular world beyond my senses is not the sort of thing that either needs or is susceptible of explanation. But what grounds could she have for thinking that the skeptic's scenarios are not explanations at all—not real possibilities?

One reason for holding this might be that she follows Wittgenstein in thinking that the relation between a referring term and its referent is paradigmatically an internal one[25]—such that I cannot understand the use of a referring term without understanding what it refers to. According to this view, the skeptic's hypothesis defeats itself because it makes nonsense of the supposition that I speak a language.[26] If I cannot understand the use of a referring term like *brain* or *vat* without understanding what it refers to, then I cannot understand the skeptic's hypothesis without knowing what its terms refer to. But I can know what those terms refer to only if the skeptic's hypothesis is false. Conversely, if the skeptic's hypothesis is correct, then I don't understand the language that I take myself to speak. This undermines the very conceptual determinacy of inner experience that the skeptic must presuppose in formulating the skeptical hypothesis, for the skeptic's scenario is intended to be explanatory of the coherence of my inner experience, a coherence that consists precisely in the conceptual determinacy made possible by language.[27]

A line of reasoning similar to this is often attributed to Putnam. For the past two decades Putnam has been an articulate critic of the position that I have been calling metaphysical realism, as well as of a number of related doctrines that the metaphysical realist often endorses, most notably the correspondence theory of truth.[28] One of his most controversial arguments takes up the sort of external-world skepticism I have been considering and concludes that it is not really possible that we have always been brains in a vat.

Most commentators have treated Putnam's argument primarily as an antiskeptical one, and many critics have suggested that it fails to show categorically that the skeptic's worries are misplaced. It would follow on this assumption that metaphysical realism also stands unrefuted. But as David Davies has observed (1995, 224–27) and as Putnam himself seems to suggest at times (1981, 6, 49), the argument is more interesting for what it shows us about the differences between metaphysical and modest realism. I think it helps to show that metaphysical realism is affected by a variety of epistemic neurosis. But let us begin by taking the argument at face value.

Consider Putnam's version of the skeptic's puzzle. Imagine that not just I, but we—all of us, indeed, all "thinking things" in the universe—are now, and always have been, brains in a huge vat of nutrient solution, being fed electrical impulses from some sempiternal computer that leave us with the collective impression that we have knowledge of the world. In fact, we are hopelessly deluded about the world around us. Is this situation possible? It violates no constraints of logic or physics (so it seems). Nevertheless, says Putnam, we could not *really* be brains in a vat, because if we were, then the words used to formulate the skeptical possibility would not refer to *brains* or *vats*, but to brains and vats "in the image" (1981, 15), illusory brains and vats, or perhaps to the computer's electrical impulses (14)—if, indeed, they referred to anything.[29] But *ex hypothesi*, we are *not* brains in a vat "in the image" or various types of electrical impulses; so whether we suppose ourselves to be brains in a vat or not, the statement "We are brains in a vat" is false, if it means anything.

The argument can be summarized as follows:

1. We speak English if and only if we are not brains in a vat.
2. If we are brains in a vat, then we speak Vat-English or no language at all.
3. Either we are brains in a vat, or we are not brains in a vat.
4. Therefore, either we speak English or we speak Vat-English or no language at all (from 1, 2, 3).
5. It is not the case that we speak no language at all.
6. Therefore, either we speak English or Vat-English (from 4, 5).
7. If we speak English, "We are brains in a vat" is false (from 1).
8. If we speak Vat-English, then "We are brains in a vat" is false, because it means that *we are brains in a vat in the image* or *we are certain kinds of electrical impulses*, neither of which is the case if we speak Vat-English.
9. Therefore, "We are brains in a vat" is false (from 6, 7, 8).[30]

It is important to be clear about the import of "We are brains in a vat." The possibility that we are brains in a vat should be understood as the possibility that we have *always been* and currently are brains in a vat (1981, 6, 15). The significance of this will become clear shortly. Also, although I have formulated the argument in terms of English and Vat-English, it ought to work for other languages; so we should think of the intent in terms of, say, natural languages and vat-languages, and statements that can be translated into the English or Vat-English statement "We are brains in a vat." I forego these emendations as possible and, for the most part, obvious.[31]

The argument is clearly valid; so any complaints must be directed either at the truth of its premises or the strength of its conclusion. With respect to the latter point two concerns are noteworthy: first, that the argument does not have the modal consequences that Putnam claims for it ("*It cannot possibly be true*" [1981, 7] that we have always been brains in a vat, he claims);[32] and second, that the falsehood of "We are brains in a vat" implies only that if we are brains in a vat, then we do not know how to say so.

The Modal Consequences

Consider the first complaint. The conclusion of the argument is that the statement "We are brains in a vat" is false. On the surface this seems merely to be a claim about what is actually the case, not about what is possible or impossible. Yet Putnam seems to want a stronger conclusion: "The existence of a 'physically possible world' in which we are brains in a vat (and always were and will be) does not mean that we might really, actually, possibly *be* brains in a vat" (1981, 15). What, if anything, justifies this move from the actual to the possible?

Interpreters of Putnam have frequently failed to notice that the sense in which he thinks we could not always have been brains in a vat is not that of logical possibility.[33] It is, rather, as Putnam's own words suggest, real possibility that is of relevance here. This means that the inference from our not being brains in a vat to our not possibly being brains in a vat is easily justifiable, for the reasoning that Putnam applies in the actual world would apply equally in any really possible world, relative to the nature and variety of our experience. The skeptic's contention, recall, is that our always having been brains in a vat would constitute just as good an explanation of the coherence of our experience as our being in epistemic touch with a world around us. But any such explanation would have to account for the possession and exercise of our linguistic abilities. So, relative to the nature and variety of our experience, any really possible world is one in which the possession and exercise of those abilities is preserved as part of the phenomenon to be explained. Moreover, any world in which we speak a language is a world in which we can apply Putnam's reasoning to our own situation.[34] If we are not brains in a vat, then only if we were not language users could we always have been brains in a vat.

But then, it is not clear that *we* is still an applicable term here. It may be physically possible that there were always brains in a vat and that none of us existed, but this is not a skeptical hypothesis. Confusing it with one is, as Putnam says, "taking physical possibility too seriously" (15). It may also be logically possible that *we* have always been brains in a vat. But a logical or physical possibility, as we have seen, poses no threat to our knowledge. So, if Putnam is right that we have not always been brains in a vat for the reasons that he gives, then there is no really possible world of the relevant character in which the skeptic's hypothesis is correct. Hence the skeptic's scenario is not a real possibility—it is no explanation at all, and we could not "really, actually, possibly *be* brains in a vat." That is, provided we are not brains in a vat.

But are we? What of the contention that Putnam has shown only that if we are brains in a vat, then we cannot knowingly say so? In order to assess this objection, we need to consider a more fundamental one concerning the soundness of the argument: that Putnam draws on a conception of language and reference that presupposes empirical premises that fall within the scope of the skeptic's doubts.

The Interactive Conception

Steps 1, 2, 7, and 8 of Putnam's argument are applications of what I shall call the "interactive conception" of reference, because this view sees reference as possible only in the context of complex interactions between an organism and the macroscopic objects and events that its environment comprises. According to this view, reference cannot be reduced to any nonsemantic relation, such as a causal chain of the appropriate type or even a complex nexus of causal relations. Referring is, above all, something that we *do*—it is an intentional notion. This is not to say that causal connections are *irrelevant* to reference. "It may well be that a certain referring use of some words would be impossible if we were not causally connected to the kinds of things referred to" (Putnam 1992a, 165).[35] The claim is, rather, that reference cannot be analyzed into nonintentional terms and that we should deny that "the referring *is* the causal connection" (165). Put another way, the relation between a referring term and its referent is paradigmatically an internal relation, not an external relation, in the sense that a competent speaker cannot understand how to use the referring term without knowing what it refers to. Such competence comes in degrees: I might incorrectly think that *dog* refers to wolves as well as to dogs and still be said to have a partial grasp of the term, but the person who thinks that *dog* refers always and only to wolves does not understand how to use the term.[36]

Putnam illustrates the interactive view of reference by an appeal to what he calls the "Turing Test for Reference" (1981, 9). Suppose, says Putnam, that I am in "conversation" by means of an electronic keyboard with a Turing machine. The machine is programmed to play the "Imitation Game"—that is, to respond eloquently and appropriately to my questions, remarks, and exclamations in such a natural manner that I think that I am conversing with an intelligent, linguistically competent speaker of English. However, suppose also that "not only does the machine lack electronic eyes and ears, etc., but that there are no provisions in the machine's program, the program for playing the Imitation Game, for incorporating inputs from such sense organs, or for controlling a body. What should we say about such a machine?" (10). Putnam would have us say that such a machine cannot *refer*, and that its inability to do so arises from its inability to interact with objects in the world, to distinguish between cats and cherries: "It is true that the machine can discourse beautifully about, say, the scenery in New England. But it could not recognize an apple tree or an apple, a mountain or a cow, a field or a steeple, if it were in front of one" (10).

If I am to be able to refer at all, then I must know at least roughly how I would succeed or fail to do so, and what counts as success or failure is as diverse and variegated as the many contexts in which I use language. If I cannot recognize apple trees and cows, what counts as successful reference to these things is precisely what I do not know. Reference is fixed by the roles that words and objects play in our daily affairs. In order to understand what a word standardly refers to, I must understand its standard use, and to understand that standard use is, in part, to know what the word refers to. If we do not suffer confusion over whether we refer to cats or to cherries when we say, "The cat is on the mat" (as analytic philosophers are wont to do), this is because cats and cherries have very different roles to play in our plans and projects, and the words that we use in the contexts of dealing with cats and cherries likewise acquire very different roles. Cherries, Ian Hacking says, "are for eating, cats, perhaps, for stroking" (1983, 104). (Hacking takes himself to be criticizing Putnam, but I think that the two are in close agreement on this point.) The fact that we can refer to apples or country fields is determined by the fact that we "are able to perceive, handle, deal with apples and fields. Our talk of apples and fields is intimately connected with our *non-verbal* transactions with apples and fields" (Putnam 1981, 11). That the Turing machine seems to be referring, seems to be "speaking," stems from the fact that we interpret its program and use it to achieve certain ends. But it has no means of relating to the world beyond its electronic keyboard. Nor has it any *need* to relate to the world. The sounds we utter are ways of *talking*, because they are embedded in the context of our many other ways of behaving and being in the world. Without that context, arising from a multitude of desires and ends that compel us to deal with the world for their satisfaction, there is no language, no meaning, and no *reference*. So says the interactive conception of reference.

According to the interactive view, then, *brain* refers to brains, *vat* to vats, *cats* to cats, and *cherries* to cherries only if we speak *English*—only if we are not brains in a vat, but interact with the world in more or less the ways that we think we do. If we *are* brains in a vat (suspending judgment on the argument's conclusion for the moment), then the things we interact with, and hence *can refer* to, are not cats and cherries, but illusory cats and cherries (if this makes sense to say), or electrical impulses of various types, or "the vat-cum-computer environment" (Rorty 1991b, 133) in which we are situated—if we "interact" with anything. This is why I suggest that "We are brains in a vat" be taken as implicitly saying that we have *always been* brains in a vat. Were this qualification omitted, it might be thought possible for us to be speaking English *inside* the vat, at least for a while, due to our prior acquaintance with the language outside the vat.

If the interactive conception of reference can be sustained, then steps 1, 2, 7, and 8 should be acceptable. The remaining steps I take to be uncontroversial. This would leave the argument vulnerable to criticism only at the point of its conclusion. But can the interactive conception be sustained?

Epistemic Neurosis

Putnam's Turing Test for Reference is not so much an argument for the interactive conception of reference as a vivid way of stating it, and it seems likely that any argument for the interactive conception would turn on empirical premises that, from the standpoint of the skeptic (and hence of the metaphysical realist), are *verboten*. Although the argument is valid, its soundness is in doubt. Putnam has not refuted external-world skepticism; hence, he has not refuted metaphysical realism.

It needs to be emphasized that the metaphysical realist who wishes to criticize Putnam's argument is not in a position to say any more than this. It will not do, for example, to criticize Putnam's reasoning by invoking another conception of reference that depends equally on empirical assumptions (unless, of course, one has a definitive or even probabilistic refutation of external-world skepticism that does not depend on empirical premises). From this perspective, the debate between Putnam and his critics reaches a stalemate.

However, Putnam makes no secret of the fact that his argument rests on empirical assumptions. He does not subscribe to the view that the "*preconditions* of reference and hence of thought" are "wholly independent of empirical assumptions" (1981, 16). "What we have been doing," he suggests, is "inquiring into what is *reasonably* possible *assuming* certain general premises, or making certain very broad theoretical assumptions" (16). Putnam, it seems, is not even *trying* to refute the skeptic. The brains-in-a-vat puzzle interests him for other reasons, as Davies points out (1995, 224–27). Although the brains-in-a-vat hypothesis is usually used to introduce the worries of the skeptic, writes Putnam, it is "also a useful device for raising issues about the mind/world relationship" (1981, 6). And "the question of 'Brains in a Vat' would not be of interest," he goes on to say, "except as a sort of logical paradox, if it were not for the sharp way in which it brings out the difference between these philosophical perspectives" (49). He refers to the perspectives he has in mind as the "externalist" and "internalist" (49) perspectives. The difference between them corresponds closely to the difference between what I have been calling metaphysical realism and modest realism, respectively. But what does Putnam's argument show us about the differences between these two kinds of realism?

I just remarked that if Putnam's argument is thought of as an attempted refutation of skepticism, then the metaphysical realist can offer no stronger criticism than to say that Putnam begs the question by assuming empirical premises. However, the compulsion to try to refute Putnam utterly is a strong one. It is thus sometimes claimed—as I noted in an earlier section—that if Putnam has proven anything, it is not what he intended to prove. In particular, what his argument shows, it is sometimes thought, is that had we always been brains in a vat, then we could not say so and know that we had. Yet, we could still *be* in a situation that we could not express or know of.[37]

The critic who reasons thus is like the person who thinks that I can experience my own death. It is certainly a logical possibility that I should now be dead, but I cannot coherently conceive of myself *as dead*. In every attempt to do so, I implicitly place myself beyond my own mortality and regard my death as the death of another who bears my name, past, features, and so on. As Sartre says, I doubt my existence "only in words and abstractly" (1956, 337). Similarly, I claim, any attempt to conceive of the possibility that we are and always have been brains in a vat involves an implicit situating of oneself *outside* the vat.

Consider what is being claimed: Putnam has shown only that if we have always been brains in a vat, then we cannot knowingly say so. Whence is this claim supposed to be made? From inside the vat? Well, if we have always been brains in a vat, then it is no more possible to say knowingly that "If we have always been brains in a vat, then we cannot say so," than it is to say that "We have always been brains in a vat." If the argument shows that we cannot say the latter, then it shows that we cannot say the former. Or is the claim supposed to be made from outside the vat? Then the critic joins Putnam in presupposing that we have not always been brains in a vat. The claim that we *could* always have been brains in a vat is, thus, tacitly counterfactual. Implicit in describing the possibility is the presupposition that that state of affairs does not obtain. It is as though, in formulating the brains-in-a-vat hypothesis, we entertain it of another group of people, not of ourselves. It is a possibility for *them*, but never really for us. In order to make his criticism of Putnam, the metaphysical realist must assume that the skeptic's hypothesis is false.

The metaphysical realist, I am suggesting, often does not take seriously the skeptic's scenario, and yet precisely what is supposed to distinguish metaphysical realism is that it does take external-world skepticism seriously. That purported seriousness in the face of skeptical doubt is embodied in the allowance that skeptical scenarios are real possibilities, not merely logical ones. As such they constitute a genuine epistemic worry even for the fallibilist. The skeptic, remember, alleges that all the marks of evidence available to us would be explained by our really being brains in a vat, and we have no good reason—epistemically speaking—to prefer the hypothesis of our epistemic contact with the real world to that of our being hopelessly deluded. Each hypothesis is as good as the other when it comes to a general explanation of the variety and nature of our experience. The strong objectivist is committed to this kind of possibility, to interpreting the claim that the world exists independently of the reliability of our epistemic capacities as saying that we might really be utterly mistaken about the way the world is. But in order to go beyond the claim that Putnam's argument does not refute skepticism, the metaphysical realist must betray this commitment.

This inadvertent betrayal of commitment is linked with a conflation that the metaphysical realist often makes of the logical possibility of skeptical scenarios with their real possibility and, hence, of metaphysical with modest realism—a conflation we met earlier. Thus, in an assessment of Putnam's work, David Anderson remarks that metaphysical realism—or "epistemological realism" as he calls it—"takes skepticism quite seriously" (1992, 67). But he interprets this as meaning simply that "It is *logically* possible that the ultimate nature of reality is, in principle, inaccessible to the cognitive and sensible faculties of human beings" (67; my emphasis). Devitt, whose views we have already encountered, allows that metaphysical realism does not take skepticism seriously, but insists that it is under no obligation to. Although, he thinks, we could always have been brains in a vat, the skeptic's hypothesis is "too implausible to take seriously" (1997, 64). Such skepticism, he says, is "unanswerable" but "simply *uninteresting*" (64).[38] But what does it mean to say that an explanatory hypothesis like the skeptic's is implausible? What does it mean to say that skepticism's puzzle is insoluble?

Devitt's position here is subtle. Like Quine, he does not believe that there is any "first philosophy," and he conceives of all propositions, even those expressing our knowledge of macroscopic objects in space and time, as hypotheses of a sort: "The world bombards us with stimuli. The innate machinery is activated, 'ordering' the resulting experience. We are theorizing. We presume that even these first steps take us 'beyond experience,' positing an external world, however primitive. In these first steps we arrive at beliefs (partly) *as a result* of experience," (1997, 76). On this view physical objects, as Quine memorably put it, are "irreducible posits comparable, epistemologically, to the gods of Homer" (1980, 44). Even our most basic beliefs about objects in the world around us are theoretical beliefs— parts of our "folk theory of the external world" (Devitt 1997, 76). Also like Quine, Devitt thinks that "Our beliefs are underdetermined by the evidence" (64), and this must include our "folk-theoretic" beliefs about the external world. But what this underdetermination shows, says Devitt, is that we do not have to justify ruling out all the hypotheses that constitute real possibilities relative to some given phenomenon. "Our best science shows us this" (75). We need only give serious consideration to those hypotheses that strike us as plausible ones, and the justification of one hypothesis is accomplished only relative to those that seem relevant.

It is a consequence of this "naturalized epistemology" (64) that a skeptical challenge inevitably arises, but because it "arises from within natural science" (Quine 1974, 2), it must be stated in terms that the natural scientist is obliged to accept by her own discursive practice. Since it is part of the practice of science that belief in a hypothesis can be justified even when not all of the possible alternatives have been ruled out, the skeptic cannot pose a challenge to the naturalized epistemologist by adopting some stronger account of justification that requires that such alternatives be ruled out before a belief can be justified. Thus Devitt complains that "The thoroughgoing skeptic sets the standards of knowledge (or rational belief) too high for them ever to be achieved" (1997, 75). The skeptic is, of course, free to challenge those standards, but she may not assume as given some other set of standards that the nonskeptical philosopher does not accept. As Michael Williams observes, "everything the skeptic needs has to be already present in our most ordinary ways of thinking about knowledge" (1996c, 17).

It seems, then, that sense can be made of claiming that skepticism is both unanswerable and uninteresting. But there are problems for this view nonetheless, and they lie, as hinted above, in Devitt's ambivalence about the relation of his "realism" to the problems raised by the skeptic. This relation he describes in passing as the "struggle with skepticism" (1997, 304). But if skepticism is really both uninteresting and unanswerable, why should there be any struggle involved? Again like Quine, Devitt wavers in his treatment of the "evidence" provided to us by our senses: "We do not . . . *infer* [our beliefs] *from* experience . . . for, inference being a relation between beliefs, that would require that our first beliefs were about experience, which is contrary to our presumption and highly implausible" (76). Such inferentialism would be an embrace of the old Cartesian self and its first philosophy, logically prior to experience. And yet, the skeptic's scenarios are conceded to be "hypotheses" that are rivals (albeit uninteresting ones) to our "folk theory of the external world" (76).

What is it that is being explained here? To introduce a general point to which I shall return repeatedly in the next few chapters, we can explain only what we can already identify and describe—only that about which we already have beliefs. And so we can give a "folk theory of the external world" only by treating our inner experience as logically, if not temporally, prior to that "theory." But to allow this just *is* to slip back into Cartesian first philosophy, and from that standpoint it is not at all obvious that the skeptic's hypothesis is uninteresting or irrelevant.[39] If inner experience is the sort of thing that admits of a unified explanation, then what grounds are there for saying that the skeptical hypothesis is too implausible to take seriously? It is, after all, the only challenger to the "folk theory of the external world"; so there is no question of having to seek out and test a potential infinity of rival explanations. A naturalistic view of hypothesis testing would seem to require that the skeptic's hypothesis be taken very seriously here.

Notice that some other standard naturalistic ploys are of no help here. We might for example be tempted to appeal to Robert Nozick's clever way of dealing with the skeptic. According to Nozick's account of knowledge as "truth-tracking," it is a necessary condition of my knowing that p that I would not believe that p unless it were true that p, and if it were true that p, then I would believe that p (1981, 172–78). In understanding these subjunctive conditional claims, we are not to imagine just any set of possible circumstances in which, respectively, I would not believe that p, or it would be true that p, but, rather, possible circumstances similar to the actual ones in which I find myself. This is in keeping with the conventions we follow in evaluating counterfactual and subjunctive conditional statements. Those conventions tell us to consider a possible world that is very much like the actual world, with the exception that the if-clause of the conditional obtains at that world. We then ask ourselves whether the then-clause would also obtain at that world. Thus, if we want to decide whether it is true that if the Nazis had won World War II, then we would all now be speaking German, we should imagine a world much like the actual one, but one in which, for example, the Allies failed to break the Enigma code or Nazi scientists succeeded in building an atomic bomb. This alone does not settle the historical question, but such a world is the one relevant to debating it. We would not, for example, think it worth considering a possible scenario in which extraterrestrials would have landed on earth in the early 1940s and formed an invincible alliance with Nazi Germany.

So, consider the question of whether, as I sit in my office typing these words, I know that I am doing so. In the nearest possible world in which I am not sitting in my office, I am, perhaps, standing in it or ascending the stairs to it. Let's assume the latter. Under such circumstances I would not believe that I was in my office. Likewise, in the nearest possible world in which I am in my office, things are much as they actually are, and I would in such a situation believe that I was sitting in my office. So by Nozick's criteria I know that I am sitting in my office. However, I do not also know that I am not a brain in a vat, because although at the nearest possible world in which I am *not* a brain in a vat, I do not believe that I am, in the nearest possible world in which I *am* a brain in a vat, I *still* do not believe that I am, because I am deceived about my real situation. According to Nozick, then, if I am *not* the victim of a skeptical scenario, then I can *know* that I am not, even though if I *were* the victim of a skeptical scenario, then I could *not* know whether I was or not.

This *conclusion* is one for which I have some sympathy. It is a conclusion shared by Michael Williams (1996c, 350–59), with whose views mine have an affinity I have already suggested. However, Nozick purchases it at the price of begging the question against the skeptic—as he explicitly concedes. "Our goal is not . . . to refute skepticism, to prove it is wrong or even to argue that it is wrong" (1981, 197). On the contrary, says Nozick, "Our task here is to explain how knowledge is possible, given what the skeptic says that we do accept" (197).[40]

The problem for the naturalist, as for more traditional metaphysical realists, is that, although there seems to be something unreasonable about external-world skepticism, strong objectivism depends on that same unreasonability. The metaphysical realist needs to have it both ways. Skepticism must be treated as a real concern, because such a concern is what gives content to metaphysical realism's claim that the nature and existence of the world are independent of the reliability of our epistemic capacities. But, unless skepticism is embraced, then what is needed is either a direct answer to the skeptic (a way of showing an admitted real possibility not to be *actual*) or a way of saying *why* skepticism is uninteresting. But the latter option is not open, since a reason to hold that skepticism is uninteresting is also a reason to hold that the account of independence and objectivity at the heart of metaphysical realism is uninteresting.

The kind of double bind in which the metaphysical realist is caught is characteristic of what I want to call "epistemic neurosis." The metaphysical realist's view is defined by its vulnerability to a skeptical doubt that threatens to interfere with the very positive philosophical programs that this view is intended to ground. We thus return finally to the theme with which we began this chapter, and we are now in a position to see how talk of mental disorder might be an appropriate metaphor to describe certain forms of philosophical thinking:

> The neurotic, we might say, doesn't believe what he says. Still he does go back at the risk of losing his train to make sure the lights are off. The philosopher doesn't. His acts and feelings are even less in accordance with his words than are the acts and feelings of the neurotic. He, even more than the neurotic and much more than the psychotic, doesn't believe what he says, doesn't doubt when he says he's not sure. (Wisdom 1957, 174)

The worries of the skeptic, Wisdom suggests, are in a sense like the worries of the obsessive neurotic, and because metaphysical realism depends on the worries of the skeptic, it is also marked by the symptoms of neurosis. There is a bit of the neurotic in us all and more than a bit of the skeptic in the metaphysical realist. The themes of neurosis are as much exaggerations *of* the norm as deviations *from* it. The neurotic shows us something about our society, our culture, and ourselves; the skeptic shows us something, indeed, even more, about metaphysical realism. Skepticism lies buried in the "soul" of metaphysical realism, and when this strong objectivism tries to distance itself from skepticism by claiming it to be *uninteresting*, it displays a fragmented self-understanding. The very position that the metaphysical realist advocates depends on the worries of the skeptic, but those are worries that cannot be taken too seriously if metaphysical realism is not simply to collapse into skepticism.

This internal conflict gives rise to another symptom that Putnam describes: "unconsciously operating with a magical theory of reference, a theory on which certain mental representations necessarily refer to certain external things and kinds of things" (1981, 15). On such a view, my being a brain in a vat is no barrier to my referring to brains and vats and, moreover, *knowing* that I am referring to those things. A magical theory of reference may not be *logically* incoherent, but it is *magical*—there is no reason whatsoever for thinking it to be true. Such a theory does not seem in keeping with the metaphysical realist's avowed acknowledgment of "our evident limitations" (Nagel 1986, 69). It seems more like what Nagel calls a "heroic" attempt to "leap across the gap" (69) that the metaphysical realist purports to discern between mind and world, while "The chasm below," as Nagel observes, "is littered with epistemological corpses" (69).

Unfortunately, such heroic wizardry seems to be just what the strong objectivist needs at this point. The metaphysical realist wants to express a possibility that in principle cannot be expressed, to say knowingly from within the vat, as it were, that we might really always have been brains in a vat. Even as she holds that skepticism is unanswerable, the metaphysical realist tries to reach out and refer to the "real" world. Even as she needs to suppose that we really could have always been brains in a vat, the metaphysical realist behaves as if our capacity to refer knowingly to things in the world were not genuinely threatened by this. Even as she supposes that we really could be utterly deluded, the metaphysical realist assumes that we could say so. How, but by magic, can such assumptions be reconciled?

The strong objectivist's inner conflict cries out for remedy. One of these competing assumptions must be forsaken: (1) that we can talk knowingly about the "external" world, or (2) that the objectivity and independence of that world are comprised by a position vulnerable to skepticism. It seems evident which is the healthier choice, but the metaphysical realist avoids deciding, objecting that the skeptic has set the standards too high or has changed the meaning of the word *know*. However, such replies, to the extent that they are compelling, also speak against metaphysical realism. If the skeptic sets the standards of knowledge too high, then so does the metaphysical realist. But the latter goes even further by supposing that the standards can then also be magically fulfilled.

Notes

1. See "Truth" in Dummett 1979, 1–28.
2. See "Realism" in Dummett 1979, 145–65. The latter two issues are indeed separate, for one may well think that truth is not "recognition transcendent" without being at all interested in issues in formal semantics.
3. Devitt is also a physicalist, holding that all entities are physical entities and that "ultimately, physical laws explain everything (in some sense)" (1997, 24). However, he distinguishes realism from physicalism on the grounds that the former is compatible with dualism. I shall not be as fastidious as Devitt in distinguishing "independence" from "objectivity," but I do not believe that any of my claims depends on a pernicious conflation of these two notions.
4. The distinction that follows is similar to one made by Maudmarie Clark between two different ways of understanding truth as correspondence. See Clark 1990, 29–61. I discuss correspondence in Chapter 3.
5. How can one be a modest realist about minds and intentional phenomena? One must hold that other minds do not depend for their existence on one's own mind, nor on the minds of *other* others, in the sense that one might cease to exist without those first other minds ceasing to exist, and *other* other minds might cease to exist without those first other minds ceasing to exist. Moreover, other minds (excluding, perhaps, the minds of one's children) might easily have existed even if one's own mind or *other* other minds (excluding, perhaps, the parents of those first other minds) had never existed. More succinctly, for any x and any y, if x and y are both minds and x is not identical to y, it is not the case that if x ceases to exist, then y must also cease to exist. And within the same scope, with the appropriate qualifications about parents and children, it is not the case that if x had never existed, then y would never have existed.
6. Realism here refers to the view that the truth-conditions of sentences of natural language are recognition-transcendent, but McGinn also seems committed to metaphysical realism. See, for example, his remarks about Davidson and global skepticism at McGinn 1986, 358f.
7. See Stroud 1996, 347, 358.
8. Williams speaks simply of "realism" in this context, and Rorty suspects him of making a conflation like the one I am considering. See Rorty 1998, 153–63. But I think that Williams's insistence on detaching vulnerability to skeptical doubt from the characterization of realism (1996c, 225ff.) makes him a modest realist in my terms.
9. Williams identifies "the foundationalist doctrine of the priority of experience" (1996c, 81) as the stage setting that makes the skeptic's entrance possible. I have no quarrel with this; I insist only that the conflation I identify here plays an important role too. Williams seems to deny this (51), but in the end the two doctrines are linked. If Williams is right about foundationalism, then the metaphysical realist's conception of objectivity presupposes foundationalist assumptions. My contention below that skepticism purports to offer explanatory possibilities for phenomena of which knowledge is *assumed* is an attempt to capture much the same point.
10. I hope it will be clear that my interest here is with modern skepticism, not ancient.

11. Epistemologists are much exercised by the problems that Gettier raised for the general account of knowledge as justified true belief, but those problems do not count against the general point that most contemporary Anglophone philosophers are fallibilists. Indeed, Gettier's problem can be stated only by assuming fallibilism—it would not have arisen for Descartes. See Gettier 1963.

12. See Williams 1996c, 73–79 for a similar point.

13. See Chisholm 1989, 1–4.

14. Goldman (1986, 32f.) comes close to this assessment, as does Devitt (1997, 62). See also Stroud 1984, 231f. and, explicitly, McGrew 1995, 116–39.

15. Indeed, the classical Cartesian skeptic holds, as Kant observed, that "inner experience" is "indubitable"—that I am actually never mistaken about my actual intentional phenomena, provided I am attentive enough in examining them. See Kant 1965, B275. This epistemic priority, whether of the strong Cartesian variety or the fallibilistic variety, is the mark of the foundationalism to which Williams traces skepticism. See Williams 1996c, 47–134. I shall make more of this point in Chapter 4.

16. Papineau claims not to grant any premise that denies that "all beliefs are initially on a par, as corrigible claims about things other than themselves" (1987, 11). But he later allows that "It is epistemologically possible that we are the playthings of a mad scientist, and if we were we'd have an erroneous intellectual system" (227). Surely this is to presuppose that our beliefs about mere appearances have epistemic priority over our beliefs about things in space and time.

17. My terminology is suggested by some of Putnam's remarks at 1981, 15. But there is an echo here of Kant's distinction between mere conformity with the law of noncontradiction and possibility as it relates "to understanding and its empirical employment" (Kant 1965, A219/B266). See A244/B302-3 for an explicit contrast between logical and real possibility. See also Brittan 1978, 20–24.

18. It might be objected that my characterization of skepticism rests on the dubious validity of abductive inference—i.e., the principle of inference to the best explanation. Why should the skeptic not be thought of as simply making the inductive claim that all experience to date provides as much evidence for thinking that I have always been a brain in a vat as for thinking that I am in epistemic contact with a world beyond my senses? Such a skeptic, however, is still drawing on a special kind of possibility—what could be called "inductive possibility"—and I can as easily draw a distinction between metaphysical realists, who allow the inductive possibility of skeptical scenarios, and modest realists, who do not. Nothing in my argument rides on the validity of abductive inference, in contrast to inductive inference.

19. I am indebted here to Brittan 1978, 20–24, but my account and my aims differ from his.

20. See, e.g., Lewis 1987.

21. I have argued against such explanatory and analytical views in Hymers 1991.

22. Those with no taste for the metaphysics of modality may want to skip this section and the section entitled "The Modal Consequences."

23. I have also discussed these possibilities in Hymers 1996a.

24. See, e.g., Papineau 1987, 227–29; McGrew 1995, 116–39; and Devitt 1997, 64, 75f. I return to Devitt's views below.

25. I shall have more to say about the notion of an internal relation in Chapter 2.

26. This general strategy is suggested by a number of passages in Wittgenstein 1972. See, e.g., §§55, 80–81, 114–15, 126, 158, 369, 383.

27. Kant tried a similar move that cited spatio-temporal objects as enabling the determinacy of inner experience. His argument, which is largely independent of transcendental idealism and may even undermine it, is that any reason I could have for doubting the existence of an external world is also a reason for doubting that my representational states are ordered in time. See Kant 1965, B275 and Hymers 1997a.

28. Putnam has been criticized for including those additional theses in his description of metaphysical realism. He has responded that although metaphysical realism does not imply those theses, the metaphysical realist usually finds them appealing. See Putnam 1990, 30–42.

29. When Putnam allows that our words might refer to brains and vats "in the image," I take him to be doing so for the sake of argument—provisionally granting part of the skeptic's description of the skeptical scenario in order to show that that description cannot really be right if the interactive model of reference alluded to below is correct. (Putnam has recently cast doubt on this assumption—see 1994a, 456–61—but I persist.) It might be less misleading to suppose that if brains in a vat refer to anything at all, they refer to the electrical impulses stimulating them or, better, to the sources of those impulses—the vat and computer. This, Rorty reports, is Davidson's view. See Rorty 1991b, 133.

30. Cf. Coppock 1987.

31. A language whose speakers had not engaged in such disputes might not have the concepts needed to formulate the skeptic's worry, but the concepts could be imported from another language.

32. Kinghan allows the modal consequences, but not that Putnam has shown us not to be brains in a vat: "Putnam succeeds in showing that if we are not brains in a vat (which he assumes) then we are necessarily not" (1986, 166).

33. See, e.g., Brueckner 1986, 149–53; Kinghan 1986; Malachowski 1986; Steinitz 1994; and Tichy 1986. An important exception is Davies 1995.

34. That is not to say, of course, that any such really possible world is one in which we *do* carry out such reasoning.

35. Many interpreters attribute to Putnam a "causal theory of reference" according to which reference either reduces to causal chains or always requires them. See, e.g., Lewis 1984, 234; Kinghan 1986, 161; Tichy 1986, 137; Devitt and Sterelny, 1987, 207; and Steinitz 1994, 213f. But in *Reason, Truth and History* he repudiates such views: "The idea that causal connection is necessary [for reference] is refuted by the fact that 'extraterrestrial' certainly refers to extraterrestrials whether we have ever causally interacted with any extraterrestrials or not!" (1981, 52).

36. This is not to say that all referring terms fit the model of internal relations. Theoretical terms like *electron* are such that one can be competent in their use without knowing what, if anything, they refer to. At issue is the contention that *all* referring terms are like *electron*. See Chapter 2.

37. See Brueckner 1986; Nagel 1986, 73; Devitt and Sterelny 1987, 207; and Martin 1992, 8f.

38. See also Devitt and Sterelny 1987, 227.

39. I return to this point in Chapter 4.

40. Nozick's argument entails the failure of the principle of epistemic closure, which says that if I know that p and I know that p entails q, then I know that q. See Nozick 1981, 204–11. Williams argues, however, that contextualism should not and need not reject this principle. See Williams 1996c, 317–59.

2

Internal Relations

> *I want to say: propositions of the form of empirical propositions, and not only propositions of logic, form the foundation of all operating with thoughts (with language).—This observation is not of the form "I know . . .". "I know . . ." states what I know, and that is not of logical interest.*
>
> *In this remark the expression "propositions of the form of empirical propositions" is itself thoroughly bad; the statements in question are statements about material objects. And they do not serve as foundations in the same way as hypotheses which, if they turn out to be false, are replaced by others.*
>
> —Ludwig Wittgenstein, On Certainty

In the preceding chapter I invoked the notion of an internal relation to explicate what I called the interactive conception of reference. The importance of internal relations, however, far outstrips the role they play in Putnam's argument. In chapters to follow I shall argue that a neglect of internal relations and an obsessive preoccupation with external relations is an important source of the epistemic neuroses of which I take metaphysical realism's disorder to be an exemplar. If I am to do this, however, I shall first need to clarify the distinction between internal and external relations that is crucial both to the interactive conception of reference and to the psycho-philosophical disorders I seek to diagnose. That is the task to which I now turn.

Since Bertrand Russell and G. E. Moore, it has often been assumed that only analytic truths can express internal relations—relations that, in Russell's words, are "grounded in the natures of the related terms" (1966, 139). An object, a, is internally related to another object, b, if and only if a is related to b in virtue of a's possessing some property, P. So if a has the property of being a branch, then it is internally related to some tree, b, as part to whole. In turn, "A branch is a part of

---

This chapter is based on Hymers 1996a.

some tree" is (at least a plausible candidate for) an analytic truth. It is true in virtue of the meanings of its terms or because the concept of the predicate contains the concept of the subject.

Quine's critique of analyticity has thus made pragmatically minded philosophers—philosophers whose views I often find attractive—wary of talk of such relations. For example, to accept Quine's view, says Rorty, "is at once to abandon the logical-empiricist notion of 'truth in virtue of meaning' and the sometime Oxonian notion of 'conceptual truth,' since there are no meanings or concepts from which truths might be read off" (1979, 193).[1]

Internal relations, on this view, are of interest only to the historian of philosophy or to the traditional metaphysician, and attempts to combine talk of internal relations with a pragmatic attitude toward meaning and truth, such as that embodied in the modest realism I am advocating, must, accordingly, seem baffling. But there is, I believe, a way of drawing a distinction between internal and external relations that is quite congenial to modest realism. It is a way that is suggested by Russell's erstwhile student, Ludwig Wittgenstein. I shall argue in this chapter that in Wittgenstein's transitional and later work a picture of internal relations emerges that (1) treats internal relations as obtaining between or among the "instruments" of language, which include not only words, but, for example, gestures, facial expressions and spatio-temporal objects used as paradigms; (2) does not entail that all propositions expressing internal relations must be analytic; (3) allows a distinction between the analytic and the synthetic; and (4) does so in a way that is compatible with Quine's critique, except where that critique is led off the rails by Quine's scientistic outlook.[2] Indeed, Quine himself has been led to reinvent a similar account.

Some History

The notion of an internal relation has a nefarious past, and an unpromising future, in the minds of some philosophers. Indeed, analytical philosophy might plausibly be said to have been born in the rejection by Russell and Moore of British Idealism's "Axiom of Internal Relations" (Russell 1966, 139).[3] This was the view that *all* relations were internal, and it entailed, roughly, that the identity of any object was constituted by its relations to all other objects. Russell complained that, on this view, there could be no relations at all and, hence, the absolute idealist could make no sense of diversity (139). Moreover, inasmuch as internal relations were expressed by analytic propositions, all truths must end up being analytic truths (144f.). Moore joined Russell in criticizing the "dogma" of internal relations, but attributed acceptance of the dogma to what modal logicians might now describe as a confusion about the scope of the necessity operator. One could be led to suppose that all relations were internal only by conflating material implication with strict entailment (Moore 1993, 89–99).[4] Though some relations were internal, conceded Moore, a great many were not (80).

Wittgenstein never propounds the idealists' view that all relations are internal, but in his early work his picture theory of meaning leaves an important place for internal relations. It is in virtue of its internal relation to the possible state of affairs (1922, §2.202) that it represents that a proposition is *able* to represent that state of affairs. "In the picture *[Bild]* and the pictured there must be something identical in order that the one can be a picture of the other at all" (§2.161)—namely, a shared "logical form" (§2.18) or "structure" (§4.014).

Logical form is no incidental feature of a state of affairs or of the proposition that represents it. It is, rather, an internal *property* such that an object that possesses it cannot cease to possess it without ceasing to exist. Change the logical form, and you change the possible state of affairs. Change the logical form, and you change the proposition. The sharing of logical form is an internal relation, and it is characteristic of this relation that "if I understand the proposition," then I also "know the state of affairs presented by it" (1922, §4.021).

This epistemic facet of internal relations—that if I can understand or identify one *relatum*, then I can also understand or identify the other—later dominates Wittgenstein's thinking about internal relations. But in the *Tractatus* his explanation of internal relations is linked with the notion of an internal property and with the "unthinkability" of an object's possibly not possessing any one of the internal properties that it does possess. "A property is internal," he says, "if it is unthinkable that its object does not possess it" (1922, §4.123). Two shades of blue, B_1 and B_2, are related as "brighter and darker," such that "It is unthinkable that *these* two objects should not stand in this relation" (§4.123). Such unthinkability is taken as a sign of what is possible for the things conceived (§3.02). It is not only the case that the property that B_1 possesses of being lighter than B_2 sets up an internal relation between B_1 and B_2, such that if B_1 ceased to possess that property it would no longer be related to B_2 in the same way. Rather, that property which grounds B_1's internal *relation* to B_2 is itself an internal *property*, such that B_1 could not cease to have it and still be B_1. So it is unthinkable that two shades of blue should be related other than as they are, *because* their relations to each other *constitute* their identities. If B_1 is brighter than B_2, then to try to think of B_2 as brighter than B_1 is to cease to think about one, or both, of these two shades.

The *Philosophical Remarks*

By the time of the *Philosophical Remarks* (1929–1930), the picture theory of meaning, with its metaphysics of "atomic facts" and "simple" objects (1922, §§2, 2.02), has begun to lose favor with Wittgenstein. But internal relations remain central to his new "picture conception" *(Bild-Auffassung)* of intentions: "The essential difference between the picture conception and the conception of Russell, Ogden and Richards,[5] is that it regards recognition as seeing an internal relation, whereas in their view this is an external relation" (1975, §21). Russell, Wittgenstein comments, insists on inserting some third thing between an intentional attitude and the object of the attitude, as though I could identify the attitude without knowing toward what object it were directed. The object of a desire, for example, is characterized in *The Analysis of Mind* as that thing whose achievement removes the desire. The desire itself, Russell says, is a state of "discomfort," provoking a "behavior-cycle" that tends "to cause a certain result, and continu[es] until that result is caused, unless [it is] interrupted by death, accident, or some new behavior-cycle." The object of a desire is "the result which brings [the cycle] to an end, normally by a condition of temporary quiescence—provided there is no interruption" (1921, 62–68).[6]

Wittgenstein responds that Russell's theory of desire leads to a kind of indeterminacy of intentional objects. According to Russell, he claims, "If I wanted to eat an apple, and someone punched me in the stomach, taking away my appetite, then it was this punch that I originally wanted" (1975, §22).[7] We might reply on Russell's behalf that a punch in the stomach is an "interruption" of the behavior-cycle initiated by the desire, not its goal. But the problem is that what counts as an interruption is relative to a prior characterization of the purpose to which the cycle is geared. There are indefinitely many ways of characterizing the behavior cycle in question, and there is no principled reason for preferring one description over the others. Only if the relation between a desire and its object is internal will we be able to say determinately what satisfies the desire.[8]

In the *Tractatus* we met with an epistemic criterion for picking out internal relations and properties: A relation is internal if it is unthinkable that its *relata* should not be so related. In the *Philosophical Remarks* another epistemic criterion takes priority: A relation is internal if identifying one of its *relata* serves also to identify the other *relatum*.

The *Philosophical Grammar*

The *Philosophical Grammar*, which follows the *Philosophical Remarks* by about three years,[9] revisits many of the themes already encountered. "Wishes, conjectures, beliefs, commands," Wittgenstein writes, "appear to be something unsatisfied, something in need of completion" (1974, 132).[10] When we try to say what their "satisfaction" amounts to, we are tempted to find an intermediary to link the wish or the belief to its conditions of satisfaction. But to search for this *tertium quid* is to construe the relation between intentional attitude and object as an external one. Consider "an expectation and a fact *[Tatsache]* which fit together": "Here one thinks at once of the fitting of a solid into a corresponding hollow. But when one wants to describe these two one sees that, to the extent that they fit, a *single* description holds for both. (On the other hand compare the meaning of: 'These trousers don't go with this jacket'!)" (134).

Nothing in the jacket intimates to me what trousers it should be worn with. Nor can I judge from the trousers alone what jacket they belong to. I also need to know some standard of fashion that proscribes, prescribes, or permits the wearing of these trousers with this jacket. Here there are three things, each of which I can identify apart from the others—the trousers, the jacket, and a convention for combining them—and I need three different descriptions, one for each, to describe the fact that these trousers don't go with this jacket. The expectation and the fact that fulfills it, however, fit a *single* description: The expectation *that it will rain tomorrow* is "satisfied" by the fact *that it will rain tomorrow*—and by nothing else.

The "fact" here, it should be noted, is not one of the atomic facts of the *Tractatus*, and it is not, I think, to be thought of in the fashion of "facts" in traditional correspondence theories of truth.[11] Wittgenstein at this point has no *ontology* of facts of the sort that comes from hypostasizing talk of facts. Facts are not a kind of self-articulating *thing* from which the world is composed independently of the reliability of our epistemic capacities—in either the sense of metaphysical realism or that of modest realism.[12] Wittgenstein's version of logical atomism has been replaced by a more holistic view in the *Philosophical Remarks* (1975, 317). But although the picturing relation of the *Tractatus* has yielded to Wittgenstein's self-criticism (1974, 163), it has been succeeded by a picture of language as a formal *calculus*. "From expectation to fulfilment," Wittgenstein suggests, "is a step in a calculation" (160). "The role of a sentence in the calculus is its sense" (130). This talk of calculi signals a further transformation in the idea of an internal relation.

Just as we are tempted to introduce a mediating term between an expectation and its fulfillment, so we are tempted to introduce some third thing between an order and what counts as its execution: "It can look as if the ultimate thing sought by the order had to remain unexpressed, as there is always a gulf between an order and its execution" (1974, 133; 1968, §433). The cases presented in the *Philosophical Remarks* might lead us to expect that this "gulf" between order and execution—this ability of the sign only to *hint* at "something it doesn't express" (1974, 133)—will close if we see that order and execution, rule and instance, are related internally.[13] But what Wittgenstein *says* is this: "The appearance of the awkwardness of the sign in getting its meaning across . . . —this disappears when we remember that the sign does its job only in a grammatical system" (133).

The contention that a sign is part of a "grammatical system," that it has a role in a calculus, thus seems linked with the claim that an order and its execution, a rule and its instances, are internally related. What could this mean? Part of the answer is this: A rule and its instances are internally related as long as expressions for that rule and its instances play a role in the calculus of our language. But this is just part of the answer.

Much of Part I of the *Grammar* examines what it means to *understand* various things: a word, a proposition, a picture, a language, a story, a piece of music. If the meaning of a word is "the role of the word in the calculus" (1974, 63), and if I must understand the meanings of words to understand a language, then it is not surprising that Wittgenstein sees understanding a language as being able to operate a calculus. Linguistic understanding is an *ability*, or perhaps a range of abilities. To understand a word or a proposition is to understand its role in the calculus, and I could neither understand a word without knowing how to use it, nor "know the use of the word and yet follow it without understanding" (65).

What is implicit here Wittgenstein will later make explicit—namely, that talk of internal relations is appropriate only where the *relata* in question are *concepts* or, more generally, "linguistic instruments."[14] Internal relations obtain only among things that play a role in a language and only in virtue of the particular roles that they play. Also implicit here is a further revision of the epistemic criterion for internal relations: two concepts, or instruments of language, A and B, are internally related if in order to understand one, I must also understand the other. This allows for three different kinds of internal relations: (1) where an understanding of A presupposes an understanding of B, (2) where an understanding of B presupposes an understanding of A, and (3) the conjunction of (1) and (2).[15]

Concepts have no existence here independent of norms and practices. To understand a concept is, paradigmatically, to be able to use a word correctly, where correctness amounts to accord with the rules of a calculus. This means that our new epistemic criterion is not merely a means of identifying internal properties or relations; it is now *constitutive* in part of the very idea of an internal relation. But lingering in the picture of linguistic understanding as the operation of a calculus is a commitment to a sharp distinction between the analytic and the synthetic—between the tautologies of logic (the rules of the calculus) and empirical propositions. Wittgenstein's loosening of this distinction marks the final stage in the evolution of his thinking about internal relations.

Wittgenstein's Later Writings

In some passages of the *Philosophical Grammar*, Wittgenstein seems to view talk of calculi as metaphorical. Languages, he says, are spoken long before an explicit grammar is formulated, and simple games are often played without explicit rule formulations: "But we look at games and language under the guise of a game played according to rules. That is, we are always *comparing* language with a procedure of that kind" (1974, 62f.; see 77).

By the time of the *Investigations* this figurative tendency predominates. The chess analogies abound, but Wittgenstein now eschews talk of the calculus of a language. "In philosophy," he says, "we often *compare* the use of words with games and calculi which have fixed rules, but cannot say that someone who is using language *must* be playing such a game" (1968, §81). A close look at meaning, understanding, and thinking, he holds, will help both to explain and to alleviate our temptation to suppose "that if anyone utters a sentence and *means* or *understands* it he is operating a calculus according to definite rules" (§81).

Understanding, however, remains a set of abilities. To understand the meaning of a word is to be able to *use* the word correctly. But correctness now amounts to accord with public criteria that vary in precision from word to word and from context to context. And understanding the use of a given word requires understanding the uses of many other words, as they are embedded in a complex set of human practices.

What began in the *Tractatus* as an epistemic criterion for recognizing an internal relation was later transformed into a partly *constitutive* characteristic of an internal relation. Two concepts are internally related if in order to understand one I must also understand the other. Now, if understanding a concept typically amounts to being able to use a word, and if "For a large class of cases . . . the meaning of a word is its use in the language" (1968, §43), then we can cautiously say that internal relations can obtain among meanings. Two meanings are internally related if in order to know one meaning I must also know the other. But the relation of a word to its meaning is not like that between "The money, and the cow that you can buy with it" (§120). Meanings are not objects, "Platonic" or otherwise.

I think these remarks allow us to capture what is plausible in traditional accounts of analyticity without also netting their defects. In particular, Wittgenstein's picture of internal relations differs from standard accounts of analyticity in four major ways: (1) It involves no commitment to Aristotelian subject-predicate logic, as Kant's did.[16] (2) It involves no commitment to what Quine has aptly called the "museum-myth" of meaning (1969, 27). (3) It does not follow from this view that a proposition expressing an internal relation is an analytic truth. (4) This view allows a distinction between the analytic and the synthetic, but it does so in a way that does not run afoul of the problems that are often thought to plague the analytic-synthetic distinction.

I shall focus on the third and fourth ways, beginning with the issue of whether an internal relation can be expressed only by an analytic proposition.

A New Picture

There is a weight of tradition behind the view that internal relations can be expressed only by analytic truths. This was certainly the view that Moore and Russell propagated in their critiques of British Idealism (Russell 1966, 144f.; Moore 1993, 85). But, as G. P. Baker and P. M. S. Hacker point out (1984b, 109), this was a view that Wittgenstein rejected.

Consider pain. In the sense of "internal relation" that we are considering, there is an internal relation between the concept of pain and instances of pain behavior (that's why it's *pain* behavior), despite the fact that a person in pain can sometimes suppress pain behavior and a person can feign pain by producing instances of pain behavior in the absence of pain. It would be wrong to say that a person is in pain if and only if she displays some "characteristic expression-behavior"

(Wittgenstein 1981, §488) of pain, and it would be wrong to hold this proposition to be not merely true, but analytic. But I would not understand the concept of pain unless I recognized winces, grimaces, cries, and the like as forms of pain behavior. One learns the concept of pain by learning to recognize pain behavior. Pain and its characteristic expressions can occur in each other's absence, but this could not always happen, or the concept of pain would be very different—if we had such a concept at all: "this would make our normal language-games lose their point" (1968, §142). If people more frequently displayed what we think of as pain behavior in the absence of pain than in its presence, then we would no longer think of such behavior as an *expression* of pain. Its *meaning* would change. And there is no sharp line between the circumstances that would lead us to change our concept and those that would not. Despite this vagueness, given our present use of the word *pain*, one must be able to recognize characteristic kinds of pain behavior to understand the concept of pain.[17]

This linkage of internal relations with the contexts of teaching and learning appears elsewhere in Wittgenstein's work. "An internal relation," he is reported to have said in a 1939 lecture, "is never a relation between two objects, but you might call it a relation between two concepts. And a sentence asserting an internal relation between two objects ... is not describing objects but constructing concepts" (1976, 73). We tend to think that when we say "This shade of blue is lighter than that one," or "White is lighter than black," we have said "something about the *essence* of the two colors" (1978, 75) or the two shades, as though we were describing two "Platonic" objects. But, Wittgenstein asks, "Whom do we tell 'White is lighter than black'? What information does it give?" (76). We say such things, ordinarily, if at all, only to someone who is learning our language—a child perhaps or a speaker of another language. And when we say such things, we impart to our interlocutor something about the standard uses of the words in question. It is an internal property of "white" to be lighter than "black," *because* for someone to understand the words *white* and *black*—to be able to use them in ways that will not occasion great confusion—she must know that white is lighter than black. By telling someone that white is lighter than black, I help her to *construct* concepts, to acquire the ability to participate in a certain array of language games.[18]

But if internal relations hold between *concepts*, what are we to make of the suggestion that the relation between pain and certain kinds of behavior is an internal one? Is this any more intelligible than thinking of internal relations as relations between or among objects?

"'Concept,'" Wittgenstein observes, "is a vague concept" (1978, 433). More to the point: Wittgenstein does not say that internal relations can obtain *only* between concepts, just that they do not obtain between objects. I take this to mean: between objects that occupy no place in a language game, real or imagined, between objects that are considered apart from the possibility of being placed under a description of some sort, between objects that have no established (or imagined) linguistic *use*. Internal relations obtain between concepts, because concepts are "instruments" (1968, §569) of language, and it is between or among the instruments of language that internal relations lie. Events like wincing and crying are among those instruments, because we use them to teach others the concept of pain.

Wittgenstein's figure of language as an array of instruments for various purposes is a familiar one. "Language is like a collection of very various tools" (1974, 67), he says. "Look at the sentence as an instrument, and at its sense as its employment" (1968, §421). We use words as instruments to further our manifold ends, and, as any technology does, words shape our ends as we grow reliant on words, as they become more complexly integrated with our ways of being and doing. But words and the sentences that we compose with them are not our only linguistic instruments. We also have at our disposal a toolbox full of gestures, facial expressions, inarticulate sounds, and macroscopic, spatio-temporal objects—objects that function, for example, as samples or paradigms. "It is most natural, and causes least confusion," says Wittgenstein, "to reckon the samples among the instruments of the language" (§16).

"The language" here refers to the language game of *Philosophical Investigations*, §8, a primitive language for builders that includes only four nouns (*block, pillar, slab* and *beam*), the letters of the alphabet, used when counting blocks and the like, the indexical terms *this* and *there*, and—most pertinent here—a number of color samples with which the building materials can be compared. But I do not think that the point of Wittgenstein's remark is limited to this particular thought experiment. Language games are not "separated by a break" (1958, 17) from more complex forms of language. We *use* objects as exemplars, just as we *use* sound patterns and visual marks as words. Words and objects do not stand on either side of an epistemic divide, waiting to be united by some external relation of fitting or correspondence, for example. They are both elements within our complex array of linguistic practices. Language and the world are continuous. That is why Wittgenstein says that "the harmony between thought and reality is to be found in the grammar of the language" (1974, 162; see 1968, §429)—that is, in the internal relations established and passed on by teaching and learning. I teach someone how to use the word *red* by showing her a red sample, and the person who cannot pick out a red sample under a range of standard perceptual conditions has at best a limited understanding of the word *red*. Because I cannot explain the use of *red* without recourse to some red object, there is an internal relation between the concept "red" and its instances. The same holds for macroscopic events. Characteristic behavioral expressions of pain are internally related to the concept of "pain" (in other words, they *are* characteristic expressions) because they serve as examples in the teaching and learning of the use of the word *pain*. But it is not even true, let alone analytic, that a person is in pain if and only if she shows characteristic pain behavior.[19]

The connection with Putnam's Turing Test for Reference, discussed in Chapter 1, should be clear. A Turing machine that had no means of relating to the world beyond its electronic keyboard, says Putnam, "could not recognize an apple tree or an apple, a mountain or a cow, a field or a steeple, if it were in front of one" (1981, 10). If internal relations obtain between the concepts "apple," "tree," and "cow," on the one hand, and their respective instances, on the other, then not being able to recognize such things amounts to not understanding these concepts. Could the Turing machine *refer* to apples and mountains if it had no understanding of these concepts? If reference is an intentional notion, like expectation and belief, then a *single* description holds for both the referring term and its referent: *apple* refers to apples, *cow* to cows. "It is trivial to say what any word refers to *within* the language the word belongs to, by using the word itself" (Putnam 1981, 52). And if we try to treat reference as reducible to an external relation, then we can expect to encounter the same bizarre kind of indeterminacy that Wittgenstein detected in Russell's behavioristic treatment of desire as an external relation between irritation and that which removes the irritation. As we shall see in Chapter 3, Putnam's model-theoretic argument against the correspondence theory of truth draws on precisely this parallel.

Quine's Critique

We come now to the issue of whether the problems sometimes taken to dog the proverbial dogmas of empiricism are also problems for this new picture of internal relations. But we need to consider what is being avoided when philosophers, influenced by Quine, proclaim their liberation from the analytic-synthetic distinction.

Quine's criticisms in "Two Dogmas of Empiricism" focus on the view that "a statement is analytic when it is true by virtue of meanings and independently of fact" (1980, 21). He discerns two kinds of analytic truths—logical truths and all the rest. A logical truth "is a statement which is true and remains true under all reinterpretations of its components other than the logical particles" (22f.). Prima facie, this category of analytic truths poses no problems. It is the remaining ones that engender difficulty. What characterizes analytic truths that are not logical truths is that they can be changed into logical truths "by putting synonyms for synonyms" (23). So synonymy is implicated from the start in analyticity. The problem, Quine argues, is that there is no clear account of synonymy.

This is not for want of candidates. Quine considers and dismisses suggestions for treating synonymy as sameness of meaning "by definition" and substitutivity *salva veritate*, and he criticizes Rudolf Carnap's proposal in *Meaning and Necessity* that analyticity be defined by an appeal to "semantical rules" (Carnap 1956, §2). But for us the most relevant of his criticisms follow directly from his holism, and they are directed at attempts to define synonymy and analyticity by appeal to a verifiability theory of meaning.

If the meaning of a statement is its method of confirmation or disconfirmation, then it seems plausible to hold that "An analytic statement is that limiting case which is confirmed no matter what" (1980, 37).[20] But this, thinks Quine, is no real option at all. "Our statements about the external world face the tribunal of sense experience not individually but only as a corporate body" (41). No statement can be (dis)confirmed in isolation, and any statement "can be held true come what may, if we make drastic enough adjustments elsewhere in the system" (43).

This appeal to holism involves two distinct criticisms. The first returns to the notion of synonymy. If a statement's meaning is its method of confirmation or disconfirmation, then two statements might seem to be synonymous if they have the same method of confirmation and disconfirmation.[21] In turn, an analytic statement would be synonymous with a logical truth. The problem is that if "The unit of empirical significance is the whole of science" (1980, 42), then no unique method of confirmation attaches to any particular statement. Thus, no precise account can be given of what it is for two statements to share such a method—hence, no account of synonymy and no account of analytic truths that are not logical truths. The notion of a logical truth, however, remains untouched by this criticism.

The same is not so of Quine's second holistic complaint: If "our statements about the external world face the tribunal of sense experience . . . as a corporate body," then in principle "no statement is immune to revision" (1980, 43). One feature that was supposed to characterize analytic truths was that their "factual component should be null" (36). "An analytic statement is that limiting case which is confirmed no matter what." And logical truths were to share this feature with their other analytic comrades. But neither sort seems to possess it, on Quine's view.

All this suggests that Quine thinks the very notion of an analytic truth that is not a logical truth is suspect, and that the boundary between the analytic and the synthetic is a fuzzy one, for although the idea of a logical truth *can* be made out clearly, such logical truths get woven into the net with all our other statements for possible revision. They avoid revision in the light of new experience only because we have a "natural tendency to disturb the total system as little as possible" (1980, 44). Attempting to revise the truth-value of a "logical truth" would have ramifications throughout our web of belief, and so we avoid such revisions. We can, if we like, retain the distinction between logical truths and nonlogical ones, but we cannot retain the distinction between *necessary* truths and *contingent* ones. The category of the a priori, meanwhile, gets relativized. What is valid a priori depends on which claims we hold immune to revision. No claims are absolutely valid a priori.

A New Picture of Analyticity

I said that Wittgenstein's picture of internal relations captures what is plausible in traditional accounts of analyticity without suffering from their problems, but I did not say what analyticity amounts to. Let me now offer a proposal.[22] We saw that on Wittgenstein's later view two expressions, or two "linguistic instruments," are internally related if in order to understand how to use one of them I must also understand how to use the other. Understanding, remember, lies in one's ability to use a term in a way that more or less accords with the mutable, often loose and informal, public standards for its application. And it is a feature of understanding, as it is of any ability, that it is fallible.

I suggest the following rough characterizations of synonymy and analyticity. A proposition is analytic if an understanding of the use of its terms requires that I understand it to be true. Whatever can be derived from an analytic truth by means of customary logical operations is likewise an analytic truth. And if a proposition is analytic, then it can be changed into a logical truth by substituting synonyms for synonyms. As for those synonyms, two expressions are synonymous if they have the same use. Or rather, since no two words have exactly the same use, two terms are synonymous if they have relevantly similar uses. In certain contexts, which admit of no sure and fast delineation, I could use either term indifferently to convey what I want to convey. This, as Rorty would say, is a "commonsensical and philosophically uninteresting" picture of "sameness of meaning" (1979, 197). This, I say—and I think Rorty would agree—is as it should be.

Now, it might be objected that this picture of analyticity runs afoul of evident facts about mathematical knowledge, for it seems that I could *understand* a mathematical proposition without knowing it to be true or false. It seems clear, for example, what is meant by Goldbach's conjecture that every even number greater than 2 is the sum of two prime numbers, but no one has been able to prove or disprove it.

I think it best to maintain that in cases that depend on novel proofs, we do *not fully* understand the proposition until that proof (or a proof of falsehood) has been given, because its meaning is so far unclear. Understanding develops by degrees, and words can be used in novel ways that outrun our current understanding. The true propositions of mathematics for which we have proofs are analytic (and the false ones self-contradictory). But the unproven proposition is neither analytic, nor self-contradictory, because the internal relations that would make it analytic do not yet obtain. They are *created* by the novel proof. "The mathematician," says Wittgenstein, "is not a discoverer: he is an inventor" (1978, 111), and what he invents are "new connexions" or "a new concept" (166).

Since concepts have no existence outside cognitive practices, internal conceptual relations and, hence, analyticity have no existence outside such practices either. "What is proved by a mathematical proof is set up as an internal relation and withdrawn from doubt" (363). By systematically putting familiar terms to a new use, the novel proof extends the meaning of the terms of the theorem. In this sense the proof of a new theorem is like the paraphrase of a new metaphor. "The proof changes the grammar of our language, changes our concepts" (166). The poet challenges our understanding and imagination when she creates a new metaphor, and we rise to the challenge (if we can) by struggling to catch up with her, relating the new to the old by paraphrase. I may well have a good command of the standard uses of all the terms in a metaphorical utterance, but it does not follow that I automatically understand the statement. In order to do so, I may have to work at relating it to what I am already familiar with, but that work—if done well—can transform my understanding of the familiar, as it enables my understanding of the unfamiliar. What counts as a good paraphrase is open to more debate than is what counts as a proof, but that difference stems from the special role that mathematical concepts play in our practices. It does not preclude the comparison of proof and paraphrase.[23]

My proposals, however, might seem to fail by the criteria that Quine employs in "Two Dogmas." H. P. Grice and P. F. Strawson once noted critically that Quine seems to presuppose both that an adequate explanation of terms like *analyticity* and *synonymy* "must not incorporate any expression belonging to the family-circle" of terms like *self-contradictory, necessary, semantical rule* and so on, and that adequate explanations must also provide necessary and sufficient conditions for the application of the terms being explained (1956, 147f.). This does seem to be Quine's attitude in "Two Dogmas," and it is puzzling in light of his insistence that Alfred Tarski had the last word to offer on the concept of *truth*, for Tarski's *starting point* was that no materially adequate, formally correct definition of truth could be given for colloquial language.[24] Quine is well aware of this point. Yet he insists that "Truth is disquotation" (1990, 80), even for colloquial language. And if this is not a "definition in the strict sense," which "tells how to eliminate the defined expression from every desired context in favor of previously established notation" (81f.), it is, he says, still a definition "in a looser sense" (82). But if a looser sense is adequate for such a central concept as truth, then why not for synonymy or analyticity?

Elsewhere Quine allows that he would settle for "a rough characterization in terms of dispositions to verbal behavior" (1960, 207). Unfortunately, he thinks, not even this approach is very promising. He offers accounts of "stimulus-synonymy" and "stimulus-analyticity" (46–57), but there is no hint that these notions explain "synonymy" or "analyticity" proper. Stimulus analyticity, says Quine, is a "behavioristic ersatz" (66) for the real thing—a "strictly vegetarian imitation" (67).

But in later work Quine is more optimistic. He insists that the notion of synonymy be restricted to intralinguistic application, but he now thinks that a "rough account of analyticity" (1990, 55) in terms of dispositions to verbal behavior is a live possibility for "domestic" (53) synonymy and analyticity. His proposal should sound familiar: "A sentence is analytic," he remarks, "if *everybody* learns that it is true by learning its words" (1974, 79). The "everybody" in this formulation is important. Some truths that I learn to be true by learning the words with which they are expressed are not so learned by others. I might learn that it is true that my dog has four legs by learning how to use *dog* or *four* or *legs*, but it is not analytic. I might learn that my sister is in pain in the process of learning how to use the word *pain*, but that does not make it analytic that she is in pain, or analytic that she is in pain if and only if she displays pain behavior. "Language," says Quine, "is social, and analyticity, being truth that is grounded in language, should be social as well" (79).

Quine's proposal, minus the behaviorist rhetoric, is much like the one that I made above. A statement is analytic if an understanding of the use of its terms depends on understanding it to be true. On this view, the social character of analyticity, which Quine emphasizes, is captured by the social character of standard use. To understand how to use a word is, in part, to understand how other speakers use it. Such use varies somewhat from speaker to speaker, but the standard use derives from a rough convergence of individual uses.[25] Quine puts the point in terms of learning, rather than of understanding. But the two are intimately related, since, as an empirical fact, I must learn a language in order to understand it. And we saw earlier how Wittgenstein explicitly ties the establishment of internal relations to contexts of teaching and learning.

Indeed, our earlier examples of failed candidates for analyticity in Quine's sense display the features of claims that express internal relations. It is not analytic that my dog (or dogs in general) has (or have) four legs, but if I am to be said to understand the general term *dog*, then I ought to be of the opinion that, by and large, dogs have four legs each. Someone who denied this would be better interpreted as having misunderstood the term *dog* than as having a false belief about dogs.

We have here a continuum of cases. At one end lie the analytic truths; at the other is the general, holistic interdependence of meaning, according to which, "To understand a sentence means to understand a language" (Wittgenstein 1968, §199). This involves, as Quine says, "no such radical cleavage between analytic and synthetic sentences as was called for by Carnap and other epistemologists" (1974, 80). But it does not render the concept of analyticity empty or useless. Quine's "rough account of analyticity" draws attention to cases that belong to the broader family of claims that express internal relations in Wittgenstein's sense. Far from conflicting with Quine's arguments against the analytic-synthetic distinction, I maintain, Wittgenstein's later views on internal relations are largely compatible with those arguments.

Necessity and Revisability

The picture of analyticity and internal relations I have drawn from Wittgenstein's work is echoed in the recent writings of a number of philosophers of a laudably pragmatic bent. Putnam, as we shall see in the next chapters, has argued that treating the relation between a word and its referent as an external one leads to a radical indeterminacy of reference and that the concepts of truth and justification are internally related. Rorty, despite his avowed suspicions, seems warm to the view that "the sentences in which our beliefs are expressed touch the world directly" (1991b, 141 n. 30) without mediation by any *tertium quid*. Philosophers who want to treat truth as an explanatory, theoretical relation between words and the world, he complains, "need, so to speak, two independently describable sets of cogwheels, exhibited in sufficiently fine detail so that we can see just how they mesh" (55). And Davidson, whose views will be of special interest in Chapter 5, has argued that we have no understanding of truth apart from our understanding of how to attribute beliefs and other attitudes to persons in a way that gives meaning to their behavior.[26] In other words, the concepts of truth, meaning, and belief are internally related. Or, as Quine says, "Truth, meaning, and belief are sticky concepts. They stick together" (1981, 38).[27] But despite the significant convergence between Quine and Wittgenstein, remarked on above, they have important differences that I shall conclude this chapter by clarifying.

First, Quine is well known for his thesis of the indeterminacy of translation, according to which, beyond the level of truth-functions, observation sentences, and terms for assent and dissent, there can be no such thing as a uniquely correct translation of another language (1960, 68–79). It is because of this thesis that Quine limits his rough accounts of synonymy and analyticity to intralinguistic application. But several critics have rightly disparaged the scientist privileging of the language of physics that underlies his allegation of indeterminacy.[28] And there seems no reason not to apply our rough and ready notion of synonymy across our rough and ready linguistic boundaries. Likewise for analyticity. The English word *dog* and the German word *Hund* are good candidates for interlinguistic synonyms, and by the criterion proposed earlier it is analytic that *ein Hund* is a dog. I cannot understand this statement without seeing it to be true.

Quine's scientism is at the root of another sort of divergence between his rough accounts of synonymy and analyticity and those that I have extracted from Wittgenstein. This divergence concerns the revisability of the truths of logic and mathematics.

Now, it may seem that our protagonists are actually in agreement at this point. Consider the seemingly nontemporal character of analytic truths: the sum of 7 and 5 is 12, even in leap years; white will always be lighter than black; no one will ever discover how to trisect an angle. It seems, Wittgenstein says, that these internal relations "are not subject to wind and weather like physical things; rather are they unassailable, like shadows" (1978, 74). But as the umbral simile hints, we should not be misled by appearances. "The picture of a black and a white patch," he remarks,

> serves us *simultaneously* as a paradigm of what we understand by "lighter" and "darker" and as a paradigm for "white" and for "black." Now darkness "is part of" black *inasmuch as* they are *both* represented by this patch. It is dark *by* being black.— But to put it better: it *is called* "black" and hence in our language "dark" too. That connexion, a connexion of the paradigms and the names, is set up in our language.

And our proposition is non-temporal because it only expresses the connexion of the words "white", "black" and "lighter" with a paradigm. (75f.)

The apparent indifference to temporality displayed by propositions that express internal relations is rooted in our tacit refusal to *let* these relations between our words change, not in the imagined essence of "whiteness" or "7" and "5." It may seem that the laws of logic have a kind of inexorability that prevents white from becoming darker than black and that ensures that 7 and 5 will always add up to 12, but "it is *we* that are inexorable in applying these laws" (82).

The suggestion that the inexorability of logic and mathematics is really the inexorability of logicians, mathematicians, and ordinary thinkers and calculators might seem to "abolish logic" (1968, §242). Some have thought the same of Quine's suggestion that "no statement is immune to revision," should only we meet with experiences sufficiently recalcitrant to merit a reweaving of our network of intentional attitudes. Could we really do away with some minimal principle of noncontradiction?[29] Suppose I find myself in the extraordinary position of the radical interpreter, trying to understand from scratch a person whose language is wholly unfamiliar to me. If I can attribute beliefs and other intentional attitudes to that person at all, what reason could I possibly have for interpreting her as believing that each and every statement is unequivocally both true and false at the time of its utterance?

It should be said that Quine is not in the habit of suggesting that the law of noncontradiction might be revised with respect to its truth-value. And he has no faith in the idea of a "prelogical mentality" (1960, 58). His favorite candidate for a "law of logic" that might be revised in light of new experience is just the law of the excluded middle (1980, 43; 1974, 80).

But there is still an important way in which the view that I have attributed to Wittgenstein differs markedly from Quine's. Consider what Quine says:

> As an empiricist, I continue to think of the conceptual scheme of science as a tool, ultimately, for predicting future experience in the light of past experience. Physical objects are conceptually imported into the situation as convenient intermediaries—not by definition in terms of experience, but simply as irreducible posits comparable, epistemologically, to the gods of Homer. (1980, 44)

This passage, despite its antireductionism, would be unacceptable to Wittgenstein, because (among other reasons) it treats physical objects as explanatory "posits." What are these posits supposed to help us explain and predict? Past and future stimulations of our sensory organs—"surface irritations"—I expect Quine would say. But, as I remarked at the end of the preceding chapter, we can *explain* only what we can already *describe*, and we can describe only what we have meaningful terms for. We understand no language prior to this alleged "positing" of physical objects. We do not begin with a way of describing stimulations of our sensory receptors and then proceed to replace or augment those descriptions with "explanations." Physical objects do not arrive on the scene as posits, introduced on the basis of some already determinate set of purposes that motivate our efforts to *explain* our sensory irritations.[30] On the contrary, objects—not to mention other minds—are implicated in the very meaningfulness of our descriptions from the moment we begin learning to communicate with language. To treat objects as posits that serve to explain the irritation of our sensory organs is to recapitulate the "Cartesian" subjectivity of which Quine seems so critical (1969, 69–90).

Quine, like Carnap (1956, 233), insists that the theory of meaning be kept separate from the theory of reference (1980, 22). He sees this as correlative of the view that meanings are not a special kind of object. But Wittgenstein—who shares the latter view—holds that, in the case of macroscopic objects and events in space and time, there is an *internal relation* between a referring term and its referent. I cannot fully understand how to use a referring term without knowing what thing or sort of thing it refers to. That is just the lesson of Wittgenstein's remark that the harmony between thought and reality lies in language. The objects to which words refer do not lie on the other side of some epistemic gap; rather, they themselves have roles to play *in* the language. To understand those roles is, in part, to understand which words refer to which objects. But in that case there is little sense to the idea that the theory of reference must be set apart from the theory of meaning. The concepts of meaning and reference are internally related, and neither is the sort of thing for which a theory is needed.[31]

"The limit of the empirical—is *concept-formation*" (1978, 237), writes Wittgenstein. The moment we try to treat macroscopic spatio-temporal objects as explanatory posits, we overstep the bounds of the empirical, because the meaningfulness of our words depends on our practical consciousness of objects. The construction of concepts, as we saw earlier, involves the setting up of internal relations among the various tools of language, including objects and events that play the role of exemplars. To treat macroscopic objects as posits is to allow that there might be some reasonable doubt about their existence. But to hold such a doubt is to call into doubt the internal relations between words and paradigms. It is to treat those relations as external ones, and that in turn is to cast doubt on my grasp of my own concepts, on my understanding of my own words. If the limit of the empirical is concept formation, then the limit of doubt for a speaker lies in the internal relations that characterize her language.

So, the contingency of our practices does not entail that we could intelligibly *deny* the truth of 7 + 5 = 12 (because, say, it helped make phrenology look more scientific). Someone who held that 7 + 5 = 13 would not be doing *addition*, because the rule for addition is internally related to its instances. Such a proposition might, of course, play a role in some other practice—for example, in a mystical, numerological rite of some sort or as part of an obscure riddle. But that would be to employ another concept, not to revise a truth-value. "The river-bed of thoughts may shift," but "the bank of that river consists partly of hard rock" (Wittgenstein 1972, §§97–99). Quine, as Grice and Strawson charged (1956, 156ff.), confuses the possibility of changing our linguistic practices with the idea that all of our judgments are hypotheses of a sort.

The notion of an internal relation is thus transformed in Wittgenstein's work from a kind of metaphysical relation between objects, which determines their identities, to a pragmatic constraint on linguistic understanding and meaning. Two linguistic instruments are internally related if in order to understand or explain the use of one, I must also understand or make use of the other. However, not just words, but macroscopic objects and events can serve as linguistic instruments, because both play crucial roles in the teaching and learning of concepts. Referring terms for such objects and events stand in internal relations to them: This is the core of the interactive conception of reference. In the next chapter I want to show how ignoring this interactive conception leads the causal theorist of reference into epistemic neurosis.

Notes

1. More recently, Rorty remarks: "I am also puzzled about Davidson's seemingly un-Quinean notion of 'conceptual content,' and by the conceptual-empirical distinction which he draws throughout his Dewey Lectures" (1993, 460 n. 26). See Davidson 1990.

2. I draw on Baker and Hacker 1985, 85–91, 338–47. See also Shiner 1977/78 and Putnam 1994b, 245–63.

3. Russell was criticizing one of the clearest, least dogmatic statements of the idealists' program. See Joachim 1969.

4. Moore takes the proponent of the dogma of internal relations to be confusing the following two propositions:

(1) = "What we assert of Φ, when we say, Φx entails $[\sim(\Phi y)\supset\sim(y=x)]$ can be truly asserted of every relational property."

(2) = "What we assert of Φ, when we say, $\Phi x \supset [\sim(\Phi y)$ entails $\sim(y=x)]$ can be truly asserted of every relational property." (1993, 96f.)

The following formal paraphrase reinterprets the confusion as one about the scope of the modal operator:

(1') $\Box(\forall x)(\forall y)(\forall \Phi)[(\Phi x \ \& \sim\Phi y)\supset\sim(x=y)]$

and

(2) $(\forall x)(\forall \Phi)[\Phi x \supset \Box(\forall y)(\sim\Phi y\supset\sim(x=y))]$,

where "Φ" designates a relational property.

5. Ogden and Richards 1923, chap. 3.

6. A related account of belief and verification appears at 269f.

7. See 1968, §440.

8. Similar considerations would apply to Freud's category of unconscious intentional attitudes, which treats the relation between intention and object as an external one insofar as I can have an unconscious intention without knowing toward which object it is directed. Russell notes this connection between behaviorist views and Freudian ones (1921, 59).

9. Many of the remarks contained in the *Grammar* were written between 1930 and 1932, but not assembled in their extant form until 1933. Remarks from the *Philosophical Remarks* date from 1929 to early 1930. See Rhees's "Editor's Note" at Wittgenstein 1975, 347–51 and "Note in Editing" at Wittgenstein 1974, 487–90.

10. See 1968, §§438ff.

11. I shall discuss correspondence in Chapter 3. Wittgenstein, I believe, deflates the correspondence theory by treating the relation between facts and statements ("propositions" in his terminology) as an internal one, and by holding that facts are individuated intensionally—or so I shall suppose. That is why in the example above "a *single* description holds for both" expectation and fulfilling fact (*that it will rain tomorrow*). This marks a change from the *Tractatus*, where facts were individuated extensionally, and a proper justification for claiming such a change would require further investigation. My main concern here is simply to show how a viable conception of internal relations emerges from Wittgenstein's philosophy.

12. Even in the *Tractatus* the independence of the atomic facts of which the world is said to be "the totality" (1922, §1.11) was only as strong as that countenanced by modest realists, for Wittgenstein's view all along was that "Skepticism is *not* irrefutable but palpably senseless [*unsinnig*]" (§6.51).

13. For an examination of the role of internal relations in Wittgenstein's remarks on rule following, see Baker and Hacker 1984b. The rule skepticism that Kripke and others have found in Wittgenstein's treatment of rules arises, Baker and Hacker argue convincingly, from neglecting Wittgenstein's belief that a rule and its instances are internally related. See Kripke 1982.

14. Wittgenstein later speaks of both concepts (1968, §569), on the one hand, and words (§§11, 23, 360) and samples (§§16, 53, 57), on the other, as being instruments or tools. Rules (§54), descriptions (§291), sentences (§421), and language or languages (§§492, 569) are also described this way. This variety should not bother us as long as we bear in mind that it is between or among the *uses* or *roles* of words or samples that internal relations obtain. See "A New Picture" below.

15. The sense in which the grasp of one concept presupposes a grasp of the other I would explicate as a material-conditional statement embedded in a stronger modal antecedent. Roughly, if in any world in which a given language, *L*, is spoken as it is actually spoken, a grasp of the use of one term, t_1, of *L* implies a grasp of the use of another term, t_2, of *L*, then the uses of t_1 and t_2 in *L* are internally related.

Notice also that the preceding gloss provides only a sufficient condition for an internal relation to obtain between two instruments of language, not a necessary one. Terms like *medical doctor* and *physician* seem internally related in their uses, but I need not be acquainted with one in order to be able to use the other, any more than I need be acquainted with the German word *Hund* in order to use the English word *dog*. Pending a plausible explication of the concept of analyticity, then, we might also say that the uses of two terms are internally related if they stand, one to the other, in a relation of predication or identity in an analytic truth, e.g., "Every physician is a medical doctor." I shall say more about analyticity later in this chapter.

16. See Kant 1965, A6–10/B10–14.

17. One might object that there will always be *some* analytic truth that expresses a given internal relation. Thus, even though (1) "For all x, x is in pain if and only if x displays pain behavior" is not analytic, it might be that some other truth about pain and pain behavior is, for example: (2) "Any world that contains pain contains pain behavior," or (3) "Other things being equal, any person who is in pain displays pain behavior." However, neither of these statements would serve to teach someone the concept of pain. The former, (2), is compatible with the bizarre scenario of, say, half the population's experiencing only unexpressed pain, while the other half experiences no pain, but goes about wincing and grimacing. Only someone who already understood the internal linkage of pain and pain behavior would know that such cases were irrelevant. The latter, (3), suffers the same fate. Unless I already understood the concepts of pain, unexpressed pain, deception, and so on, I would not know what it would be for other things *not* to be equal. Statement (3) amounts to the tautology, "Any person who is in pain displays pain behavior, unless he or she does not." This statement will be useless if I am trying to teach someone the concept of pain. Not every analytic consequence of an internal relation "expresses" that relation in the sense of being useful in the contexts of teaching and learning that relation.

18. Such "construction" is not explicit in the way that the construction of a concept in a mathematical proof might be. The point is simply that I help a person to acquire a certain competence in using words by saying that "white" is lighter than "black."

19. This does not settle whether Wittgenstein thinks "criteria" are decisive or defeasible. On the former, see Cavell 1979; Canfield 1981; and McDowell 1982. On the latter, see, e.g., Hacker 1972, chap. 10. Passages from Wittgenstein 1978 and 1976 suggest that in at least some cases Wittgenstein held criteria to be decisive—for a proof is conclusive, constitutes a new criterion for the concepts of its theorem, and is definitive of those concepts. See 1978, 161, 187, 317, 319, and 1976, 54, 73, 127, 131, 164, 286. However, the urge to equate Wittgenstein's views with a single thesis about the nature of criteria is a reductive impulse that is better resisted. Hacker now holds that criteria can be either decisive or defeasible depending on the case. See Hacker 1993, chap. 13.

20. Cf. Wittgenstein 1975, §225.

21. Cf. Wittgenstein 1975, §225.

22. Given what Wittgenstein says about the standard meter (1968, §50), it might seem that the idea of extracting remarks about analyticity from his work is inappropriate. But I take the point of the example to be not that there is no truth-value that can be assigned to "The standard meter is a meter long," but that any truth-value that we do assign must apply for reasons very different from those for which we might say "This table is one meter long." See Baker and Hacker 1985, 343 and Allen 1993, 121–32.

23. The evidence for attributing to Wittgenstein the view that established mathematical truths are analytic is not unequivocal. One might argue that the influence of Gestalt theories of perception on Wittgenstein led him to treat mathematical truths as synthetic a priori. See Dwyer 1990, 148–66. Wittgenstein himself remarks of "the propositions of mathematics" that "their being synthetic . . . does not make them any less a priori" (1978, 246). However, this "synthetic character" is said to appear "most obviously in the unpredictable occurrence of the prime numbers," because "The distribution of primes . . . is . . . not dis-

coverable by an analysis of the concept of a prime number" (246). That mathematical propositions are synthetic "in this sense" (246) consists in the fact that they "determine a concept by synthesis" (246). Given the way in which I have defined "analytic," it is not clear to me that these remarks or the passages cited by Dwyer are in any conflict (except a terminological one) with the view that I have developed here. It is compatible with the "Gestalt" nature of seeing a mathematical proof as a proof that in so seeing it I should understand that its theorem is true, and I should not have a full grasp of the theorem until I see its proof as a proof.

Perhaps relevant here is Kant's conflation of the alleged existence of synthetic truths knowable a priori with the existence of a special kind of intuition by means of which such truths might be known (see Coffa 1991, 7–21). The Gestalt character of a proof is more akin to a variation on Kant's pure intuition, whereas my claims concern successors for the notion "true in virtue of meaning." The two points are distinct.

24. Tarski 1949, 52–84. For related criticism of Quine, see Lewis 1969, 206, and Putnam 1988, 61–68.

25. This is not, however, intended as a *reduction* of the normative character of use to statistical generalization. The point is, simply, that it does not make much sense to suppose that all the speakers of a language might be mistaken about the correct uses of their words. Quine's behaviorism, as Hacker notes, makes it difficult for him consistently to admit normativity, though his discussion seems to presuppose it. See Hacker 1996b, 207–11.

26. See, e.g., Davidson 1996, 274f.; 1986a, 319.

27. As Davidson has noted, it seems odd for Quine to hold this and also to hold that the theory of meaning must be kept utterly separate from the theory of truth. See Davidson 1996, 271.

28. See, e.g., Chomsky 1969; Rorty 1972; and Hockney 1975.

29. See Putnam 1983, 98–114.

30. Quine sometimes speaks of physical objects as "cultural posits" or "myths" (1980, 44). This is at best a misleading metaphor. A *cultural* posit is as different from a *posit* as an *unconscious* intention is from an *intention*. See also Quine 1960, 21–25.

31. This is not necessarily to say that reference must always be an internal relation. Talk about the macroscopic world of objects and events differs from talk about, say, electrons precisely insofar as the latter is hypothetical, while the former is not. So it might be possible to make a case for saying that, with electrons and other unobservable entities posited by the natural sciences, a person can be competent using a term for a theoretical posit without knowing its referent. It can be a matter of dispute (the argument might go) what the referent of a term like *electron* is, even when proponents of different subatomic theories use terms like *electron* in significantly similar ways. Denying that macroscopic objects and events are posits, then, does not automatically commit one to instrumentalism about unobservable entities on the grounds that posited entities are ineligible referents. On the other hand, perhaps such an argument against scientific realism could be constructed—I am indifferent between the two conclusions, and the issue is not of consequence for my concerns here.

3

Truth and Reference

> *In fact the skeptical philosopher never succeeds in killing his primitive credulities which, as Hume says, reassert themselves the moment he takes up the affairs of life and ceases to murmur incantations which generate his philosophic doubt. More than that, most philosophers refuse to be Skeptics even in their philosophic moments; these travelers on the road to Nothing mostly look back and would return whence they have come, but cannot.*
>
> —John Wisdom, Philosophy and Psycho-Analysis

Now that we have a firmer grasp on the notion of an internal relation, it is time to resume the diagnostic task I began in Chapter 1. I pointed there toward a tension that characterizes the work of metaphysical realists who refuse to acquiesce in skepticism, but who think that a refutation of the skeptic's doubts is either unavailable or unnecessary. Epistemic neurosis, I suggested, is a psycho-philosophical disorder that afflicts any position that is committed simultaneously to asserting and denying skeptical theses. And metaphysical realism, I argued, is marked by the symptoms of such a neurosis when it tries to go beyond asserting the real possibility of the skeptic's scenarios.

It is important to notice that the tension at work here is not just the cleavage that Hume describes between his "reflections very refin'd and metaphysical" and the "current of nature" which dispels the "philosophical melancholy and delirium" (1978, 268f.) brought on by his skeptical thoughts. It is a tension that characterizes metaphysical realists "even in their philosophic moments," as Wisdom observes. My complaint is not just that as a metaphysical realist I cannot take skepticism seriously when I drink with my friends or take to bed with my lover, but that I cannot afford to take skepticism too seriously when I philosophize—unless I have the Humean resolve to become a philosophical skeptic. The threat of skepticism usually does not stop the metaphysical realist from proceeding with an examination of other philosophical problems. But with no categorical or probabilistic refutation of the external-world skeptic to illuminate matters, it is difficult to see how the metaphysical realist can turn to those other philosophical questions without assuming that the skeptic is, as a matter of fact, wrong. In making this assumption, the metaphysical realist assumes everything that Putnam helps himself to. This disorder, I suggested, is displayed prominently in the desire to refute Putnam by recourse to an externalist account of reference. In this chapter I shall argue that such accounts of reference are themselves epistemically neurotic, leading to unanswerable skeptical worries, even while they purport to explain reference and truth. First, however, we need more context.

Correspondence Theories of Truth

In the Chapter 1, I outlined some features of the interactive conception of reference, to which I take Putnam to be committed. Putnam, I suggested, views reference as an intentional notion: Referring is something that we *do*, and the reference of words derives from their acquisition of standard uses in our linguistic practices—from the fact, that is, that we generally use them to refer to particular things or kinds of things.[1] In order to understand what a word standardly refers to, then, I must understand its standard use, and I cannot understand its standard use without knowing to what it standardly refers. I glossed this point by saying that there is an internal relation between a referring term and its referent, and I contrasted this view with the view that the reference relation is an external one such that I can understand the standard use of a term without knowing what it refers to. If reference is an external relation, then I can understand quite well how to *use* terms like *brain* and *vat*, without knowing what their referents are. The "real" referents of these terms might be forever hidden from me, so that I could always have been a brain in a vat, "speaking" (in my vattish way) a complex language without, however, knowing what any of its terms referred to.

Now, I have already objected to the dialectical use of an externalist account of reference as a response to Putnam, on the grounds that it appeals to empirical premises as much as Putnam's interactive conception does, and, more particularly, that one can no more knowingly say that, had we always been brains in a vat, we could not knowingly say so, than one can knowingly say that we have always been brains in a vat—unless we have not always been brains in a vat.

But it might seem that this view has independent merits that go beyond its attraction—and spurious support—for metaphysical realism. Indeed, it might reasonably be thought to be independent of metaphysical realism. One version, the treatment of reference as a causal relation of some sort, might seem especially attractive insofar as it raises the hope of satisfying the naturalistic impulses of many contemporary philosophers. Reference, it might be plausibly thought, is a natural phenomenon among others, not some mysterious act of mind. As such, it calls out for a naturalistic theory, not a "magical theory of reference" (1981, 15), to borrow Putnam's own words.

In addition to its obvious naturalistic appeal, a causal treatment of reference holds out the promise of rescuing the correspondence theory of truth from some traditional objections—especially the claim that correspondence is rendered a trivial notion by the inability of the correspondence theory to distinguish one fact—to which a true statement is said to correspond—from another. Let me make my way to these points gradually.

I have spoken of "the" correspondence theory of truth, but there are many things that might potentially be meant by saying that a statement is true if and only if it corresponds to reality, or the world, or the "facts." In particular, the features of a potential correspondence theory can be mapped from the ways in which it lets us respond to the following three questions:

1. Does the alleged relation of correspondence imply the doctrine of metaphysical realism?
2. Are the portions of reality to which a statement is thought to correspond to be individuated extensionally or intensionally?
3. Is the alleged relation of correspondence between a statement and reality an internal relation or an external one?

On the assumption that there are two possible answers to each of these questions, they yield—at least numerically—eight different possible ways of being a correspondence theorist (2^3 unique yes-no combinations). It is possible that there are additional questions that would yield additional possible combinations and, so, additional permutations of the idea of correspondence. But these three will prove complication enough for now.

The first thing to note is that not all of these combinations are likely to yield something that is appropriately thought of as a correspondence *theory* of truth. Some of them effectively deflate the notion of correspondence so that it does no explanatory work. In my opinion this is as it should be. But my present point is that it is not clear without further consideration just how the notion of correspondence is to be understood, and I think that debates over the validity of correspondence sometimes become bogged down because these questions have not been clarified and answered beforehand.[2]

My first question, or at least a variation on it ("Are we obliged to accept metaphysical realism if we want to be realists?"), has so far supplied a major theme of my discussion and needs no further explanation. The point of asking the question, simply, is that prima facie there is no necessary connection between being a metaphysical realist and being a correspondence theorist. (But as we shall see, efforts to explain correspondence by appeal to causal theories of reference are hard to hold apart from metaphysical realism.)

My third question is closely related to my remarks in Chapter 1 about the interactive conception of reference, and its significance should be clear from my examination of Wittgenstein in Chapter 2. A relation of reference is an internal relation, I said, if I cannot understand how to use the referring term without understanding what the term's referent is. Similarly, to say that there is an internal relation between a true statement and the fact that—as it were—"makes it true"[3] is just to say that someone cannot understand the statement without knowing which fact it does correspond to (if it is true) or would correspond to (if it were true). As we have seen, Wittgenstein held such a view as early as the *Tractatus*. So, for example, if I say, "There are a lot of magpies around here," you understand what I have said only if you understand what circumstances would have to obtain in order for my statement to be true. A likely candidate for those circumstances in this case would be the fact that there are a lot of magpies around here. (Of course, in the *Tractatus* Wittgenstein held that it was the atomic propositions, into which all statements of natural language could be uniquely analyzed, that were internally related to atomic facts.) I shall give further attention to this concern when I turn to causal theories of reference later in this chapter.

The Individuation of Facts

This leaves my second question: "Should facts be individuated intensionally or extensionally?" *Intensional* here is spelled with an *s* not a *t*, and it is closely associated with what logicians think of as nontruth-functional or "opaque" contexts. Truth-functional or transparent contexts allow for substitutivity *salva veritate*—that is, truth-preserving substitutivity. Thus, if P and Q are truth-functionally equivalent expressions (that is, if P is the case if and only if Q is the case), then the one expression can be substituted for the other in any context without altering the truth-value of the context in which they are embedded. Expressions of natural language, however, often fail to live up to this standard. "George Sand" and "the Baroness Dudevant" refer to the same person—George Sand *was* the Baroness Dudevant. But in some contexts it is doubtful that they can be interchanged without altering the truth-value of the expression in which they occur. For example, it seems plausible that I might believe that George Sand was a French writer without believing that the Baroness Dudevant was a French writer. Verbs like *believe, hope, fear,* and so on are often treated by logicians as intensional operators. The substitution of co-referring terms into contexts governed by such operators can change the truth-value of the overall formula.

In less technical terms, the relevant application of the term *intensional* is to what we might loosely call the "connotation" of an expression, in contrast to its "denotation" or "extension." To borrow an example from Gottlob Frege,[4] we might say that the expressions "Morning Star" and "Evening Star" have the same denotation or extension, but different connotations or intensions. Both refer to the planet Venus, but they do so in different ways.

Now, what is in question when it is asked whether facts are to be individuated intensionally or extensionally can be illustrated by recurring once again to the example of beliefs and posing a similar question. When I see Venus shining in the western sky, I may believe that "That heavenly body I see is the Evening Star." But the Evening Star is the same object as the Morning Star—namely, the planet

Venus. So, do I also believe that "That heavenly body I see is the Morning Star"? If beliefs are individuated intensionally, or according to connotation, then the belief that "That is the Evening Star" is a different belief from the belief that "That is the Morning Star." I can believe one without believing the other. However, if we choose to individuate beliefs extensionally—and some philosophers do[5]—then the belief that "That is the Evening Star" is exactly the same belief as the belief that "That is the Morning Star." If I believe the one, then I believe the other—even if I would never say so.

The case with facts is similar. If facts are individuated intensionally, then the fact that the Evening Star is in the western sky is not the same fact as the fact that the Morning Star is in the western sky. But if facts are individuated extensionally, then we have here not two distinct facts, but one. The belief or claim that that is the Evening Star is made true by the very same fact that makes it true that that is the Morning Star.

Indeed, critics of correspondence, most notably Donald Davidson, have argued that if facts are individuated extensionally, then there is only one fact—period.[6] And every true statement corresponds to this One Big Fact. The argument for this conclusion is sometimes called the "slingshot" argument (Barwise and Perry 1983, 24), and it goes roughly like this. Take a true statement like:

(1) *De Caelo* was written by Aristotle.

If we are individuating facts extensionally, then the fact that makes this statement true is surely the same fact that makes it true that

(2) Aristotle was the author of *De Caelo*.

Statements (1) and (2) vary in the ways in which they pick out this fact, one using the passive, the other the active, voice. But the fact remains the same. Now, by substituting a coextensional expression for "the author of *De Caelo*" we get, for example,

(3) Aristotle was the most famous student of the philosopher Plato.

"The author of *De Caelo*" and "the most famous student of the philosopher Plato" each uniquely refers to the same thing, Aristotle. They refer to Aristotle in different ways, but for an extensional account of facts the ways in which they refer are irrelevant. What matters for the composition of facts is what things are referred to by the expressions that compose statements about those facts. Consequently, statement (3) is made true by the same fact that makes (1) and (2) true.

Now, extensionally speaking, the fact that makes it true that Aristotle was the most famous student of the philosopher Plato is the same fact that makes it true that

(4) Plato was the philosopher whose most famous student was Aristotle.

Again, all that differs from (3) to (4) is the way in which the fact that makes each of them true is individuated. If, again, we substitute a co-referring expression for "the philosopher whose most famous student was Aristotle" we can get the result that

(5) Plato was the author of *The Republic*.

And if facts are individuated according to denotation, not connotation, then this is made true by the same fact that makes it true that

(6) *The Republic* was written by Plato.

On this view, then, it seems that the fact that makes it true that *De Caelo* was written by Aristotle is the same fact that makes it true that *The Republic* was written by Plato. "That *De Caelo* was written by Aristotle" and "that *The Republic* was written by Plato" are merely two different names or definite descriptions for the same fact. If we continue to apply this sort of co-referential substitution with sufficient ingenuity, it begins to look as though we can never tell one extensionally individuated fact from another. There is, it seems, just One Big Fact, and all true statements correspond to it, or perhaps to the world as a whole. This result, as Davidson has urged, trivializes the correspondence relation.[7] The term *correspondence to reality*, as Rorty remarks, becomes little more than "a stylistic variant" of the term *truth* (1991b, 138).

So it might seem that the correspondence theorist should retreat to the view that facts are individuated intensionally—according to connotation. On a charitable construal this route also leads to triviality. For now, when called on to identify the fact that makes it true that Plato is the author of *The Republic*, we can say only that this statement is "made true" by the fact that Plato is the author of *The Republic*. And that is just an awkward way of saying that it's true that Plato is the author of *The Republic*, if and only if Plato is the author of *The Republic*. Correspondence is once again rendered trivial.

On a less charitable construal, a doctrine of the intensional individuation of facts leads to some peculiar difficulties. First, if it is to avoid the triviality encountered above, it requires us to suppose that the world divides into precisely as many facts as we have names for those facts. But there is no limit to the number of such names we can justifiably generate, as Morning-Star/Evening-Star examples suggest. All we need do is give another name, N, to the planet Venus, and it seems that there is automatically a fact in the world to fit the statement that N is in the western sky. Moreover, it would seem that speakers of different languages make assertions that are not rendered true (or false) by the same facts, simply because they speak different languages. Translation, on this view, is always wide of the mark. And, even more strangely, if there must be a unique, independent fact for every true statement we can make, then it seems as though we must countenance the existence of negative facts. What exactly would such a thing be like? Perhaps Sartre's example of looking for Pierre in the café and, on failing to find him, being confronted by the Nothingness of his absence would fit the description (1956, 40ff.). But although this might be a plausible description of the phenomenology of thwarted expectation, it is implausible to suppose that such Nothingness is an objective property of the world—something about whose presence I could be mistaken.

Causal Theories of Reference

A causal account of reference might seem to provide a solution to the difficulties that have been raised for a correspondence theory of truth, for those difficulties stem from the attempt to provide some kind of substance for the term *fact*. However, what exist independently of our descriptions (the modest realist and the metaphysical realist agree) are not facts, but objects. And what "correspondence" really amounts to, it might be said, can be broken down piecemeal into relations of reference between the terms of a statement and objects in the world. This is Devitt's view:

> The only entities we need are the familiar ones we already have, objects of one sort or another; and the only relations we need are ones of reference between the parts of the sentence and the objects. If we could generalize this approach to cover the many structures of natural language and explain the appropriate reference relations, then we would be well on the way, at least, to explaining the correspondence notion of truth. (1997, 28)

The criticism that there is just One Big Fact that acts as an all-purpose truth-maker is dulled considerably once we allow that particular objects that had been thought to compose a fact can be uniquely picked out by way of their individual causal relations to speakers and their words. The "fact" that Plato is the author of *The Republic* is not the same "fact" as the "fact" that Aristotle is the author of *De Caelo*, because the terms "Plato" and *"The Republic"* stand in different causal relations to the world from those in which "Aristotle" and *"De Caelo"* stand. But this view can be expressed without any talk at all of facts or similar entities (such as "states of affairs" or "propositions"). The question of whether such entities are individuated extensionally or intensionally accordingly goes by the board.[8]

Now, causal theories of reference come in a number of shapes and sizes. One need not hold that all referring terms can be accounted for by a causal theory. One might for example find it plausible to claim that the reference of proper names can be explained causally, but deny a similar explanation for general terms on the grounds that such an account would require the existence of real universals like "Redness" and "Roundness" to stand at one end of the causal chain. Or one might maintain that an appropriate nominalism about universals will yield an adequate causal account of the reference even of general terms. But more important, there are different accounts of just what role the notion of a cause is supposed to play in so-called causal theories.

Saul Kripke and Hilary Putnam are sometimes regarded as causal theorists, but, as Putnam has observed, the views of both are best thought of as accounts of how the reference of proper names (in Kripke's case) and natural-kind terms (in Putnam's case) is *fixed* "although no definite description is associated with any term by all speakers who use that term" (1983, 17).[9] Frege had held that the *Bedeutung* of a referring term was fixed by its *Sinn*,[10] or, in the less technical terminology I employed above, that the denotation was fixed by connotation. The definite description "the Morning Star" picks out one thing, namely, the brightest planet that appears in the eastern sky before sunrise, and which thing it picks out is determined by its connotations—a "star" in the morning sky. Russell, in turn, argued that proper names were all disguised definite descriptions: "Walter Scott" is to be analyzed as "the author of *Waverly*."[11] And from here it was a small step to the conclusion that the reference of a proper name was determined by the connotations of the definite description that could be substituted as a proper analysis for the name. But, as Wittgenstein argued, there is no one description uniquely associated with a proper name. "We may say, following Russell: the name 'Moses' can be defined by means of various descriptions," he writes:

> But when I make a statement about Moses,—am I always ready to substitute some *one* of these descriptions for "Moses"? I shall perhaps say: By "Moses" I understand the man who did what the Bible relates of Moses, or at any rate a good deal of it. But how much? Have I decided how much must be proved false for me to give up my proposition as false? Has the name "Moses" got a fixed and unequivocal use for me in all possible cases?—Is it not the case that I have, so to speak, a whole series of props in readiness, and am ready to lean on one if another should be taken from under me and vice versa? (1968, §79)

The fact that no one description—or even necessarily a determinate "cluster" (Kripke 1980, 55)[12] of descriptions—can stand in for a proper name is among the reasons that Kripke cites in favor of the view that the reference of a proper name is fixed by an "initial baptism" (78), followed by a shared intention among members of the linguistic community in which the baptism occurs to use that name to refer to the person or thing baptized:

> Someone . . . is born; his parents call him by a certain name. They talk about him to their friends. Other people meet him. Through various sorts of talk the name is spread from link to link as if by a chain. A speaker who is on the far end of this chain, who has heard about, say Richard Feynman, in the market place or elsewhere, may

be referring to Richard Feynman even though he can't remember from whom he first heard of Feynman or from whom he ever heard of Feynman. He knows that Feynman is a famous physicist. A certain passage of communication reaching ultimately to the man himself does reach the speaker. (91)

This view is plausible and surely tells us something about the transfer of linguistic information—what Devitt calls "reference borrowing" (1981, 137). But to the extent that it is correct it is merely a description of one aspect of what I have been calling the interactive account of reference. "Richard Feynman" refers to Richard Feynman because that is how we use the name. Causality certainly plays a role here. The person who mentions the name "Feynman" to another depends on the laws of physics for the sound waves created by her voice to impinge on the ears of another, and so on. But to call it a "causal theory of reference" is misleading. If anything, it is a *historical* account of reference relying on "historical chains" (Devitt 1981, 8 n. 9)[13] to explain how certain words came to be used as they are, and it offers us no *theory* at all about what reference *is*. It certainly makes no effort to reduce reference to some nonintentional, nonsemantic notion.

The idea that reference must be reduced to physicalistic terms if it is not to seem in some way mysterious gets one of its most influential statements in Hartry Field's paper "Tarski's Theory of Truth" (Field 1972). On Field's account reference and truth are to be treated as phenomena on a par with chemical valence. In such a case we want to explain some regularity or similarity among particular instances, and so we offer hypotheses that would account for the phenomena by seeing them as the consequence of some simpler facet of nature underlying the phenomena. A proper reduction of reference to a physicalistic level would thus have to be something more than a list, even a recursive "list" of the sort that Tarski's notion of "satisfaction" invokes (1949, 62f.). An alleged reduction of chemical valence that merely eliminated the word *valence* by pairing every known element and compound with an integer would be no genuine reduction at all, thinks Field (1972, 362ff.). What is needed is a reduction—or an "approximate reduction" (374)—of the "laws" of reference to succinctly worded causal laws. Field wants what we might call a type-type identity theory that identifies types of referential relations with types of causal relations. The presence of identifiable types would then yield lawlike generalizations.

Devitt sympathizes with Field's criticism of Tarski (Devitt 1997, 29) and with the general thesis that "The overall aim in semantics is to explain semantic relationships like designation in nonsemantic terms," though he is uncertain about the prospects for a successful type-type reduction of reference (1981, 8). However, the difficulty of finding type-type identity relations need not result in difficulty for identifying particular reference relations with particular causal relations. Devitt has, in effect, a token-token identity theory, according to which reference in general (or "designation," as Devitt prefers) is "a functional relation which can be realized by various physical relations" (29). His plan is to incorporate much of the Putnam-Kripke treatment of how reference is fixed, but also to insist that particular reference relations can be explained in terms of formative confrontations between minds and objects, which ground the abilities of speakers to refer to, or designate, particular objects. Such a primal confrontation produces a "grounding thought" (133) in the mind of the speaker, a thought that "includes a mental representation of that object brought about by an act of perception" (133), and which might be expressed by a speaker by means of a demonstrative like "That cat is friendly." However, it is the "demonstrative representation" (133) that is primary for Devitt. All linguistic reference is ultimately traceable to designation "in thought" (130), and all such designation depends causally on the causal relation that brings about the demonstrative representation. This causal relation does not merely fix reference, it instantiates reference—it *is* reference in this particular case. And the thing referred to is the perceptual cause of the grounding thought.[14]

How does a causal theory, in either Field's or Devitt's sense, save the correspondence theory? It might be tempting at first to think that the move to causal theories of reference again has the effect of trivializing the correspondence theory of truth, for once all talk of facts and states of affairs has been replaced by talk of objects and reference, all that the causal theorist of reference might seem to be saying is—to take cases of simple predication, for example—that it is true that *Px*, if and only if (1) "*x*" refers to *x*, (2) "*P*" refers to *P*, and (3) *Px*. And this sounds like a variation on the observation that it is true that *S*, if and only if *S*.

However, Field's criticism of Tarski should make us wary of any such conclusion, and Devitt makes it clear that he has something more in mind than this deflated notion of correspondence. The reason that a causal theory can rescue a substantive correspondence theory, thinks Devitt, is that it provides us with a wholly objective relation, or set of relations, between words and the world. Classical correspondence theories, which made reference to facts, are better thought of as embodying three central elements. The relation of correspondence "(1) . . . holds of a sentence . . . partly in virtue of the structure of the sentence. (2) It holds of a sentence partly in virtue of the relation the sentence has to reality. (3) It holds of a sentence partly in virtue of the objective, mind-independent nature of reality" (Devitt 1997, 27). By satisfying this call for a relation to a mind-independent reality, thinks Devitt, a causal theory of reference contributes to a rehabilitation of the correspondence theory of truth.

Putnam's Argument

Devitt's insistence on the "objective, mind-independent nature of reality" builds metaphysical realism right into the correspondence theory of truth (given Devitt's conflation of metaphysical and modest realism—see Chapter 1). But the problem for causal theories of reference transcends any explicit commitment that its proponents might have to metaphysical realism. Prima facie, one might hold a causal theory without being a metaphysical realist. The problem arises from the fact that causal relations are external relations, and to treat reference as an external relation is to court skeptical doubts about the determinacy of reference. This is the insight that drives Putnam's "model-theoretic" argument against the correspondence theory of truth.

Variations on Putnam's argument against the correspondence theory appear in an essay entitled "Realism and Reason" (1978, 123–40) in *Reason, Truth and History* (1981, 29–48, 217f.), in the introduction to a collection of essays also entitled *Realism and Reason* (1983, viii–xii), and in a paper reprinted in that collection, "Models and Reality" (1–25). Much of Putnam's argumentation is rooted in technical considerations concerning model theory and the Skolem-Löwenheim Theorem, but I shall ignore these technicalities wherever possible, because I believe that the central insight of the argument is easily summarized in terms I have already introduced.

In *Meaning and the Moral Sciences* Putnam presents his case as follows. Suppose that there is a determinate reality independent of the reliability of our epistemic capacities in the way characteristic of metaphysical realism. Suppose further that this determinate, strongly objective reality contains or can be broken down into infinitely many objects. When we speak whatever language we speak, we take ourselves to be referring to these objects, or sets of them. That is to say that there is an intended interpretation of the words of our language according to which certain parts of the world, rather than others, are picked out by certain bits of language.

According to the correspondence theory of truth, it is in virtue of this determinate correspondence that what we say stands a chance of being true. Of course, it is not a 100-percent chance, because many of the things we have wanted to say about the world have proved—as far as we can tell—to be false, or at least unjustified, and this gives us some reason to suppose that we are now discussing the world in terms of a theory that is only partially or approximately true. Worse yet, metaphysical realism's vulnerability to skeptical worries means that no matter how ideal our theory of the world might be—in terms of standardly recognized theoretical constraints, such as consistency, simplicity, or predictive power, and in terms of particular operational constraints within the theory[15]—there is always a skeptic's chance that it is false. But just as the truth of any statement is due to the satisfaction of the proper correspondence, so the falsehood of any statement is due to a failure of that correspondence. Whether a key is the right key or not depends on whether or not it fits the lock that is to be opened.

Now, let us assume that we have such an ideal theory, T1:

> Lifting restrictions on our actual all-too-finite powers, we can imagine T1 to have every property *except objective truth*—which is left open—that we like. E.g., T1 can be imagined complete, consistent, to predict correctly all observation sentences (as far as we can tell), to meet whatever "operational constraints" there are ... to be

"beautiful," "simple," "plausible," etc. The supposition under consideration is that T1 might be all that *and still be* (in reality) *false*. (1978, 125)

In order to allow for the skeptic's chance that T1 might be wrong, however, the metaphysical realist must have a way of singling out what the intended interpretation of the terms of the theory is, because—and this is what the model-theoretic argument is meant to show—for a consistent set of statements that can be interpreted to be about objects in some infinite set of objects there will always be some model, consisting of an interpretation and an infinite domain, according to which the terms of T1 *correspond* to the objects of that model's domain.[16] But then, insofar as there is such a correspondence, the theory T1 will be true on that model. There will always be *some lock* that the key fits and some key that fits a given lock. A key is the *right shape* only relative to some particular lock. There is no key that is *absolutely* the right shape—apart from any particular lock.

Unless the metaphysical realist can give a reason for choosing one specific correspondence between the terms of T1 and one specific domain of objects—one way of "carving up" the world—then, Putnam claims, there is no reason to think that truth is independent of theory interpretation. Moreover, as we shall see, Putnam holds that the realist *can* give no principled reason for choosing one interpretation over another.

This version of the argument emphasizes showing that an "ideal" theory could not be false, unless there is some principled method for restricting the many ways of interpreting the terms of a language. In *Reason, Truth and History* Putnam takes a slightly different tack, but with similar results. Suppose again that we have an ideal theory, as above, but let it also be the case that that theory is *true*, and not just true on any old interpretation. In other words, on the "intended" interpretation of the terms of T1, there is a correspondence between every statement of T1 and some set of pieces of the world. But if that is the case, then we can tell for any statement of the language what its truth-value is, simply because our theory correctly predicts the truth-values of all observation statements and tells us what theory statements are made true by what observations, and so on. Putnam argues that even if a theory is true on the intended interpretation, there is still nothing privileged about that interpretation, because there will always be other interpretations that assign exactly the truth-values to all statements that the intended interpretation does. Thus, correspondence on the intended interpretation does not *explain* truth, for there are other correspondences on other interpretations that could do the job just as well. In fact, Putnam claims that there are interpretations according to which the truth-value of every statement will remain unchanged *in every possible* world from the truth-value it is assigned under the intended interpretation.[17]

The argument can be made clearer by applying it to a few simple terms of English. Putnam has us consider the statement "A cat is on a mat." We can interpret this statement such that *cat* may be taken to refer to cherries and *mat* to trees in the actual world without changing the truth-value of the statement in any possi-

TABLE 3.1   Cat*hood

	Some cat is on some mat	No cat is on any mat
Some cherry is on some tree	(a) x is a cat* iff x is a cherry	
No cherry is on any tree	(b) x is a cat* iff x is a cat	(c) x is a cat* iff x is a cherry

TABLE 3.2   Mat*hood

	Some cat is on some mat	No cat is on any mat
Some cherry is on some tree	(a) y is a mat* iff y is a tree	
No cherry is on any tree	(b) y is a mat* iff y is a mat	(c) y is a mat* iff y is a quark

ble world—provided we give the proper sort of interpretation to "A cat is on a mat" at each world. We could, for instance, reinterpret "A cat is on a mat" to mean "A cat* is on a mat*," where we can define cat*hood and mat*hood in worlds where some cat is on some mat, some cherry is on some tree, no cat is on any mat, no cherry is on any tree, or where the noncontradictory conjuncts of the preceding conditions are true. Thus, we can give a simple visual display of Putnam's reinterpretation by constructing what we might call "transworld definition matrices" for cat*hood (Table 3.1) and mat*hood (Table 3.2).

The conditions expressed outside the matrices specify, when taken in row-column conjuncts, classes of worlds. The statements inside the matrices indicate the truth conditions at these worlds of the statements "x is a cat*" and "y is a mat*." Brief scrutiny should reveal that in worlds of type (a) "A cat* is on a mat*" is true, because some cherry is on some tree, but additionally, "A cat is on a mat" is true, because some cat is on some mat. In worlds of type (b) "A cat* is on a mat*" is true, because some cat is on some mat, but this also means that "A cat is on a mat" is true. In worlds of type (c) "A cat* is on a mat*" is false, because cherries cannot sensibly be said to be on quarks, but likewise "A cat is on a mat" is false, because no cat is on any mat. Therefore, in all possible worlds—that is, necessarily—a cat is on a mat, if and only if a cat* is on a mat*. By extending this method and playing a similar game with *all* of the statements of the language, we arrive at the result that the intended interpretation is not needed to preserve the truth-values of our statements in all possible worlds. It seems then that we have no reason to think that we know what our words refer to, and so we are left without any clear explanation of the truth of our statements in terms of their correspondence with the world. But surely it is the goal of a correspondence *theory* of truth to *explain* truth.

Objections

Some critics of Putnam's argument have objected to his reasoning on technical grounds. Hacking, for example, complains that Putnam's use of the Skolem-Löwenheim Theorem jeopardizes the interest of the argument, because that theorem is restricted in its application to sentences of first-order logic, and it is unlikely that natural language can be completely formalized without going beyond the unquantified, truth-functional expressions of first-order calculus (1983, 105). Putnam has responded that although the original inspiration for the argument was the Skolem-Löwenheim Theorem, the version presented in *Reason, Truth and History* relies, rather, on the "permutation of individuals—which does apply to second-order logic, modal logic, tensed logic, etc.!" (1994b, 372 n. 11).[18] However, as will become clearer below, I think that such technical disputes are extraneous to the central point of Putnam's argument.[19] That point is that to treat reference as an external relation is automatically to invite skeptical doubts about our knowledge of reference.

Three objections to Putnam's reasoning are particularly important for my purposes. The first of these is that Putnam's argument is hopelessly intertwined with his talk of "ideal theories" and that, because no clear sense can be made of the notion of an ideal theory, no clear sense can be made of the argument. The second objection maintains that Putnam has begged the question against the causal theorist by implicitly assuming that a causal theory could not explain the reference of its own terms. The third objection insists that Putnam's conclusion goes through only because he implicitly assumes determinate reference for the terms of a stable metalanguage—he assumes that we can know what words we refer to when we discuss questions about reference, but that we cannot in turn know the reference of those words.

I shall take these points in turn, extending my examination of the first two over this section and the next. As we shall see in the next chapter, the third objection is really an objection against efforts to treat reference as a theoretical notion and, as such, is not in conflict with Putnam's position. It is, rather, a restatement of his main point. The second objection rests on a misinterpretation of Putnam's argument, confusing an objective indeterminacy of reference with our inability to know what we refer to, but this confusion is abetted by Putnam's own tendency to make the same conflation at times. The first criticism, I shall argue in this section, forces us to clarify Putnam's argument further, at which point we shall see that ideal theories play no substantive role in his reasoning. Let me begin, then, with ideal theories.

When Putnam first introduces his model-theoretic argument, remember, he invites us to suppose that we are in possession of a theory that is "imagined complete, consistent, to predict correctly all observation sentences (as far as we can tell), to meet whatever 'operational constraints' there are . . . to be 'beautiful,' 'simple,' 'plausible,' etc." (1978, 125). It is an *ideal* theory that wants for nothing in the way of things that make a theory virtuous. However, the idea that we could make sense of what having such a theory would amount to is not free of controversy. Michael Williams objects that "we have little or no idea what it would be for a theory to be ideally complete and comprehensive in the way required, or of what it would be for inquiry to have an end" (1996c, 233).[20] We could never have a good reason for thinking that we had arrived at an ideal theory that could answer all of our questions, because the mere fact that all of our questions could be answered by such a theory might as easily be a consequence, as Rorty puts it, of our "merely having gotten tired or unimaginative" (1991b, 131). Moreover, if, with Williams, we hold to a contextualist picture of justification (1996c, 114–21)—a picture for which Putnam's work since *Reason, Truth and History* displays some affinity—then it is hard to see how any theory could have the kind of global, acontextual character suggested by Putnam's description of an ideal theory.

This is important, because the possibility that even an ideal theory might be false is used by Putnam to characterize metaphysical realism (1978, 125). However, metaphysical realism will be distinguished from modest realism by the possibility of a false ideal theory, only if we assume (1) that there is no distinction to be drawn between statements and hypotheses, and (2) that the explanatory coherence of the totality of a belief system is what constitutes its justification.

Consider the first assumption. As we saw in the preceding chapter, if we suppose that the meaning of a word is, paradigmatically, its use in the language, then we can distinguish common or garden-variety claims about macro-level objects and events from theoretical claims about the explanatory micro-structures of these things. If we do draw this distinction, however, then the possibility of a false ideal theory no longer divides metaphysical from modest realism. For now this possibility leaves untouched our quotidian judgments about the spatio-temporal objects and the macroscopic phenomena that are implicated in the meaningfulness of our words. Since, on my reading, Putnam is moving toward an interactive conception of reference that treats reference as an internal relation, in the spirit of Wittgenstein's later views, it is not clear that he is entitled to such talk of ideal theories.

But even if we allow Putnam to join Quine in denying this distinction, his apparent commitment to contextualism about justification would seem to rule out the intelligibility of a unified, ideal theory, the possibility of whose falsehood would distinguish strong objectivism from its modest alternative. That Putnam has contextualist leanings is made clear by his attempt to respond to criticisms of his apparent equation of truth with idealized rational acceptability:[21]

> People have attributed to me the idea that we can sensibly imagine conditions which are *simultaneously ideal* for the ascertainment of any truth whatsoever, or simultaneously ideal for answering any question whatsoever. I have never thought such a thing. . . . I do not by any means *ever* mean to use the notion of an "ideal epistemic situation" in this fantastic (or utopian) Peircean sense. . . . One cannot say what are good or better or worse epistemic conditions in quantum mechanics without using the language of quantum mechanics; one cannot say what are good or better or worse epistemic situations in moral discourse without using moral language; one cannot say what are good or better or worse epistemic situations in commonsense material object discourse without using commonsense material object language. (1990, viii–ix)

A belief or claim is not justified in virtue of its coherence with the totality of a knower's existing beliefs (or in virtue of its coherence with some other total belief system to which the knower might be tempted to move by a new belief's failure to cohere with some antecedent totality of beliefs). Rather, it is justified by its coherence with some subset of beliefs that are deemed relevant in a particular context, and such a context will take a great many other beliefs for granted. The historian, as Williams is fond of remarking, need not bother to ascertain whether the earth has existed for more than 150 years in order to be justified in believing that Napoleon was victorious at the battle of Austerlitz.[22]

If Putnam both allows a distinction between theoretical and nontheoretical claims and embraces a contextualist picture of justification, why does he persist in talk of ideal theories?

In the period that extends from his initial rejection of metaphysical realism in "Realism and Reason" until his writings of the mid-1980s, Putnam displays considerable ambivalence about the kind of position that he is arguing for: "'Coherence theory of truth'; 'Non-realism'; 'Verificationism'; 'Pluralism'; 'Pragmatism'; are all terms that have been applied to the internalist perspective; but every one of these terms has connotations that are unacceptable because of other historic applications" (1981, 50). His frequent references to Kant in *Reason, Truth and History* sometimes give the impression that he is advocating an updated, linguistic version of transcendental idealism (60–64). But his retention of some arguments from his earlier writings (e.g., 22–25) might be thought to suggest that he does not see his new views as a complete overthrow of his earlier ones. As well, his remarks in "Realism and Reason" about Peirce and ideal theories (1978, 125, 130) can give the impression that he wants some kind of Peircean pragmatism in which truth is linked to what would be believed at "the end of inquiry"—an impression strengthened by his apparent identification of truth with "idealized rational acceptability" in *Reason, Truth and History* (1981, 55).[23] Moreover, his favorable comments on Dummett's "verificationist semantics" (1978, 129) invite the label of "antirealist" to join an already confusing blend of terminology. And there is also a Wittgensteinian strand to his arguments, which has become prominent in his more recent work and which I am trying to uncover in his transitional writings. This engagement with a motley of competing ideas (sometimes similar, sometimes not) is one reason for Putnam's use of ideal-theory talk. I think he has not at this point clearly settled on what position he wants to take, and so he retains his earlier treatment of metaphysical realism as characterized by the possibility of a false ideal theory without seeing that this treatment conflicts with what will later become a dominant strain in his thinking.[24]

Another, related reason for his persistence in such talk is his tendency to link metaphysical realism with a correspondence theory of truth and a causal theory of reference. If reference is assumed to be an external relation, then the distinction between statements and hypotheses cannot be made in the way I have suggested, because I have based that distinction on the assumption that a referring term is internally related to its referent. Thus, unless the causal theorist can find another way of distinguishing between theoretical and nontheoretical discourse, ideal-theory talk will divide metaphysical realism from modest realism. All truth-claims about the world around us will then be part of the ideal theory, and the possibility of that theory's falsehood will raise skeptical worries about our knowledge of the external world.

The temptation of taking metaphysical realism to entail an externalist account of reference is understandable, for if externalist accounts of reference do raise skeptical worries, then they amount to applications of a strong objectivism to the notions of reference and truth. However, my claim is that Putnam's argument is really an argument against externalist accounts of reference, not against metaphysical realism as such.[25] Putnam should, therefore, not be so eager to identify metaphysical realism with the real possibility of a false ideal theory. The modest realist is free to allow that an ideal theory could be false as long as she distinguishes hypotheses from judgments, and Putnam's own arguments, in my opinion, commit him to this distinction.[26]

These remarks should not be interpreted as saying, however, that the problems raised by Williams's objection are compounded by Putnam's wavering. Rather, if Putnam's argument is thought of as a variation on Wittgenstein's critique (considered in Chapter 2) of Russell's theory of desire—as I am suggesting it should be—then the notion of an ideal theory does no real work; it is merely an artifact of Putnam's linkage of metaphysical realism with causal theories of reference and of the transitional nature of his views. "Idealness of the theory," as David Lewis says, "doesn't figure in the proof" (1984, 230). All that matters for Putnam's argument is (1) that to treat reference as an external relation is to concede that I could be able to use my terms without understanding what they refer to, and (2) that the reference of my terms and the truth of true statements would be explained just as well by causal* relations as it would be by causal relations.

These two points are crucial to rebutting the second, and most common, objection to Putnam's position. This complaint rests on an important misreading of the argument, but Putnam does not help matters by phrasing his position somewhat carelessly at times. The complaint is that Putnam *assumes* the correspondence theory of truth to be false "in order to show that it is false" (Devitt 1997, 228). Putnam, say his critics, begs the question.

Putnam is indeed unclear at times about how appeals to the appropriate causal chain between referent and word fall short. Consider what he says in response to Field's suggestion (1972, 367ff.) that there might be a physicalistic relation, R, such that "(1) x *refers to* y if and only if x bears R to y": "If reference is only determined by operational and theoretical constraints . . . then the reference of 'x bears R to y' is *itself* indeterminate, and so knowing that (1) is true will not help" (Putnam 1981, 45f.). Prima facie, this response is not very compelling. Holders of a causal theory of reference are trying to provide something *in addition to* the "operational and theoretical constraints," and they argue that it is this additional constraint that explains reference, where the initial constraints failed. A later remark does nothing to assuage the impression that Putnam is begging the question:

> If I say "the word 'horse' refers to objects which have a property which is connected with my production of the utterance 'there is a horse in front of me' on certain occasions by *a causal chain of the appropriate type,*" then I have the problem that, if I am able to specify what *is* the appropriate type of causal chain, I must *already* be able to refer to the kinds of things and properties that make up that kind of causal chain. But how did I get to be able to do this? (1981, 66)

It is tempting to reply with the causal theorist that I got to be able to do this *by means of a causal chain of the appropriate type*. If people can refer determinately at all, then they have been doing so longer than anyone has been discussing causal theories of reference. To suppose that a causal chain of the appropriate type cannot explain the reference of the terms of a causal theory of reference itself is, as Devitt complains, to *presuppose* that a causal theory of reference is false.

Lewis mirrors Devitt's criticism of Putnam.[27] Putnam's critique of causal theories can be seen as a conviction that any effort to produce the causal theorist's desired additional constraint—call it C—will result only in an extension of the original theory, T1, and that T1 will simply annex this extension, so that the terms of C will meet with the same indeterminacy as those of T1. If T1 really is a true, ideal theory, and if reference is a theoretical notion, then presumably C will be part of T1. Lewis replies, "C is *not* to be imposed just by accepting C-theory. That is a misunderstanding of what C is. The constraint is *not* that an intended interpretation must somehow make our account of C come true. The constraint is that an intended interpretation must conform to C itself" (1984, 225). Which interpretations of our language and theory are most likely to be correct will be selected for by some objective, determinate relation between the world and the terms of our theory—whatever we might happen to think about that relation. There is nothing wrong with holding that the reference of the terms of a causal theory is to be explained by that very theory.

Epistemic Neurosis—Again

The Devitt-Lewis objection presupposes that Putnam's argument is meant to show that reference itself is indeterminate. But his real point—which he sometimes misrepresents—is that if reference is an external relation, then *I cannot know* what my words refer to, even if they do refer determinately. Of course, if I cannot know this, then I have little reason to think that my words do refer determinately, but it cannot be claimed that reference is indeterminate for the externalist, without the further assumption that determinate reference requires that a competent speaker know what her terms denote—and that *is* to beg the question by assuming that reference is an internal relation. Putnam, in his zeal, sometimes runs the two points together. All this, however, leaves the real point untouched: Externalist accounts of reference lead to skeptical worries about our knowledge of reference.

Lewis seems at times to recognize that Putnam is trying to draw a skeptical consequence from premises taken for granted by causal theorists (and by natural-property theorists like Lewis himself).[28] But he still misreads Putnam as calling the determinacy of reference into doubt, rather than as expressing doubt about how we can know what our words refer to, given the externalist's assumptions. "The rules of disputation sometimes give the wrong side a winning strategy. In particular, they favor the skeptic. They favor the ordinary skeptic about empirical knowledge; they favor the logical skeptic, Carroll's tortoise or a present-day doubter of non-contradiction; and they favor the skeptic about determinate reference" (1984, 225). The implicit suggestion is that the skeptic has an *unfair* advantage when it comes to the "rules of disputation." Says Lewis, "truth is one thing, winning disputations is another" (226).

But why should the skeptic's alleged advantage be thought unfair? This charge, I suspect, is motivated by sympathy for the attitude to skepticism that Devitt displayed for us in Chapter 1. Skeptical doubts are *unanswerable* (they have an advantage), but they need not be taken seriously (that advantage is unfair). As we saw, however, the fact that metaphysical realism rests on the real possibility of the skeptic's scenarios makes this response a symptom of epistemic neurosis, for skepticism and metaphysical realism are linked (in spite of themselves, in Devitt's case) by the controversial assumption that skeptical scenarios would explain so-called inner experience. The problem that faces the externalist about reference, similarly, is that if a diagnosis of epistemic neurosis is to be avoided, then some good reason must be given for thinking that the skeptic's complaints are mistaken or irrelevant. Devitt and Lewis, having misread Putnam's intentions (with a little help from Putnam), provide us with no such good reason, for they overlook the fact that Putnam's skeptical argument turns on a premise that is central to theoretical treatments of reference. Consider why.

The problem for causal theories of reference is not simply that "causes" is itself a victim of the indeterminacy of reference—that is, indeed, true only if causal theories of reference are false. The problem is, rather, that for any external relation between the terms of our language and the objects of some domain, there will always be countless other external relations between the terms and the objects of other domains and no reason for preferring one over another. Although there may be some causal relation between *cat* and cats, there will also be a causal* relation between *cat* and cats*. And even if "'Causally related' is 'glued to one definite relation' [viz., a causal relation] by causal relations, not by metaphysical glue" (Devitt 1997, 227), it is equally the case that "causally related" is "glued" to some other definite relation (a causal* relation) by causal* relations (see Putnam 1983, 296). Rorty summarizes Putnam's point succinctly: "No matter what nonintentional relation is substituted for 'cause' in our account of how the things in the content reach up and determine the reference of the representations making up the scheme, our theory about what the world is made of will produce, trivially, a self-justifying theory about that relation" (1979, 295). There is nothing wrong with holding that the reference of the terms of a causal theory is to be explained by that very theory—except that if a competing causal* theory is capable of a similar self-application, then there will be little reason for thinking that a causal theory is superior to its causal*-theoretical rival.

Now, the causal theorist will want to say that a causal* relation cannot do the theoretical work expected of a causal relation, and therefore if I can have knowledge of a causal theory of reference, then I can know what my words refer to.[29] (It might even be held that ordinary speakers have long held some kind of undeveloped "folk theory" of the causal nature of reference.) But any reason for thinking that a causal theory is correct is as much a reason for thinking that a causal* theory is correct, because causal* explanations *look just like* causal explanations—they just place a different interpretation on the terms used in explanations, and the claim that causal relations explain the reference of the terms of a causal theory of reference can be interpreted just as easily as the claim that causal* relations explain the reference of the terms of a causal* theory of reference.

Causal relations are external relations, because, as Hume elegantly argued, I can be well acquainted with a particular event without being able to identify its cause or, indeed, its effects. And if reference is a causal relation, then I can understand the use of a referring term without knowing what it refers to. *That is just what it is for reference to be an external relation.* So the very idea of giving a causal theory (or some other externalist theory) of reference automatically opens up the possibility that a causal* theory of reference is true—that is just what it would be for us to be ignorant about the reference of our terms. When Putnam says, "how 'causes' can uniquely refer is as much of a puzzle as how 'cat' can" (1978, 126), he is being sloppy. But when he points out that there is more than one relation that constitutes a model of our language—maybe causal relations constitute one such model—he is pointing out that the causal theorist owes us an *explanation* of why it is this particular relation that constitutes the "correct" model rather than some other relation. To the extent that no such explanation can be given, the "causal theory of reference" proves simply to be a "magical theory of reference" (1981, 15).

At this point it is reasonable for the externalist to respond that the truth of a causal* theory, or some other perverse account, of reference is indeed a possibility that is raised automatically by treating reference as an external relation, but, like the skeptic's hypothesis about the external world, it is "too implausible to take seriously" (Devitt 1997, 64).[30] But as in the case of confronting the external-world skeptic, there is no demand here that the causal theorist refute a potential infinity of rival explanations, one by one. All that is needed is a reason for thinking that some representative rival to a causal theory of reference is not as good an explanation of our behavior as a causal theory is. And it happens that in this sort of case the only representative rivals are skeptical hypotheses.

The causal theorist—or more generally, the externalist about reference—purports to be offering an empirical explanation. But that very attempt to *explain* gives rise to skeptical doubts that the causal theorist then wants to regard as uninteresting in much the way that the metaphysical realist is tempted to treat external-world skepticism as uninteresting. Once again, to treat such doubts as uninteresting is to treat the position that engenders them as uninteresting. The causal theorist cannot avoid skeptical worries without avoiding causal, and other externalist, theories, and this ambivalent relation with the skeptic is a symptom of the externalist's epistemic neurosis. "To adopt a theory of meaning according to which a language whose whole use is specified still lacks something—namely its 'interpretation'—is to accept a problem which *can* only have crazy solutions" (Putnam 1983, 24).[31]

Notes

1. When I say that reference is an intentional notion, I do not mean that intentions to refer can be determinate prior to our acquisition of language. The point is simply that the standard reference of a term is determined by the way in which it is standardly used by speakers, who might well have used the term differently from the ways in which they do and who might well come to use it differently, either by way of stipulation or by way of gradual linguistic evolution.

2. E.g., the engaging exchange between Austin and Strawson, in which Austin argues for rehabilitating correspondence, while Strawson insists on abandoning it. See Austin 1964 and Strawson 1964. See also the criticisms of Rorty and Davidson in Callinicos 1995, 80–82, which, moreover, follow Devitt 1984 in conflating metaphysical realism with modest realism.

3. Like Rorty, I do not want any special ontology of "truth-makers." See Rorty 1992a, 415. But like Putnam, I think that there is an innocuous use of such verb phrases as "makes it true that" and "is made true by." See Putnam 1992c, 431–35.

4. The terminology, of course, is not Frege's. He speaks of *Sinn* and *Bedeutung*. The former is usually translated as "sense," while the latter is variously rendered as "meaning," "reference," or "*nominatum*." In addition to capturing the intuitively obvious distinction between connotation and denotation, these terms have special technical roles to play in Frege's philosophy of language—so I prefer to avoid them. See Frege 1984, 162.

5. In the *Tractatus*, for example, Wittgenstein remarked with some overstatement: "It is clear that 'A believes that p,' 'A thinks p,' 'A says p,' are of the form "'p" says p': and here we have no co-ordination of a fact and an object, but a co-ordination of facts by means of a co-ordination of their objects" (1922, §5.542). A more explicit example is Martin 1987, 182–89.

6. See Davidson 1984b, 37–54; Frege 1984, 163f.; Linsky 1992; Barwise and Perry 1983, 24f.; and Church 1956, 24f. In what follows I take some liberties with the "carving" of content (see Linsky, 1992) to which a critic might object—e.g., in the move from "was writ-

ten" to "is the author of." But I am content to retreat to the more cautious version offered by Church 1956, if pressed on this point.

7. Alex Callinicos treats this conclusion as a triumph for correspondence: "As to Davidson's charge that 'there is nothing interesting or instructive to which true sentences might correspond,' what about the world itself?" (1995, 82). In "True to the Facts" (1984b, 37–54) Davidson took himself to be advocating a modest version of correspondence, but he now gives the same argument as a reason for rejecting correspondence: "There is no interest in the relation of correspondence if there is only one thing to which to correspond, since, as in any such case, the relation may as well be collapsed into a simple property: thus, '*s* corresponds to the universe,' like '*s* corresponds to (or names) the True,' or '*s* corresponds to the facts' can less misleadingly be read as '*s* is true'" (1990, 303).

8. Of course, the causal theorist typically wants to distinguish extension from intension, or the theory of reference from the theory of meaning. That distinction goes naturally with the decision to treat reference as an external relation.

9. See also Putnam 1992a, 221 n. 4.

10. Or, in one translation, its meaning was fixed by its sense. See Frege 1984, 157–77.

11. "On Denoting" in Russell 1994, 423.

12. Kripke mistakenly attributes the "cluster-theory" to Wittgenstein. See Kripke 1980, 31. See also Devitt 1981, 31.

13. Devitt also suggests the adjective "historical" (1981, 8), but he tends to use "causal" for reasons that will become clear shortly.

14. Devitt's talk of grounding thoughts is reminiscent of the foundationalists' side of the Vienna Circle's debate over verification and correspondence theories of truth, especially Schlick's *Konstatierungen* ("confirmations"); see Schlick (1959). This debate was strongly influenced by the Circle's transmutation of Wittgenstein's internalist conception of reference into a relation of verification, as is hinted at by Schlick's curious attempt to compare *Konstatierungen* to analytic truths (1959, 225).

15. E.g., "Probably, if red litmus paper turns blue when immersed in a solution, then that solution is a base."

16. We can do the same thing for a finite world by taking our sentences to refer to objects in a finite domain. See Putnam 1978, 139 n. 3.

17. As I remarked in Chapter 1, talk of possible worlds should not be taken with any ontological seriousness, nor should it be taken to explain modality. See "Possibility and Necessity" in Putnam 1983, 46–68 and Putnam 1992a, 51.

18. Putnam also complains that Hacking ignores the discussion of second-order logic in "Models and Reality." I assume he refers to Putnam 1983, 23.

19. See Lewis 1984, 229 for a similar point.

20. See also Williams 1980, 269.

21. I shall argue in Chapter 4 that this identification is only apparent.

22. See Wittgenstein 1972, §§183ff.

23. All that Putnam actually claims is that metaphysical realism cannot be consistently distinguished from Peircean pragmatism, not that he himself wishes to embrace Peircean pragmatism. See Putnam 1978, 130.

24. Putnam uses the notion of an ideal theory to distinguish Peircean pragmatism from "realism" in his John Locke Lectures before developing the model-theoretic argument and so, before avowedly abandoning metaphysical realism. But he criticizes such talk as senseless in the absence of a substantive correspondence to "a framework of space-time loca-

tions, objects, etc., to specify the manner in which and the conditions under which scientific investigation is to proceed to the limit" (1978, 36).

25. Cf. Devitt 1997, 331.

26. In more recent work Putnam hints at such a distinction, and he explicitly commits himself to the related distinction between the analytic and the synthetic, sometimes making use of the term *internal relation* as well. See especially, Putnam 1994a, 458, 513 and 1992b, 374, 388, 393, 402, 408 n. 82.

27. The reading of Putnam common to Devitt and Lewis is identified and criticized in LePore and Loewer 1988.

28. Lewis does not think that a causal chain of the appropriate type is sufficient to explain reference. He also wants to restrict the class of models of our language according to their domains. Certain pieces of the world are more eligible referents because they have relatively *natural* properties: "the ones whose sharing makes for resemblance, and the ones relevant to causal powers" (Lewis 1983, 347). But the notion of a natural property is less helpful if we consider the possibility of natural* properties. See Putnam 1990, 38. See also 1981, 37, where Putnam rebuts a similar attempt to distinguish intrinsic from extrinsic properties.

29. Devitt has recently advanced an objection like this. See Devitt 1997, 334–36.

30. Devitt does not make this move—perhaps because he thinks that nonstandard interpretations of reference relations would not be explanatory. See Devitt 1997, 334–36.

31. See also the remarks that follow this one and Putnam's comments on his changing conception of "use" at 1994a, 457.

4

Renouncing All Theory

> *Where does our investigation get its importance from, since it seems only to destroy everything interesting, that is, all that is great and important? (As it were all the buildings, leaving behind only bits of stone and rubble.) What we are destroying is nothing but houses of cards and we are clearing up the ground of language on which they stand.*
>
> —Ludwig Wittgenstein, Philosophical Investigations

The modest treatments of truth and objectivity I am advocating avoid the epistemic neuroses that trouble metaphysical realism and externalist treatments of truth and reference. Because the modest realist does not allow that skeptical scenarios are real possibilities, she is in a position to avoid the fragmented self-understanding that threatens the metaphysical realist, and by denying that truth and reference are notions that can be explained by external relations she avoids the psycho-philosophical disorder characteristic of the causal theorist's efforts to save a substantive correspondence theory of truth.

But, as we saw in Chapter 1, Putnam's argument against the real possibility of our always having been brains in a vat does not work as an antiskeptical argument, because it uses empirical premises that are called into doubt by the skeptic. So it would seem that no justification has been given for modest realism, beyond the prospect of avoiding epistemic neurosis, and such a justification will not likely convince the dedicated metaphysical realist, who will probably want to respond that the mere absence of some metaphorical "neurosis" is no indicator of the *truth* of modest realism. After all, it may be that the skeptic is right, and that the only mistake on the part of the metaphysical realist consists in failing to acquiesce in skepticism. Nor, I must concede, has any conclusive reason been given for thinking that reference is an internal relation. All that I have argued is that to treat reference as an external relation is to become a metaphysical realist about reference—to invite the real possibility of skeptical scenarios regarding my knowledge of the reference of my words. But perhaps we *are* in the position of not knowing the real reference of our terms—perhaps we are and always have been brains in a vat.

The causal theorist would be wiser to avoid drawing this connection between skeptical doubts about the reference of our terms and skeptical doubts about our knowledge of the world around us. As I argued in Chapter 1, we can no more try to justify an externalist account of reference without begging the question against the external-world skeptic than we can try to justify treating reference as an internal relation without similarly begging the question. It would, however, be odd to suppose that reference and truth possessed the kind of strong objectivity characteristic of metaphysical realism while denying that the world itself possessed such objectivity. If I cannot be radically mistaken in my beliefs about the world in the way imagined by the external-world skeptic and, yet, I *can* be so mistaken about the reference of my words, then it seems that the "aboutness" of my beliefs must be altogether different from the referentiality of my words. There would have to be an internal relation between belief and object, but an external relation between word and referent, such that I would typically know what my beliefs were about, but not necessarily what my words referred to. It is unlikely that such a view could be made plausible. So it seems that externalist treatments of reference are not quite as independent of strong objectivism as they might at first have seemed to be in Chapter 3.

Nonetheless, my emphasis on the metaphor of neurosis invites a question about the nature of my criticisms. What, exactly, is the objection to metaphysical realism, as long as its adherents refrain from begging the question against the skeptic?

Part of what I am trying to do is to follow Rorty's advice for pragmatists: "offer the skeptic a way of speaking which would prevent him from asking his question" (1991b, 138). Such a way of speaking would, of course, also prevent the metaphysical realist from stating a view that depends on the real possibility that the skeptic's hypothesis might be right. That there is such a way of speaking is part of the argument in favor of modest realism and the treatment of reference as an internal relation: The presence of a coherent alternative to metaphysical realism and related doctrines suggests that the strong objectivist cannot claim uncontroversially to reflect the natural opinion of prereflective reason. But, additionally, I want to lighten the burden of proof that modest realism must bear by arguing that, far from being natural or inevitable—far from being "a conception of an objective world" that relies on "nothing but platitudes we would all accept" (Stroud 1984, 82)—metaphysical realism turns on substantive philosophical assumptions. I will approach this task by considering an important respect in which the views of the metaphysical realist and the causal theorist are formally similar.

The causal theorist's position, I shall argue, depends on the contentious assumption that truth and reference are unified phenomena that are amenable to theoretical explanation. Unfortunately, critics of the correspondence theory and its causal-theoretic crutches tend not to recognize this assumption, even when—

as in Putnam's case—their own arguments call it into question. Rather, they are tempted to offer alternative "theories" of truth, because it seems difficult to imagine what it would mean for an apparently substantive notion like truth not to stand in need of explanation. But if truth seems to require a theoretical explanation, then that is because we lack a clear overview of the contexts in which we learn to employ the concept. We learn how to use words like *true* in contexts that we do not usually learn to describe.

Much the same, I shall suggest, holds for the metaphysical realist's assumption that our beliefs and experience need to be explained by postulating the existence of an "external" world. Like the correspondence theory, metaphysical realism rests on a contentious methodological presupposition about its objects of inquiry. If metaphysical realism seems natural or inevitable, then that is partly because we lack a perspicuous representation of our epistemic practices and of the "inner experience" that strong objectivism takes for granted in stating its own case. The point of my arguments is, thus, also to place a greater burden of proof on the doctrines that I am criticizing. If that can be done, then we will have further reason to think that modest realism is, in John McDowell's words, "intellectually respectable" (1994, 113).

Epistemic Privilege

In Chapter 3, I presented three objections to Putnam's provisional skepticism about our knowledge of reference. Two of these have been dealt with already. First, the notion of an ideal theory, I argued, plays no essential role in Putnam's argument; that argument rests, rather, on the claims that to treat reference as an external relation is to open the possibility that we do not know the reference of our own words and that, when this idea is coupled with attempts to explain reference as an object of theory, the possibility of such ignorance becomes a real possibility. Second, once we recognize the centrality of these two claims, we can clarify Putnam's argument sufficiently to absolve him of the charge of begging the question against his opponents. Putnam's point is not that an externalist treatment renders reference indeterminate, but that it casts doubt on our knowledge of reference simply by presenting it as a phenomenon that stands in need of empirical explanation.

We are returned now to the third objection—that Putnam's argument presupposes, controversially, our ability to know what we refer to when we use words to refer to other words. According to this criticism, Putnam needs to presuppose our knowledge of reference in a stable metalanguage that remains mysteriously insulated from the skeptical worries said to threaten our knowledge of reference in the object language, if those worries are even to be formulated. In order to argue that we do not know whether *cat* refers to cats or to cats*, Putnam must assume that we know how to refer to the word *cat* and, also, that we know how to refer *in the metalanguage* to the cats and cats* that we are supposed to be confused about referring to in the object language.[1]

The trouble with this objection is that it undercuts the very assumption against which Putnam is arguing—namely, that reference and truth are theoretical notions.[2] Putnam's point is that by treating reference as something that stands in need of, and is amenable to, explanation, the causal theorist automatically admits skeptical doubts, for the assumption that an explanatory theory can be had here presupposes a split between the "observable" phenomena of language use and the underlying reality that is alleged to explain those phenomena—whether that underlying reality should take the character of posited theoretical entities and processes (particular causal relations) or merely (as the instrumentalist might have it) some lawlike regularity in events. The very suggestion that the reference of our words needs an explanation—in terms of an empirical causal theory, for example—presupposes that we have access to linguistic phenomena at a level that is epistemically prior to our knowledge of reference. We can explain only what we can already identify and describe, and the supposition here is that we can identify and describe the uses of linguistic expressions, that we can understand how to use expressions, without yet knowing how and to what those expressions refer. (In other words, reference is an external relation.)

This supposition, as we have encountered it, is made in the service of another—namely, that we can identify and describe some range of expressions as true statements distinct from false statements and distinct from other kinds of utterances (questions, commands, requests, and so on) that are neither true nor false. And this is just the supposition of stable metalinguistic reference. It is the goal of a correspondence theory of truth to explain the truth of true statements, and the point of a causal theory of reference is, in part, to make such a correspondence theory viable. But we can identify the true as an *explanandum* only if we understand the various uses to which expressions are put and only if we can knowingly refer to them. These are constraints that come with the project of treating truth as the object of an explanatory theory. The reason that bizarre causal* theories of reference constitute skeptical worries for the causal theorist is that they are real possibilities relative to the uses of our words and the truth of our statements. And real possibilities, remember, are possibilities whose actuality would explain some given phenomenon or phenomena of which we are assumed from the start to have knowledge.

The point here is a general one about empirical explanation (in contrast to "explaining" the use of a word, for example). Before I can go looking for explanations, I must have in mind some determinate phenomenon that, from the perspective of my interests, needs to be explained. And from this perspective the phenomenon to be explained is always more certain than the explanation that I seek. That is a methodological constraint on explanatory investigations: I must provisionally regard the *explanandum* as already known and the *explanans* as—

to begin—unknown. The latter is something to be hypothesized and tested, and my confidence in it can never rationally be greater than my confidence in my knowledge of the former, for the justification of the *explanans* derives precisely from its explanatory value. (Or, for inductivists, my confidence in the available evidence must always be greater than my confidence in the conclusion that such evidence is taken to support, since evidential support is not a deductive relation.) Moreover, the explanation must compete with rival explanations, other real possibilities, and so my confidence in it must be lower than my confidence in my initial knowledge of the phenomenon to be explained—unless I have some independent reason for trusting in the truth of the hypothesis. Of course, any particular theoretical statement can play the role of either *explanandum* or *explanans*.[3] But for as long as it takes the role of *explanandum*, it must be regarded as more certain than the real possibilities that might serve to explain it.

Now, I have no complaint with the granting of epistemic privilege for standard methodological purposes. But it is by no means clear that we either can or need extend this methodological procedure to "phenomena" like truth and metalinguistic reference. Skepticism about our knowledge of reference gets off the ground only with help from the noncompulsory assumption that the use of a word is more certain than its reference—an assumption that entails both that metalinguistic reference is more certain than object-language reference and that a sharp distinction can be drawn between the theory of meaning and the theory of reference. But this is just another way of saying that skeptical doubts about reference rest on the substantive philosophical assumption that truth, meaning, and reference are appropriate objects for an explanatory theory—that truth, meaning, and reference possess hidden natures. Putnam's argument assumes nothing about metalinguistic reference that is not assumed by the enterprise of trying to give a theoretical explanation of truth. If those assumptions seem questionable, then so much the worse for theories of truth.

Renouncing Theory

In "Pragmatism, Davidson and Truth" Rorty reaches a similar conclusion about the theoretical status of truth. Pragmatists, Rorty suggests, are better off without a theory or definition of truth, and they should stick to the purely "negative point" (1991b, 127) that "one [can]not use truth as an *explanatory* notion" (127). Some philosophers, notably, Richard Boyd (1973) and an earlier incarnation of Putnam (1978, 18–33), have thought that metaphysical realism and a correspondence theory of truth could be justified on the grounds that they provided an explanation for the apparent success of the natural sciences. Any such explanation hinges on the viability of explaining truth as a substantive, external relation between words and the world. Otherwise, when we say that some theory, T, is successful because it is true, we will simply be reasserting the claims made by T. In other words, to say, "T is successful because (1) T entails that S, and (2) it is true that S," will amount to saying no more than "T is successful because (1') T entails that S, and (2') S," unless, that is, truth itself can be given an explanation in terms of, say, a causal theory of reference. The problem, as we have seen, is that bizarre relations of reference to gerrymandered objects like cats* and mats* manage to "explain" truth just as well as causal theories do. Because truth is not itself fit for theoretical investigation, it can do no explanatory work in theories about the success of science or the evolutionary advantages of particular "systems of belief" or "conceptual schemes."

Unfortunately, critics of correspondence often are not themselves free of the impulse to treat truth as a theoretical notion—to give a rival account that will fill the emptiness of our metaphysical longing. It is, after all, not immediately obvious what we are to do with the concept of truth, if we are denied the chance of explaining it theoretically. This is, as Wittgenstein remarked of such matters, "The difficulty of renouncing all theory: One has to regard what appears so obviously incomplete as something complete" (1980a, §723).

Such difficulty is apparent in much of Putnam's work.[4] Until quite recently he has held that truth should be viewed as a "substantive" or "substantial property of assertions" (1983, 280f.). Truth, he has repeatedly said, is "some kind of correctness which is substantial and not merely 'disquotational'" (246), a "genuine property" (1990, 276) or a "*normative* property" (1988, 69). He has praised those "who see truth as a substantial notion which still remains to be philosophically explicated in a satisfactory way " (1994b, 315). And he has chastised Rorty's alleged "denial that truth is a property" (321).

But for truth to be a genuine property for a pragmatist is just for truth-talk to be irreducible. And *every* case in which Putnam presses the point is, indeed, one in which he criticizes views that he takes to be reductive.[5] There is nothing here for Rorty to disagree with.[6] He himself has sometimes said that "truth is a property . . . of sentences" (1989, 7).[7] Why think that to call truth a "property" is to say something more?[8]

One answer Putnam gives is that if truth were not a property, then we could give no "rationale" for the "laws and inference procedures" (1992c, 436) of logic—we could not say that the laws and procedures of logic are *truth-preserving*. But since, as Putnam observes, "Logical inference does not carry truth from premises to conclusion in the way a pipe carries water from one place to another" (436), it is hard to see how this comes to saying more than *if an argument is valid, then if its premises are true, so is its conclusion*. Putnam and Rorty agree that the laws of logic "are connected with our understanding of truth itself" (436). As Rorty says (perhaps too strongly), "We should hardly call something 'logic' or 'valid inference' if we did not think it preserved truth" (1992a, 417).[9]

Putnam's insistence on a substantive notion of truth seems at times to lead him to try defining truth as "some sort of ideal coherence of our beliefs with each other and with our experiences *as those experiences are themselves represented in our belief system*" (1981, 50). Thus in *Reason, Truth and History* he speaks of "the idealization *theory* of truth" (56; my emphasis) and tells us that truth is "(idealized) rational acceptability" (49) or "an *idealization* of rational acceptability" (55), that "*Truth is ultimate goodness of fit*" (64). Summarizing his views in the introduction to *Realism and Reason* he says that "truth is to be identified with justification in the sense of *idealized* justification" (1983, xvii) and he polemicizes against "disquotational" treatments of truth:

> If a philosopher says that *truth* is different from *electricity* in precisely this way: that there is room for a theory of electricity but *no room* for a theory of truth, that knowing the assertibility conditions is *knowing all there is to know* about truth, then . . . he is denying that there is a *property* of truth (or a property of rightness, or correctness), not just in the realist sense, but in *any* sense. (xv)

More recently, Putnam notes his passing fancy for "the identification of truth with idealized warranted assertibility" (1992b, 364) and "the view that a statement is true if and only if acceptance of the statement would be justified were epistemic conditions good enough," saying that he "no longer defend[s] that theory of truth at all" (1994b, v). It was, partly, "the hope that truth might actually be reduced to notions of 'rational acceptability' and 'better and worse epistemic situation' . . . that was responsible for the residue of idealism in *Reason, Truth and History*" (1992b, 373).

Any attempt to reduce truth to idealized rational acceptability faces serious problems. As Putnam himself observes, "rational acceptability is both tensed and relative to a person" (1981, 55). Is ideal rational acceptability similarly relative? If so, then truth becomes relative too. If not, then we seem forced to exclude from our list of truths any claim that is not ideally warranted for every epistemic agent to make. But this leaves out a lot of claims that we ordinarily—and justifiably—regard as true. If I am stranded on Europa, I may be the only person who is justified in claiming that there is a volcanic eruption taking place there. It is counterintuitive to suggest that for that reason alone what I say, as I record my last explorer's log, is not true.[10]

The problems do not end here. The better our warrant for a statement, it might be plausibly maintained, the more likely it is (from our evidence-relative perspective) to be true. But does this mean that we could—in "theory," if not in practice—have perfect justification for asserting a statement? Does it mean that we could have *conclusive* reasons for asserting or believing the statement?[11] In the introduction to *Realism and Reason* Putnam rejects this proposal, along with the view that "ordinary-language-sentences about material objects outside of theoretical science could be conclusively verified" (1983, xvii). But if idealized justification does not consist in having conclusive reasons, then an ideally justified statement can still be *false*.[12] So truth and ideal justification cannot be identified.

But there are other, antitheoretical tendencies in Putnam's earlier presentations of his view—tendencies that are masked by his recent self-descriptions. In

Reason, Truth and History he writes, "I am not trying to give a formal *definition* of truth, but an informal elucidation of the notion" (1981, 56). He elaborates in "A Defense of Internal Realism": "Now, the picture I have just sketched *is* only a 'picture.' If I were to claim it is a *theory* I should be called upon at least to sketch a theory of idealized warrant; and I don't think we can even sketch a theory of actual warrant" (1990, 42). "For a variety of reasons," he is not "offering . . . a definition of truth" (viii). "The suggestion," he clarifies elsewhere, "is simply that truth and rational acceptability are *interdependent* notions" (1988, 115).

Indeed, it is this antitheoretical strain in Putnam's thinking that has come to dominate his talk about truth. Only a metaphysical realist, he now maintains, should have any interest in "a view of truth as a 'substantive property'" (1994a, 501)—one that can be ascribed "to all and only true sentences" (501). And he confesses, "I fell into this error myself in my previous published criticisms of deflationism" (501 n. 34). This change of heart is reflected in his opinion of the relation between truth and warrant. "Our understanding of conjecture, speculation, etc.— and of what warrants *all* of the various uses of statements—undergirds our understanding of truth, and conversely" (1992b, 365). Putnam no longer identifies truth with ideal warrant (if he ever unequivocally did), but rather insists "that our grasp of truth depends on our grasp of warranted assertibility" (365) and that "*belief* and ideal justification are internally related" (374). "'Assertibility' and 'truth,'" he writes in a discussion of Wittgenstein, "are internally related notions: one comes to understand both by standing inside a language game" (1994b, 271).[13] This, I maintain, was the real insight of Putnam's model-theoretic argument against correspondence theories of truth all along, even if it has taken him nearly two decades to pry that insight free from competing philosophical opinions and deal with the difficulty of renouncing all theory.

The Uses of *True*

Truth, I am claiming, is not a fit object for theoretical explanation. What, then, are we to say about it? And why does it seem so obvious that we need a theory of truth?

At least part of the answer to the latter question, I think, is that the scientific temperament of our age and culture encourages us to think in terms of theoretical explanations. But this cannot be the entire answer. After all, very few thinkers are tempted to offer theories of chairs and tables—it seems abundantly obvious that a theory of tables will not teach us anything more about what tables are than we already know. An analogous claim about truth, however, seems far from obvious.

I think some light is shed on both our questions by those same contexts of teaching and learning that we noted when we considered Wittgenstein's conception of internal relations in Chapter 2. There is much about the context in which we learn the use of an expression that is not articulated to us and that we do not learn to articulate ourselves, despite our learning to employ the expression.

Wittgenstein makes some instructive remarks in *Zettel* about learning to use the word *think:*

> One learns the word "think," i.e., its use, under certain circumstances, which, however, one does not learn to describe.
> But I *can teach* a person the use of the word! For a description of those circumstances is not needed for that.
> I just teach him the word *under particular circumstances.*
> We learn to say it perhaps only of human beings; we learn to assert or deny it of them. The question "Do fishes think?" need not exist among their applications of language, *it is not raised.* (What can be more natural than such a set-up, such a use of language?)
> "No one thought of *that* case"—we may say. Indeed, I cannot enumerate the conditions under which the word "to think" is to be used—but if circumstance makes the use doubtful, I can say so, and also say *how* the situation is deviant from the usual ones.
> If I have learned to carry out a particular activity in a particular room (putting the room in order, say) and am master of this technique, it does not follow that I must be ready to describe the arrangement of the room; even if I should at once notice, and could also describe, any alteration in it. (1981, §§114–19)

Our trouble is that we sometimes mistake all that we cannot describe about the context of learning for a hidden essence that we have failed to grasp. When someone, for whatever reason, asks us "What is thinking?" or "What is truth?" we find ourselves unable to respond immediately, and we are misled into thinking that there is something in the nature of these things that we cannot easily grasp, like the flame of a candle. "And how is the riddle of thinking to be solved?—Like that of flame?" (1981, §125). But there is no alethic analogue for chemistry and plasma physics, and if what we cannot at first describe is not an essence, but features of context that we have not articulated, then our investigation must focus on getting an overview of those circumstances—a "perspicuous representation" (1968, §122) of the uses of the word *true* and the concepts to which truth is internally related. Our philosophical investigation must become a "grammatical" one.

A comprehensive investigation of this sort would require more space than I can afford here. The roles played by the word *truth* and its cognates are complicated and pervasive. But maybe a sketch of what such an investigation might look like will serve to make clear the alternative I am proposing. Such a sketch has been given by Rorty, who suggests that there are three standard ways in which the word *true* is used: an endorsing use, a cautionary use, and a disquotational use (1991b, 128).[14] Let me consider these in order.

Other writers have commented on the role that truth places in the endorsement of particular claims. As Strawson observes, we typically insist on the truth of a claim in contexts in which that claim is up for assessment (1949, 96). Indeed, to insist on its truth is to invite its assessment. And as pragmatists have long emphasized, we often use the word *true* to commend a statement or belief. *"The true is the name of whatever proves itself to be good in the way of belief, and good, too, for definite, assignable reasons"* (1974, 59), says William James. By this he does not mean to reduce truth to justification, but to give "a genetic theory of what is meant by truth" (53)—that is, an account of why we come to call a claim or a belief "true." The pragmatist Robert Brandom has argued (1987), is interested in the performative aspect of saying that something is true, not in giving a theory about the essence of truth, and part of the performative aspect of truth is that it is used to pick out particular propositions as "good in the way of belief." To acknowledge this function of the truth-predicate is to recognize that I could not understand the concept of truth—that is, know how to use the word *true* in ways that do not tend to cause confusion amongst my co-linguists—without having any concept of warrant or justification. Truth is, to this extent, an epistemic concept.

This last remark may seem to place me in direct conflict with an influential proponent of the view I have been calling modest realism—Donald Davidson. According to Davidson, attempts to see truth as epistemic are "untenable" (1990, 298), because they "reduce reality to so much less than we believe there is" (298f.). What he seems to mean by this is simply that truth cannot be reduced to epistemic notions like warrant and justification. He labels supporters of epistemic accounts of truth "relativists," who hold that truth is reducible to justification according to culturally relative standards, or "idealists," who hold that truth is reducible to some sort of coherence of our empirical representations (298).

As we have seen, the existence of an endorsing use of *true* has sometimes made it tempting to suppose that truth can be defined in some way with reference to such epistemic notions as justification or warrant. (This problem is exacerbated by a failure to recognize that an internal relation does not always require an analytic truth to give it expression.) And identifying truth with warrant is clearly not a plausible option, for though it was once warranted to say that the earth is flat, it is not and never was true to say this (Putnam 1981, 55). But to say that truth is an epistemic concept, in my parlance, is just to say that truth and justification are internally related, and that means simply that in order to understand truth I must also have some concept of justification. There is no reduction of truth here and none of the "Relativism about truth" that Davidson thinks is "a symptom of infection by the epistemological virus" (1990, 298). Someone who understands the concept of truth must have some grasp of such notions as warrant, justification, and verification. But someone who understands the concept of truth also understands that what a person says may well be justified and, yet, not true. To recognize that truth outstrips verification in this way is to acknowledge that *true* has what Rorty calls a "cautionary use."

Nonetheless, there is an additional sort of conflict between my view and Davidson's, as becomes apparent when we turn to the third of Rorty's uses of *true*, the "disquotational use." Rorty's preference for the term *disquotation* suggests an allegiance, via Davidson, to some variation on Tarski's "semantic conception of truth" (1949). This is an aspect of Rorty's position that I would sooner avoid. Like a number of other philosophers, I am inclined to see truth as a pragmatic notion, rather than a semantic one.[15] My qualms here may simply point to a minor squabble among pragmatists, but let me try to explicate my concerns briefly.

Davidson thinks that truth is a property of sentences (1990, 309) and the concept of truth for a particular language is to be elucidated by a "truth theory" that is modeled on Tarski's notion of a recursive truth definition. Tarski's view (1949, 52–58) was motivated in part by a pessimism about the prospects of being able to provide a rigorous definition of truth for natural languages. Any attempt to fill in the blank of "For all S, S is true if and only if ____," thought Tarski, would founder on the liar paradox and other paradoxes of truth. If, for example, we substitute "This sentence is false" for S in the preceding generalization and then try to pair it with some set of truth-conditions, we simply succeed in reproducing the paradox in our metalanguage. The only way to make truth a rigorous concept, he believed, was to restrict its application to formalized languages, which would rule out the paradox-generating sentences as ill-formed formulae.[16]

Davidson is less pessimistic than Tarski was about the prospects of extending such a formalized treatment to natural languages, and he wants further to link Tarski's view to a story about how we should go about interpreting another speaker. But for the moment these differences are unimportant, and we can regard Davidson's approach—which Rorty endorses—as much like Tarski's.

There are several reasons for wanting to avoid this approach. First, if we think of truth as predicated not of sentences, but of *statements*—that is, of what we use individual sentence-tokens to *say*—then the paradoxes of truth look more tractable. Suppose that we allow the possibility of saying, "This sentence is false." Then it seems as though we can readily identify the particular sentence-token that is taken to be the referent of *this*. More sophisticated versions forego indexicals by the use of such formulations as "The nth sentence on page k of *Philosophy and Its Epistemic Neuroses* is false," where the sentence just quoted is taken to be the nth sentence. But in these cases, too, predicating truth and falsehood of sentences allows us to identify readily the alleged bearer of the appropriate property, and the paradox ensues forthwith. Now suppose, instead, that we insist on reformulating the claim that leads to the paradox as follows: "This statement is false" or "The nth statement on page k of *Philosophy and Its Epistemic Neuroses* is false." If, as in these examples, truth (or falsehood) is predicated of a statement, then, before any paradox can arise, it must be possible to identify what statement a particular sentence-token is used to make. However, it is not at all clear what statement—if any—is made by the utterance or inscription of either of these sentence-tokens. The paradox does not seem to be generated, because it is always open for an interlocutor to ask, "Which statement do you mean?" If a genuine statement is made by either of these sentence-tokens, then it ought to be possible to paraphrase it in a way that eliminates such constructions as "this statement" and "the *n*th statement on page *k*." That does not seem possible here.[17]

Second, sentences are not bearers of truth and falsity, as Tarski's treatment would have it, because tokens of the same sentence can be used on different occasions to express either a truth or a falsehood. Davidson has been careful to indicate that it is particular token-utterances of type-sentences that he regards as true or false (e.g., 1984b, 34). But it seems odd to say that the particular tokens I use to say something true or false are themselves true or false, for they seem to have properties not possessed by what I say when I use them. Sentence-tokens may be longer or shorter than my index finger, but what is true or false has no length at all. Sentences may be written in French or English or Inuktitut, but what is true or false transcends individual languages and the opinions of their speakers (though not language and belief in general). And as Hacker remarks, "What we suspect or fear may be true, but we do not suspect or fear sentences" (1996b, 288 n. 65). It is what one says with a sentence-token on a particular occasion that is true or false. And this places truth in the realm of what is typically thought of as pragmatics.[18] (If the meaning of a word is determined by its standard use, then there is no *absolute* distinction between semantics and pragmatics, although in understanding the speech behavior of another I often need to distinguish between the standard use of a term and the idiosyncratic use to which she might put it on a particular occasion.)

In place of Rorty's "disquotational use" I propose including what might be called the "redundant" use of *true*. And the significance of this use is this: that if I am to be said to understand the concept of truth, then I must see that by and large it is true that *S*, if and only if *S*. Anyone who seriously doubts this does not have a firm grasp on the notion of truth, just as anyone who does not think that white is lighter than black does not grasp the roles of these color terms. Anyone who thinks that snow is white, but that it is not true that snow is white misunderstands the role that *true* plays in our language.[19]

A description of these three uses of *true* thus expresses three truisms about truth. They are truisms akin to those truisms (like "White is lighter than black") that a person must learn if she is to have a competent grasp of the terms *white*, *black*, and *lighter*. They are things that a speaker must know in order to have a competent grasp of the notion of truth. Of course, we can, and typically do, learn how to use the word *true* under circumstances that we do not learn how to describe. But we know these truisms in the sense that we can use the word *true* as it is standardly used under "normal" circumstances, and we can recognize misuses of *true* and occasions on which circumstances are not normal. The grasp of truth that we competent speakers have is evinced in our sense that there is something trivial and uninformative in formulations like "It is true that snow is white, if and only if snow is white," and something manifestly perverse in denying such formulations. Our grasp of truth is evinced in our appreciation that there is something self-defeating in saying (to vary Moore's example) "It's true that it's raining, but I don't believe it" or "It's true that Jupiter has a nickel core, but we have no reason for thinking so." And it is evinced in our occasional persistence in believing that *p* is the case, in the face of good reasons for thinking that *p* is not the case, and in our (sometimes grudging) concessions that what another says may be reasonably believed, even though it is not true.

Truth is not a fit object for theoretical investigation because truth does not have an essence or a hidden nature of which competent *truth*-users might be ignorant, any more than functional concepts like "can opener" or "shopping cart" have hidden essences. All that truth has is a complicated context of standard usage that we do not learn to describe, but that we can typically recognize when the conditions sweet for truth turn sour. Nothing hidden awaits our discovery in some science of the truth in the way that subatomic particles and quasars remained unimagined for millennia. If something were hidden here, then we could be completely mistaken about the meaning of *truth*. But the meaning of *truth* is determined by the way (or related ways) in which *truth* is used, and if we speak English, then we cannot be completely mistaken about that—though we may have some difficulty in perspicuously representing it, and our desire for a "scientific" treatment of truth can worsen that difficulty. There is nothing here that wants explaining—except in the sense in which we explain the meanings of words—and, so, no need for an empirical theory. To ask for something more than an overview of the uses of truth-talk, to ask for something deeper than a list of truisms that any competent speaker must know in order to give *truth* its standard employment, to ask for a *theory* of truth—is like asking for a theory of goal scoring: If you know how to play the game, then you know everything that there is to know, even if you have trouble describing it.[20]

"Experience" and Theory

I have been considering how to make sense of the idea that notions like truth and reference might not be fit objects for explanatory theories. The need to do so was provoked by my suggestion that one can explain only what one can already identify or describe independently of giving the explanation. However, more is at stake here than the fate of one objection to Putnam's "model-theoretic" argument. We are dealing with a general attitude about the proper treatment for concepts like truth and reference, and we are also dealing, I think, with an even more general principle: that skeptical doubts arise when a nontheoretical term is treated as designating some phenomenon that stands in need of empirical explanation.

This idea has been with us since Chapter 1, when I criticized Devitt for his talk of our "folk theory of the external world" (1997, 76). It reemerged in Chapter 2, when I suggested that Quine's treatment of spatio-temporal objects as "posits" was indicative of a latent Cartesianism in his conception of our knowledge of the world around us. We do not bring an already determinate language or "conceptual scheme" to bear on a reality that is, at first, nothing but surface irritations of our sensory organs. Scheme and content, as Davidson has helped us see, are not so easily separated (1984b, 183–98).

But the paradigmatic case—the one that drives my treatment of Putnam's model-theoretical argument—is Russell's theory of desire. Russell, recall, wanted to identify an organism's desire with a state of discomfort that initiated a behavior cycle, which, unless interrupted, would continue until the discomfort were removed. The object of the desire would be whatever removed the discomfort. To characterize desire in this way is to see the relation between a desire and its object as an external one, such that the desire might be identified independently of knowing what would satisfy it.

Now, it is true that we sometimes speak of not knowing what we want, but this is typically said in cases that present us with an array of alternatives, all of which we desire in some degree and which compete for our attention. And although there are cases in which we seem to experience an indeterminate craving for something that we cannot immediately identify, it is not clear that such cases are really cases in which we possess any desire prior to our arriving at a decision about what we want. Our vague discomfort is transformed into a desire. To suppose that I might be ignorant of the object of my desire and yet know with some greater assurance that I actually have a desire that needs an explanation is to invite skeptical doubts about the determinacy of my desire. Unless I already know what the object of my desire is, then I will not be able to say what constitutes an interruption of my "behavior cycle" in contrast to a fulfillment of my desire. "I should like to say, if there were only an external connection no connection could be described at all, since we only describe the external connection by means of the internal one" (Wittgenstein 1975, §26).

None of this rules out inventing a theoretical category called "desire" (though we might well wish for another name) and using it for some explanatory purposes that empirical investigation or clinical practice has found fruitful. The point here is simply that *if* I can identify a desire, then I can identify its object too. So, what I have been saying is not *automatically* an objection to, for example, a psychoanalytic category of unconscious desire. However, we should not be misled by a superficial similarity of terminology into thinking that psychoanalysis reveals something hitherto unknown about our ordinary attributions and avowals of intentional attitudes. As Wittgenstein held, the "Extension of a concept in a *theory* (e.g., 'wish-fulfilment dream')" (1981, §449) or "unconscious thoughts" (1958, 23) should not be confused with a "stupendous discovery" (23). It is, rather, the adoption of a "new convention" (23) for a specific practical purpose. Thus, nothing in psychoanalytic theory or clinical investigation could reasonably convince us that we *never* know what we want or, for that matter, that we never understand the meanings of our words.[21]

The latter point has been an implicit theme in my discussion in the preceding chapters. Suppose that I try to doubt that I understand my words and insist that I merely seem to do so, that my words merely seem to be meaningful. (One can also imagine a would-be skeptic about the external world making this rejoinder to the suggestion that if I had always been a brain in a vat, then I could not understand my own words or the skeptic's hypothesis.) If I seem to myself to use words, then I seem to use them in some particular ways and not in others. Otherwise, there is no content to the notion of seeming. Seeming to use words and to understand them is not like having a headache; it is not a brute sensation that happens to accompany some instances and not others. There must be cases that count as my seeming to speak a language and cases that do not if I am to be said to seem to speak a language, and I must be able to distinguish among them. If there are such cases among which I can distinguish, however, then meaning has been smuggled in by the back door, and I no longer merely seem to understand my words.

My general principle, then, is this: We can explain only what we can already identify and describe, and efforts to treat internal relations as external, explanatory relations lead invariably to skeptical doubts. If this principle is valid, then it is overwhelmingly tempting to apply it in another context that we have encountered, that of external-world skepticism. This temptation is best gotten rid of by yielding to it.

Experience is no more externally related to the world than terms that refer to macroscopic objects or events are to their referents. Internal relations, remember, do not obtain strictly among concepts, but among the various instruments of language, including spatio-temporal objects and events. Experience fits the latter category. It consists of events that have roles to play in our linguistic practices, and it is internally related to the world, such that I cannot have knowledge of my "inner experience" without having knowledge of things in the world around me.[22] Skeptical doubts arise about the "external" world, as a result of (1) assuming that knower and known are related only externally, and (2) assuming that a knower's inner experience as of a world of spatio-temporal objects and events is to be explained by the knower's being externally related to such a world.

Notice that these two assumptions run parallel to the two assumptions I suggested in Chapter 3 are central to Putnam's model-theoretic argument. Doubts about our knowledge of the reference of our terms arise from assuming, first, that reference is an external relation and, second, that our ability to identify and describe some range of expressions as true statements, distinct from false statements, and distinct from other kinds of utterances that are neither true nor false, is to be explained by the presence of such an external relation between word and object. And just as I cannot, according to the interactive, internalist conception of reference, understand a language without knowing what its nontheoretical terms refer to, neither can I know my own mind without knowing something of the world around me.

Notice also that my suggestion about the internal relation between mind and world meshes neatly with my description in Chapter 1 of the congress between metaphysical realism and external-world skepticism. (This meshing, of course, is no mere coincidence.) There I described the metaphysical realist as someone who thinks that the scenario painted by the external-world skeptic is a real possibility—a possibility that would explain both the nature and variety of "inner" experience and our coming to hold the many beliefs that we do. By contrast, I said, the modest realist thinks that the skeptic's scenario is no explanation at all. But this is not necessarily to say that the hypothesis of our epistemic contact with a world beyond our senses is a good explanation of that inner experience. The skeptic's hypothesis is no explanation of our inner experience, but neither is the external-world hypothesis. That is because, like reference and truth, neither so-called inner experience nor the totality of our beliefs is the sort of thing that demands, or is amenable to, theoretical explanation.

It is difficult to say this, however, without being misunderstood, for the very vocabulary of "inner" and "outer," of "internal" self and "external" world, goes hand in hand with the treatment of experience as an independent phenomenon that can be identified and explained apart from any empirical knowledge. Thus to deny that inner experience or our system of beliefs about the world is something unified that stands in need of explanation is to deny something that seems evident. It is, once again, to ask us to regard as complete something that appears so obviously incomplete. We need to consider then, as we did with regard to the seeming obviousness of truth's theoretical status, what the source of this obviousness is, and what the appropriate alternative is to offering a theoretical explanation of our "inner" experience and of our beliefs about the "external" world.

Answers immediately suggest themselves. If experience and knowledge are really like truth in being nontheoretical concepts, then it would seem that their examination must also focus on providing an overview of the contexts in which they and related terms are used, and this is once again because we learn the use of experience-talk—and knowledge-talk—in contexts that we do not learn to describe.

The role of talk of inner experience, however, is not at all easy to summarize. It is even more complicated and variegated than the role of truth-talk in our linguistic practices. "The whole complex of ideas alluded to by this word [inner] is like a painted curtain drawn in front of the scene of the actual word use" (Wittgenstein 1992, 84). One function the discourse of inner experience and subjectivity plays is simply that of drawing a distinction between what seems to me to be the case and what is in fact the case, regardless of how it seems to be. Our perceptual systems and our belief-forming mechanisms are fallible, and sometimes we acquire false beliefs. We mark this fact, much as we distinguish truth from justification, by acknowledging that an individual's inner experience may fall short of veridicality at times, by allowing that her assessments of what is the case may at times be merely subjective and idiosyncratic.

It is this feature of experience-talk that is exploited, and misrepresented, by the metaphysical realist and the external-world skeptic. Each group would have us believe that we could really be mistaken about *all* our beliefs about the "external" world at once. Each would have us believe that talk of inner experience, instead of merely marking our epistemic fallibility, points to the presence of a unified phenomenon that can be explained. Of course, they are right to suggest that talk of subjectivity does more than acknowledge our capacity for error, for our experience includes our pains, our pleasures, and our desires, and though I do not think that we can sharply delineate these phenomena as "noncognitive," in contrast to cognitive categories like "belief," they do plainly differ.

But this very difference points to the difficulty in treating "experience" as a unified phenomenon.[23] Experience and subjectivity seem mysterious to us, and, like the candle flame that we cannot grasp, they thus seem to stand in need of a theoretical explanation. But we mistake the unarticulated contexts of learning for the hidden nature of subjectivity. These terms name a blanket category that we throw over a whole array of very different psychological phenomena, and it is not clear that they possess any common essence, any underlying unity, that justifies the substantive assumption of their theoretical status. What do imagining the sun setting as it illuminates my office door, fearing the haggard face that stares at me through the window from the darkness, thinking of my absent lover, and believing that the square root of 2 is an irrational number have in common?

Perhaps, as Wittgenstein suggested, it is characteristic of the "verbs of experience *[Erlebnisverben]*" that "their third person but not their first person is stated on grounds of observation . . . of behavior" (1980a, §836). I judge, for example, that a person is in pain on the basis of winces, grimaces, flinching, and so on, but I need not make such observations in my own case. But beyond this, it is difficult to find any generalizations that subsume all the phenomena of subjectivity.

When I see the light from the setting sun shining on my door, my impression lasts for a definite period of time, and it changes in color, contrast, and intensity. It blends with other impressions of sound, smell, taste, and texture, and it stands in spatial and temporal relations to my other impressions. I see the doorway here, next to the wall, now, after I have walked into my office, not before. Much the same holds true when I try to imagine such an event, but my image is "voluntary"—I do not "behave as an observer in relation to the image" (Wittgenstein 1980a, §885).

Emotions also have duration and a course of development, but they do not stand in spatial relations with each other and have no location. I do not feel sadness or joy in my left arm, or even in my breast. I do not perceive one in the corner and another on the bookshelf. But my emotions may well be accompanied by "characteristic 'undergoings' and thoughts" (Wittgenstein 1980a, §836). I may feel nauseated with fear, worry, or excitement, and in my despair I may remember a melancholy musical theme or a passage from a novel or simply other moments of despair. In the midst of my self-loathing I may contemplate suicide or self-abasement, and these thoughts will be colored with emotion. Unlike images and impressions, emotions can have characteristic behaviors or expressions: I smile in delight, I wince in disgust, I shudder with fear. My emotions can be directed toward an object: I fear the face in the window. Or they may be undirected:

I may be *anxious* with no particular object for my anxiety (1981, §489). But images and impressions are always of something.

Beliefs differ in additional ways from impressions, images, and emotions. They need have no course of development, and my having a belief does not consist in my attending to its object for any definite period of time—thinking is yet another phenomenon.[24] My foot can throb with pain for several hours, aching with varying intensity, but I do not believe for several hours, now strongly, now moderately, that the dinosaurs perished 64 million years ago or that the root of 2 is irrational. I cannot be interrupted in the activity of believing or disturbed from a state of belief by someone's knocking at my door, whereas my thinking about what groceries to buy can be disrupted by an errant visitor (Wittgenstein 1980b, §45; 1981, §85). If I claim to have believed something for many years, I am not claiming that it has been constantly on my mind for that time. And even if I claim only to have had an occurrent belief for some short period of time, that belief does not consist in my thinking about the object of belief—though such thinking may well characterize in part my occurrent belief that someone is trying to enter my apartment. And beliefs do not color my thoughts in the way that emotions do. I may think longingly of my absent lover; I do not think believingly of her. But like "thinking," "belief" is a "widely ramified concept" (1980b, §218), applying in different ways to many different kinds of cases, among which we may find a family resemblance, but certainly no essence.

Much the same could be said for experience in general. What we want to unify as an object of study under the title "experience" exhibits much less unity when we try to taxonomize it. But without the appropriate unity, there is no phenomenon here that calls for an overarching explanation of the sort that is offered by the hypothesis of an external world.

Theories of Knowledge

A similar claim has recently been argued by Michael Williams with respect to the alleged nature of our "knowledge of the external world." Williams emphasizes Stroud's characterization of the skeptic's doubts as arising naturally from traditional epistemology's attempt to assess and justify "all our knowledge of the world at once ... from what looks like a detached 'external' position" (Stroud 1984, 209).[25] One of the central troubles for this traditional project, and hence for the naturalness of skeptical doubt, is that it presupposes all of our knowledge of the world to be bound together by some underlying unity. But what kind of unity could it be? It is not a topical unity, as many advocates of the unity of science hoped:

> "Knowledge of the external world" covers not only all the natural sciences and all of history, it covers all everyday, unsystematic factual claims belonging to no particular investigative discipline. Since, even within a single subject, theories, problems and

methods tend to proliferate with the progress of inquiry, so that even the most systematic disciplines tend to become less rather than more unified, it is doubtful whether we can take a synoptic view of physics, never mind everything we believe about the external world. It is not obvious that it makes sense even to try. (Williams 1996c, 103)[26]

Just as there are many different concepts of experience, so are there many different kinds of knowledge, which vary according to the kinds of justification that they require, the kinds of explanation or clarification that they provide, their degrees of systematicity, the effects of inquiry on the objects of inquiry, and so on.

But, of course, the traditional epistemologist, the metaphysical realist, and the external-world skeptic will all want to say that it is not any kind of topical unity that is relevant here, either in the case of experience or in the case of knowledge. The fact that terms like *mental state, subjectivity,* and *experience* are rubrics for a diversity of phenomena is unimportant, because the many concepts of experience all share the characteristic that the phenomena they classify are the effects of sensory stimulation. Likewise, although there may be many different kinds of knowledge—or purported knowledge—about the external world, what all such knowledge shares in common is its origin in the senses. This is why talk of inner experience does not simply gesture at our epistemic fallibility, but signifies a unified theoretical phenomenon, and this is also why our would-be knowledge of the external world must be subject to the comprehensive and systematic examination and justification that is the task of traditional epistemology. The only plausible kind of unity for knowledge is an epistemological unity, according to which all of our beliefs about the "external" world

> might be subject, in so far as they are meant to be justified or to amount to knowledge, to the same fundamental, epistemological constraints. This is what is usually suggested, or rather assumed. Thus Descartes ties his pre-critical beliefs together, thereby constituting their totality as an object of theoretical inquiry, by tracing them all to "the senses." No matter how topically heterogeneous, and no matter how unsystematic, his beliefs have this much in common: all owe their place to the authority of the senses. (Williams 1996c, 104)

The problem with this response, as Williams argues at length (1996c, 47–88), is that the dependence of our empirical beliefs on the senses amounts either to a "causal truism" or "a contentious epistemological doctrine" (104). The truism is that our knowledge, like our subjective experience, does depend on the senses as effect on cause. In order to acquire beliefs about the world, we must have some means of acquiring them. Such a claim, however, is insufficient to ground the kind of unity that is needed for traditional epistemology or metaphysical realism, which (it is becoming apparent) depends on epistemology for its expression.

The traditional epistemologist aims at a theoretical explanation of our beliefs and experience as a central component in the project of *justifying* our claims to have knowledge of the world. Knowledge is thought to depend on the senses in the sense that our beliefs about the world are justified only if they are formed or retained on the basis of sensory evidence. If epistemology is to get off the ground, then we must assume that some kinds of beliefs and experiences are intrinsically better known than others—that some beliefs are intrinsically credible, bringing with them their own justification, whether certain or fallible. The senses must not merely link us causally with the universe; they must provide us with *evidence* for its nature and existence, which we can then infer from the evidence.

Tracing our beliefs about the world around us to the senses will serve to explain inner experience and, hence, to justify those beliefs, only if we assume that we can identify and describe those beliefs and the experience in which they are rooted prior to explaining and justifying them. (Or, again for the inductivist, we can infer the existence of an external world from our beliefs and experience only if we can identify and describe them independently of identifying and describing that world.) This, as we saw earlier, is a methodological constraint on any explanatory inquiry. But for the metaphysical realist and the traditional epistemologist a methodological constraint is not good enough. If the attempt to examine all of our knowledge of the world at once is not to be merely optional, then the assumption of epistemic priority must be forced on us as soon as we begin to ask questions about our knowledge. That is why some beliefs must be held to be intrinsically evidential.[27]

Epistemology and metaphysical realism, then, are fed on a diet of substantive assumptions, and the truism that all knowledge and experience depend causally on the senses will not serve to replace those assumptions. If this is so, then skeptical doubts are a long way from being natural doubts. This is Williams's conclusion. My additional conclusion is that the metaphysical realist is in no position to cite the real possibility of skeptical scenarios as evidence that his or her view has, if nothing else, the endorsement of "common sense." The modest realist has as much claim to that endorsement.

Of course, none of this refutes skepticism categorically. By extension none of it refutes metaphysical realism, construed as vulnerability to skeptical doubt, nor do my earlier points refute externalist—theoretical—treatments of reference and truth, which we have seen amount to applications of strong objectivism and its accompanying threat of skepticism to reference and truth. However, it does suggest that there is nothing simply "intuitive" about these views, that they rest on controversial theoretical assumptions. As such, the mere fact that a position gives rise to skeptical doubt is not automatically a mark in its favor. We are, rather, in a position to see a liability to skepticism as an objection, and the strong objectivist's tendency to underestimate the importance of skeptical doubt as symptomatic of a troublesome psycho-philosophical disorder that does not affect the rival views I have been recommending. We are in a position to take seriously the idea of renouncing all theories of truth and knowledge.

Notes

1. See Lewis 1984, 230.
2. As we shall see in the next section, Putnam displays some ambivalence about this, but there is clearly an antitheoretical current in his work of the past two decades. Rozema (1992) criticizes Putnam for allegedly holding that reference is a theoretical concept. But unlike such critics as Lewis, Rozema does not "play fair" (Lewis 1984, 222), citing passages out of context in a way that is highly prejudicial to Putnam's position. Thus, he writes of an example from Chapter 1 of *Reason, Truth and History*: "It seems that we are to take seriously the possibility of a conceptual scheme within which the word 'elm' refers to beeches and vice-versa. But Putnam has already said that 'it is trivial to say what any word refers to *within* the language by using the word itself.' So how could 'elm' refer to beeches in *any* language?" (Rozema 1992, 299). However, the latter remark of Putnam's—from Chapter 3 (!) of *Reason, Truth and History*—is the conclusion that Putnam hopes to draw, relying in part on the cited remarks about elms and beeches. It is Rozema who has already cited this remark, not Putnam who has already made it. Moreover, those remarks are directed at holders of a doctrine that Tyler Burge (1986) has named "psychological individualism." The sort of individualist whom Putnam is addressing is someone who holds that "the difference between the reference of 'elm' and the reference of 'beech' in *my* speech is explained by a difference in my psychological state" (1981, 18). Notice that Putnam does not use Rozema's term *intentional state* (Rozema 1992, 298), but the term *psychological state*, because he is criticizing the assumption that "same psychological state" entails "same intentional attitude." If, as Rozema maintains, there really is a difficulty in stating Putnam's Twin-Earth examples, then this is a criticism of psychological individualism's identification of psychological states with intentional attitudes, not of Putnam's arguments against this equation.
3. By "theoretical statement" I mean any statement whose truth-value is not bound up with the meaningfulness of my words in the way that the truth-values of statements like "There is a world beyond my senses" and "I have not always been a brain in a vat" are. This distinction was introduced in Chapter 2.
4. The members of the Vienna Circle provide another example. Before their encounters with Tarski they could see no alternative to correspondence but coherence. Hempel, describing Neurath's criticisms of Schlick, remarked, "Obviously, these general ideas imply a coherence theory of truth" (1935, 54). However, every occurrence of *obviously* in Hempel's article masks a contentious assertion about the theoretical status of truth.
5. See 1994b, 264–78, 320–27, 330–50; 1992c, 435ff.; 1990, 31f., 106f., 113ff., 276; 1988, 68f.; 1987, 16, 77; and 1983, xiii-xv, 278–82, 245ff.
6. For a similar point, see Ramberg 1993, 237.
7. See also 1982, xiii-xiv.
8. More recently, Rorty has said that *truth* is a "nominalization" (1991a, 10) or "reification" of an "approbative adjective" (1998, 53). See also 1992a, 418. But this does not imply that truth is reducible to assertibility or approbation. The point is merely that only claims and beliefs can have truth-values, and where there are no speakers or believers there are no truth-values.

9. In *Reason, Truth and History* Putnam seemed still to hold that truth was an explanatory property (1981, 39), but he rejected this view soon after. See 1983, 232.

10. See Field 1982. Field also wonders how to specify ideal epistemic conditions in contrast to less than ideal ones and how to make sense of being in a position to evaluate every sentence. For Putnam's response to the latter point, see 1990, viii. Rorty (1993, 452) presses the former criticism, contending that ideal epistemic conditions require dubious talk of ideal epistemic communities. If the account proposed in Chapter 2 is accepted, then we can regard some *nontheoretical* judgments as ideally justified in the sense that any reason to doubt them would be a reason to doubt our grasp of the terms used to formulate our original doubt. However, this explication requires that ideal warrant be a sufficient, but not a necessary, condition for truth.

11. This is less worrying if my proposal in the preceding note is accepted.

12. See Goldman 1986, 146.

13. See also 1995, 49 and, for more talk of internal relations, 1994a, 458.

14. For competing overviews see Austin 1964; Strawson 1949, 1964; and White 1971. I take Rorty's overview as a recent, succinct example of the sort of description needed, though modifications and elaborations may be appropriate. Rorty's picture leaves implicit the function of truth emphasized by Frank Ramsey (1990, 1991) and propounded more recently by Paul Horwich (1990): The truth-predicate lets us affirm a claim or belief without actually stating that claim or belief, as in "The special theory of relativity is true." This use intertwines with Rorty's "endorsing use" and with what I call below the "redundant" use of *true*.

15. See, e.g., Strawson 1964, 33; White 1971, 3–6; Habermas 1973, 212; and Baker and Hacker 1984a, 180–90. For more on Tarski and Davidson, see Chapter 5.

16. See Tarski 1949, 62–64. For a lucid discussion, see Putnam 1988, 61–66. In order to "formalize" a language, says Tarski: "We must indicate all words which we decide to use without defining them, and which are called 'undefined (or primitive) terms'; and we must give the so-called rules of definition for introducing new or defined terms. Furthermore, we must set up criteria for distinguishing within the class of expressions those which we call 'sentences.' Finally, we must formulate the conditions under which a sentence of the language can be asserted" (1949, 57).

17. See Strawson 1949, 92 and Austin 1964, 23 n. 13.

18. To say that truth is a property of what one says or believes is not to propose an ontology of propositions. There is no saying what one says or believes without resorting to words, and there is no canonical form of things said or believed. What I believe or assert when I believe or assert that *p*, is neither a proposition nor a sentence, but simply that *p*. That truth attaches only to what is said or believed is intended, one might say, as a "grammatical remark." Making this plausible would probably require undermining Quine's claim that there is no distinction "between the 'there are' of 'there are universals,' 'there are unicorns,' 'there are hippopotami,' and the 'there are' of '(∃x),' 'there are entities x such that'" (1980, 105). See Dilman 1996 and Arrington 1996. Schiffer (1989, 139–78) makes another proposal that might prove useful here.

19. But we could hold that there was a time when snow *was* white, but when it was not *true* that snow was white. The redundant use of *true* permits a convention according to which, although it *is* true that snow was white a billion years ago, and although snow *was* then white, it was not then *true* that snow was white. Similarly, we need not conflate the truth of a counterfactual conditional claim with the counterfactual conditional truth of a

claim, as Allen seems to when he argues that counterfactual conditionals that presuppose the absence of believers lack truth-values (1993, 113–48). See Hymers 1999. Schmitt (1995, 132–36) thinks that a deflationary view of truth must make this conflation, but his argument conflates the indicative mood with the subjunctive.

20. "Doesn't understanding how to play a game require understanding the rules?" Well, yes. "And isn't this theoretical knowledge?" This question conflates theoretical knowledge with propositional knowledge. Someone who doubts that scoring a goal in hockey, for example, entails putting the puck in the net is not someone whom we credit with an alternative "theory" of goal scoring, but someone who does not understand the game. Moreover, understanding the rules does not require me to be especially articulate in explaining them. Correcting the flawed attempts of a novice player to imitate my behavior (which I have learned by imitating others) may be enough to impart a good deal of what is known here.

21. Both claims—that we never know what we want and mean—are sometimes associated with the influential French psychoanalyst Jacques Lacan. See Bouveresse 1995, 39f. I return to Lacan in Chapter 8.

22. This proposal has some affinities with McDowell's "conception of experiences as states or occurrences that are passive but reflect conceptual capacities, capacities that belong to spontaneity, in operation" (1994, 23). But I find McDowell's attempt to rehabilitate Kantian language more distracting than helpful—however interesting it may be. Williams (1996a) has suggested that McDowell's views harbor a lingering impulse toward theoreticism.

23. Of course, there is a formal unity to experience, which Kant referred to as the transcendental unity of apperception. (I shall discuss a variation on this kind of unity in Chapter 8.) But the sort of unity that is at issue here is something more than this; it is the sort of unity that would serve to constitute an object of theoretical inquiry. Kant criticized Descartes for inappropriately inferring from transcendental apperception to the claim that he was conscious of himself as *res cogitans*, a thinking substance (1965, A341–405/B399–432). Such an inference contributes to the illusion of the theoretical integrity of experience by treating experience as the "modes" of a special substance. See Descartes's *Principles of Philosophy*, Part I, §64 in Descartes 1984, 1:215f.

24. Sometimes Wittgenstein suggests that "thinking" is not even "a concept of an experience" (1981, §96). See the example at 1968, §330.

25. See Williams 1996c, 22.

26. But such ideas die hard. See Wilson 1998. For a summary of Williams's position, see Williams 1996b.

27. As Williams argues compellingly (1996c, 292–303), this substantive foundationalism is also a feature of coherence theories of knowledge and justification, for the coherentist must treat the "criteria of coherence" as having a "privileged status" (302) and must also assume the unconditional epistemic priority of the belief that other of her beliefs are members of a (more or less) coherent system or face an infinite regress of reasons.

5

Conceptual Schemes

> "Relativism" is the view that every belief on a certain topic, or perhaps about any topic, is as good as every other. No one holds this view. Except for the occasional cooperative freshman, one cannot find anybody who says that two incompatible opinions on an important topic are equally good. The philosophers who get called "relativists" are those who say that the grounds for choosing between such opinions are less algorithmic than had been thought.
>
> —Richard Rorty, Consequences of Pragmatism

My discussion in the preceding chapters has taken metaphysical realism and the related causal theory of reference as representative of theoretical approaches to truth and knowledge. And I have argued that these theoretical approaches result in varieties of epistemic neurosis. But, of course, these do not come close to exhausting the possible ways in which one might be a philosophical theoretician about problems that I have maintained are better seen from the perspective of the philosophical therapist. As we saw in Chapter 4, renouncing philosophical theory is a difficult thing to do, and critics of metaphysical realism and causal theories of reference can themselves be easily tempted to propose some alternative account of truth or knowledge. One such alternative is offered by epistemic relativism, which holds that truth is relative to cultures or groups. The epistemic relativist may claim that truth reduces to the consensus of the community, or to an idealization of that consensus with no guarantee that the ideal consensus of different communities is in any way convergent.

Epistemic relativism is generally thought to be self-refuting, because any argument that can be given in support of the thesis that truth is relative must either presuppose a nonrelativist notion of truth or must beg the question by presupposing that truth is relative. The availability of such a quick refutation makes it clear why metaphysical realists might want to saddle their critics with such an implausible view, and philosophers who freely express their reservations about strong objectivism are often criticized for their alleged relativism. What is less clear, on this rendering, is why epistemic relativism would seem attractive to its proponents.

Part of the answer is that it is difficult to find a real, live relativist—even among those who call themselves relativists. Occasionally, says Rorty, a "disillusioned" philosopher will "play at being" a relativist (1982, 167), but no one really believes the relativist's doctrine, just as no one really believes the conclusions drawn by the would-be skeptic about the external world. But, although there is some truth in this contention, it does not fully explain why there are philosophers who do call themselves "relativists." In order to understand that, we need to understand the attraction of relativism. How are we to do this?

Part of the answer is implicit in my raising of the issue. As long as one holds to the assumption that truth and knowledge are fit objects for theoretical explanation, then any reasonable alternative to the views I have considered will have to be an alternative theory of truth and knowledge. Relativism satisfies this requirement. However, this can be only part of the story. Two other elements also enter. First, according to some of its relativist critics, realism has pernicious ethical and political consequences that can be avoided only by embracing relativism. Second, while epistemic relativism might look frail when left to stand alone, it acquires greater plausibility when it is coupled with the doctrine of incommensurable conceptual schemes. In Chapter 6, I will consider the ethical-political argument for relativism, but in this chapter I want to turn my attention to conceptual relativism. I shall argue that, though it makes good sense to suppose that different cultures give rise to different concepts, this fact can give no support to epistemic relativism. At the heart of conceptual relativism, I shall argue, is the same substitution of external relations for internal relations that characterizes metaphysical realism and the causal theory of reference. The conceptual relativist thinks of concepts and their content as related only externally, so that the same content can be differently articulated by a variety of concepts. Like the correspondence theorist, the conceptual relativist also holds that reference and meaning have only an external link to each other. Conceptual relativism thus proves to be a kind of metaphysical realism—metaphysical realism about conceptual schemes.

So-called Relativists

Not all so-called relativists are "would-be" relativists. Some are modest realists who are labeled "relativists" with little heed for their own testimony or for countervailing evidence. This is because, as we have seen, it is difficult to stop thinking of truth and knowledge as things that are amenable to theoretical investigation, whether in the form of old-style metaphysical theories or currently fashionable scientific ones. The complexity of the contexts in which we speak of truth and knowledge and the centrality of science to the cultural self-image of the Western democracies, a self-image reinforced by the institutions of learning that produce philosophers and theoreticians of the humanities and social sciences, make it difficult to believe that anyone would doubt that knowledge and truth were fit objects for theory. And so, the position of the modest realist is apt to look like another *theory* of truth and knowledge, rather than like an eschewal of explanatory treatments of these notions. Rorty has made this point (his "realist" is my "metaphysical realist"):

> The reason that the realist calls this negative claim "relativistic" is that he cannot believe that anybody would seriously deny that truth has an intrinsic nature. So when the pragmatist says that there is nothing to be said about truth save that each of us will commend as true those beliefs which he or she finds good to believe, the realist is inclined to interpret this as one more positive theory about the nature of truth: a theory according to which truth is simply the contemporary opinion of a chosen individual or group. (1991b, 24)

Rorty should know. Few philosophers have received this sort of misplaced criticism more than he, or from as many quarters. But it is not just metaphysical realists who have difficulty believing that truth has no intrinsic nature. As we saw in Chapter 4, Putnam has taken years to disentangle his own criticisms of theoretical philosophy from his recurrent urge to give an alternative theory of truth as idealized warrant—an account of truth as a "substantive" notion. Indeed, some of the most strident criticism of Rorty's antitheoretical attitude has come from Putnam.

At times Putnam compliments Rorty, calling him "a thinker of great depth" (1987, 16), whose work addresses "profound questions head-on" (1983, 236) and with whom he has had "a very fruitful ongoing exchange" (1990, 19). But it is more common for him to attribute to Rorty a "self-refuting relativism" (1981, 216) that "identifies truth with right assertibility by the standards of one's cultural peers" (1983, 235). Such "Cultural relativism of the Rortian variety" (1988, 69), "even if it is given a new name, such as 'deconstruction' or even 'pragmatism'" (1990, 18), holds that rightness "is defined by the 'standards of one's culture'" (125). According to Putnam, even nihilism can characterize Rorty's position: "*all* discourse can be understood without presupposing the notion of truth at all" (15). And when he examines Rorty's responses to charges of relativism, he first pleads that "Rorty is too hard to interpret," substituting "a typical relativist" (1992a, 69) as the object of his criticism, and then changes tack, holding that Rorty has moved from "physicalism to an extreme linguistic idealism which teeters on the edge of solipsism" (1994b, 306) and which is "largely a fashionable 'put-on'" (1995, 75).[1]

Rorty has often agreed that epistemic relativism is "self-refuting" (1991b, 23),[2] though he reserves doubts about the importance of this observation, given his conviction that there are no relativists. And when, for example, he says that "truth is made rather than found" (1989, 7), he is not claiming that our agreeing that something is true *makes* it true. His point is, rather, "that *languages* are made rather than found, and that truth is a property of linguistic entities" (7). Truth is not found, because it does not exist independently of epistemic and linguistic practices, and it has no hidden nature after which to inquire. Rorty, by my reckoning, is a modest realist, and he "does not have a theory of truth, much less a relativistic one" (1991b, 24).

Other thinkers happily identify with the label that Rorty rightly rejects. Thus, Barry Barnes and David Bloor insist that "the balance of argument favors a relativist theory of knowledge" (1982, 21). Paul Feyerabend advocates "epistemic relativism" (1987, 73) as "a weapon against intellectual tyranny and as a means of debunking science" (19). And Barbara Herrnstein Smith insists that critics of relativism make the mistake of "taking for granted as unquestionable or irreplaceable the orthodox concepts or explanations at issue" (1997, 78).

However, these cases provide us not with thinkers who hold the self-refuting view that I have been calling "epistemic relativism," but with proponents of varieties of modest realism, as closer inspection makes clear. Barnes and Bloor, for example, reject the postulate that "all beliefs are equally true" and the postulate that "all beliefs are equally false" for the reason that both "run into technical difficulties": "To say that all beliefs are equally true encounters the problem of how to handle beliefs which contradict one another. If one belief denies what the other asserts, how can they both be true? Similarly, to say that all beliefs are equally false poses the problem of the status of the relativist's own claims. He would seem to be pulling the rug from beneath his own feet" (1982, 22f.). In other words, relativism, as traditionally construed by its critics, is self-refuting. If relativism is true, then it is only relatively true, but if it is only relatively true, then it is not true *simpliciter*.[3] And if all beliefs are false, then so is the belief in relativism. In contrast to this self-defeating view, Barnes and Bloor hold "that all beliefs are on a par with one another with respect to the causes of their credibility. It is not that all beliefs are equally true or equally false, but that regardless of truth and falsity the fact of their credibility is seen to be equally problematic" (23).

This formulation is just the denial, encountered in Chapter 4, that truth is an explanatory concept. The fact that a belief is true does not explain why it is held—only details peculiar to the particular belief can do that, and such details attend false beliefs as much as they do true ones. There is no way of identifying true beliefs apart from identifying beliefs that we regard as justified, and among the beliefs that we regard as justified there will be some that are false. A belief can be justified without being true, and a belief can be true without being justified. But we have no understanding of truth apart from having an understanding of justification. As Barnes and Bloor put it: "Validity totally detached from credibility is nothing" (1982, 29).

Feyerabend is more explicit in pointing out that his "relativism" is not a "theory" (1987, 80) about "the nature of reality, truth and knowledge" (78). "A relativist who deserves his name," he says, "will have to keep to specifics" (78) and avoid theorizing about such notions. This is just the advice that I have given as a therapeutic alternative to traditional epistemology and truth theory. Feyerabend's position, as Rorty has suggested, "seems misdescribed, by himself as well as by his critics, as 'relativism'" (1991b, 28). Relativism *is* a theory of truth and knowledge, not a resolution to avoid such theorizing.

Feyerabend disagrees. Protagoras, sometimes regarded as a paradigmatic relativist,[4] "would not," he says, "have called conflicting positions 'equally right'" (1987, 81). In Feyerabend's eyes, as seemingly in Barnes and Bloor's, critics of relativism tend to construe relativism too narrowly—there are other kinds of relativism that are untouched by the argument from self-defeat, and one such is Feyerabend's antitheoretical position.

Smith takes a similar line (1988, 151). She joins with Rorty in eschewing theories of truth (155f.), but her preference is to accept the label "relativist" and to dispense with talk of "'reality,' 'validity,' 'justification,' 'reason,' 'truth,' 'facts,' and so forth" (156) in favor of "an alternate structure of conceptions of what [the objectivist] calls 'truth'" (113). The charge of "relativism," she suggests, will "continue to be generated unavoidably and unwittingly through the self-inversion of objectivist thought" (156). Rather than reject a label that will be continually applied despite her protestations, the modest realist ought simply to accept it and proceed to articulate an intelligible alternative with a new vocabulary and a different understanding of the conceptual structures that tempt us into treating truth and knowledge as fit for theoretical explanation.

We have here a disagreement about terminology and rhetorical strategies. What critics of relativism identify as a self-refuting theory of truth and knowledge is precisely that. But it is not the position that any of the self-proclaimed relativists whom we have just encountered can properly be said to hold. I shall adhere to the antirelativist tradition of identifying relativism with a self-defeating theory for three reasons. First, I think that such a theory is immediately suggested by claiming that truth is relative to cultures or persons (in contrast to claiming that what is called "true" is so relative). Second, since I am rejecting theoretical treatments of knowledge and truth, I do not want my view (similar in ways to those of the "relativists" considered above) to be thought of as itself just another explanatory theory about these notions. Finally, I see Smith's proposal as potentially raising as many difficulties as it is designed to overcome. Philosophical puzzlement is something that arises from failing to get a clear overview of the uses of our words. No set of terminology is immune to such puzzlement, and the best thing we can do is to try to alleviate the puzzlement we feel about the words we already use, rather than hope that replacing them will leave our problems behind. What is more likely is that our old difficulties, or comparable ones, will arise again with our new terminology, and we will be even less well prepared to obtain a clear overview of the uses of our new terms. The therapeutic philosopher's advantage, both philosophical and rhetorical, lies in avoiding the term *relativism*.[5]

But there are some thinkers for whom "relativism" seems to be more than a rhetorical commitment. Thus Anne Seller suggests that "all ways of making sense of the world are equally valid" (1988, 170) provided they are held by groups, not by single individuals. And Joyce Trebilcot remarks that for her "the notions of true and false, right and wrong, and reality and fantasy do not have ... the absolute and universal meanings that they usually have in patriarchy" (1988, 12).[6] What is it that makes epistemic relativism look like an attractive position? Part of the answer lies, I think, in the acceptance of a firm distinction, an *external relation*, between conceptual scheme and empirical content.[7]

Other Schemes

A few years ago Agence-France Presse (AFP) reported a number of "mob attacks" in Lagos in which apparently innocent citizens were beaten, sometimes to death, for allegedly stealing men's genitalia.[8] These thefts were thought to have been accomplished by means of "bodily contact such as handshakes" or by asking "the time of day or for directions." According to Reuters, which also reported the alleged theft of women's breasts, medical examinations of complainants showed that "organs were in their natural place and functioning,"[9] but this empirical disconfirmation did not deter those who put faith in the rumor. "Many Lagos residents," said AFP, "now go about the streets checking ... their genitals immediately after a handshake or after bodily contact with a stranger."

The cheeky tone of the AFP report suggests that we are to regard this tale as one of the eccentricity, incomprehensibility, and general lack of "scientific" sophistication of Nigerian culture.[10] When we consider that vigilantism—even lynching—is a "frequent popular reaction to the police's corruption and perceived indifference at the city's high rate of robberies and muggings,"[11] the *extremity* of the reaction to the "bizarre rumor" is less baffling. And if we think of the "superstition" that breasts and genitals can be stolen by casual contact as a metaphor for our own culture's fear of diseases like AIDS, the whole series of events makes yet more sense.[12]

But even if we are critical of the obvious ethnocentrism of this story, I think it is difficult for Westerners to shake the feeling that a belief in the magical theft of genitalia is beyond our abilities to grasp properly. Are the people described simply *irrational*? Do the alleged "thefts" bear any resemblance to what we would normally think of as theft? And, if not, are there any criteria for deciding whether or not the thefts really took place?

The anthropologist Dan Sperber tells of an elderly Southern Ethiopian acquaintance named Filate, who "in a state of great excitement" asks Sperber to "kill a dragon" whose "heart is made of gold" and which "has one horn on the nape of its neck" (1982, 149). Sperber is bewildered: "How could a sound person believe that there are dragons, not 'once upon a time,' but there and then, within walking distance? How am I to reconcile my respect for Filate with the knowledge that such a belief is absurd?" (150).

This sort of question might prompt us to embrace what I call the "ethical-political argument" for relativism (though Sperber is not so prompted). If we are to make sense of Filate or of the angry crowds in the Nigerian capital, the argument goes, then we must interpret their actions and beliefs as shaped by a very different set of concepts from our own. If we abandon our urge to force our views on them, then we see that their ways of conceiving of the world make sense of these incidents which, to English-speakers with a modern European cultural heritage, for example, seem bizarre. And if we have difficulty grasping how anyone might rationally believe that his penis had been stolen—despite evidence to the contrary—or that nearby there is a golden dragon with a horn on the nape of its neck, then that is just because our "conceptual scheme" has no room for their ways of thinking. In a manner of speaking, we live in "different worlds," and we cannot reasonably fault them for not living in ours. In our world there are no dragons, and the theft of someone's breasts or penis would be a different and, we may think, more horrific happening. But Filate inhabits a world in which there *are* dragons and the angry Lagonians have something real to fear. Their conceptual schemes, their ways of carving up the world, are incommensurable with our ways, and we cannot criticize them in any way that does not beg the question, because our concepts do not get any purchase on their beliefs. What are we to make of this position?

Such thinking, Davidson has argued, rests on a dubious "third dogma" (1984b, 189) of empiricism—the dogma that there is a sharp division to be made between a conceptual scheme and its empirical content. In Davidson's view, the only intelligible account of what a conceptual scheme could be is captured by saying that a conceptual scheme is a language (or a group of intertranslatable languages), and the only sense to be made of the idea of *different*, incommensurable conceptual schemes lies in saying that there could be languages that could not be translated. I shall call this view *conceptual relativism*. Such failures of translatability might be complete or partial. But, argues Davidson, a language that we could not possibly translate would not be recognizable *as a language*. So, it is idle to suppose that there could be different conceptual schemes, as well as to speak of there being *one* conceptual scheme.

Whether commensurability is best captured by intertranslatability is a point to which I shall return below, but for now let us see where Davidson's assumption takes us. As Rorty notes (1979, 261), the scheme-content dogma that interests Davidson is not just a dogma of empiricism; it has a central role in the Kantian synthesis of intuitions in accord with the pure concepts of understanding.[13] But Davidson was responding to a trend in Anglophone philosophy that he saw as partly a result of Quine's rejection of synonymy and reductionism, empiricism's first two dogmas:

> The dualism of the synthetic and the analytic is a dualism of sentences some of which are true (or false) both because of what they mean and because of their empirical content, while others are true (or false) by virtue of meaning alone, having no empirical content. If we give up the dualism, we abandon the conception of mean-

ing that goes with it, but we do not have to abandon the idea of empirical content: we can hold, if we want, that *all* sentences have empirical content. (1984b, 189)

The notion of a conceptual scheme had already been entertained by the logical empiricists. In "Empiricism, Semantics and Ontology" Carnap suggests that there may be a variety of "linguistic *framework[s]*"—that is, "systems" of "ways of speaking" that recognize rules appropriate for discussing a "kind of entities" (Carnap 1956, 206).[14] Examples include "thing language" in which we discuss "the spatio-temporally ordered system of observable things and events" (206f.) and the frameworks in which we discuss natural numbers, propositions, or spatio-temporal coordinates. Within each of these frameworks it makes sense to raise certain questions: "Is there a white piece of paper on my desk?" or "Did King Arthur actually live?" for example. These are *internal* questions—in this case, internal to the linguistic framework of thing-language. Such internal questions, says Carnap, should not be confused with *external* questions, or rather, with external *pseudo*-questions that purport to address matters of *ontology* before accepting a particular linguistic framework. We might be tempted to ask whether there are any spatio-temporal objects in general. But such a question, says Carnap, is senseless, because its intelligibility presupposes the very linguistic framework that it calls into question. The only way to make sense of the query, he claims, is to see it as a *pragmatic* question about whether or not to talk in thing-language (207f.). We might choose to abandon thing-language for some other "form of language" (208), but to do so is not to exchange one set of ontological commitments for another; it is merely to settle on a new way of talking, and this we do for such pragmatic reasons as "efficiency, fruitfulness and simplicity" (208).

Unlike the conceptual schemes of the conceptual relativist, Carnap's frameworks do not put up barriers to understanding, because regardless of which frameworks we use, we can always ground communication across frameworks on what is objectively given us in experience. Observations may not uniquely confirm a specific linguistic framework, but they *are* given, regardless of one's choice of frameworks. And although Carnap allowed for the possibility of different frameworks even at the level of observation statements, he also endorsed the possibility of determinate translation from one observation language to another.[15]

This idea of a theory-neutral set of intertranslatable observation languages and the sharp distinction between "questions of meaning and questions of fact" (1956, 215 n. 5), as Carnap acknowledged, rest on the notion of a strict synonymy of terms in different observation languages and an absolute distinction between "logical and factual truth" (215 n. 5).[16] And, according to Quine, abandoning these two dogmas of empiricism requires that we forego theory-neutrality and regard scientific hypotheses as having ontological import.

We encountered Quine's general strategy in Chapter 2. Analytic truths comprise, as proper subsets, the set of logical truths and the set of truths rendered analytic by synonymy of certain of their subject and predicate terms. If sense is to be made of analyticity, then sense must be made of synonymy. However, Quine argues, no clear account of synonymy can be given. Hence, synonymy—sameness of *meaning*—goes by the wayside, and so then does the verification theory of meaning assumed by the logical empiricists. Without bridge laws that let us reduce theory sentences to sets of observation sentences with which they are synonymous, the central project of logical positivism collapses.[17] With it collapses the idea of a theory-neutral language—a language of sense data or of physicalism that could bridge the gaps between rival sets of theory sentences, providing a ground for common understanding. As Davidson says, "To give up the analytic-synthetic distinction as basic to the understanding of language is to give up the idea that we can clearly distinguish between theory and language" (1984b, 187).

However, being awakened from this dogmatic empiricist slumber does not entail being dragged from the comfy bed of empirical content, and it is this fact that gives the idea of a conceptual scheme a new, dreamlike quality. Even if we reject the first two dogmas of empiricism, analyticity and reductionism, we may be tempted to keep our old talk of frameworks or of "the conceptual scheme of science" (Quine 1980, 44) without any theory-neutral observational bridge between alternative frameworks. Thus, Quine says that his "pragmatism" is "more thorough" than Carnap's, which "leaves off at the imagined boundary between the analytic and the synthetic" (46). Choosing a "convenient conceptual scheme or framework for science" (45) implicates not just scientific hypotheses, but our whole ontology. Faced with the changing flux of empirical content, bereft of a neutral language of sense data or physics, we need schemes or frameworks to *"organize"* or *"systematize, divide up* (the stream of experience)" (Davidson 1984b, 191). And there seem to be diverse ways of doing this.

In Chapter 2, I took issue with some of the details of Quine's position. Analyticity, I argued, can be made sense of in a way that does not violate Quine's critique, and Quine himself has adopted a notion of intralinguistic analyticity similar to the interlinguistically applicable notion that I propose. A statement is analytic, I said, if I cannot understand its terms without understanding that it is true. And with the treatment of internal relations on which this notion of analyticity depends comes a distinction between quotidian statements about the macroscopic world of spatio-temporal objects and the explanatory hypotheses of theoretical discourse. So we *can* draw a rough distinction between language and theory. I can intelligibly doubt the hypothesis of quantum indeterminacy, though it may be well enough confirmed that such doubt is unjustified. However, under ordinary circumstances I cannot doubt, for example, that I am seated in my office composing a paragraph at my word processor (if I am), without thereby casting doubt on my grasp of terms like *seated, office,* and *word processor*. It is part of my understanding of these words that I do not have such doubts, unless circumstances are recognizably extraordinary.

For the moment, I want to set such worries aside. The important point here is to see why Quine's views helped to change the role of "conceptual schemes" in philosophical debate: If one rejects the analytic-synthetic distinction, but retains the notion of "empirical content," then one will be tempted to apply pragmatic criteria of theory choice to ontology itself. And although Davidson's remark about the consequences of giving up the analytic-synthetic distinction sounds very Quinean, "to give up the idea that we can clearly distinguish between theory and language" (1984b, 187) is not to give up the idea that we can distinguish between theory and language at all. As we shall see, Davidson's arguments against the scheme-content distinction rest on the very notion of an internal relation central to my arguments.

Incommensurability

If "Two Dogmas of Empiricism" suggested a revision of the idea of a conceptual scheme, its dry (though lucid) discussions of definition, interchangeability, and semantical rules still required a little help to become influential in enacting this revision. Such help came from the engaging studies of philosophers and historians of science like Thomas Kuhn. Kuhn, who cites Quine as an important influence (1970, vi), is known for disputing a conception of scientific-theory change, according to which science is cumulative or accretive—that is, according to which scientific discoveries are really *discoveries*, and when old theories are rejected in favor of new ones, those new ones can tell us new things about the objects studied by the old theory.

The apparent continuity in the history of science, Kuhn argues, is largely an illusion brought about by scientists and historians of science, who tend to view the science of their day as having *progressed* from the science of earlier times. There is great resistance to theoretical change in the natural sciences, and to understand this resistance we cannot treat the history of science as one of continuous dialogue against a background of shared criteria of relevance. So-called crucial experiments, Kuhn says, seldom settle a current dispute between two theories that aim to explain roughly the same phenomena. Such experiments are usually carried out after a new theory has already been adopted, and it often remains open for the holder of an obsolete theory to interpret the results as confirming, rather than falsifying the old approach, assuming that advocates of the older "paradigm"[18] have not all died off.

Thus, theorists of opposing schools often talk at cross-purposes—if they bother to talk with each other at all—for, it seems, they cannot even agree on their standards of warranted assertibility. This communicative gulf is broadened by the fact that terms from an older theory can survive to play a role in the newer theory, but often the role will be slightly different, suggesting that, for example, what Thomson meant by *atom* is not what Bohr meant by *atom*. In short, practitioners of one paradigm may not even be talking about the same things as are practitioners of another paradigm. This casts doubt on the idea that scientists gradually acquire more and more knowledge about the same things with each theory change. A cumulative account of science applies only to "normal science," research carried out *within* a paradigm.

Kuhn imputes the communicative breakdowns that separate scientists in different traditions or eras to the incommensurability of their respective paradigms. After a scientific revolution, he seems at times to say, a whole new ontology confronts the researcher.[19] "In so far as their only recourse to [the] world is through what they see and do, we may want to say that after a revolution scientists are responding to a different world" (1970, 111). If scientists following a new paradigm live in "a different world," then similarities of the vocabulary that they retain are no more than that—the reference of the terms involved will have shifted with their new situation in a new paradigm. The atoms that Thomson investigated were not the atoms that Bohr investigated—indeed, they did not even belong to the same world. But if the reference of a term changes along with its use, we have no reason to think that the same concept is at work in different paradigms, even though the same term is. We are left with conceptual relativism. And if concepts, reference, and meaning change utterly from one paradigm to the next, then what we knew—what was *true*—before the shift of paradigms, seems no longer to be true. Either those former truths are now false, or they are neither true nor false, because they purport to talk about entities peculiar to that erstwhile world of the prerevolutionary scientist. Truth is relative to incommensurable conceptual schemes, and anything that we are epistemically justified in saying or believing is similarly relative.

In the 1969 postscript to the second edition of *The Structure of Scientific Revolutions,* Kuhn repents of his more relativistic-sounding formulations. Scientists working with different paradigms do not inhabit different worlds, because "they share a history, except for the immediate past" and so they share "their everyday and most of their scientific world and language" (1970, 201). They can thus come to understand what it is that they disagree about by trying to "translate" from one paradigm to another: "What the participants in a communication breakdown can do is recognize each other as members of different language communities and then become translators.... Having isolated ... areas of difficulty in scientific communication, they can next resort to their shared everyday vocabularies in an effort further to elucidate their troubles" (202).

But the influence of Kuhn's views on critics of strong objectivism is often independent of this fact, I think. Although Kuhn himself may not be a relativist, his views have helped to make relativism seem attractive.

Scheme and Content

The attraction of a relativism of concepts and truths to "schemes" that divide the world into different ontologies is not felt so strongly by Davidson. The problems, as Davidson sees them, are two: (1) it makes sense to talk of different schemes carving up the world, only if it makes sense to say that it is the same world that is carved up by each, but if it is the same world that is differently carved, then there is a shared basis for understanding across schemes; and (2) we have no concept of truth apart from having concepts of translation and interpretation, so we cannot attribute to members of another culture (or our own) a set of true beliefs which we cannot in principle understand. As I shall try to clarify, the former point amounts to saying that there is an internal relation between concepts and their empirical "content," and the latter points to the presence of an internal relation between the concept of truth and the concepts of understanding and interpretation.[20]

Take the first point. Davidson skillfully dissects the metaphors used to illustrate what it would mean for there to be different conceptual schemes. Such schemes are thought of as carving up, dividing, or organizing their empirical content, which is variously referred to as "the world" or as "nature, reality, sensory promptings" (1984b, 191). For the relativist there are, as we saw, different "ways of making sense of the world," all of which "are equally valid" (Seller 1988, 170). But what exactly would it be to "make sense" of the world as a whole, as opposed to making sense of the many determinate facets that get grouped together under the rubric "the world"? What could it mean for a scheme to "organize" something like nature or reality or "experience" as a whole? "Someone who sets out to organize a closet arranges the things in it. If you are told not to organize the shoes and shirts, but the closet itself, you would be bewildered. How would you organize the Pacific Ocean? Straighten out its shores, perhaps, or relocate its islands, or destroy its fish" (Davidson 1984b, 192). Of course, it is not the things *in* nature or experience—shoes and shirts, shores and fishes—that are supposed to be organized, for those things are supposed to be the *results* of conceptual "organization": an ontology relative to the particular scheme employed. If there already were determinate things in nature or experience, then holders of different schemes would share a basic ontology; they would live in, and respond to, the same world, though they might not wear the same shoes or eat the same fish, and they might not all classify fish (or shoes) in the same way. However, without any determinate things in nature prior to the application of concepts, we are returned to the problem of what it means to organize nature or experience as a whole.

For a distance, the problem here runs parallel to a problem encountered in earlier chapters. The metaphysical realist, the external-world skeptic and the traditional epistemologist, we saw, are all in agreement that my experience as of a world beyond my senses is a unified phenomenon that requires, and is amenable to, overarching explanation. Or, to vary the point of consensus, experience constitutes a unified body of evidence that can be taken to provide inductive support for the conclusion that there is an external world (or that I have always been a brain in a vat). My experience of the world is thus taken to be related to the world only externally. Being able to identify my experience does not ensure that I can say what it is experience of. Much the same assumption is at work in the sharp distinction between conceptual scheme and empirical content, for that empirical content is taken to comprise an identifiable totality that can then be subject to the organizing—or, as Kant would have said, "synthesizing"—powers, both of our concepts and of others'. Being able to identify the empirical content does not ensure that I can identify any particular conceptual scheme that might be brought to bear on it. Content and scheme are externally related.

What makes the problem worse in this case, however, is that this totality of empirical content is flat and featureless. It has no determinate structure of its own prior to our imposing a conceptual regimentation on it. It is amorphous and undifferentiated, like the metaphysical realist's mind-independent reality stripped of any determinate features—bare being, a mere thing-in-itself. And how we could ever identify it in the first place, independently of attributing a determinate structure to it, is a mystery. But then, if empirical content is variegated in the way it would have to be for anything at all to be said about it, we can no longer make sense of the suggestion—in the way that the conceptual relativist requires—that we and Filate and victims of "genital theft" live in different worlds.

So conceptual relativism and strong objectivism alike see experience as related to the world only externally—strong objectivism, because it conceives the world as having a determinate structure independently of the real possibility of our knowing anything of it; relativism, because it conceives of the world as undifferentiated matter for a variety of incommensurable conceptual forms and a variety of incommensurable experiences. It should not surprise us, then, that a predilection for external relations also troubles the relativist's treatment of truth. Davidson's second criticism helps to make this clear.

Radical Interpretation

Davidson's second complaint, recall, is that we have no grasp of truth apart from understanding translation and interpretation, and therefore we cannot attribute to members of another culture (or our own) a set of true beliefs which we cannot in principle understand, rooted in a set of concepts that we cannot in principle grasp.[21] The question of whether we can characterize alternative conceptual schemes as "largely true but not translatable," says Davidson, "is just the question how well we understand the notion of truth, as applied to language, independent of the notion of translation. The answer is, I think, that we do not understand it independently at all" (1984b, 194). Nothing, Davidson suggests, could count as a good reason to suppose that we had encountered speakers of an untranslatable language, because any evidence that would count in favor of untranslatability would also count in favor of believing that the behavior manifested by these alleged speakers "was not speech behavior." "If this were right," he continues, "we probably ought to hold that a form of activity that cannot be interpreted as language in our language is not speech behavior" (185f.). We could not even recognize such a "language" as a language.

To understand Davidson's argument we need to review his conception of radical interpretation and his use of Tarski's work on truth.[22] Take the latter. Tarski proposed that for any formalized language, L, a truth definition could be given by providing a recursive method for pairing sentences of the object language, L, with metalinguistic descriptions of their truth-conditions.[23] Given a finite vocabulary, a set of rules for forming sentences from the vocabulary, and a list of the "satisfaction"-conditions of terms of that vocabulary (their reference, more or less), it would then be possible to say for any well-formed combination of terms what were its truth-conditions on the basis of already knowing the satisfaction-conditions for its constituent terms. All such "truth theorems" given in the metalanguage would take the form

"s" is true if and only if p,

where "s" names an object-language sentence to which are assigned truth-conditions, p, described in the metalanguage. Tarski's much-used example (1949, 54) is

"Snow is white" is true if and only if snow is white,

where the metalanguage includes the object-language, and the truth definition is, therefore, "homophonic."

Tarski's view gives us a different truth-predicate for each artificial language with an appropriately specified structure, and in eschewing the messiness of natural language, it may seem to leave the general notion of truth untouched.[24] But Davidson thinks that we can reasonably apply a technique like Tarski's to natural languages, and he thinks that, though there must be more to the notion of truth than Tarski's account makes available, nonetheless "Tarski has told us much of what we want to know about the concept of truth" (1990, 295). What we want to know further is what all of Tarski's individual truth-predicates have in common, and we find this out, says Davidson, by examining truth's "essential connections with the concepts of belief and meaning" (295).

To this end, Davidson wants to apply Tarski's conception of a truth definition to natural languages in such a way that it takes on the characteristics of a truth *theory*, and such a truth theory will be part of an overall empirical theory of interpretation for a given speaker. A "truth theory" here is not a "theory of truth" in the sense that I have disparaged in earlier chapters. It does not seek to explain the nature of truth; it simply tries to employ a particular regimentation of the use of the word *true* in order to help us detect the "pattern truth must make" (Davidson 1990, 295) in a particular language. By formulating hypotheses about the truth-conditions for object-language sentences to which the speaker gives prompted assent, we can, as it were, work backwards to a constituent vocabulary, an account of the satisfaction-conditions for particular terms and rules for the combination of terms. Along the way, we manage to interpret the speaker's utterances. So if we ask what would be sufficient to understand a language, says Davidson, we should be content with the answer that we could understand a given language, L, if we could formulate a truth theory for L that were well confirmed by the empirical trials of radical interpretation.[25]

Suppose I want to understand a speaker of a language wholly unfamiliar to me. Understanding her amounts, roughly, to attributing to her beliefs and desires that make sense of her behavior by assigning meanings to her utterances. But, as I remarked in Chapter 2, the thesis that the concepts of truth, meaning, and belief are internally related is central to Davidson's position. Davidson does not use such terminology, but he does offer this description of the "interdependence" of meaning and belief:

> What a sentence means depends partly on the external circumstances that cause it to win some degree of conviction; and partly on the relations, grammatical, logical or less, that the sentence has to other sentences held true with varying degrees of conviction. Since these relations are themselves translated directly into beliefs, it is easy to see how meaning depends on belief. Belief, however, depends equally on meaning, for the only access to the fine structure and individuation of beliefs is through the sentences speakers and interpreters of speakers use to express and describe beliefs. (1986a, 315)

We do not get much of an impression of what a speaker believes, save by recourse to what she says.[26] But at the same time what we interpret a speaker to mean in uttering certain words depends in part on what other beliefs (and desires) we presuppose her to have. Such interdependence poses a problem for the radical interpreter, since she can neither assume knowledge of a speaker's beliefs in order to assign meanings to terms, nor assume meanings in order to attribute beliefs:

> If we want to illuminate the nature of meaning and belief, therefore, we need to start with something that assumes neither. Quine's suggestion, which I shall essentially follow, is to take *prompted assent* as basic, the causal relation between assenting to a sentence and the cause of such assent. This is a fair place to start the project of identifying beliefs and meanings, since a speaker's assent to a sentence depends both on what he means by the sentence and on what he believes about the world. Yet it is possible to know that a speaker assents to a sentence without knowing either what the sentence, as spoken by him, means, or what belief is expressed by it. (1986a, 315)

We need to identify which statements a speaker will assent to—that is, which statements she holds true—and the best place to start is with statements about the macroscopic world of objects and events, these being the easiest things to represent or reenact in an attempt to elicit the speaker's assent to an interpreter's utterance of some candidate-statement of the object language. What we take to constitute assent, of course, is a matter for trial and error, and our decision is subject to the possibility of later revision in the light of recalcitrant evidence. But we have no other recourse in such a situation of radical linguistic difference.

Notice first that the idea of a truth theory for L has a formal notion of translation built into it. Each theorem of a Tarski definition is a translation of a sentence of the object language into a sentence of the metalanguage. This fact is hidden if the object language is part of the metalanguage, so that truth theorems are homophonic, as in:

"Snow is white" is true if and only if snow is white.

But if the metalanguage is English, and the object language is German, then our theorems begin to look more interesting:

"*Der Schnee ist weiss*" is true if and only if snow is white.

If we understand this metalinguistic claim as a hypothesis about the truth-conditions for "*Der Schnee ist weiss*" to be tested together with similar hypotheses for other sentences of the object language, then we can see how such a theory might serve in interpreting a speaker of the object language.

Now, I do not share Davidson's confidence in the applicability of Tarski's work to natural languages. As I confessed in the preceding chapter, I think that truth is a pragmatic concept, a property of what is said, not a property of sentences, as it is construed by Tarski. As well, there is a wide range of linguistic utterances that do not come in the form of assertions with truth-conditions. Questions, exclamations, commands, requests, avowals, and so on constitute a huge portion of most natural languages, and it is highly contentious to suppose that these linguistic phenomena can be made to fit into the straitjacket of a recursive truth theory.

Moreover, it may seem that we can make sense of truth without invoking translation. Tarski-style truth theories matter to Davidson because he thinks that they have a role to play in radical interpretation. But the goal of interpretation is understanding, and although translation often facilitates understanding, it is neither necessary nor sufficient for it.[27] It is not necessary, because I can learn to understand a speaker of another language by learning to speak that language as a native speaker would, without recourse to translation; I understand speakers of my own language this way. Indeed, as Davidson has emphasized in recent years, I can also interpret a speaker of another language without either translating or learning her language. As long as both she and I have sufficient linguistic competence to employ marks and noises as words, all that matters is that I can understand how she uses particular marks and noises on a particular occasion, even if her use deviates wildly from the standard practices of her co-linguists (Davidson 1986b).

Translation, in the sense employed in a Tarski-style truth theory, is not sufficient for understanding a speaker, because I could translate statements of one language, L_1, into another, L_2, with nothing more than a truth theory for the object language, L_1, written in the metalanguage, L_2. I could have such a theory (assuming truth theories could be given for natural languages) without understanding either L_1 or L_2 and without engaging in any interpretation at all. Translation for Davidson, as for Quine, is a "syntactic notion" (Davidson 1986a, 315).

For much the same reasons, the question of whether there are incommensurable conceptual schemes, which Davidson construes as a question about whether some languages can fail to be intertranslatable, should really be thought of as a thesis about whether we can be incapable in principle of interpreting and understanding the behavior of the speaker of another language, or the holder of another "conceptual scheme." Davidson suggests as much, when he defines "conceptual relativism" in a more recent paper as "the idea that conceptual schemes and moral systems, or the languages associated with them, can differ massively— to the extent of being mutually unintelligible or incommensurable, or forever beyond rational resolve" (1989, 160).

There is, however, a more general consideration that underlies Davidson's position, and it can be stated without recourse to talk of translation or Tarski. Prompted assent, we saw, gives us a foothold for attributing meanings to the speaker's words and beliefs to the speaker. However, if we are to decide *what* statements a speaker holds true, and hence what she believes, then we need an additional leg-up. It is the principle of charity that gets us climbing.

The principle of charity says that we can get beyond the methodologically basic attitude of holding true, only by assuming that the speaker's beliefs about the macroscopic world of objects and events are largely true and largely like our own. Without this assumption, we cannot even begin to try to interpret another: "If all we know is what sentences a speaker holds true, and we cannot assume that his language is our own, then we cannot take even a first step towards interpretation without knowing or assuming a great deal about the speaker's beliefs. Since knowledge of beliefs comes only with the ability to interpret words, the only possibility at the start is to assume general agreement on beliefs" (Davidson 1984b, 197). General agreement is to be supposed because our only way to figure out what a speaker holds true in a situation of prompted assent is to consider what we hold true in that situation and because, from the standpoint of the modest realist, we cannot be massively mistaken about the macroscopic world of objects and events. Neither, then, can our potential interlocutors. Only the metaphysical realist's insistence on the real possibility of the external-world skepticism can stand in the way of this assumption.

Metaphysical realists have objected to just this aspect of Davidson's position. Devitt once insisted that Davidson must be an antirealist, because the principle of charity's denial of the real possibility of skeptical scenarios "makes reality dependent on our opinions in a way that is inconsistent with the independence dimension of Realism" (1984, 180).[28] This is not the sort of objection from which a conceptual relativist should take encouragement, however, for the typical conceptual relativist is also committed to attributing a great many true beliefs to holders of other conceptual schemes. And here we encounter a new problem. (Or is it so new?)

We have no resources for identifying true statements, except those that we employ in deciding (1) what constitutes a statement and (2) what is true. And the attribution of true beliefs to language users rests largely on our ability to identify certain utterances as true statements. Now, the central motivation for conceptual relativism is to give the epistemic relativist a rationale for holding that what is true for one culture or social group need not be true for another. So the relativist is committed to holding that we can identify true statements in the language of a cultural other without our being able ever to understand those statements.[29]

The assertion that a recognizable language could be forever beyond our grasp thus embodies an assumption that we have already encountered—that the theory of reference is to be kept separate from the theory of meaning, or that reference and use are externally related. That thesis, recall, is held in common by Carnap, Quine, and causal theorists of reference. It is also, I am suggesting, an important assumption for conceptual relativists. To suppose that we could identify certain kinds of behavior as speech behavior is to suppose that we could trace in that behavior the sorts of patterns typical of linguistic usage—reporting, exclaiming, querying, promising, requesting, assenting, joking, and so on. Maybe not all of these need feature in every language, but the relativist needs to suppose at least that we can trace the patterns left by *assertions* of cultural others. To suppose that we can trace such patterns, however, is to suppose that we can map the *uses* of utterances of the language at hand. Yet, even as we can do this, we allegedly still do not understand what the terms of the language refer to—we supposedly do not know what ontology is selected for by this alternative conceptual scheme; we do not live in the same world.[30]

It is no surprise that the epistemic relativist who seeks refuge in the idea of alternative conceptual schemes should also be committed to the correspondence theorist's sharp distinction between meaning and reference. Epistemic relativism is a theory of truth and knowledge, and the epistemic relativist is attracted to conceptual relativism, because the latter doctrine seems to make sense of how truth can be relative. If each scheme slices the world into a different ontology, then each scheme will admit a different set of truths. We have seen, moreover, that the conceptual relativist's distinction between scheme and content is tied to the strong objectivist's insistence that there is only an external relation between our experience of the world and that world itself. The conceptual relativist is, we could say, a kind of metaphysical realist—a metaphysical realist about conceptual schemes. Just as the metaphysical realist needs the real possibility that we might be utterly mistaken about the nature and existence of the external world, so the conceptual relativist needs the real possibility that there be "worlds of meaning" about which we are irremediably ignorant. The conceptual relativist, like the metaphysical realist who will not acquiesce in external-world skepticism, must both affirm and deny a skeptical thesis central to her own position: that we cannot understand the holders of a radically different conceptual scheme. Such tension is the classic symptom of epistemic neurosis.

Other Concepts

Davidson's argument from the internal relation between truth and understanding has been criticized on the grounds that it is ethnocentric and parochial. Alasdair MacIntyre, for example, thinks that there is something fundamentally wrongheaded about Davidson's approach here:

> Antirelativism pictures us first as necessarily inhabiting our own conceptual scheme, our own *weltanschauung* . . . and second as necessarily acquiring whatever understanding we may possess of the conceptual schemes and *weltanschauungen* of others by a process of translation so conceived that any intelligible rendering of the concepts and beliefs of the others must represent them as in all central respects similar to our own. (1987, 404)

Davidson wants to discourage us from using terms like *conceptual scheme*. We do not inhabit our own conceptual scheme "necessarily" because we do not inhabit our own conceptual scheme. We do use concepts, but they are not welded into a steel-plated "scheme" that is crafted to bump up roughly against any other scheme it meets. But of course, MacIntyre's complaint is with the Davidsonian principle of charity. MacIntyre fears that this principle translates into a wielding of cultural hegemony, a willful ignorance of cultural differences elevated to the level of a methodological procedure and a logical principle, which implies that members of other cultures must believe what we believe in order to count as language users.[31]

This criticism misconstrues its object. Davidson's argument is not designed to show that other cultures must conform to our way(s) of life or our vision(s) of the good in order for their members to count as persons. The point is not that people from other cultures cannot possess other *concepts*. Ways of life diverge, and with them so do cultures and concepts. Although human beings share many basic ends, the means that they arrange for the attainment of those ends vary widely, and in the course of devising means we also acquire new and divergent ends. The *interests* of a foraging people differ in important ways from the interests of an agrarian people, which in turn differ in important ways from the interests of a people devoted to the manufacture and trade of commodities. Different concepts are needed to serve these different interests. The urban commodity consumer does not need to know which roots and berries are safe to eat, any more than the forager needs to know not to cross on a red light. "An education quite different from ours," Wittgenstein suggests, "might also be the foundation for quite different concepts" (1981, §387). "For here life would run on differently.— What interests us would not interest *them*. Here different concepts would no longer be unimaginable. In fact, this is the only way in which *essentially* different concepts are imaginable" (§388). Elements of the practices that serve our basic needs come to matter to us in themselves—familiarity breeds dependence—and their attainment and preservation give rise to new practices, linguistic and otherwise. To the extent that such changes take place in settings isolated from one another, different courses of development and different concepts are to be expected.

But the would-be relativist who cites MacIntyre's objection for support confuses the true observation that there is *no canonical description* of "the world" or the things of which it is composed with the self-defeating claim that any description will do. Despite our differences, we all occupy a shared world of spatio-temporal objects and events. We are all biological organisms with needs and desires, most of us under three meters tall, most of us slower than a bear or a tiger or a speeding bullet. We are all vulnerable to illness, disease, injury, and the betrayal of trust. Our lives have beginnings and ends and are filled to varying degrees with pain and pleasure, expectation and disappointment, fear and security, anger and joy. This core of commonality, Wittgenstein suggests, "is the system of reference by means of which we interpret an unknown language" (1968, §206). It is the system of reference for Davidson's principle of charity: Do not attribute to others the belief that what we call "rocks" and "trees" do not exist because in so doing you undermine the intelligibility of your own interpretation; do not attribute to others the belief that they can walk on water without any special aid because you will then be able to make no further sense of them.

> We are bound to suppose someone we want to understand inhabits our world of macroscopic, more or less enduring, physical objects with familiar causal dispositions; that his world, like ours, contains people with minds and motives; and that he shares with us the desire to find warmth, love, security, and success, and the desire to avoid pain and distress. (Davidson 1982, 302)

Only once a certain amount of agreement is in place does it make sense to consider the possibility of disagreement about additional matters. If I say at a party "The man with a martini is a philosopher," and if the man in plain view to whom I refer is a nonphilosopher, drinking water from a cocktail glass, then I plainly have at least two false beliefs, even if at the party there is some other man who is a philosopher drinking a martini.[32] But the principle of charity does not require that my remark be interpreted as true. What it does require is that to interpret my remark an auditor should suppose that I correctly believe, as she does, that there is a person in plain view, that he is a man (though we can also imagine "his" turning out to be a woman), that he is drinking something, or holding something in his hand as one would a drink, or standing next to a table with a glass on it. Without attributing true beliefs *such as* these, it is unclear how even to begin to interpret my words. The principle of charity, as B. T. Ramberg observes, is not a pragmatic constraint on interpretation, but *"a precondition for interpretation"* (1989,

77). It is the radical interpreter's correlate of the unintelligibility of doubt about the external world as a whole.

By applying the metaphysical realist's conception of objectivity and mind-independence to conceptual schemes, conceptual relativism reifies cultures and languages, as though they possessed discrete structures that we could hold up, in imagination or otherwise, for the purposes of point-by-point comparison, much as we might compare two photographic transparencies by laying one atop the other and holding them up to the light. When we try to lay one language or culture atop the other to compare them, we find that their figures do not mesh. We see only a confused jumble of partial images.

But cultures and languages are not like this. What the relativist wants to call a "conceptual scheme" is not a formal, eternal structure—a synchronic time-slice of a language made general and implicitly diachronic. It is a motley assortment of related (but different) practices that can grow and change to embrace new practices. Rorty puts the point clearly: "Alternative cultures are not to be thought of on the model of alternative geometries. Alternative geometries are irreconcilable because they have axiomatic structures, and contradictory axioms. They are *designed* to be irreconcilable. Cultures are not so designed, and do not have axiomatic structures" (Rorty 1991b, 26). We compare our language and concepts to others not by holding up formal structures, but by using our language and concepts, and this process of comparison automatically alters the things being compared, for we now have to extend our language in ways that will account for the differences we find. It need not be the case, to use Feyerabend's formulation, "that English *as spoken independently of the comparison* already contains native [i.e. other-cultural] ideas." However, "languages can be *bent* in many directions and ... understanding does not depend on any particular set of rules" (Feyerabend 1988, 197). It remains possible for us to come to fathom another culture, to learn to interpret its language, even if we cannot adequately translate all of it, because understanding need not be a matter of translation, and because we all inhabit the same world of macroscopic objects and events.[33] We can come to understand by a judicious mix of interpretation and—if we are allowed—participation in the activities that embed the language whose speakers we are trying to comprehend.[34]

Practical differences remain. There can, indeed, be practices that are "incompatible in principle," as Charles Taylor puts it (1985b, 144). And with these incommensurable practices go incommensurable interests and problems of communication. If my goal is to acquire and exploit natural resources to further what I call my economic well-being and power, and if your interest is in maintaining what you call a spiritual connection with the land, taking from it only what you think you need without thought to ownership, then our interests will likely collide when we meet. And we will likely not understand each other. I will have to acquire the concept of having a spiritual connection to the land in order to understand you, and you will have to acquire the concept of owning land and natural resources in order to understand me. We will have to bend our languages if we are serious about understanding each other. Failures of communication may well be the norm rather than the exception here, and this is not inconsequential. But there is no "philosophical" problem about how communication is possible for us, for our differences are readily comprehensible—I have just described them.

Notes

1. For similar charges see Farrell 1994, 117–47.
2. See also 1991b, 24, 25, 49–51, 202; 1982, 167; and 1993, 450, 457.
3. See Putnam 1981, 119–24 for a more thorough version of the self-refutation argument. See also Putnam 1983, 234–38, where Rorty is miscast as the relativist.
4. See, e.g., Rorty 1982, 167 and Putnam 1981, 120.
5. I also suspect that Smith's proposal that we adopt "an alternate structure of conceptions of what [the objectivist] calls 'truth'" (1988, 113) is apt to sound to the strong objectivist like just another theory, perhaps analogous to eliminative materialism in the philosophy of mind. Is this point decisive? Perhaps not. I can say only that the philosophers (and my own earlier selves) with whom I have discussed such issues seem at least to see the possibility of modest realism if it is so labeled, whereas the label *relativist* typically inspires their suspicion. There is, I think, no substitute for emphasizing that truth and knowledge neither need nor are amenable to theoreticization. So I say it again.
6. In fairness, it is not clear to me that either Seller or Trebilcot is *unequivocally* committed to epistemic relativism. Many of Seller's arguments for relativism seem really to be arguments against scientism, and Trebilcot remarks at one point that her main concern is with "methods for using language" (1988, 1). It is primarily the rhetoric associated with claims to know the truth that seems to bother her.
7. This is confirmed in Trebilcot's case when she says, "I *think* . . . that I can imagine being with, communicating with, another being with whom I share no beliefs" (1990, 142). The importance of shared belief will become clearer below.
8. See "Lagos men"; "Nigerians fear"; "Vanishing organs." Similar events were more recently reported in Accra, Ghana. See "Vanishing penises."
9. "Sex organ scare."
10. The Reuters report is somewhat more reserved.
11. "Lagos men."
12. The proliferation of reports in Western nations, particularly the United States, by people who claim—seemingly sincerely—to have been abducted by extraterrestrial beings is surely no less bizarre than stories of genital theft. But such stories seldom provoke any recourse to conceptual relativism.
13. See also my 1997a.
14. See D'Amico 1989, 32f. for his account of Carnap's influence.
15. Carnap came to prefer a language of physics to one of sense data for observation statements, but not because he saw the choice as a "cognitive" one and not because he saw talk of physical objects as constitutive of the meaningfulness of our words. Physicalist language is preferable to phenomenalist language because of its "intersubjectivity, *i.e.*, the fact that the events described in this language are in principle observable by all users of the

language" (Carnap 1963, 52). But this advantage is of a kind with the criteria of "efficiency, fruitfulness and simplicity." Physicalism was for Carnap a question of "'attitude' and not 'belief' because it was a question of practical preference, not a theoretical question of truth" (51).

16. Responding to Quine's and White's (see White, 1950) criticisms of the analytic-synthetic distinction in "Meaning and Synonymy in Natural Languages," Carnap observes that an Anglophone linguist who tries to understand a German predicate through radical translation must assign a property to that predicate as its intension. This assignment "may be made explicit by an entry in the German-English dictionary, conjoining the German predicate with an English phrase. The linguist declares hereby the German predicate to be synonymous with the English phrase" (1956, 237).

17. Of course, logical positivism was never quite so simple or so homogeneous among its proponents in the Vienna Circle, but that is not my topic here. See Coffa (1991).

18. Kuhn's use of the word *paradigm* is typically held to be ambiguous, but I do not intend to explore that issue of interpretation here. I shall use the word in fairly innocuous contexts.

19. This initial estimate will be revised below.

20. P. M. S. Hacker, a leading proponent of the importance of internal relations and an interpreter of Wittgenstein from whose work I have learned a great deal, has recently argued against Davidson that there are such things as conceptual schemes. But the modifications I suggest below to Davidson's reasoning show, I think, that there is a kernel of insight here that is quite compatible with what Hacker wants to say. See Hacker 1996a.

21. We can think of the sense of "in principle" here as pertaining to real possibility, as outlined in Chapter 1. The conceptual relativist is denying that any set of interpretive hypotheses that we might formulate would suffice to explain the behavior, linguistic and nonlinguistic, of the holders of certain alternative conceptual schemes.

22. The best comprehensive discussion of these issues is given in Ramberg 1989, 64–97.

23. See Tarski 1949, 62–64.

24. See Tarski 1949, 52–8 and Putnam 1988, 60–66.

25. Such a theory, says Davidson, is not necessary for understanding any particular L; rather, a speaker's competence can be succinctly represented by saying that his or her linguistic competence can be *modeled* by the grasp of a theory of truth-in-L. See Davidson 1986b, 438. I share Schiffer's puzzlement about the exact import of such claims. See Schiffer 1989, 116f.

26. Linguistic behavior is not the only kind of behavior relevant to interpreting a speaker, but the present point concerns how to interpret what manifestly includes linguistic behavior. We need to be able to say that the intentional attitudes of a competent speaker are expressed by what he or she says.

27. For an extended discussion of the distinction between translation and interpretation as it applies to Davidson, see Malpas 1992, 24–50, 180–85. Still, I think that Davidson is correct to say that a language that could not in principle be translated *at all* would be no language at all.

28. Devitt has since withdrawn this charge, but still harbors doubts about the principle of charity. See Devitt 1997, 199–201.

29. It would be odd, indeed, to hold that another culture possessed a conceptual scheme incommensurable with our own, but that most of the beliefs of members of that culture were false. Even this eccentric thesis, however, rests on the assumption that we can

attribute beliefs of some sort to other-cultural speakers and, hence, that we can identify statements of some sort. So even such an eccentric conceptual relativist is committed to our being able to identify statements in the language of a cultural other without our being able to understand those statements.

It might be pleaded that we need not be able to *identify* any true statements in order for there to *be* any. But now the relativist sounds like the metaphysical realist: If the possibility of conceptual relativism is to be more than an idle, logical possibility, then, like the skeptic's hypothesis that we have always been brains in a vat, it must be warranted by the evidence. That evidence includes our identification, or probable identification, of certain utterances as true statements.

30. Or at least, this is one variation. We might alternatively see the relativist as driving a wedge not between reference and use, but between use, on one hand, and meaning and understanding, on the other. The point might be that we can trace linguistic patterns in the behavior of other-schemers—recognize patterns of use—without understanding those patterns. On this picture there would be an external relation between knowing the use of a term and understanding its meaning. From the point of view of someone who treats both reference and use and use and understanding as internally related, these two options are just variations on the same dissonant theme.

31. For related, but distinct, criticisms, see Code 1991, 59 and Hacking 1982, 62.

32. See Grandy 1973, 445.

33. For an expansion of this "same-world" theme, see Malpas 1992, 94–103, 138–47, 164–65, 186, 206–8. Should we encounter a species whose practices are rendered very different by their different sensory apparatuses or whose biological composition is so different that their "basic" interests seem obscure to us, then the scope of practical difference would be broadened—but it would remain practical, and interpreting them would require assuming that we share some beliefs with them, though it might be harder to discern which ones.

34. See MacIntyre 1987, 393 for similar remarks. Hacker (1996b, 220f.) rightly emphasizes the importance of participation to the acquisition of understanding. On the need for a "participant perspective" in the philosophy of language, see Ebbs 1997.

6

The Ethical-Political Argument

> *One of the most important tasks is to describe all the blind alleys of thought so vividly that the reader says "Yes, that is just what I meant." To hit off exactly the features of every error. You see, it is the right expression only if he recognizes it as such. (Psychoanalysis.)*
> *What the other person recognizes is that the analogy I am offering him is the source of his way of thinking.*
>
> —Ludwig Wittgenstein, "The Big Typescript,"
> in The Wittgenstein Reader

When Wittgenstein analogizes philosophy to therapy, he sometimes emphasizes the importance of describing a person's views in a way that she herself will concede to be accurate. The point here is not simply that one must be charitable in interpreting the views of another, but that if one wants to alleviate philosophical puzzlement, one must display both the contingency of the position held and the factors that make such a contingent position seem necessary or inevitable, and one must do this in such a way that the holder of the view will say, "Yes, that is what led me to such an opinion."

In the preceding chapter I tried to show that conceptual relativism gets its bite from the same set of assumptions that makes metaphysical realism and contemporary versions of the correspondence theory of truth attractive. But even if seeing that she shares such assumptions with her objectivist opponents gives the would-be relativist pause, I do not believe that this discovery by itself is likely to break the attraction of relativist views. Many such thinkers are attracted to relativism by the perceived political or ethical perniciousness of realism, and I think it is only by taking this attraction seriously and trying to trace it to its sources that one can hope to weaken it.[1] The would-be relativist needs to see her motivating concerns represented in a portrait of relativism before she can acknowledge it as presenting her own view and before she can allow that what she wants from such a view might be better had elsewhere.

What I shall call the "ethical-political" argument has sometimes been recognized by critics of relativism. Thus, Charles Taylor writes that relativism is tempting, because "It takes the heat off; we no longer have to judge whose way of life is superior" (1985b, 146). And Putnam observes that the relativist wants "to convince us to stop destroying primitive cultures by attacking our belief in the superior rationality and morality of our own" (1981, 161). But although this motivation for relativism has been correctly identified, there has been little sustained discussion of why it might *seem* that realism is morally or politically suspect, and as long as this appearance remains in place, the ethical-political argument will remain a perennial attraction.

In this chapter I shall argue that the would-be relativist conflates not only metaphysical and modest realism, but also realism and scientism. This latter conflation is encouraged by the frequent concurrence of these doctrines in both post-Viennese analytical philosophy and, more importantly, in influential strains of Marxist theory. The would-be relativist thus sees an internal relation between scientism and realism where there is only an external, historical one. In the process, the most subtle alliance of realism and scientism is overlooked: that which consists in seeing truth and knowledge as fit objects for explanatory theories, where science provides the model for such explanation.

Some realist philosophers will find positions of the sort I shall outline below to be naive—not worth discussing. But the truth here is that intelligent, educated people are tempted by these views, and if we want to understand why this is so, then it is poor interpretive practice to begin with the gratuitous assumption that such people are simply irrational or "naive." One might, with as much justification, say that the would-be skeptic about the external world is irrational or naive, and that to treat his position in the straight-faced manner that it is often accorded would be embarrassing—beneath the dignity of a serious philosopher. Many philosophers would not find this contention satisfactory, and yet in both cases we are dealing with views that circulate in the same conceptual economy as metaphysical realism. The relativist, I suggested in the preceding chapter, shares the metaphysical realist's conviction that we need to have theories of truth and knowledge and simply applies the metaphysical realist's own conception of objectivity to recognized facts about cultural difference. Any reason for thinking relativism (or idealism) to be naive would be likewise a reason for thinking that metaphysical realism is naive.

Nietzsche, Inc.

Some philosophers wear on their sleeves their political commitment to relativism. Anne Seller criticizes realism, under the name "rational-scientific epistemology," for what she sees as its antidemocratic stance:

> Although this epistemology, which I call rational-scientific, is politically appealing (it enables us to say to the sexist "you are wrong"), it also raises political problems. First, it is an élitist epistemology. Only some women have the resources (time, library, etc.)

to conduct such research, other women will simply have to accept it on authority. . . . Secondly, women have often experienced the scientific-rational approach as oppressive both in its process and in its findings. (1988, 170f.)

A stronger point is put rather more bluntly by Joyce Trebilcot: "To use the concept of truth—to claim that what you believe is true and what others believe is false—is a way of controlling others: of making them attentive and supportive, of getting them to do what you want, of having access to your own resources" (1992, 97). She thus prefers not to claim truth for any of her own beliefs, but allows that "when there is no alternative for defending [her]self or others," she "might use the concept of truth as a weapon" (97).

Paul Feyerabend makes a similar move. "Debating with objectivists," he writes, the relativist "may of course use objectivist methods and assumptions; however his purpose will not be to establish universally acceptable truths . . . but to embarrass the opponent" (1987, 78). Because "the idea of Reason and the idea of Objectivity have often been used to make Western expansion intellectually respectable" (5), says Feyerabend, "Epistemic Relativism" (73) is needed as "a weapon against intellectual tyranny and as a means of debunking science" (19), or at least its title to paradigm of knowledge.

I have already suggested that Feyerabend's position is better thought of as a variety of modest realism, inasmuch as he explicitly distances himself from offering an alternative theory of truth and knowledge. But here I am interested in the questions of why it should seem plausible to link realism with oppression, and why something called "relativism" should thus seem more attractive than something called "realism"—so that even thinkers, like Feyerabend and Barbara Herrnstein Smith, who explicitly distance themselves from theories of truth and knowledge should want to be known as relativists.

It is not just relativism that can be rendered attractive by such ethical and political considerations. It is natural to think of the scheme-relative ontologies on which conceptual relativism relies as in some way constituted by the application of schemes to neutral empirical content in a manner very reminiscent of Kant's transcendental idealism. Minds "make up" the world that they inhabit, but they do not follow one shared set of categories in doing so, as Kant thought. Even if one gets beyond the temptations of relativism, the attraction of idealism can remain. Thus, the literary theorist Ross Chambers remarks that "one must be ready to conceive discourse, not as a representation whose power depends on its adequacy to a (preexisting) real, but as a mediating practice with the power to produce the real" (1991, xvi). Particular "context[s] of reference," says Chambers, are not "givens . . . whose nature language attempts to reproduce," but "products of the functioning of language itself" (37).

Paul A. Bové, espousing a variety of discourse criticism, writes that "'true statements' are always relative to the authority of empowered discourses" (1990, 59). This view, he says, arises from a "radical skepticism about 'truth' and the correspondence of fact and concept" (55), which, he continues, "celebrates ... the increasing impossibility of defending 'truth' in any metaphysical way and welcomes the political possibilities for self-determination inherent in a recognition that 'truth' is made by humans as the result of very specific material practices" (55). The claim that truth is "made rather than found" (Rorty 1989, 7), as we saw in Chapter 5, need not be interpreted as an espousal of linguistic idealism. Indeed, I have hinted that it might be better to analogize truth and knowledge to artifacts than to natural kinds, and doing so does not entail that truth and knowledge are not objective, any more than tables and chairs are not objective for not being natural kinds. But there are more explicit examples. In the article "Literary History," for instance, Lee Patterson contends that "the 'linguistic turn' initiated by Saussure" has shown that "all forms of writing" are "as distant from the real world ... as literature had been thought to be" (1990, 257). This includes the "sciences," whose "very name," he remarks obscurely, implies "a claim to referentiality" (257). And Jacques Lacan, whose psychoanalytic theory has left a mark on the writings of many contemporary literary theorists, declares bluntly: "It is the world of words that creates the world of things—the things originally confused in the *hic et nunc* of the all in the process of coming-into-being" (1977, 65).[2]

The charge that concepts like truth and objectivity conflict with certain "political possibilities for self-determination" (Bové 1990, 55) or are "tools of a domination that is fundamentally phallic" (Trebilcot 1990, 143) turns in part, I think, on an implicit assumption that presuming to know or speak the truth is somehow immodest: Truth and a grasp of an objective world are beyond us, and any claim to possess them implicitly marginalizes competing views of the world, which have as much (or as little) right to the honorific "true."

One motivation for this assumption might be an identification of truth with a substantive correspondence between statements or beliefs and the strongly independent world of the metaphysical realist, combined with an acknowledgment of what Stroud calls the "conditional correctness of skepticism" (1984, 132). If one thinks that truth is correspondence to a strongly objective and independent world, and if one thinks that no refutation of the skeptic is possible, then one may be tempted to conclude that "we should not aspire to firm truths about how things are" (37).

The charge of immodesty can also be a response to the absolute idealists' conception of truth, according to which knowing one truth about a particular thing requires knowing all truths about everything. Truth, on this view, is a "significant whole" (Joachim 1969, 66) that cannot be grasped piecemeal, but only in its entirety, by possessing *the* ideally coherent system of beliefs. No one among us can rightly claim such cognitive achievement. As Lacan remarks, "We are some way yet from this ideal!" (1988, 264). "Every emission of speech," he continues, "is always, up to a certain point, under an inner necessity to err" (264), and "we are led," therefore, "to a historical Pyrrhonism which suspends the truth-value of everything which the human voice can emit" (264).

But the greatest modern philosophical source of the charge of immodesty is undoubtedly Nietzsche. In *The Gay Science* he asks, "What are man's truths ultimately?" only to answer, "Merely his *irrefutable* errors" (1974, §265). "Truth," he says in *The Will to Power*, "is the kind of error without which a certain species of life could not live" (1968b, §493). Those things we call "true" we value for their apparent utility or their perceived conduciveness to our survival as individuals and as a species. But such conduciveness is no guarantee of truth. "Life is no argument," says Nietzsche. "The conditions of life might include error" (1974, §121). Indeed, he sometimes suggests that error is unavoidable, because there is no stable *being*, only what Lacan called above "the *hic et nunc* of the all in the process of coming-into-being" (1977, 65), and all attempts to categorize *becoming* force it into a falsifying mold. "In a world of becoming, 'reality' is always only a simplification for practical ends, or a deception through the coarseness of organs, or a variation in the tempo of becoming" (Nietzsche 1968b, §581). There can be no truth as a correspondence to reality in itself, because there is no reality in itself—no truth and no knowledge: "Knowledge and becoming exclude one another" (§517). Our faith in the possibility of knowledge and truth is an immodest and self-deceiving expression of our aspiration for control.[3] The "will to truth" (1974, §344)[4] is just another aspect of the will to power. "Those who feel 'I possess Truth'—how many possessions would they not abandon in order to save this feeling! What would they not throw overboard to stay 'on top'—which means, *above* the others who lack 'the Truth'!" (1974, §13). "To impose upon becoming the character of being," he later writes, "—that is the supreme will to power" (1968b, §617).

However, it is not obvious that Nietzsche's mature views on truth involved either its rejection or its relativization. Maudemarie Clark (1990) has argued convincingly that Nietzsche's later published writings display an effort to reconceptualize the notions of truth and objectivity in a way that is friendly to what I have been calling modest realism. In *Twilight of the Idols*, for example, Nietzsche describes "How the 'True World' at last Became a Fable" (1968a, 40f.): "We have abolished the true world," he says, but *"with the true world we have also abolished the apparent world!"* (41).[5] Abolishing the "True World"—a world whose nature and existence are independent of the reliability of our epistemic capacities in the proto-skeptical sense of the metaphysical realist—does not leave us with the subjective idealist's world of mere appearances. Nor are we left with the skeptic's veil of illusion, for both these ideas get their sense from their contrast with the so-called True World. It is not claiming to know some truth about an objective world that is an immodest expression of the will to power, but claiming, if only implicitly, to see the world from a God's-eye view or the vantage of Absolute Mind. Nietzsche's relentless questioning of truth, as Barry Allen argues (1993, 41–69), is in the end a questioning of truth's alleged inherent value, but one can hold that truth gets its value extrinsically, when it gets it, from its role in an array of contingent social practices without holding that there is no such thing as truth.[6]

The Nietzschean linkage of truth and power has been made much of by Michel Foucault, whose influence, in turn, has been considerable. Many critics have charged Foucault, like Nietzsche, with propagating relativism and irrationalism,[7] and I suspect that, as in the case of Nietzsche, this popular image of Foucault has encouraged some radical critics to identify themselves as relativists. But, as with Nietzsche, the case is not so clear-cut. Gary Gutting, for example, has argued that criticisms of Foucault, "based on the charge of global skepticism or relativism, are unfounded" (1989, 272).[8] And Foucault himself did take the time to observe that when he spoke of the "'political economy' of truth" (1980, 131), by "truth" he did not mean a property of assertions and beliefs or "the ensemble of truths which are to be discovered and accepted," but, instead, "the ensemble of rules according to which the true and the false are separated and specific effects of power attached to the true" (132). Foucault's concern, this remark might suggest, is with the influence of power on practices of epistemic justification, with how what is *called* "true" can have a lot to do with the social distribution of power, and with how that distribution both enables human agency and limits it. None of this need reflect any particular understanding of what truth is, let alone skepticism about truth.[9]

Another influential French thinker, Jacques Derrida, is also often portrayed as being skeptical about the very possibility of objectivity, truth, and determinate meaning. Such *skepsis*, it is thought, rubs off on his attitude toward normative epistemic concepts. Thus, Putnam contends: "The problem is that notwithstanding certain moments of argument, the thrust of Derrida's writing is that the notions of 'justification,' 'good reason,' 'warrant,' and the like are primarily repressive gestures" (1992a, 132). Elsewhere Putnam attributes to Derrida a "radical linguistic idealism" (1990, 264), referring later to Derrida's oft-cited remark, "There is nothing outside the text" (1995, 75). Habermas complains similarly that Derrida "is particularly interested" not merely in drawing attention to the function of rhetorical features in philosophical writing, but in "standing the primacy of logic over rhetoric ... on its head" (1987a, 187). Derrida, thinks Habermas, holds that "'deconstruction' is an instrument for bringing Nietzsche's radical critique of reason out of the dead end of its paradoxical self-referentiality" (191).

One need only read Derrida's "Toward An Ethic of Discussion" to wonder if something might be awry in these assessments. "I have never," he laments, "'put such concepts as truth, reference and the stability of interpretive contexts radically into question,' if 'putting radically into question' means contesting that there *are* and that there *should be* truth, reference, and stable contexts of interpretation" (1988, 150). The phrase "there is nothing outside the text," far from being an avowal of linguistic idealism, he suggests, should simply be interpreted as "there is nothing outside context" (136). In other words, given the appropriate circumstances, anything at all can be relevant to the interpretation of a text. Contexts of interpretation do not have metaphysically rigid boundaries; those boundaries are, rather, normative ones. And to Habermas's charge that he views rhetoric as prior to logic, Derrida responds bluntly, "That is false. I say *false*, as opposed to *true*" (157 n. 9).

Of course, an author's work and an author's self-interpretations are two different things. So, the protestations of Foucault and Derrida do not alone settle the interpretive issues (but neither should their protests be dismissed out of hand), and I do not claim to have, in a few lines, cleared either of them, or Nietzsche, of the harsher charges of their critics. But that is not my aim here.

I *do* want to claim that, given the influence of these thinkers, popular readings of their work as skeptical, relativist, or idealist have likely played a role in the motivation of some would-be relativists. But I also want to claim that this surely cannot be the whole story, given the possibility of interpreting these thinkers in nonrelativist ways. Plainly there is something deeper in our intellectual, ethical, and political cultures that makes the relativist interpretations seem plausible. So the whole story would have to be a complicated one. Part of it might involve the romantic, "expressivist" reaction to the "disengaged reason" of Descartes, Locke, and the subsequent Enlightenment—a variation on part of the elaborate story that Charles Taylor (1989) has given us about the origins of the "modern identity." But I shall limit myself to narrower considerations: I think that friends of the ethical-political argument for relativism confuse realism with scientism, and I think that they are encouraged to do so by certain historical, but contingent, alliances of the two doctrines. My concern in the remainder of this chapter will be to elaborate this claim.

Realism and Scientism Conflated

I argued in Chapter 1 that it is commonplace for philosophers to conflate metaphysical realism with modest realism, and I claimed in subsequent chapters that the would-be relativist is tempted to offer a competing theory of truth and knowledge, once she becomes convinced that metaphysical realism is problematical. These two factors collude with each other. If I think I need a theory of truth and knowledge, and if I have conflated metaphysical realism and modest realism, then I may be tempted to conclude that the objectivity and independence of the world are ideas that I must do without. From here it is a short step to thinking that truth is relative or that I must do without it as well.

The ethical-political argument needs this conflation of realisms if relativism (or idealism or skepticism about truth) is to seem an obvious alternative. But it also turns on an additional conflation that makes the charge against realism of political or moral turpitude seem plausible. That is a conflation of realism with the doctrine that all and only science is to count as knowledge—that is, with *scientism*.

Anne Seller is a case in point. Speaking of feminist aspirations for a "democratic epistemology," she writes that, *contra* traditional "realist" epistemology, "We do not have necessary and sufficient tests of the truth, which we can individually apply, such as Descartes and so many since him have sought, but a process of conversation which may allow the truth to emerge" (1988, 179).

The phrase "necessary and sufficient tests for truth" is confusing. Part of what it suggests is an infallible method for distinguishing truth from falsehood—a reading confirmed by Seller's mention of Descartes. As I argued in Chapter 1, metaphysical realism is not committed to any such Cartesian quest for certainty, and it should be clear that modest realism has no such aspirations either. But Seller also seems to be objecting to the idea that a belief is justified if and only if it is arrived at, or subsequently confirmed by, a unique right method, where that unique right method prescribes a series of tests that any rational individual can, in principle, apply.[10] And she is trying to distance feminist "consciousness-raising" from both the individualism of this view and the scientistic doctrine of the unity of method.

The idea that consciousness-raising is the *method* of feminist theory is closely associated with the legal theorist Catharine MacKinnon. "Feminism," she writes, "does not appropriate an existing method—such as scientific method—and apply it to a different sphere of society to reveal its pre-existing political aspect" (1982, 535). Rather, feminism's distinctiveness lies in its emphasis on dialogue and the discussion of women's experience. MacKinnon's case for viewing consciousness-raising as a method rests on a list of epistemic advances that she takes feminism to have made by means of such shared discussion. Seller gives a similar, but briefer, account:

> Women's oppression has partly been understood in terms of the silencing of women, the denial of their experience as valid, or the treatment of it, when discovered, as neurotic. The woman who failed to find satisfaction in the fulfilment of domestic duties or who did not want to have babies was treated as a suitable case for treatment. The apprehension that such women were not sick but oppressed by a false view of what they should be came about only through women sharing these feelings and experiences with each other. (1988, 176)

The banal observation that two heads are better than one intimates that consciousness-raising could be a means of acquiring knowledge. One does learn things by talking to others. Indeed, one can learn about oneself by talking to others. The *differences* in another's experiences allow her to see my experience differently from the way I do and, so, to give me possible new descriptions of those experiences and of myself (see 1988, 180). And to the degree that we are similar, her sharing views with me may reinforce my conviction in matters about which I had only tentative and insecure suspicions, or which I had not admitted to myself. Intersubjectivity is a mark of objectivity, though not a sufficient condition.

So Seller's complaint seems to be that doctrines of the unity of method ignore the epistemic importance of dialogue. This, however, is not a complaint with realism, but with scientism—for it is the latter doctrine that seeks to reduce all inquiry to a single canonical method. The metaphysical realist is free to concede that a correct description of women's social reality depends on the kinds of epistemic practices that fall under the rubric "consciousness-raising." If Seller supposes otherwise, it is because of the liberal way in which she defines realism:

> It is the view that there is an objective order in human affairs, independent of people's beliefs about it, which can be discovered by some methodology generally characterized as rational and scientific. Thus, on this view, both Marxists and positivists might be characterized as realists because they believe in a social reality discoverable by the use of a method they specify as scientific. (1988, 183 n. 2)

Like some views canvassed in Chapter 1, this account of realism—"a view that . . . is best understood in opposition to relativism" (183 n. 2)—does not distinguish metaphysical realism from modest realism (though it is "social reality" and "human affairs" that concern Seller, not "the external world" in general). But more important here is Seller's qualification of social reality as knowable "by some methodology generally characterized as rational and scientific." Adopting a "scientific method" is not logically decreed by the metaphysical realist's notion of the world's objectivity, and certainly not by the modest realist's less demanding conception. Metaphysical realism *is* subject to scientistic influences of a subtler kind, as I hinted in earlier chapters, because it treats knowledge of the world as a theoretical notion, but this does not imply that "social reality" is knowable only by means of a science. Moreover, the alternative to metaphysical realism that abandons the view that we need a theory of truth or knowledge is not relativism, which is also a theory of truth and knowledge, but modest realism. Seller sees relativism as the only alternative to realism because she does not distinguish between metaphysical and modest realism, and she thinks realism is politically suspect because she confuses realism with scientism.[11]

Other writers have suggested, however, that scientism presupposes a "realist" conception of objectivity. The reason that scientism is problematical is not simply that not all knowledge is scientific, but that science is committed to "the view from a distance and from no particular perspective" (MacKinnon 1982, 538). Thus, Catharine MacKinnon writes that it is inappropriate to use science to understand women's oppression, because science draws a sharp distinction between epistemic agents and a mind-independent reality:[12] "The problem with using scientific method to understand women's situation is that it is precisely unclear and crucial what is thought and what is thing, so that the separation itself becomes problematic" (1982, 527 n. 23). Overcoming women's oppression, therefore, requires dissolving the objective-subjective distinction: "Disaffected from objectivity, having been its prey, but excluded from its world through relegation to subjective inwardness, women's interest lies in overthrowing the distinction itself" (536).

Elsewhere, she criticizes strong objectivism more directly: "Cartesian doubt... comes from the luxury of a position of power that entails the possibility of making the world as one thinks or wants it to be" (1987, 58). A position of relative power, thinks MacKinnon, makes it possible for men to confuse "what [they] think" with "the way the world is" (58), because although the world is taken as an independently existing thing that places constraints on behavior, men's behavior toward women is in important ways *un*constrained.[13] It thus becomes possible for men to doubt whether women possess any independent reality. Much as the skeptic wonders whether there is anything real beyond experience, so men may wonder whether women are mere phenomena with no underlying reality.[14]

Feyerabend also sees scientism as rooted in realism, and he portrays "relativism" as a response to "the idea of Reason and the idea of Objectivity," which, he says, "have often been used to make Western expansion intellectually respectable" (1987, 5). He is not hostile to science, but he insists—rightly, I think— that "science" taken as the paradigm of rationality with exact and authoritative methods is a "fictitious unit" (36). The idea that there is a single scientific method that trumps all other means of epistemic justification is an idea that Feyerabend sees as imposed on science by a reverence for Objectivity and Reason:

> To say that a procedure or a point of view is objective(ly true) is to claim that it is valid irrespective of human expectations, ideas, attitudes, wishes. This is one of the fundamental claims which today's scientists and intellectuals make about their work. *The idea of objectivity*, however, is older than science and independent of it. It arose whenever a nation or a tribe or a civilization identified its ways of life with the laws of the (physical and moral) universe and it became apparent when different cultures with different objective views confronted each other. (1987, 5)

Once again the two senses of objectivity that I have tried to distinguish are run together in this passage. But clearly Feyerabend regards realism as objectionable simply in virtue of its attachment to "Objectivity." Just as the standpoint of objectivity, in MacKinnon's story, is supposed to make it easy for men to confuse what they think with the way the world is, so "Objectivity," in Feyerabend's story, is supposed to allow a civilization to confuse "its ways of life with the laws of the ... universe."

But why does Feyerabend blame objectivity? There are two responses to the idea of objectivity with which he expresses some sympathy, "opportunism" and "relativism." The former, he writes "is closely connected with relativism; it admits that an alien culture may have things worth assimilating, takes what it can use and leaves the rest untouched" (1987, 86). It is only a third response, "persistence," that incurs his displeasure, and that disapproval is not unequivocal:

> One reaction was *persistence*: our ways are right and we are not going to change them. Peaceful cultures tried to avoid change by avoiding contact. The pygmies, for

example, or the Mindoro of the Philippines did not fight Western intruders, they did not submit to them either, they simply moved out of their sphere of influence. More belligerent nations used war and murder to eradicate what did not fit their vision of the Good. (1987, 5f.)

But persistence in its belligerent guise seems not unlike Reason on Feyerabend's account: "This belief . . . may be formulated by saying that there exists a right way of living and that the world must be made to accept it" (1987, 11). It would seem, then, to be the *combination* of some form of realism with some authoritative (or authoritarian) form of "Reason" that troubles Feyerabend, and realism enters the picture only because it facilitates hegemonic Reason. At this point, Feyerabend's views strongly resemble MacKinnon's, for part of her concern is that objectivity facilitates *objectification*, and in her opinion science is a key method of objectification: "What is objectively known corresponds to the world and can be verified by pointing to it (as science does) because the world itself is controlled from the same point of view" (1982, 538).

Are Feyerabend and MacKinnon right? Is the "conflation" of realism and scientism that I have cited as a source of relativist temptation really an insight about the logical presuppositions of scientism? I think not.

Each Without the Other

The metaphysical realist—as I never tire of saying—holds that the world's existence and nature are independent of people's capacities to know or describe them in the sense that it is really possible for us always to have been brains in a vat. But holding such a view is compatible with believing in similarly objective grounds of moral or aesthetic value and with thinking that science tells us nothing of morals or aesthetics. Think of the ethical and aesthetic nonnaturalism of G. E. Moore and the Bloomsbury group. If we contemplate an "exceedingly beautiful" world and "the ugliest world [we] can possibly conceive," says Moore, we should conclude that it is better that the former exist even "supposing them quite apart from any possible contemplation by human beings" (Moore 1959, 83f.). Moore commits himself here to a strong conception of objectivity indeed, but there is no hint of scientism.

Also possible are other varieties of realism that have little taste for scientism. Platonism, for example, centers on the claim that the world of sense is mere appearance and that only the Forms, which depend on nothing else for their existence, are real.[15] But this view antedates modern science by two millennia. Some kind of realism is also the implicit metaphysics of strains of religious fundamentalism, whose supporters seldom feel much sympathy for the claim that all and only scientific knowledge counts as knowledge.[16]

It might be objected, however, that all of these positions, despite their great differences, display just the sort of élitism to which Seller objects when she links scientism with realism. Dialectic is a discipline for which, according to Plato, few are suited, and his *Republic* is premised on the idea that such élitism is the best way of choosing a ruler. Fundamentalism, similarly, often takes some holy text as the final authority and only the chosen few have access to knowledge by way of the word of God, Allah, or whomever. And even Moore's nonnaturalism, or at least its appropriation by the writers and artists of Bloomsbury, was seen in its day as an élitist view.[17] It might seem that realism really is the problem, and scientism merely a manifestation.

But surely there are nonfundamentalist religious views that belie this suggestion—resolutely realist, nonscientistic views that hold, for example, that the word of God is there for all to hear. As well, some environmental philosophers have argued for metaphysical realism on the grounds that strengthening our conception of the world's objectivity and independence helps ensure that the natural world can be viewed as valuable in itself, quite apart from our evaluative or epistemic capacities. And I have argued in earlier chapters that one can deny the metaphysical realist's treatment of the world's independence and objectivity without denying the very concepts of independence and objectivity and without adopting a scientistic point of view. On my view there are a great many things about the world of spatio-temporal objects and events that we all know and that no pronouncement from scientists or other cultural authorities could undermine without calling itself into question.

So we can have realism—even metaphysical realism—without scientism. We can also, I think, have scientism without realism. First, we can have scientism without metaphysical realism. Consider Carnap's views on "frameworks," encountered in Chapter 5. The concerns of the external-world skeptic can get no hearing from Carnap, for doubts about the external world undermine the linguistic framework of "thing-language," presupposed by the very expressions used to formulate the skeptic's doubt. Questions like "Might we not be completely mistaken about the external world?" must be regarded as nonsense, or as implicitly pragmatic questions about which linguistic framework to employ. In neither case can they express the doubt that the Cartesian skeptic wants to express (see Carnap 1956, 207f.). A. J. Ayer reaches a similar conclusion, drawing on a principle of verifiability: "We say that the question that must be asked about any putative statement of fact is . . . Would any observations be relevant to the determination of its truth or falsehood? And it is only if a negative answer is given to this . . . question that we conclude that the statement under consideration is nonsensical" (Ayer 1952, 38). But the skeptic's worry gets no grip here: no series of sense experiences could give evidence for believing that we were deceived about that same sense experience as a whole. So, says Ayer, "anyone who condemns the sensible world as a world of mere appearance . . . is saying something which, according to our criterion of significance, is literally nonsensical" (39).

The emphasis on sense experience may remind us that the logical positivists were scientific through and through. It was "The Scientific Conception of the

World" (Hahn, Neurath and Carnap 1973, 299) that announced the program of the Vienna Circle in 1929 with the goal of *"unified science"* (306). And according to Ayer, we must not be deluded by the belief "that there are some things in the world which are possible objects of speculative knowledge and yet lie beyond the scope of empirical science" (1952, 48).

Seller, we saw, treats positivism as a *form* of realism, and it might be argued that there are certain affinities between the modest realist's treatment of objectivity and the logical positivists'. After all, any good scientist would be prepared to admit that the universe existed much as it is long before creatures with beliefs blundered onto the scene, and that is all that modest realism requires of the world's "mind-independence." However, the version of modest realism I have proposed is resolutely antiscientistic inasmuch as it insists that many of our ordinary beliefs about middle-sized dry goods are not justified by any probabilistic confirmation of the sort enjoyed by some scientific hypotheses. As long as modest realism does not *entail* scientism, the suggested affinity between my views and those of the logical positivists makes no difference to my claim that would-be relativists sometimes mistake scientism for realism.

Moreover, we might put the following rhetorical question: What barrier stands in the way of being a *relativist* and also embracing scientism? After all, if truth and rationality are relative to cultures, then the thesis of scientism is "true" for a scientistic culture. "Scientism," says the scientistic relativist, "may not be true for you, but it's true for me."

If scientism and realism (metaphysical or modest) are distinct doctrines, such that neither entails the other, we are left with an additional question about the attractiveness of "relativism" for the radical theorist: Why do scientism and realism seem so closely related that one can be mistaken for the other? Part of the answer, I think, is that there is a contingent historical connection between realism and scientism that begins with the rise of science in the seventeenth century and has persisted in two intellectual traditions of importance to English-speaking, "relativist" philosophers: a strain of analytical philosophy that has inherited its scientism from the logical positivists, but which is metaphysically realist, and an influential trend in Marxism to which feminist theorists such as Seller and MacKinnon find themselves responding.

As I remarked above, this is only part of the story, but I think it is nonetheless suggestive of a deeper explanation for the ethical-political attraction of relativism.

Analytic Philosophy

The principle of verifiability was a centerpiece of logical empiricism, and the apparent unverifiability of statements about morality, aesthetics, and metaphysics suggested that such claims possessed no truth-values—that they were literally meaningless (Carnap 1959, 61). But the pervasion of such *"pseudo-statements"*

(61) demanded some explanation, which for ethics and aesthetics came in the forms of emotivism and prescriptivism. Value judgments were expressions of feeling or prescriptions aimed at influencing the behavior of others.[18] Metaphysical assertions, in turn, were held to be confusions arising from the improper analysis of language or implicit recommendations for the adoption of new linguistic frameworks. And knowledge claims in the human or social sciences were pressured to fit the prevalent philosophical conception of practices in the natural sciences, especially physics. The *unity of science* dictated that such disciplines be able to share methods of verification thought to be specifiable for the natural sciences. The "work of the Vienna Circle," included "creating the often neglected 'cross-connections' between the individual sciences so that it is possible to relate the terms of each science to every other science without effort" (1983, 98), Otto Neurath wrote. So, psychology was pushed toward an exclusive "behavioristics" (98), while social scientists were to look for "general laws" (Hempel 1965, 231) required to explain historical events. Sociology was to be guided by "social behaviorism" (Neurath 1983, 71).[19]

Logical positivism has since met its official downfall, but although the formal commitments of this view have been cast aside, its scientism has left a lasting mark on Anglophone philosophy. This scientism is apparent, I suggested in Chapter 2, in Quine's contention that all judgments are hypotheses. It is also present, I think, in the desire to give theories of truth and knowledge—especially in contemporary efforts to rescue the correspondence theory of truth by appeal to a causal theory of reference—and in the tendency to treat truth as an explanatory concept that accounts for the success of scientific theories or for the survival value of our beliefs. This latter tendency helps, in turn, to broaden the apparent applicability of abductive inference—a tidy dialectical circle from which escape can seem imponderable. Let's consider how this alliance of correspondence and "explanationism" works to uphold scientism.

If for the Viennese positivists verifiability was the standard of *meaningfulness* for statements, for the postpositivist analytical philosopher explanatory coherence became the standard of *justifiability* for statements. Quine's critique of the logical-empiricist dogma of reductionism signaled a shift away from "enumerative induction" toward abduction or "the inference to the best explanation" as an account of scientific reasoning (Harman 1965). If one could not reduce theory statements to statements in the language of sense data or physicalism, then one faced questions about the ontological status of unobservable entities. As Gilbert Harman pointed out, "the inference from experimental data to the theory of subatomic particles certainly does not seem to be describable as an instance of enumerative induction" (1965, 90). A noninstrumentalist account of the truth of scientific statements and theories requires reasons for believing in the existence of such entities. Explanatory coherence thus acquires a new importance for anyone interested in denying instrumentalism about theoretical posits. We are justified in positing electrons because their existence would explain observable phenomena like electrostatic attraction.

So the value that many contemporary philosophers place on explanatory coherence is partly clarified by their differing from the logical positivists in rejecting enumerative induction. But we should also attend to what many contemporary philosophers hold in common with their Viennese predecessors: a faith in the general scope of scientific reasoning. Quine's critique of reductionism and the analytic-synthetic distinction does not merely make inference to an explanation seem more central to scientific reasoning; it also encourages us, as we saw in Chapter 2, to forsake talk of internal relations and to blur the distinction between theoretical and nontheoretical statements. In the process, even macroscopic physical objects take on the character of explanatory "posits." The scope of abductive inference is thus greatly broadened to include potentially any object or property whatsoever.

So it is that treating truth as an explanatory concept can seem natural. Quine does not treat truth this way, but broadening the scope of inference to the best explanation makes it possible to think of truth as an explanatory notion. The belief that truth is an external relation of correspondence between statements or beliefs and a world about whose nature and existence we might always have been mistaken is justified, on this view, because this belief accounts for the success of our scientific theories and explains why our ancestors, in their wild youth, did not all fall off cliffs.

And so it is that truth itself seems to have a nature that needs explanation, lest its apparent explanatory power prove illusory. We have already seen how invoking a causal theory of reference for this purpose leads to skeptical worries. But faith in the scope of abductive reasoning also puts pressure on those normative concepts that the logical positivists saw as merely expressions of "an attitude toward life" (Carnap 1959, 78), and it is abetted by its ostensible justification of truth as correspondence to the metaphysical realist's self-articulating world. Here is how.

Abandoning positivism might tempt us to think that moral claims have truth-values after all. But then we face the question of whether or not moral properties, whose existence seems to be posited by moral statements, make up part of our best overall account of the world. It seems that either we must admit that moral claims are *all false* because their terms fail to refer, or we must show how to give a naturalistic account of moral properties, preserving the status of science as, if not the final judge of all epistemic claims, at least the epistemic protection-racketeer.

J. L. Mackie urges the former course. If we are to make true moral statements, then there must be objective moral properties attaching to situations, events or persons. Moreover, we need some way of acquiring knowledge of such properties. But, according to Mackie's "argument from queerness," neither requirement is easily fulfilled: "If there were objective values, then they would be entities or qualities or relations of a very strange sort, utterly different from anything else in the universe. Correspondingly, if we were aware of them, it would have to be by some special faculty of moral perception or intuition, utterly different from our ordinary ways of knowing everything else" (1977, 38). Thinking of truth as correspondence to the metaphysical realist's world pressures us to find things or features of things to which we can point for confirmation of our moral claims as we would point to observable happenings, including instrument readings, as confirmation of scientific hypotheses. But the sciences have found no such things or features, and the motivational force of these things or features makes it hard to imagine what they would be like—let alone how we could know of them—when our best scientific theories show no trace of them. Thus, Mackie concludes, moral claims are all false, because moral terms lack referents. Values are not part of the ultimate furniture of the objective world, but appearances that we project onto that world. Truth, therefore, must be something value-free or value-neutral. If truth is a metaphysical correspondence to a world whose constituents are picked out by the natural sciences, then to the extent that our knowledge claims are value-laden, they will likewise be further from the truth, distorted by our subjective preferences. To have knowledge one must purge one's views of the warping influence of one's values. So knowledge and truth appear all the more like strongly objective phenomena with hidden natures.

The second option—naturalism—responds to the argument from queerness. What we need, says the moral naturalist, is an abductive argument for the existence of moral properties: We are justified in believing in objective values if they offer the best—or at least a useful—explanation of some facet of human behavior.[20] Such arguments, good or bad, take for granted the terms of adequacy imposed by the scientific credo. This kind of naturalism derives its credibility from scientism, and in the face of a metaphysical correspondence theory may seem the only viable alternative to subjectivism or the positivists' noncognitivism.[21]

My point, then, is that metaphysical realism and its correspondence theory of truth, in a culture that values science and its authority, buoy up that authority by forcing candidates for nonscientific knowledge into a framework that mars their credibility. If we compare values to the posits of natural science, they do seem to be "queer" sorts of things. This is just what the ethically or politically motivated, would-be relativist does not want, for she begins with the belief that there is something wrong with the existing social order, and she does not see this belief as a mere subjective preference that she projects onto the world. In an attempt to escape the scientistic pressure on values, she rebels against realism.

But the perceived oddity that attaches to values arises from assuming that moral claims must be true or false in virtue of correspondence to a metaphysical world that has been impressively described by the natural sciences, where correspondence is lent specious credence by a scientistic broadening of the notion of explanatory coherence. Scientism has had other nutrients in the past, but in the late twentieth century it thrives on correspondence and strong objectivism. This is one reason that the would-be relativist philosopher mistakes realism for the source of her worries.

Marxism

Another likely source of the relativist's conflation of realism and scientism is traditional Marxist theory. Marx's later writings are clearly realist, as are the writings of Engels and Lenin. As well, the dominant strains of Marxist theory and Marx's own views are scientistic. But it is most interesting that historical materialism, especially in versions that emphasize ideology and false consciousness, merges realism and scientism in functional explanations of the development of class relations in history—and functional explanations ignore the self-descriptions of individual agents. Such self-descriptions are particularly important to the feminist notion of consciousness-raising, and the desire to rescue them can translate into an emphasis of "subjectivity" over objectivity.

Thus, in a definite conflation of realism and scientism, Catharine MacKinnon first describes Louis Althusser's Marxist epistemology as one "that claims to portray a reality outside itself" (1982, 527 n. 23) and then goes on to criticize its failure to "see the scientific imperative itself as historically contingent" (527 n. 23).[22] And Anne Seller argues that "the political problems of the rational-scientific epistemology are made more acute" for feminism "when questions of ideology and false consciousness are introduced." "At best, the use of this epistemology appears to be profoundly undemocratic. At worst, it is an exercise in domination. At best, some women are telling other women what they are like, what their interests are, and how they might best be served. At worst, some women are imposing their own interests on the movement as a whole" (1988, 172).[23]

It is odd to think that relativism would be of help here. Seller explicitly distances relativism, "which may be a coherent position, from subjectivism"—the view that truth is relative to *individuals*, rather than to communities—"which is certainly not" (1988, 170) a coherent position. The views of the individual, she thinks, should be subject to correction by a broader "community of resistance" (179), provided that community attends to "individual experiences" and "seeks to understand them through conversation" (180). But what of the individual who belongs to more than one community? (And how do we individuate communities here?) How is she to decide what her experience teaches her if the verdict of her A-community clashes with the verdict of her B-community? If we think of relativism on the model of incommensurable conceptual schemes, how can her A-communal self even recognize her B-communal self as having intelligible beliefs and desires? Self-knowledge here seems problematized by an internal division of the self, as disruptive as any intrusion of functional descriptions of an agent's reasons and motivations would be.

But the temptation of these views becomes easier to understand when we look more closely at the Marxist tradition, which long set the agenda for radical theory. Marx's realism is evident in his historical materialism, described in *Capital* as an inversion of Hegel's dialectical idealism (1967, 19). In *The German Ideology* he and Engels give an early account of the materialist conception of history:

> The premises from which we begin are not arbitrary ones, not dogmas, but real premises from which abstraction can only be made in the imagination. They are the real individuals, their activity and the material conditions of their life, both those which they find already existing and those produced by their activity. These premises can thus be verified in a purely empirical way. (Marx and Engels 1975–, 5:31)

Here the "real" and the "material" are emphasized in contrast to the "ideal," and the relevance of science is suggested by the reference to empirical verification. Marx clearly viewed his methods as scientific: "Where speculation ends, where real life starts, there consequently begins real, positive science" (1975–, 5:37). Elsewhere he compares his inquiries to those of the physicist (Marx 1967, 8) or the evolutionary biologist (Marx and Engels 1975–, 41:246f.)—Marx's correspondence is full of references to Darwin. And in a passage from the preface to *A Contribution to the Critique of Political Economy,* he writes of conflicts between the productive forces and the relations of production in a way that ostensibly sets his method apart from the falsehood of ideology: "it is always necessary to distinguish between the material transformation of the economic conditions of production, which can be determined with the precision of natural science, and the legal, political, religious, artistic or philosophic—in short, ideological forms in which men become conscious of this conflict and fight it out" (1975–, 29:263). Science and technology are to revolutionize the forces of production so that "the necessary labor of society" is reduced to a "minimum" (91),[24] leaving individual talents to flourish in fulfilling activity, rather than stagnate in the satisfaction of basic needs.

Both science and realism are themes emphasized by the subsequent Marxist tradition. Engels, for example, insists in his critique of Dühring that it is the task of "modern materialism" to "discover the laws of motion" that govern "the process of evolution of humanity" (Marx and Engels 1975–, 25:25). The scientific investigation of "nature and human history" is concerned with "forms of *being*, of the external world, and these forms can never be created and derived by thought out of itself, but only from the external world" (34). Lenin, in his *Materialism and Empirio-Criticism,* cites the findings of the sciences as support for realism: "Natural science positively asserts that the earth once existed in such a state that no man or any other creature existed or could have existed on it" (1962, 75). Russian followers of Mach's positivism, he insists, are idealists, whose arguments "do not differ in the least from Berkeley's" (25) and whose views are "*thoroughly reactionary*" (357). And Louis Althusser, in a passage criticized by MacKinnon (1982, 527 n. 23), insists that: "We know that a 'pure' science only exists on condition that it continually frees itself from ideology which occupies it, haunts it, or lies in wait for it" (Althusser 1969, 170). To the extent that radical theorists respond to the long tradition of Marxist theory, it should not be surprising that a rejection of Marxist scientism should issue forth in a rejection of realism. If metaphysical and modest realism are conflated, then relativism may seem once again to be the appropriate radical stance.

The conflation of realism and scientism is further encouraged by scientific Marxism's focus on functional explanations of history. Marx's conception of ideology, when joined to his overall theory of history, tries to explain why particular ideas are the "ruling ideas" (Marx and Engels 1975–, 5:59) of an era, and such explanations take the form "the cause occurred because of its propensity to have that effect" (Cohen 1978, 281). That is to say, the "ruling ideas" are accepted by a significant number of people because it serves the interests of the ruling class that those ideas be found credible. Such functional accounts of the social genesis of belief, if taken to an extreme, tend to rule out entirely the validity of self-interpretation. If one asserts that only the theorist's interpretation of the experience of the oppressed has a purchase on the truth and that all else is false consciousness or ideology, then one risks incurring skeptical doubts about self-knowledge. This tendency finds influential expression in the critical theory of the Frankfurt School and the structuralist Marxism of Louis Althusser.

The former case is exemplified by Herbert Marcuse, who in *One-Dimensional Man* warned that "advanced industrial civilization" had developed "new forms of control" that ensured that a "comfortable, smooth, reasonable, democratic unfreedom prevails" (1964, 1). Central to his assessment of advanced industrial culture was the thesis that technological society produces a condition in which "individuals identify themselves with the existence which is imposed upon them and have in it their own development and satisfaction" (11). By offering enough people the conveniences of technological innovation, advanced industrial society effects a form of control that shapes the very desires of its subjects, discouraging the growth of criticism and stifling opposition by satisfying and then reproducing those desires. Social reality itself becomes ideological, signaling the end, not of ideology, as proclaimed by some of Marcuse's contemporary opponents, but rather, of reality. One-dimensional "men" are "swallowed up" by their "alienated existence" (11) and identify with needs and desires that help maintain the *status quo* of their own subordination to technology and capital.

On Marcuse's analysis, the validity of individual agents' self-descriptions in our century is threatened by a new kind of ideology, which differs from the old kind in two ways. First, it presupposes that class antagonism, which was controlled and masked by the old ideology of nineteenth-century capitalism, has been recognized, so that the old ideology has been rendered ineffective. Recent capitalism with its "technocratic consciousness" (Habermas 1970, 112) cannot afford to indulge in the same degree of unbridled oppression and exploitation (at least in the North Atlantic and Oceanic democracies), and so must make concessions to the oppressed without relinquishing power. Nineteenth-century socialism played the Ghost of Christmas-Yet-to-Come to capitalism's Scrooge, and capitalism has reacted accordingly. Its new ideology must mask the fact that, although Scrooge keeps Christmas in his heart, an unjust distribution of power remains. Second, the "new" ideology operates "with the aid of rewards for *privatized needs*" (1970, 112). The oppressed learn to enjoy their oppression and find fulfillment in social and political inequality.

Althusser ascribes to ideology a similar pervasiveness, but his reasons for doing so have more to do with formal elegance than with cultural pessimism. Althusser's work shows a tension between accepting a sharp distinction between science and ideology and holding that *"ideology has the function (which defines it) of 'constituting' concrete individuals as subjects"* (1971, 171). Like Marx and the Frankfurt school, Althusser separates knowledge (Marxist science) from ideology. But whereas Marx might be taken to hold that ideology is an abuse of abstraction—a depiction of contingent and local features (real or imagined) of the human world as necessary and universal, in a way that benefits the ruling class[25]—Althusser adds his own twist. "Ideology," he says, is a "necessarily imaginary distortion" that represents "the (imaginary) relationship of individuals to the relations of production and the relations that derive from them" (1971, 165).

This talk of the "imaginary" is inherited from the psychoanalytic theory of Jacques Lacan. In his *Écrits* Lacan offers an interpretation of Freudian psychosexual development that invokes the notion of a "mirror stage" in that development. "The child," he claims, "at an age when he is for a time ... outdone by the chimpanzee in instrumental intelligence, can nevertheless already recognize as such his own image in a mirror" (1977, 1). This alleged recognition of self, Lacan seems to suggest, is analogous to the "I's" immediate consciousness of itself as pure thought in the Cartesian *cogito*.[26] However, the child identifies, not with *res cogitans*, but with a mirror *image*, an *"imaginary"* representation of itself. Such simple identification masks "the turbulent movements that the subject feels are animating him" (1977, 2), the desires and sensations not displayed in the mirror. This "primordial form" in which the "I" is "precipitated" (2), then, is a distortion, but it constitutes for the child "the model and basis for all its future identifications" (Rose 1982, 30). It is this fiction of simple self-unity that "situates the agency of the ego, before its social determination" (Lacan 1977, 2).

In a similar sense Althusser takes ideology to involve an "imaginary distortion." In ideology individuals "misrecognize" themselves, finding their identity automatically and unreflectively in the existing social order.[27] The existence of subjects and the existence of the current regime are as *one*, and the subject can envisage the persistence or cessation of one only with the persistence or cessation of the other. Thus, she experiences her own worth and sense of "freedom" in her subordination. Moreover, without ideology there would be no subjects, since "ideology has the function (which defines it) of 'constituting' concrete individuals as subjects." Individuals are constituted as subjects by an ideology that "interpellates" or "hails" them, as though each were a free, conscious agent, responsible for her actions, able to do as she wants, a "centre of initiatives" (Althusser 1971, 182). But, as with Lacan's "mirror stage," this simultaneous "situation" of the "agency of the ego" and "imaginary" awareness of self, according to Althusser, masks the unconscious factors influencing the subject's constitution: the subordination of the subject both to capital and to the mechanisms, ideological and other, needed to reproduce the existing relations of production.

Althusser distinguishes between particular ideologies and ideology in general. Although particular ideologies may come and go, "ideology *in general has no history*" (1971, 160f.). It exists "outside" history in the sense that historical events are always structured and influenced, in part, by ideology. Ideology, says Althusser, is "an *omni-historical* reality" (161), and "there is no practice except by and in an ideology" (170). Paradoxically, then, the very thing that enables purposeful, reflective action (practice)—that which "constitutes" individual human organisms as "subjects"—also makes the subject systematically self-ignorant, since it oversimplifies and distorts the relationship of individuals to the relations of production. And this holds for a proletarian ideology—the existence of which Althusser must allow, given the "omnihistorical reality" of ideology—as much as for bourgeois ideology.

Another worry about self-ignorance lurks here as well. It would seem that Althusser's dichotomy of science and ideology prevents him from making sense of the idea of a reflective, critical practice opposed to the ruling ideology. If practice requires an ideology, then a practice of resistance requires an ideology of resistance. However, it is implausible to suppose that there could be a reflective practice of resistance without a *critique* of the ruling ideology—and that is the role played by Marxist *science* in Althusser's scheme. But if science is opposed to ideology, and if ideology is necessary for practice, then there can be no reflective activity of resistance. Althusser's account, as Ted Benton says, "leaves no theoretical room for a discourse and practice of ideology which *resists and opposes*" (1984, 105) the machinations of the ruling ideology. Althusser has, Benton suggests, confused an analysis of the ruling ideology with one of ideology in general, and the consequence is that each subject is seen to experience her own worth and sense of "freedom" in her own subordination.

Both Marcuse and Althusser, then, provide us with radical critiques of capitalism that stress the pervasiveness of ideological control. And even if one has some sympathy for the suggestion that advanced industrial society is stabilized by the creation and satisfaction of "false needs" (Marcuse 1964, 4), the sheer generality that these accounts attribute to ideological influence is likely to provoke two related responses: indignation at the perceived portrayal of the oppressed as helpless dupes and concern that radical theory has defeated its own purposes by "portray[ing] oppression in its full force, as inescapable" (Lugones 1990, 501).[28]

If, as in Marcuse's case, "the subject which is alienated is swallowed up by its alienated existence" (1964, 11), then, as he himself concluded, "The critical theory of society possesses no concepts that could bridge the gap between the present and its future" (257). If, as in Althusser's case, ideology constitutes individuals as subjects, if *"individuals are always already subjects"* (Althusser 1971, 172), if "there is no practice except by and in an ideology," and if ideology is an "imaginary distortion," then the chances of freedom and self-knowledge are greatly limited, even ruled out. How one reaches the "subject-less discourse" (171) of science is a mystery.

A predictable response to these problems is to reject functional explanations of the genesis of beliefs and desires. If realism and scientism have already been conflated, as their concurrence in the Marxist tradition encourages, then this rejection will seem to require a rejection of realism as well, and the classic alternatives are idealism and relativism. But scientism and realism are different things, even if their concurrence in influential strains of radical theory have made them seem like one. Failing to distinguish them makes it easier to overlook the scientistic assumption that relativism shares with contemporary metaphysical realism: that truth and knowledge are proper objects for explanatory theories.

Notes

1. Such perceptions are not universal, but they do exercise a hold over some thinkers who believe that philosophy should be put to work in the service of struggles against power and injustice. Another ethical motivation for relativism is endorsed by Barnes and Bloor: "A plausible hypothesis is that relativism is disliked because so many academics see it as a dampener on their moralizing. A dualist idiom, with its demarcations, contrasts, rankings and evaluations is easily adapted to the tasks of political propaganda or self-congratulatory polemic. *This* is the enterprise that relativists threaten, not science" (1982, 47 n. 44).

2. See Lacan 1988, 228.

3. The suggestion that claiming or seeking to know the truth is immodest has for Nietzsche sexual connotations, as well. See, for example, 1966, 2; 1968a, 50; and 1974, 38, §64.

4. See Nietzsche 1967, 97–163.

5. I have modified Hollingdale's translation. See Nietzsche 1969, 74f.

6. See also Clark 1990, 180–93.

7. See Putnam 1981, 155–63; Merquior 1985, 146–47, 159–60; Taylor 1985b, 174–84; 1989, 99, 488–90, 504; and Habermas 1987a, 238–93.

8. Gutting accuses Foucault's critics of ignoring "the explicitly local or regional nature of his analyses" (1989, 273), the exclusion from Foucault's critique of "sciences like physics and chemistry" (273), and the fact that "even for the dubious disciplines that are the objects of his critique, Foucault does not deny all truth and objectivity" (273), and he rebuts interpretations of passages from Foucault's writings that might be taken to lead implicitly to relativism.

9. Foucault remarked in a late interview, "All those who say that for me the truth does not exist are simple-minded" (1989, 295). For a lucid discussion of Foucault's views on truth, see Allen 1993, 149–76.

10. The phrase "necessary and sufficient tests for truth," could also be read as a complaint with the idea that there are conditions necessary and sufficient for a belief's or proposition's being true. There is little textual evidence to support this reading, though it might seem consonant with rejecting the theoretical status of truth—if one allows that

there will always be trivial statements of necessary and sufficient conditions like "It is true that p if and only if p."

11. These conflations, and the assumption that valuing science requires scientism, explain Seller's worry that scientific feminist critique excludes the epistemic value of consciousness-raising (1988, 170). It is undoubtedly true that "women have often experienced the scientific-rational approach as oppressive" (171), but this is explicable by the past absence of scientific feminist critiques and by the treatment of science as an authoritative discourse in societies that treat women and men as of unequal worth. On the compatibility of feminism and science, see Nelson 1990 and Campbell 1998. Seller also gives an argument based on the interest-relativity of causation (1988, 174), but such considerations do not lead to epistemic relativism.

12. MacKinnon is sometimes called a relativist, because she thinks that the meaning of the category "woman" is exhausted by the social construction of "women" as objects of male desire and as subordinate to men, so that genuine social change would not result in the liberation of women, but in the acceptance of a new set of social categories. See MacKinnon 1982, 532. This reading of MacKinnon is like the relativist reading of Kuhn, examined in Chapter 5, according to which a scientific revolution does not yield more knowledge about posited entities, but a new ontology. I am not convinced that MacKinnon is a relativist (though she might be an idealist), because her style displays an element of what might be called "French hyperbole."

13. When MacKinnon writes of "the male pursuit of control over women's sexuality," she intends "men not as individuals nor as biological beings, but as a gender group characterized as socially constructed" (1982, 532).

14. This remark blurs skeptical doubt and idealism. But, as Kant noted, the "transcendental realist" is driven toward idealism in order to avoid skepticism (1965, A369), and the problem then arises that idealism's attempted escape from skepticism can seem simply like a concession of the skeptic's main point (Williams 1996c, 17–22). The idealist risks dissatisfaction with the world he creates, whose *esse* is *percipi*. See MacKinnon 1987, 58 for an amusing parallel between Cartesian doubt about the external world and male doubt about female orgasms.

15. It is probably anachronistic to call Plato a metaphysical realist in the sense in which I use the term, for although he thinks that most live in ignorance of the Form of the Good, he never doubts that the proper education of those suited to rule will turn their souls to an awareness of their innate knowledge of the Good. See Plato 1974. It is not part of Plato's worldview that dialectic should forever fail to lead a proto-ruler to knowledge. (See Taylor 1989, 122.) A residue of this problem can be found in interpreting Descartes as a metaphysical realist, because, though his type of skeptical doubt is the model that is adapted to the contemporary metaphysical realist's purposes, Descartes does not think that it is logically possible for us to be massively mistaken about the world of space and time, provided we make our ideas clear and distinct. God's benevolence precludes such systematic error. Plato's Good and Descartes's God are heavy with being in just the way that the metaphysical realist takes the world to be, but they reach out and touch the knower, laying to rest the skeptical doubt that such heaviness provokes. The strong objectivist's tendency to fall back on a magical theory of reference (see Chapter 1) marks a lingering affinity for this Platonic-Cartesian heritage.

16. The difficulty of categorizing fundamentalism as a kind of metaphysical realism is similar to the difficulty with Plato and Descartes. The fundamentalist never doubts that at

least some of us have access to "the truth," while most of the world lives in ignorance everlasting. Plainly, though, fundamentalism's metaphysics, like Plato's and Descartes's, is a cousin of metaphysical realism.

17. See Leonard Woolf's attempt to absolve the habits of "*altifrons aestheticus*" of this charge in Woolf (1970).

18. See Stevenson 1959.

19. However, Neurath had rather complicated views about the so-called unity of science, which he sometimes compared with the unity of an encyclopedia. See Neurath 1983, 145–58.

20. See Sturgeon 1985, 1986.

21. The dominant trends of contemporary ethical theory, at least in North America, are contractarianism and constructivism. But the existence of neither approach to ethical theory threatens the contingent link I am proposing between scientism and metaphysical realism. Contractarian moral theory typically concedes Mackie's argument and takes *subjectivism* as its starting point. "The theory of rational choice treats value as a subjective and relative measure, not as an objective and absolute standard" (Gauthier 1986, 25). Moral constructivism, popularized by Rawls (1971), starts by assuming that moral theory must forsake correspondence with a metaphysical reality. Indeed, Rawls has been championed by two liberal critics of strong objectivism: Rorty (1991b, 175–96) and Putnam (1983, 302).

22. The Hegelian Marxism of Lukács, she suggests, "is more hospitable to feminism" (1982, 528 n. 23).

23. This reaction recalls a standard criticism of Marxist and Marxist-influenced claims to be able to tell knowledge from ideology: What makes it the case that radical theory is not itself ideological? Karl Mannheim uses this point to justify replacing "the simple theory of ideology" with "the sociology of knowledge" (1936, 78). Some Marxists also abandon the science- or knowledge-ideology distinction and speak of proletarian ideology. For discussion, see McLellan 1986, 21–34 and Eagleton 1991, 90–123.

24. Habermas (1971, 48–50) emphasizes this passage as evidence of Marx's scientism.

25. See Hymers 1996b for an elaboration of this reading.

26. For this reading of Descartes, see Gueroult 1984, 27–74.

27. Lacan writes of "the *méconnaissances* that constitute the ego" (1977, 6).

28. Marcuse responds to the former charge: "No tribunal can justly arrogate to itself the right to decide which needs should be developed and satisfied. Any such tribunal is reprehensible, although our revulsion does not do away with the question: how can the people who have been the object of effective and productive domination by themselves create the conditions of freedom?" (1964, 6).

7

Realism and Self-knowledge

> *I feel that I am moving all right, and I can also judge roughly* how *by the feeling—but I* simply know *what movement I have made, although you couldn't speak of any sense-datum of the movement, of any immediate inner picture of the movement. And when I say "I simply* know . . . *" "knowing" here means something like "being able to say" and is not in turn, say, some kind of inner picture.*
>
> —Ludwig Wittgenstein, Remarks on the Philosophy of Psychology

The excursions of the preceding chapter have led us into the province of self-knowledge. This is no surprise. By accepting the premise that I might really always have been a brain in a vat, the metaphysical realist accepts a certain epistemic priority for inner experience (or some analogue thereto) over outer experience. That, as we saw in Chapter 4, is just part of what it means to treat the external-world skeptic's scenarios as explanatory hypotheses. And the relativist, we have seen, accepts the metaphysical realist's conception of objectivity, treating experience as related to the world only externally, but exposing our knowledge of other cultures to the problems of skeptical doubt.

A corollary of this acceptance must be that no agent of another culture—or even of my own—can know my mind as well as I can. (My self-descriptions have epistemic priority over another's descriptions of me.) And as we saw in the preceding chapter, these problems come to a head when the Marxist theorist tries to give functional explanations of human behavior that seem to deny epistemic priority to the self-descriptions of those whose behavior is explained.[1]

This dynamic is not confined to the circles of radical theory, however. Recent work in the philosophy of mind has revealed a tension between a view known as "anti-individualism" and the special authority that is traditionally thought to attach to "first-person" utterances about intentions and sensations. Anti-individualism holds that our beliefs and other intentional phenomena are to be individuated or classified partly by our relation to the world we inhabit. What we believe depends in part upon what things and sorts of things there are in our environment for us to have beliefs about. At first glance, such a view might seem to threaten first-person authority in much the way that functional explanations would, for it might seem that I can be wrong—sometimes, often, or maybe even always—about *what* I believe, insofar as I can be wrong about what things or kinds of things are present in my environment. This is a matter of some concern for my position, which is committed to a variety of anti-individualism.

Recently, Tyler Burge has argued that this tension can be resolved by distinguishing several different claims that are latent in the traditional "Cartesian" conception of first-person authority. In this chapter, I shall argue that Burge's attempted reconciliation fails. However, the modest realist, by treating experience as linked to the world internally, is automatically in a position to make sense of both anti-individualism and first-person authority. In seeing mind and world, word and object, as internally related, the modest realist builds the world and its objects right into our intentional phenomena, and by linking meaning and understanding with use, she makes first-person authority a straightforward aspect of linguistic competence. This view clarifies the normal justificatory asymmetry that obtains between first- and other-person utterances, but it is also compatible, I shall argue, with the possibility of certain kinds of self-ignorance and with the prospect of Socratic self-knowledge, construed as an epistemic achievement.

Burge's Anti-individualism

The psychological individualist is someone who thinks that, in Tyler Burge's metaphor, "the mind is somehow self-contained" (1986, 118)—the nature of my beliefs and other intentional attitudes is independent of the world, though many of those beliefs still pertain to the world. In other words, the psychological individualist is someone who thinks that intentional attitudes are only externally related to the world, for they can be identified without identifying their referents. Although there are many different kinds of psychological individualists, they all agree that "the nature and individuation of an individual's mental kinds are 'in principle' independent of the nature and individuation of all aspects of the individual's environment" (117). Such an individualist, Burge indicates, need not deny that the beliefs that I in fact have were, for example, contingently caused by features of my environment, but need merely assert that they did not have to be so produced, and that being produced in another fashion would not alter the kinds of beliefs that they are. My beliefs about water may owe their origins to a complex relation between me and water, but, says the individualist, I could have *all* the beliefs about water that I actually have without being in any way causally related to water. There is, thus, an external relation between my beliefs and the world, for my beliefs can be identified independently of knowing what they actually refer to.

The *anti*-individualist, as one might guess, denies individualism. That is to say that she thinks that the nature and individuation of an individual's intentional phenomena are dependent upon some aspect(s) of that individual's environment. Our beliefs and other intentional phenomena are to be individuated or classified partly by our relation to the world we inhabit. What I believe, on Burge's account, depends partly upon what there is in my environment about which I can have a belief. This position can be illustrated by means of Twin-Earth thought experiments of the sort devised by Putnam.

In "The Meaning of 'Meaning'"[2] Putnam argued that the "narrow" psychological states of a speaker do not determine the extensions of her terms. Such "psychological states in the narrow sense" (1975, 220) are compatible with the assumption "that no psychological state, properly so called, presupposes the existence of any individual other than the subject to whom the state is ascribed" (220). Indeed, they are the sorts of psychological states recognized by versions of individualism. According to Putnam, on the assumption of such narrow psychology, two speakers might be in qualitatively identical psychological states, and yet their utterances might have different meanings, because their environments differ in subtle ways. One might live on Earth where the word *water* refers to a substance with the chemical composition H_2O, while the other might live on Twin Earth, a distant planet that is almost a phenomenological duplicate of our own and whose inhabitants have evolved, biologically and culturally, in ways parallel to our own, but where there is no H_2O to be found—just a lot of XYZ, known to Twenglish speakers as *water*. So, the respective extensions of the term *water* on Earth and Twin Earth differ. Yet, the "narrow" psychological states of our two speakers are the same. It follows, says Putnam, that those psychological states do not determine extension. Unless one is willing to maintain that extension is neither a part of meaning, nor in any way determined by it, and that meaning is exhausted by narrow psychological state,[3] one should conclude, says Putnam, that meanings "ain't in the head" (227). Meaning, on his view, is an ordered n-tuple, of which extension is a term (246). Thus, not just the extension, but the meaning of *water* differs from Earth to Twin Earth.

Now, what Putnam tried to do for meaning Burge has tried to do for intentional attitudes and perceptual phenomena. But whereas Putnam's arguments concede to "traditional philosophers" (1975, 220) the idea of narrow content, Burge's arguments make no use of this notion.[4] Even the "meanings" of beliefs and other intentional phenomena "ain't in the head" on Burge's reckoning. He has us consider an English-speaking Earthling named "Al." Al has "a variety of beliefs and occurrent thoughts involving the notion of aluminum" (1982, 284).[5] Al believes that aluminum is a metal, that it is relatively light and pliable, that beer cans are made of aluminum, and so on. Al has a *Doppelgänger* on Twin Earth, whom Burge names "Al_i." Al_i is not assumed to share with Al the same "narrow" psychological states, but his personal history is remarkably similar to Al's:

> He undergoes the same stimulations of his bodily surfaces, excepting minor micro- and gravitational differences, engages in the same motions, utters the same sounds, has the same experiences—insofar as these stimulations, motions and experiences

are nonintentionally described. This physical and phenomenal similarity—virtual type-identity—is preserved from birth to present. I will suppose also that there are internal-causal, functional, and syntactical similarities as long as they are specified nonintentionally and defined on the individual in isolation from his social and physical environment. (1982, 284f.)

Much as Putnam's Twin Earth flowed with XYZ but not H_2O, Burge's Twin Earth has no aluminum. To be sure there is a light, flexible metal on Twin Earth, which Twin-Terrans use in the manufacture of beer cans and which shares many of the phenomenal properties of aluminum. And Al_j, like his co-linguists, calls this metal "aluminum." But sophisticated laboratory tests would reveal that middle-class Twin-Terrans wrap their leftovers, not in aluminum, but in $aluminum_2$. Accordingly, says Burge, Al_j has beliefs not about aluminum, but about $aluminum_2$. The nature and individuation of belief kinds varies with the different environments of different believers.

Such anti-individualism seems incompatible with what we could call the "Cartesian" conception of first-person authority.[6] We can, for now, think of first-person authority roughly as the thesis that each person knows her own mind better than others do. First-person authority would seem to require at least that each person is not generally mistaken about her own intentional phenomena or about her sensations and perceptions. In turn, the Cartesian conception of such authority can then be taken to specify that, so long as she is sufficiently attentive, a person cannot be mistaken about her own intentional phenomena, sensations, or perceptions.

Now, Burge thinks that this version of the Cartesian conception is not explicit enough. For one thing, he wants to restrict its application to what he calls *"basic self-knowledge"* (1988, 649). Here he has in mind cases in which I both judge that *p* and judge that I am judging that *p* at the same time. Descartes's *cogito* is an obvious example, but, Burge suggests, so are "'I think (with this very thought) that writing requires concentration' and 'I judge (or doubt) that water is more common than mercury'" (649). These are cases of "strict cogito judgments," or "cogito-like judgments" (658) or "cogito-like thoughts" (662). They form a subset of the set of "all cases of authoritative knowledge," and about them "No errors at all are possible" because "they are all self-verifying" (658). Other cases of authoritative self-knowledge admit of errors, but only errors "which indicate something wrong with the thinker" (658).

But, as well, Burge thinks that there are really three separate claims implicit in the Cartesian conception, and when we make these claims explicit, we shall be able to see how first-person authority and anti-individualism can be reconciled. These claims can be formulated as follows:

1. I am actually *never* mistaken about my cogito-like thoughts.
2. In any counterfactual situation I would *never* be mistaken about my cogito-like thoughts in that situation.

3. I am actually *never* mistaken about what my cogito-like thoughts would be in any counterfactual situation.[7]

Burge contends that it is perfectly intelligible to deny the third of these claims while accepting the first two and that doing so is the key to reconciling anti-individualism with first-person authority. Consider why.

The focus of Burge's argument is on the conventions we follow in evaluating counterfactual conditional statements. As we saw in Chapter 1, those conventions tell us to consider a possible world that is much like the actual world, but for the fact that the if-clause of the conditional obtains at that world. We then consider whether the then-clause would also obtain at that world. Nozick, as we saw, thinks that these conventions, together with his account of knowledge as "truth-tracking," explain how we can have ordinary empirical knowledge without knowing that we are not victims of one of the skeptic's scenarios.

Burge wants to make a related point about the possible world relevant to evaluating counterfactual conditionals of the sort entertained by the external-world skeptic. The skeptic insists that if I had always been a brain in a vat with exactly the same beliefs and perceptions that I actually have had, then I would be deluded about the world around me. To evaluate such a counterfactual, says Burge, "We hold our thoughts constant. We consider situations in which the thoughts that we have would be false. And we concede that we could in principle be mistaken in thinking that the world is not arranged in one of the ways that would make our thoughts radically false" (1986, 122).[8] However, says Burge, we have to distinguish such skeptical scenarios from another sort of counterfactual that becomes relevant as soon as we ask, "What thoughts would we have if our relation to the world were radically different from what we take it to be?" If the "contents" of beliefs are determined by what things or sorts of things are present in the environment of the believer, then our conclusion ought to be that we would not have the same beliefs if circumstances were very different. In this case, we cannot hold the interpretation of our thoughts constant. That interpretation is just what we want to settle; so, it would be question begging to decide it beforehand. On Burge's view, the Cartesian cannot insist from the outset that the "possible world" at which we evaluate the skeptic's hypothesis is the same world at which to interpret our beliefs. Is it compatible with our having all our actual beliefs that we should be brains in a vat? Yes, thinks Burge. But *were* we brains in a vat, then our beliefs would be not about brains and vats, but, perhaps, about computer-generated electrical impulses.

Now all this matters because it is the third clause of the Cartesian conception that comes into conflict with anti-individualism. Although (1) and (2) attribute to each person a special authority regarding her basic putative self-knowledge, they do so in a way that is compatible with the claim that our intentional attitudes get their "content" from the world we occupy. As Burge observes (1988, 654), in order to be thinking about water, it is enough that I stand in the appropriate sorts of interactive relations with water—I need not be able to describe those relations with any perspicuity. And, in turn, the "content" of my belief that I am thinking about water derives from the "content" of my first-order beliefs about water. "So any conditions that are necessary to thinking that p will be equally necessary to the relevant knowledge that one is thinking that p. Here, again, to think the thought, one need not know the enabling conditions. It is enough that they actually be satisfied" (654). I need not be able to say what makes my second-order belief about my first-order belief possible in order to have such a belief, any more than I need be able to say anything about what makes my first-order belief possible in order to have that belief. And that is partly because they share certain necessary conditions.

On the basis of Burge's reasoning, it seems possible to accept a constrained version of the Cartesian conception of first-person authority by endorsing claims (1) and (2) and rejecting claim (3), while at the same time being an anti-individualist. I think, however, that Burge is mistaken about this.

A Problem for Burge

In Chapter 1, I presented four kinds of responses that seem available, if one does not want to concede the skeptic's case:

1. Argue that the skeptic's account of justification or knowledge is faulty, so that I could be justified in believing in the "external" world, despite the explanatory power of the skeptical hypothesis.
2. Deny that knowledge requires justification at all.
3. Argue that although the skeptical scenario is a real possibility, it does not give as good an explanation of my intentional phenomena as does the external-world hypothesis.
4. Deny that the skeptical scenario is a real possibility at all.

The modest realist, I said, embraces the fourth strategy. But this is something that the metaphysical realist cannot do, because metaphysical realism just is the view that external-world skepticism raises a real possibility.

Now some interpreters take Burge to be rejecting the tradition of metaphysical realism. But the problem with Burge's attempted reconciliation of first-person authority and anti-individualism is that, in fact, he remains committed to metaphysical realism. My evidence for this claim is that Burge *explicitly rejects* strategy (4). In "Cartesian Error and the Objectivity of Perception," for example, he gives qualified support to "the oft-repeated slogan that error presupposes a background of veridicality," but continues, "I think that this slogan is sometimes misused. I think that we are not immune from fairly dramatic and wholesale error in characterizing the nature of the empirical world" (1986, 130f.). "Quine and Davidson," he notes, "sometimes use this important idea with insufficient discrimination" (131 n. 4). His own "qualified" support for this slogan stems from his conviction that intentional and perceptual phenomena are to be individuated nonindividualistically. If I seem to see small shadows on the side of a brick building, then I typically do see them, because I would not have the perceptual type "seeming to see small shadows" if there were no, or very few, small shadows in my environment. But this thesis he finds compatible with "fairly dramatic and wholesale error" for reasons considered above—the Cartesian confuses the evaluation-conditions for two sorts of counterfactual conditional claims, and I need not know the enabling conditions of my intentional phenomena.

In "Individualism and Self-knowledge," Burge rejects strategy (4) thus: Some philosophers, he says, "have thought that anti-individualism, combined with the view that we are authoritative about what thoughts we think, provides a 'transcendental' response to skepticism.... I believe, however, that there is no easy argument against skepticism from anti-individualism and authoritative self-knowledge" (1988, 655 n. 6).

In reply to the skeptic Burge offers, instead, a version of strategy (1), arguing that the skeptic's account of justification is faulty. The antiskeptic, he says, should deny "that perceptual knowledge must be justified by separately insuring that the enabling conditions [for perceptual knowledge] hold and the skeptic's defeating conditions do not hold" (1988, 655f.).[9] That is, the skeptic puts unreasonable demands on the concept of justified belief and, hence, on the concept of knowledge. Just as I need not know the enabling conditions of my intentional phenomena to know what my intentional phenomena are, according to Burge, neither need I know the enabling conditions of my perceptual beliefs to be justified in holding them. "It is a fundamental mistake," he says, "to think that perceptual knowledge of physical entities requires, as a precondition, knowledge of the conditions that make such knowledge possible" (654).

So Burge is a metaphysical realist. But how does this undercut his reconciliation of first-person authority and anti-individualism? The skeptic, as we saw in Chapter 1, thinks that in some sense it is *possible* that I have always been in the deceptive grip of an evil demon or that I have always been a brain in a vat. But if these "doubts" are to be compelling, they must be based on something stronger than logical possibility. For the fallibilist, the logical possibility that p is not generally a reason for thinking that p or even that probably p.[10]

Instead, we should interpret the skeptic as presenting us with an explanatory possibility, a "real" possibility whose actuality would explain some given phenomena of which we are assumed to have knowledge. And the given phenomena in this case are the deliverances of our senses—our inner experience as of a world of objects and events in space and time. This experience, holds the skeptic, would be explained just as well by our always having been brains in a vat as by our having epistemic contact with an "external" world of spatio-temporal happenings and things.

Now, the role of real possibility in explicating skeptical doubt poses a problem for Burge. A real possibility is one whose actuality would explain some actual phenomenon of which we are *assumed* to have knowledge. Here we are assumed to have knowledge of what seems to be the case about the world. But *given* that we can individuate our beliefs about the world, and given (were the skeptic or the metaphysical realist right) that we might really be mistaken in holding those individuated beliefs, it follows that we might be completely mistaken about the external world and still know our own beliefs, if we know them at all. *Thus, for a range of counterfactual situations—skeptical scenarios that would explain our having the intentional phenomena that we know ourselves actually to have—we do know what our intentional phenomena would be in those situations, if skeptical scenarios are real possibilities.* If we have authority about what beliefs we have concerning the world, then we also have authority about what our beliefs would be in any world that would explain our having the beliefs that we know ourselves to have. If I actually never err about my intentional phenomena, then for a distinct range of counterfactual situations, I actually never err about what my intentional phenomena would be in those situations. This assumption is central to external-world skepticism and, hence, to metaphysical realism. Thus, because the skeptic's case rests on granting epistemic priority to my inner experience, and because metaphysical realism consists in granting the real possibility of the skeptic's scenarios, metaphysical realism implies a strong "Cartesian" variety of first-person authority. Metaphysical realism and anti-individualism are incompatible. So unless Burge is prepared to abandon metaphysical realism, there is no consistent way he can deny the third claim of the Cartesian conception of first-person authority. But this is just what he does.[11]

Self-knowledge as "Knowing How"

As I remarked earlier, the problematic that Burge is trying to avoid is one that also thematizes the relativist's response to scientistic forms of radical theory, though the relativist confuses scientism with realism and fails to set metaphysical realism and modest realism apart from each other.[12] As long as one clings to scientism, metaphysical realism and relativism will remain tempting positions, because one will want to treat inner experience as though it were a unified phenomenon that admitted of a unified explanation, and one will treat that experience as related only externally to the manifest world of objects and events. As long as one feels tempted by these alternatives, one will tend to blur the distinction between metaphysical realism and modest realism. And as long as one fails to distinguish between metaphysical and modest realism, one will be further tempted to conclude that one must choose between first-person authority and anti-individualism. The two will seem irreconcilable.

Things stand quite differently for the modest realist. Once we let go of the idea that our experience of the world is the sort of thing that stands in need of a general explanation, we can readily endorse Burge's denial that "the mind is somehow self-contained" (1986, 118). Because experiences are internally related to the manifest world of happenings and things, there is no question of knowing one's mind without knowing something of the world as well. But modest realism's anti-individualism does not engender any threat to first-person authority, because it does not countenance skeptical doubts about the macroscopic world of spatio-temporal objects and events that gives content to our intentional phenomena.

Is this to say that we are free to make much the move that Burge wants to make by accepting a constrained Cartesian conception of first-person authority? Here we must tread carefully, for the "Cartesian" explains first-person authority by treating self-knowledge as a kind of inner observation of private mental objects. On this view the special access that I have to my own mental things results in an asymmetry in the justification of knowledge claims about myself. My claim to know what I believe and desire trumps your claim to know what I believe and desire—at least as long as I have taken the time to make my ideas clear and distinct.

Some of Burge's discussion of basic self-knowledge suggests that claims like "I am thinking about Vienna" embody just such a special knowledge of facts about myself based on my privileged access to my own mental world. "Crudely put," says Burge, "our knowledge of our own thoughts is immediate, not discursive. Our epistemic right rests on this immediacy" (1988, 656). But it is not clear how we are to refine this crudity. Talk of immediacy in contrast to discursiveness makes it tempting to think that a special kind of knowledge by acquaintance is at work in first-person authority. And the fact that cases of basic self-knowledge involve thoughts that are "self-referential in a way that insures that the object of reference just is the thought being thought" (1988, 659) seems to rule out any comparable knowledge of things in the world around us by acquaintance. This is to say that the contents of one's own mind are better known to oneself than is the manifest world of objects and events, and we seem led here down the road to granting to inner experience the sort of epistemic priority that is characteristic of external-world skepticism and strong objectivism.

If this is the view that Burge is seeking to retain, then it is not one that the modest realist can accept. But then how do we do justice to the apparent immediacy of our basic self-knowledge? And what of other cases of non-Socratic self-knowledge that do not fit Burge's model of "cogito-like thoughts"—such as my knowing that I want a pint of beer or that I like French modernist cinema? It might seem that the relativist was right to worry about anti-individualism after all. It might seem that giving up the Cartesian conception amounts to giving up on first-person authority.

This was Gilbert Ryle's view of the matter, but it did not trouble him in the way that it has troubled some would-be relativists. The apparent asymmetry between knowledge of self and other, he held, is merely a matter of degree. Self- and other-knowledge differ only in the way that one's ability to know what a close friend or lover is thinking differs from one's tendency to make mistakes about the thoughts of casual acquaintances and to miss the mark utterly with strangers. I know my own mind better than other minds, simply because I spend more time with myself: "I learn that a certain pupil of mine is lazy, ambitious and witty by following his work, noticing his excuses, listening to his conversation and comparing his performances with those of others. Nor does it make any important difference if I happen myself to be that pupil. I can indeed then listen to more of his conversations, as I am the addressee of his unspoken soliloquies; I notice more of his excuses, as I am never absent, when they are made" (1963, 169). The same effect could be achieved if I were forever joined to another who gave voice to everything that entered his head.

But perhaps one of Ryle's own distinctions can help us here; perhaps we should think of our non-Socratic self-knowledge as embodying a kind of "knowing how" (1963, 29) rather than a kind of "knowing that." A suggestion much like this has been made by Donald Davidson (1984a, 1987).

The fact, Davidson argues, that my self-knowledge is not based on a special power of introspection does not show an absence of asymmetry in the *authority* attributed to such judgments, in contrast with other kinds of knowledge claims. The Rylean position, Davidson says, citing the similar views of Ayer, amounts to likening self-knowledge to an eyewitness report and knowledge of others to secondhand news. As such, he claims, it falls short of explaining the asymmetry: "First person attributions are not based on better evidence, but often, at least, on no evidence at all. The authority of the eyewitness is at best based on inductive probabilities easily overridden in particular cases: an eyewitness is discredited and his evidence discounted if he is a notoriously unreliable observer, prejudiced, or myopic. But a person never loses his special claim to be right about his own attitudes, even when his claim is challenged or overturned" (1984a, 104). I usually do not rely on evidence to decide, for example, what I believe about everyday objects that surround me. I don't have to check to see whether I believe there is milk in the fridge or coffee in the canister, any more than I usually have to examine the position of my limbs to determine whether I am walking or sitting, writing or making pastry. "One does not infer one's own conviction from one's words; nor yet the actions which arise from that conviction" (Wittgenstein 1968, 191).

Here lies the key, thinks Davidson, to explaining the asymmetry between self- and other-knowledge: a speaker cannot be utterly mistaken about the meanings of her own words. What distinguishes my knowledge of my beliefs and desires from my knowledge of another's is that, since I typically know what my words mean, I typically know what beliefs, desires, and hopes they express when I utter them. Says Davidson, "the assumption that I know what I mean necessarily gives me, but not you, knowledge of what belief I expressed by my utterance" (1984a, 110). For me to be able to speak a language just is for me to be able, among other things, to express my beliefs and wishes. If I cannot do this, then I am not a capable speaker of the language. Since it is not really possible that I should be totally deluded about the meanings of my words, it is a consequence of the fact that I am a language user that I know, by and large, what I believe.

By contrast, my linguistic competence is not sufficient for me to able to express the beliefs and wishes of another. Knowing what another believes or fears or hopes or wishes, thinks Davidson, depends on *interpreting* that person. To understand what belief I express when I say "Wagner died happy," you must devise a hypothesis and check it against the available evidence. That you might not know what I believe in this case stems from the fact that the process of interpretation "cannot be the same for the utterer and for his hearers" (1984a, 110). He continues:

> A hearer interprets (normally without thought or pause) on the basis of many clues: the actions and other words of the speaker, what he assumes about the education, birthplace, wit, and profession of the speaker, the relation of the speaker to objects near and far, and so forth. The speaker, though he must bear many of these things in mind when he speaks, since it is up to him to try to be understood, cannot wonder whether he generally means what he says. (110)

This does not mean that I cannot know what you are thinking, that I am ignorant of your hopes and ambitions, your beliefs and desires. There is no serious *philosophical* threat to my knowledge of others, but I can misunderstand you, and you can conceal your attitudes from me. There can be an intelligible asymmetry between first-person claims and second- and third-person claims.

Expressivism

Davidson's approach suggests an important departure from more traditional ways of thinking about self-knowledge. His emphasis on linguistic competence encourages us to think of self-knowledge not as an epistemic achievement, but as the mastery of a technique, and his description of the asymmetry between first- and other-person utterances captures something important: the fact that "My own relation to my words is wholly different from other people's" (Wittgenstein 1968, 192).

However, Davidson seems to build into his explanation the claim that I know about other people's mental lives *only* by way of interpretation. Much as Quine thinks that "radical translation begins at home" (1969, 46), Davidson seems closed to the idea that some of our knowledge of each other can be quite direct and unmediated by any sort of interpretive hypothesis. But it is implausible to think that I am *always* interpreting when I listen to another, just as it is implausible to think that all of my beliefs about the world of things and events are explanatory or inductive hypotheses, as Quine would have it. I do not learn my first language by interpreting from the ground up. Undoubtedly, interpretation enters at some stage. Having acquired a certain degree of competence and a basic vocabulary, I am then in a position to get caught in misunderstandings, and the practical need to avoid such incidents will teach me to look for other possible ways of understanding what others say to me. Correction, explication, and clarification are all skills that I learn along with my language. But I no more learn to pick out "Mummy" and "Daddy" by means of interpreting the utterances of others than I come to believe in the existence of spatio-temporal objects on the basis of evidence.[13] It is because I learn to take certain sorts of cases for granted that I can later consider the possibility of deviations from these cases—and that I can subsequently recognize a whole range of cases as ones in which interpretation is not called for.

Consider the case in which I formulate my belief that the milk is in the fridge by saying, "The milk is in the fridge." Typically, when I say this, I know what the words mean and, so, what I believe. I have no need of interpretation in order to understand myself here. But *neither do you*. Provided you understand English and do not come from a part of the world where my accent is too unusual, or there are no refrigerators, or they are not called "fridges," you typically know what I believe in making this utterance, and you do not know it by *interpreting* my behavior, because I behave in just the way that you expect me to.[14] It's not that you don't have access to my nonlinguistic behavior; rather, you don't need it. I might be in another room, when you shout to me, "Where's the milk?" And I respond as loudly, "It's in the fridge!" To be sure, you *can* be mistaken about what I believe when I say this, but so can I, and there are cases in which neither of us is wrong and in which it would be as strange for you to raise doubts as it would be for me.

If I respond to your question by pointing at the grocery bag by the doorway as I say, "It's in the fridge," then you must resort to interpretation. But it doesn't follow that your understanding of me is always like this, nor that our understanding of others *could* always be like this. If you know that I can be mistaken about myself or that you can be mistaken about me, it is because you have *learned* that there are exceptions to a frequent tendency to get things right. I can no more learn a language if, in the process of learning, I usually get things wrong about others than I can learn a language in which everyone always lies to me. If lying were the standard case, if everyone lied all or most of the time, it would not be lying—those words and behaviors would have a different standard use and a different meaning. (And if I were the only one to whom everyone always lied, then I would be deluded about standard use; I would speak a contingently private language, provided that the lies were sufficiently consistent.) My linguistic competence *does* require that over a range of cases I can understand sincere linguistic expressions of another's psychological phenomena.

There is, however, an important difference between cases in which I know without interpretation what another thinks or feels and cases of self-knowledge. The difference is that even when you know without pause or interpretation what my expression of belief means, your understanding it or reporting it is not also an expression of my belief.[15] The circumstances in which one's utterances can count as *expressions* of another's sensations or intentional attitudes, rather than as mere *reports* about them, are very special, as when, for example, a lawyer expresses the wishes of a client, or a translator expresses the thoughts of a visiting dignitary or the fears of a political refugee.

The view that I am advocating, then, is a variety of *expressivism*. A *purely* expressivist construal of first-person utterances holds that the role of first-person claims is not to make any assertion about the speaker, but to express some state or attitude of the person.[16] Utterances like "I am in pain" or "I believe that it is raining" are not reports about the speaker, but linguistic extensions of expressive nonverbal behavior. "I am in pain" expresses my pain much as an inarticulate cry or a grimace might, and "I believe that it is raining" expresses my belief in much the way that my saying "It is raining" might. In the latter case, according to this view, my words say something about the world, not about me; in the former case, my words say nothing "about" anything, just as my cry is not "about" anything.

This view is often attributed to Wittgenstein, who claims in an important passage that when a child learns the use of the word *pain* and its cognate terms, "the verbal expression of pain replaces crying and does not describe it" (1968, §244). Like wincing and moaning, my saying "I am in pain" or "That hurts!" is a form of "pain behavior" (§244).

But some of Wittgenstein's remarks might suggest that his view is not mine at all. I have adopted Davidson's locution in speaking of expressive linguistic abilities as self-*knowledge*, whereas Wittgenstein sometimes speaks as though the idea of self-knowledge had no content whatever: "It can't be said of me at all (except perhaps as a joke) that I *know* I am in pain. What is it supposed to mean—except perhaps that I *am* in pain?" (1968, §246). And again: "'I know what I want, wish, believe, feel, . . . ' (and so on through all the psychological verbs) is either philosophers' nonsense, or at any rate *not* a judgment *a priori*" (221).

The difference here is not as deep as it might at first seem. Wittgenstein wants to emphasize that my being in pain is not ordinarily something that I can find out about or something that I can doubt. "The truth is: it makes sense to say about other people that they doubt whether I am in pain; but not to say it about myself" (1968, §246). I can discover that the book I misplaced was sitting on the shelf, unnoticed. And this can happen despite my having looked on the shelf and not seen the book. I thought it was there, but when I checked, I couldn't find it, and so I came to doubt my earlier belief. In one of its standard uses *knowledge* is a term that we apply to cases like that of the discovered book. "One says 'I know' where one can also say 'I believe' or 'I suspect'; where one can find out" (221). It is because there is some possibility of doubt that it makes sense for me to say that I know where the book is. "'I know'. . . may mean 'I do not doubt'. . . but does not mean that the words 'I doubt'. . . are *senseless*" (221). But none of this talk makes sense in typical cases of pain. Where there can be no intelligible doubt, there can be no knowledge either, Wittgenstein holds.

Wittgenstein himself is fond of reminding us, however, that terms like *knowledge* have a range of different uses that vary from case to case. If we understand Wittgenstein as being concerned to deny that we know about our own sensations and intentional attitudes on the basis of some kind of inner observation—and he surely is so concerned—then I think there is no harm in saying that he allows self-knowledge in the sense of *being able to articulate* one's sensations and attitudes. In standard cases, knowing what I believe, hope, and fear is like knowing what movement my finger makes or what position my arm is in. Ordinarily, I do not infer what movements my body makes from some "immediate inner picture of the movement" (1980a, §390) or from any kind of evidence. Knowing in such cases "means something like 'being able to say'" (§390) or "being able to describe it" (1968, 185). And my knowing *how* to do something does not require the possibility of doubt. It makes sense to say either "I know that I left the book on the shelf" or "I doubt that I left the book on the shelf." But there is no expression of doubt that parallels my claim that I know how to ride a bicycle. Of course, I can doubt *that* I know how to ride a bicycle—if, for example, I have suffered a serious injury that has affected my motor control, and I can *wonder* how to ride a bicycle before learning. But it does not clearly mean anything to say "I doubt how to ride a bicycle."

Similarly, if my non-Socratic self-knowledge simply consists in my ability to say that I am in pain or that I believe it is raining, there is no room here for doubt. This, however, is neither because my intentional attitudes and my sensations possess some extraordinary property—a self-presenting clarity and distinctness—nor because I possess some extraordinary epistemic ability—the capacity for incorrigible introspection of my own "inner" states. Rather, it is a simple consequence of my having mastered a certain linguistic technique.

Self-ignorance

Knowing one's own mind, then, is not so much a variety of "knowing *that*" as a variety of "knowing *how*." Since I cannot in general doubt that I know what attitudes I express by the words I use, there is normally no question of my doubting that I believe and want what I say I do.[17]

But surely, it will be objected, there is more to self-knowledge than this! The Socratic injunction, "Know thyself!" would be pointless if self-knowledge were exhausted by one's linguistic capacities. The injunction presupposes that there is something difficult and important about self-knowledge—that self-knowledge can be an occasional epistemic achievement, rather than a standing ability. Others have dismissed the injunction as an "empty adage" (Lacan 1977, 174) on the ground that there are truths about oneself that one cannot attain on one's own. But this view, too, assumes that self-knowledge cannot be had so easily as my view might so far suggest. Talk of self-knowledge, it seems, must allow for talk of self-ignorance, and it behooves me to say something about the latter.

Like any ability, my ability to speak (or to write or to sign) is fallible. There is no perfect speaker of the English language (or of any other). This is not only because it is unclear what "perfection" would be here—the finer points of correct usage are a matter of continual dispute and changing fashion—but because manifestly everyone makes what we recognize as mistakes about the uses of words. If a person can make such errors, then she can also err in the articulation of her intentional phenomena. Of course, the occasional mistake does not undermine our confidence in a person's linguistic competence. My having the *ability* to say what I think and feel does not mean that I do it correctly every time. But too many mistakes, continual repetition of the same sorts of mistakes, or an error of particularly bizarre proportions will call my competence into doubt. And if the deficiencies in my competence run deep—if, for example, I think that my head is "made of earthenware" (Descartes 1984, 2:13) or that all my friends are extraterrestrial beings—or if these deficiencies seem especially to manifest themselves in my attempts to say what I think and feel, then doubt is thereby cast on my self-knowledge. In short, if self-knowledge is paradigmatically the ability to say what I think and feel, then at least one kind of self-ignorance consists in an impairment of that ability. Examples that fit this characterization might include varieties of what psychological theorists and therapists once called "psychosis"—disorders whose sufferers have been consumed by their own delusions and have "lost touch" with the world around them.[18] More obvious examples, perhaps, are to be found in the cases of prelingual infants and nonlingual animals.

But plainly, not all kinds of self-ignorance can be clarified in this way. There are cases in which I can, for example, have active doubts about my attitudes, and the very fact that it is relatively clear to me what I am doubting counts in favor of my linguistic competence, not against it: Do I really love this person, or am I blinded by sexual attraction? Do I really want to accept a job offer that my mentors regard as inferior, or do I simply want to demonstrate my independence by not following their advice? Do I really want to join the Resistance, or am I trying to avoid the responsibility of caring for my ailing mother? Am I really an atheist, or does my behavior at times of crisis display the patterns of a believer?[19] In such cases I cannot easily articulate what I think and feel, but this inability does not reflect poorly on my linguistic capacities as such. Coming to know my own mind in instances like these is not so much a matter of acquiring, consolidating, or repairing a standing *ability* as it is an interpretive, epistemic *achievement*. In this respect it is much like those cases of other-knowledge that Davidson regards as paradigmatic: cases in which I must try to interpret another's words against the background of that person's past and present behavior, linguistic and nonlinguistic, cases in which it makes sense to doubt that I have understood what intentional attitudes another's words express. How am I to make sense of this?

There is, I believe, no real conflict between treating self-knowledge as paradigmatically the ability to articulate one's attitudes and allowing the possibility of Socratic self-knowledge and -ignorance. But before justifying this claim, it is important to see why a critic might think the contrary.

I remarked above that treating non-Socratic self-knowledge as the mastery of a technique rules out the possibility of intelligible doubt about my non-Socratic self-knowledge. It makes no sense to say that I doubt how to express my intentional attitudes, just as it makes no sense to say that I doubt how to ride a bicycle. And though I might doubt *that I know* how to ride a bicycle, I cannot intelligibly doubt that I know how to express any of my intentional attitudes. To try to do so is itself to express such an attitude. I can, of course, doubt that I know how to express my love or my anger in the sense that I am unsure what kind of expression is socially appropriate. And I may, as a result, suppress my spontaneous expressions as a matter of habit. But this is clearly a different matter.

It is, however, just this exclusion of doubt about self-knowledge that can make it seem as if self-ignorance is possible only given a lack, or an impairment, of linguistic abilities. After all, it was the absence of any room for doubt that led Descartes to avow the certainty of the *cogito*. And Descartes, contrary to the readings of many Anglophone philosophers, did not think of the *cogito* as a *judgment*, but as an immediate intuition of "pure intelligence" (Gueroult 1984, 31). Only the "simple natures" (Descartes 1984, 1:44f.) displayed the certainty sought by Descartes's inquiry, because only what was absolutely simple could be perceived clearly and distinctly.[20] Judgment was an operation of the mind that produced a complex of simple natures, and wherever there was complexity there was room for doubt, as Descartes clarified in the Third Meditation (1984 2:26). So the kind of "knowledge" afforded by the *cogito* is not propositional knowledge, not a knowing *that*, but a direct intuition.

Now, a "direct intuition" of myself as "pure intelligence" is not obviously required by saying that self-knowledge is the ability to say what one thinks and feels. But I think we can see why this line of objection might be tempting, especially to some thinkers who steadfastly "oppose any philosophy directly issuing from the *Cogito*" (Lacan 1977, 1), particularly "the contemporary philosophy of being and nothingness" (6).

In *Being and Nothingness* Sartre puzzles over how Descartes's *cogito*—which he seems to interpret as a judgment, rather than an intuition—could ever induce the conviction that one had knowledge of oneself, and not merely of some object other than oneself. How am I supposed to know that I am identical with that upon which I reflect in the *cogito*, when typically knowledge is "a complete consciousness directed toward something which is not it" (1956, 12)? "Consciousness of self is not dual" (12), and only some further judgment could unify the knower of the *cogito* with the known, producing yet another duality in the subject and object of this further judgment. "If we wish to avoid an infinite regress," claims Sartre, "there must be an immediate, non-cognitive relation of the self to itself" (12). And only such a "pre-reflective" or "non-thetic" (13) self-consciousness, he thinks, could explain how it is that I can say what the position of my body is or what activity I am performing without pausing to reflect. A nonthetic self-awareness must bring unity to "those fleeting consciousnesses which have passed without being reflected-on" (13).[21] "It is not reflection which reveals the consciousness reflected-on to itself" (13); indeed, my self-knowledge is not grounded in any kind of *evidence*. And much as Wittgenstein insists that I do not know that I am in pain—because knowing requires the possibility of doubt or discovery, and I can neither doubt my own pain nor discover it—Sartre insists that "Pleasure cannot be distinguished—even logically—from consciousness of pleasure" (14). And later: "I *am* this jealousy; I do not *know* it" (348). Expressivism, it might seem, lies coiled at the heart of the *cogito* like a white worm.

But even if some version of the *cogito* or some variety of existential phenomenology fits with some version of expressivism, it does not follow that all versions of expressivism are committed to such mystifications as the immediate intuition of self or nonthetic self-consciousness. It is, indeed, in criticism of the Cartesian picture of private inner objects that Wittgenstein tells his expressivist story of how words can refer to sensations. So let me simply say why I see no real conflict between self-knowledge as linguistic ability and self-knowledge as Socratic self-discovery.

The situation here is analogous in one respect to that of knowledge of macroscopic objects and events. Given that there is an internal relation between a referring term and its referent, there are many things that under normal conditions it makes no sense to doubt. In normal circumstances any reason that I could have for doubting that I am seated at my desk typing these lines, if I am, is a reason for doubting that I understand what it means to say that I am seated at my desk typing these lines. But conditions *can* be unusual. If I have knowingly taken a hallucinogen or if I have reason to believe that an ill-willed neurosurgeon has implanted radio-controlled electrodes in my brain, then my doubts need show no linguistic deficiency. Learning the use of a word depends on my being taught to use it in certain circumstances without necessarily learning to describe those circumstances. But an ability that I thereby acquire is the ability to understand when circumstances deviate from the norm. Coming to know how things stand with the world around me in such cases demands something extra.

By analogy, just as it would make no sense to doubt my perceptual judgments under ordinary conditions, it would ordinarily make no sense for me to doubt what attitudes or sensations my words express. That is one side of the asymmetry that characterizes first-person authority. But conditions are not always ordinary, and one of the abilities I acquire when learning first-person expressions is the ability to recognize or understand when circumstances deviate from the norm. There are conditions in which it can make sense for me to doubt whether I can say what I think and feel and conditions in which I can "find out" what my own intentional attitudes are. Why suppose that treating self-knowledge as paradigmatically a linguistic capacity requires denying such Socratic self-ignorance and -knowledge?

The idea that there is some serious conflict here gets much of its credence from a reading, widely received among analytical philosophers, that Wittgenstein's commitment to expressivism was general and exclusive.[22] But even where expressivism seems most plausible—the linguistic expression of sensations like pain—

Wittgenstein's expressivism is not exclusive: "We surely do not always say someone is *complaining*, because he says he is in pain. So the words 'I am in pain' may be a cry of complaint, and may be something else" (1968, 189). Saying "I am in pain" can, for example, constitute an answer to the question "Why are you walking so oddly?" Here it serves as an explanation, not simply as a form of pain behavior. (Indeed, we can imagine instinctive pain behavior filling this role on a limited basis: Someone asks "Why are you walking so oddly?" and I clutch my knee and grimace in response.) Wittgenstein's concern is not to show that first-person uses of psychological predicates are always expressive, but that they are not always reports or descriptions of the speaker's state. The importance of expressive uses lies not in their exhausting the field of uses, but in the need for such uses in the learning and teaching of the language game of sensation-talk: "How do words *refer* to sensations?—There doesn't seem to be any problem here; don't we talk about sensations every day, and give them names? But how is the connexion between the name and the thing named set up? This question is the same as: how does a human being learn the meaning of the names of sensations?—of the word 'pain' for example" (1968, §244).

I learn how to use words like *chair* and *table* and *dog* and *cat* by being presented with exemplars of these things and by being made familiar with how these things function in my life and in the lives of those around me. I learn what running and walking and sitting and eating are by being presented with tokens of these events and learning how they function in the stream of life. But my pain is not an object that can be pointed out to me and put to use in a language game. It is not an event that I can observe, alone or together with other observers. So how do I learn to use the word *pain?* "Here is one possibility: words are connected with the primitive, the natural, expressions of the sensation and used in their place. A child has hurt himself and he cries: and then adults talk to him and teach him exclamations and, later, sentences. They teach the child new pain-behavior" (1968, §244). Part of learning how to use the word *pain* consists in learning how to extend my nonlinguistic expressions of pain with words that play a similar role. There is *an internal relation* between the concept of pain and pain behavior, so that I would not understand the concept of pain if I could not recognize typical pain behavior.

But this need not exhaust my learning. I also learn to say that others are in pain, to answer questions like "Are you in pain?" or "What's wrong? Why are you crying?" or "Where does it hurt?" or "Is it a sharp pain or a dull ache?" Holding that expressive uses of the first-person have a crucial role to play in language is compatible with holding that sometimes I do make reports about my sensations, because more complicated language games can be built on our expressive behavior.[23]

The case with intentional attitudes is similar. Belief has no characteristic expression behavior like wincing or grimacing, but, like the vocabulary of pain, the vocabulary of belief has an expressive aspect. "I believe . . ." like "I order you . . ."

or "I beg you . . ." or "I promise . . ." typically plays a performative role, not a descriptive one. Typically, "I believe that it is raining" expresses my belief, as does "It is raining," and both of them are reports about the world, not about me. But, again, holding this is compatible with holding that sometimes my utterance of "I believe that p" or simply "p" is a report about me, not about the world: "The language-game of reporting can be given such a turn that a report is not meant to inform the hearer about its subject matter but about the person making the report" (1968, 190). And I think it is also compatible with holding that sometimes I can have doubts about what I believe, hope, fear, or desire. Wittgenstein concurs:

> Does it make sense to ask "How do you know that you believe?"—and is the answer: "I know it by introspection"?
> In *some* cases it will be possible to say some such thing, in most not.
> It makes sense to ask: "Do I really love her, or am I only pretending to myself?" and the process of introspection is the calling up of memories; of imagined possible situations, and of the feelings one would have if . . . (1968, §587)

Socratic self-knowledge is the result of a kind of investigation into one's attitudes, and without such an investigation a person will live in self-ignorance. But an investigation that aims at Socratic self-knowledge is quite compatible with the first-person authority that I have claimed characterizes non-Socratic self-knowledge. Indeed, it is an investigation that presupposes first-person authority, for it can be carried out only against a background of knowing how to give linguistic expression to one's attitudes. Without such a background, there would be no questions to raise and no way of answering them.

Notes

1. It should be added that, inasmuch as cultural boundaries are not precise things, what begins as cultural relativism can easily turn into subjectivism. And by the same dynamic, the alleged incomprehensibility of other cultures can easily turn into the classical problem of other minds.

2. Putnam 1975, 215–71.

3. Putnam complains that this option treats terms like *beech* and *elm* as if they were "*absolutely* indexical" like *I* and *now* (1975, 245f.).

4. Putnam seems to grant the idea of narrow content for the sake of argument. But, as Burge complains, many of Putnam's remarks have "a distinctly individualistic ring" (1979, 118 n. 2). Putnam has acknowledged this even about some of his later writings (1994a, 456–65).

5. See Burge 1981, 97–120, and 1979, 117 n. 2. Burge (1979) argues for the social individuation of intentional types.

6. I use Burge's terminology and avoid the issue of interpreting Descartes's own views for now.

7. See Burge 1986, 123f. Burge leaves the term *authoritative* unanalyzed, whereas I take it to mean—in the "Cartesian" version—that an agent cannot be mistaken about things regarding which she has authority. The force of this "cannot" is, largely, captured by the combination of clauses about actual and possible situations. One could specify clauses (2) and (3) as saying that in counterfactual situations I *could* not be mistaken, rather than that I would never be mistaken. Which one is preferable depends on abstruse issues in modal logic, but for my purposes "would never" is as good as "could not." A problem for the former is a problem for the latter, and I shall present a problem for the former. For a more detailed critique of Burge, see Hymers 1997b.

8. Burge earlier remarks: "It is a well-known point that in considering counterfactual situations we hold constant the interpretation of the language whose sentences we are evaluating in the counterfactual situations. It is quite possible to consider the truth or falsity of interpreted sentences even in counterfactual situations where those sentences could not be used or understood. Similarly for our thoughts when we are considering the Cartesian situations" (1986, 122). This is more controversial than the suggestion that we evaluate counterfactuals by considering the "nearest possible world." It presupposes an application of the metaphysical realists' conception of objectivity to meaning and truth. This is the same doctrine that the metaphysical realist makes use of when claiming that we could really be brains in a vat, even if we could not knowingly say or believe so. See Chapter 1.

9. See Dretske 1970 and Nozick 1981.

10. Burge seems to acknowledge this, when he says that the skeptic's doubts raise not just a logical, but an *epistemic* possibility (1986, 122). But, as we saw in Chapter 1, the notion of epistemic possibility needs careful spelling out if it is not to beg the question.

11. Someone who sympathizes with Burge might object thus: "Your argument presupposes that the relation between experience and objects and events in the external world is an *internal relation*. But, as you have insisted, the metaphysical realist think that experience is related to the world only externally. Thus the intentional properties of experience are external properties, not internal ones. The metaphysical realist need claim only that the internal properties of experience would be explained by skeptical scenarios. So for a range of counterfactual situations—skeptical scenarios that would explain my experience's having the phenomenological properties that I know it actually to have—I do know what the internal properties of my experience would be in those situations, if skeptical scenarios are real possibilities. But this does not mean that I also actually know what *intentional* properties my experience would have in those situations. Thus, Burge can allow the real possibility of skeptical scenarios while also holding that the Cartesian requirement on first-person authority is too strong: metaphysical realism, first-person authority, and anti-individualism stand reconciled."

I am no friend of the distinction between intentional and intrinsic properties of experience, and I doubt that Burge would make this response, given his conviction that "the idea that we classify our perceptual phenomenology without specifying the objective properties that occasion it is wildly out of touch with actual empirical theories of perception as well as with common sense" (1986, 127). However, even were he to make this move, he would still have to concede that anti-individualism breaks down when we consider the contents of thoughts about the so-called internal or intrinsic properties of appearances. My being generally correct about the intrinsic properties of my experience requires my being able to say or think that my experience possesses certain properties. And if the skeptics' hypothesis is that my experience's possessing those properties would be explained by my having always been a brain in a vat, then I am also generally correct about what intrinsic properties my experience *would have* in counterfactual situations that would explain my having such experience. The contents of thoughts about the intrinsic properties of my experience, at least, would be determined independently of my environment—that is, *individualistically*.

12. If Rorty (1992b, 40) is right, this shared problematic is no mere accident, for Putnam's early theory of meaning, discussed above, was motivated by now abandoned Marxist views.

13. Davidson qualifies his remarks about interpretation in a way that is meant to accommodate such counterexamples: "A hearer interprets (normally without thought or pause) on the basis of many clues" (1984a, 110). But this qualification involves a sleight of hand similar to Quine's remark, noted in Chapter 2, that physical objects are not ordinary posits, but "cultural posits" (1980, 44).

14. The frequency with which interpretation will be necessary between two people, I would suggest, will be influenced by such factors as the degree of experience and background knowledge shared by speaker and auditor, and also by the degree of justifiable trust that obtains between speaker and auditor. A trust relation is justifiable, as Annette Baier proposes, to the extent that "its continuation need not rely on successful threats held over the trusted, or on her successful cover-up of breaches of trust" (1986, 255), but also, I would argue, to the extent that its continuation does not depend on the self-ignorance of the truster. On self-ignorance, see the next section, as well as Chapter 8.

15. For an alternative proposal, see McGeer 1996. McGeer relies on talk of "folk-theories" too heavily for my liking, but her positive proposal regarding the "commissive" nature of first-person psychological claims seems plausible at least for some cases (though perhaps not all). For related considerations, see Bilgrami 1992.

16. I shall argue below that being an expressivist does not commit one to being a pure expressivist, but I set that refinement aside for now.

17. I can lie about these things, but my lying presupposes that I can say what I think and feel, though I choose to say something else. "The awareness that one is lying is a knowinghow" (Wittgenstein 1981, §190).

18. See Malpas 1992, 58ff., for an example.

19. See Szabados 1981b, 610f., for this example.

20. On the relation between the *cogito* and the other simple natures known "per se," see Gueroult 1984, chaps. 2 and 3 and Schouls 1980, 109.

21. This noncognitive awareness plays a central role in Sartre's answer to the problem of other minds (1956, 340–400). The phenomenology of being looked at, he thinks, shows that my consciousness of the Other who looks at me is nonthetic, because I am undeniably aware of being looked at, but I am so aware only insofar as I am aware of the Other as another consciousness. That in turn, he argues, is possible only insofar as I do not apprehend the Other as an object, which is the mode in which reflective consciousness operates. "If I apprehend the look, I cease to perceive the eyes" (346).

22. For criticism, see Szabados 1981a; 1981b; and Hacker 1993, 83–96.

23. Strawson famously objected that Wittgenstein's expressivism entailed the "needlessly paradoxical" (1959, 134) consequence that psychological terms do not have the same *meanings* when applied in the first and third persons. Rebutting this objection requires showing that expressive uses can also be truth-assessable. Wittgenstein seems to hold such a view in a number of passages from the second part of the *Investigations*. See, for exam-

ple, 1968, 187–89. Jacobsen (1996) argues inventively that this is not a problem as long as we can treat Wittgenstein as having had a distinction between "sense" and "force." Since I think that there is no sharp distinction to be drawn between semantics and pragmatics, and so between sense and force, I am not entirely happy with this solution, but I think that it points the way to another: All we need do is avoid *identifying* meaning with use. As long as not every difference in use is a difference in meaning, Wittgenstein need not be committed to the consequence that the difference between first- and third-person uses entails a difference in meaning. What can be more cautiously said is that meaning is determined by use, but is not identical with it, and that every difference of meaning entails a difference of use. For this suggestion, see Hacker 1996b, 248f. The passages that could be cited to support this reading are much the same ones that Jacobsen cites in support of his stronger claim. See, for example, Wittgenstein 1968, §§197, 532, 556–57 and 1968, 175. Millikan (1996) makes some suggestions that might be useful here, but there are other elements of her position that I would wish to avoid.

8

Self-knowledge and Self-unity

> *"Suppose that it's raining and I don't believe it"—when I assert what is supposed in this proposition,—then, so to speak, my personality splits in two.*
>
> *"Then my personality splits in two" means: Then I no longer play the ordinary language-game, but some different one.*
>
> —Ludwig Wittgenstein, Remarks on the Philosophy of Psychology

In the preceding chapter I held with Davidson that non-Socratic self-knowledge is the ability to give linguistic articulation to one's sensations and attitudes. But such a view, I proposed, is best linked with a mitigated expressivism about first-person uses of psychological verbs. And I concluded by arguing that adopting such expressivism about self-knowledge is compatible with allowing both for the possibility of achieving Socratic self-knowledge and for the possibility of failing to achieve such self-knowledge and, so, suffering from a kind of self-ignorance.

However, self-ignorance also raises questions about self-*unity*. To be ignorant about oneself, it might be thought, is to have intentional attitudes that one does not know one has, and this has suggested to many that forms of self-ignorance involve a kind of "partition[ing]" (Davidson 1982, 300) of the self. Accounting for such self-fragmentation, according to some popular views, requires a rejection of the idea of a Cartesian "unified subject." Moreover, some thinkers have claimed that self-unity is not only an unattainable ideal, but a harmful one and that the ends of political liberation are better served by a preservation and celebration of one's plurality. Political agency, it is suggested, depends on fragmentation and self-ignorance. These concerns, interesting in themselves, would also seem to pose an objection to my position, since my use of the term *epistemic neurosis* seems to valorize a kind of self-unity, thereby presupposing both the possibility of self-unity and the possibility of self-division.

My discussion in this chapter will focus on two issues: First, is a unified self an attainable goal—even only as an *ideal*? And second, is unity of the self as an ideal a *desirable* goal? I shall argue that abandoning the Cartesian "unified subject" does not entail abandoning all self-unity. Indeed, the very possibility of recognizing oneself as "plural" or "fragmented" depends on a kind of grammatical unity of the subject of one's self-articulations. That there is such a thing as language at all implies that there are selves—grammatical unities—for whom language has meaning. The question of whether self-unity is desirable, then, is one about whether a particular array of self-articulations is desirable, and this question can properly be asked and answered only in specific cases.

The Decentered Subject

Wittgenstein's expressivism explains his attitude to Moore's paradox. Statements like "It's raining, but I don't believe it," Moore points out, seem self-defeating in some way, and yet they involve no contradiction of any sort. One can perfectly well imagine that it should be raining, but that I should not believe that it is— and yet, for me to assert that these things are the case sounds odd (see Moore 1993, 207–12). The reason for the oddity, Wittgenstein suggests, is that both "It's raining" and "I believe it's raining" are typically expressions of belief, whereas in stating hypothetical scenarios they are not: "Imagine that it's raining, but I don't believe it" does not express any belief; it proposes a hypothetical scenario. Thus, although there is no contradiction involved in the hypothesis that it's raining but I don't believe it, the statement, "It's raining, but I don't believe it," amounts pragmatically to saying something like "It's raining, and it's not raining." However, the fact that Wittgenstein's expressivism is not exclusive is shown by his allowance that such statements might play a role in some suitably fleshed-out linguistic context: "One would here have to fill out the picture with behavior indicating that two people were speaking through my mouth" (1968, 192; see 1980a, §495).

It might be tendentious to interpret this passage literally as saying that two persons might occupy the same body.[1] Perhaps Wittgenstein is merely thinking about cases of ambivalence: Not two minutes ago when I arrived the sky was perfectly blue, and now it's raining! It's raining, but I don't believe it! I see it with my own eyes, but I don't believe it![2]

But others have held that some forms of self-ignorance might require a self that is internally divided, "partitioned into quasi-independent structures," as Davidson says (1982, 300). The most famous advocate of this view was Freud, who took "the splitting of the mind and dissociation of the personality" (1962, 45) as central to psychoanalysis. There are precursors of the idea, of course. By Freud's own testimony (45) he and Breuer were inspired to think about "psychical splitting" (50) by the early theorist of multiple personality disorder, Pierre Janet, though it was Freud who introduced the notion of "repression" to explicate such splitting. But well before Janet there were Leibniz's *"petites perceptions"*— "alterations in the soul itself, of which we are unaware" (1981, 53)—and, later, Nietzsche's proclamation that "our body is but a social structure composed of many souls" (1966, §19). And Hegel's notion of alienation ties a thesis of self-division to a thesis of self-ignorance, but with the teleological faith that division and ignorance will be overcome in Absolute Knowledge. Freud, says Lacan, drew on "the dialectic of the consciousness-of-self, as realized from Socrates to Hegel" (1977, 79f.), but his contribution "was to demonstrate that this verifying process authentically attains the subject only by decentring him from the consciousness-of-self, in the axis of which the Hegelian reconstruction of the phenomenology of mind, maintained it" (80).

Lacan here alludes to Freud's fondness for comparing his dynamic theory of the unconscious to the changes in worldview wrought by the Copernican revolution and the Darwinian explanation of evolution by natural selection, each of which called into question the centrality that older views accorded to humanity. The earth is not the literal center of the universe, and humanity is not the metaphorical center of nature. "But human megalomania will have suffered its third and most wounding blow from the psychological research of the present time which seeks to prove to the ego that it is not even master in its own house, but must content itself with scanty information of what is going on unconsciously in its mind" (Freud 1963, 285).

However, it is Lacan, even more than Freud, who has made the "the self's radical ex-centricity to itself" (1977, 171) a recurrent theme for more than a generation of French philosophers and Anglophone literary theorists. It is Lacan who treats the unconscious as "that part of the concrete discourse, in so far as it is transindividual, that is not at the disposal of the subject" (49) and who sees the self as "fragmented in that it bears speech, and whole in that it helps in not hearing it" (137). And it is Lacan to whom Althusser turns when he reinterprets Marx's treatment of ideology as a "necessarily imaginary distortion" (1971, 165).

Althusser, recall from Chapter 6, thinks that *"ideology has the function (which defines it) of 'constituting' concrete individuals as subjects"* (1971, 171). But just as he thinks that ideology needs the category of the subject, which is "constitutive of all ideology" (1971, 171), he also holds that the "real subject" is "de-centred, constituted by a structure which has no 'centre' either, except in the imaginary misrecognition of the 'ego,' i.e., in the ideological formations in which it 'recognizes' itself" (218f.).

What does the "decentering" of the self amount to? In Chapter 7, I construed the "Cartesian conception" of first-person authority in the idiom of analytical philosophy: the Cartesian sees self-knowledge claims as incorrigible and infallible. But it is not free of controversy to attribute this "Cartesian" view to Descartes. He presents his position in terms of *ideas*, and he views *judgments* as unreliable (as I noted in Chapter 7)—at least until justification has been found for them in the simple ideas disclosed by analysis. Even then I must be careful not to judge, if my perceptions are not clear and distinct. But Descartes has an analogue for incorrigibility in the simplicity and consequent indubitability and certainty of the *cogito*. On Gueroult's reading, this immediate certainty is an "exact coincidence between my thought and existence" in which "the object posited is nothing but the subject" (1984, 27). In the *cogito* pure thought is immediately and fully *present* to itself. Nothing intervenes and nothing is hidden. Pure thought in the *cogito* is "my pure self, which has nothing in common with my individual, personal, concrete self, which can only be captured empirically" (32). But even if this pure self is—again in Gueroult's (translated) words—a "self common to all men" (32), it remains the epistemic and metaphysical focus on which the empirical self is centered and in which it has its unity.

It is something like this version of the *cogito*, taken as a model for all self-knowledge, to which Lacan and Althusser are reacting. The "philosophical *cogito*," writes Lacan, "is at the centre of the mirage that renders modern man so sure of his being" (1977, 165). But it is part of a "mirage," and "modern man's" certainty masks a pervasive self-ignorance—or better, self-misrecognition.[3]

For Althusser this misrecognition of self is a general effect of ideology, whose role, we have seen, is to "'constitut[e]' concrete individuals as subjects" (1971, 171). Part of the function of ideology, is to render, *as though indubitable and necessary*, contingent features of the real conditions of existence that obtain at a certain point in history. It does so through subjects who—like the Cartesian subject in the *cogito*—find their identity in those conditions so represented. Doubting the necessity of the current socioeconomic order thus seems like doubting the very conditions of one's own existence. Ideology, says Althusser, "imposes . . . obviousnesses as obviousnesses which we cannot *fail to recognize*" (1971, 172). But, unlike the *cogito* in Descartes's scheme, this intuitive awareness of the "self-evident," "simple" "truths" of ideology is illusory.

The unconscious, for Althusser, is linked with the ideological subject's obliviousness to her constitution *as* subject *by* ideology. We ideological subjects find our identities in the "obviousnesses" of ideological depictions of material conditions. A threat to current social relations seems a threat to us, and by the same bond we come to feel that society "could not get on without us" (Eagleton 1991, 143), that we are "concrete, individual, distinguishable and (naturally) irreplaceable subjects" (Althusser 1971, 173). But—if talk of degree is permissible—to the extent that I find my identity in ideology I cannot see that I am constituted as subject by ideology. Only if I remain unconscious of it can it constitute me as a subject. Self-ignorance is not only possible on this view, but necessary for my constitution as subject (see Eagleton 1991, 141).

Lacan, similarly, accepts a kind of "historical Pyrronism" (1988, 264) about self-knowledge. For this he seems to offer two major reasons: (1) "in discourse it is contradiction which sorts truth from error" (264); and (2) "We are forced . . . to accept the notion of an incessant sliding of the signified under the signifier" (1977, 154). Let me examine these reasons in turn.

We met the former reason in Chapter 6, when I suggested that the charge that claims to truth are immodest can be motivated by a reaction to absolute idealism. Lacan's insistence that "Reality is defined by contradiction" (1988, 267) amounts to accepting the absolute idealists' coherence theory of truth. Truth is attained only when "the totality of discourse closes in on itself in a perfect non-contradiction" (264). However, Lacan seems to think not only that "We are some way yet from this ideal!" (264), but that its possibility is an illusion. Truth (with one qualification that we shall consider below) is not a possible goal to which we might aspire, and this caution applies as much to self-knowledge as to any other kind of knowledge. "Every emission of speech is always, up to a certain point, under an inner necessity to err" (264). As I suggested in Chapter 6, such a view will tempt us only if we persist in thinking that truth is the sort of thing about which one needs to have a theory.

The second reason, the "incessant sliding of the signified," is a little harder to grasp. But it seems to amount to the claim that the conscious intentions with which a word is uttered are always accompanied by a series of unconscious intentions whose content is bound up with the possible figurative uses to which the word can be put.

The unconscious in Lacan's view is not a set of "unconscious tendencies" (1977, 50) residing in a single individual, but a part of "transindividual" (49) discourse, and as such it is amenable to study in a manner directly analogous to the investigation that structural linguistics makes of language itself. According to Lacan, "what psychoanalytic experience discovers in the unconscious is the whole structure of language" (147). But whereas structuralists like Saussure had thought of linguistic signs as composed of two elements, the signifier (the sound-pattern or inscribed mark) and the signified (the concept that a given signifier designates), Lacan wants to insist that it is the former of these whose properties must be understood if the functioning of language, and of the unconscious, is to be grasped. He urges us to abandon "the illusion that the signifier answers to the function of representing the signified, or better, that the signifier has to answer for its existence in the name of any signification whatever" (150). The realm of the signifier is radically autonomous, comprising what Lacan calls "the signifying chain" (153), and the "laws" of this "closed order" (152) are the determinants of all "signification."

Lacan's point seems to be that signification is not determined by, say, ostensive definition or teaching—"the index finger pointing to an object" (1977, 149f.)—but by the holistic interconnection of particular signifiers. Signifiers alone seem to be the functional element in language, and which signifieds are associated with them is incidental to their function. What a sound pattern signifies depends on how it is used, and its use for Lacan consists entirely in its possible contextual connections with other signifiers: "It is easy to see that only the correlations between signifier and signifier provide the standard for all research into signification, as is indicated by the notion of 'usage' of a taxeme or semanteme which in fact refers to the context just above that of the units concerned" (153).

Such "correlations," however, do not simply yield a conventional designation of object by word, according to Lacan. Rather, they operate according to the principle of metonymy, the part standing in for the whole, because each word belongs to a signifying chain that connects it with a host of terms related by "a whole articulation of relevant contexts" (1977, 154). Any one of these terms can go proxy for any of the others. But the use of a term is not confined to a single context. Each signifier is a member of other signifying chains, all of which are "rings of a necklace that is a ring in another necklace made of rings" (153). The result, thinks Lacan, is that a given signifier always does more than it at first appears to do: "What this structure of the signifying chain discloses is the possibility I have, precisely in so far as I have this language in common with other subjects, that is to say, in so far as it exists as a language, to use it in order to signify *something quite other* than what it says" (155). This, says Lacan, is the "properly signifying function ... depicted in language" (156). "For the function of language is not to inform but to evoke" (86). In order to determine what is signified by a speaker's utterance we must determine what is the relevant signifying chain, and then, what is the relevant portion of that chain. And *none* of this need be apparent to the speaker herself. Every so-called conscious intention to say something is accompanied by a string of unconscious intentions to which the conscious intention is related only as part to whole or as metaphor. Consequently, even when the Cartesian philosopher utters the *cogito*, she need not be saying what she means to say. The problem of self-knowledge thus becomes not merely one of deciding whether I know what I think and feel, but of "knowing whether I am the same as that of which I speak" (165).

Despite the poor prospects for self-knowledge this view would seem to suggest, one does find in Lacan something like the conviction that psychoanalysis can attain the truth about the subject. The novelty of the techniques that Freud pioneered, thinks Lacan, is that "during analysis, within this discourse which unfolds in the register of error, something happens whereby the truth irrupts, and it is not contradiction" (1988, 265). In the subject's "free associations, dream images, symptoms, a word bearing the truth is revealed" (265). Such phenomena, thinks Lacan, reveal the unconsciously intended significations of the subject's words. They help the psychoanalyst identify the relevant signifying chains from which an interpretation of the subject's hidden meanings can be constructed, and they lay the ground for the emergence of the truth "in the most clearcut representative of the mistake—the slip" (265). It is the patient's slip of the tongue or the word that "escapes" (269) her that reveals most clearly what she unconsciously intends.

Lacan's picture of psychoanalysis sounds oddly like the early Wittgenstein's distinction (1922, §4.1212) between "saying" and "showing," but whereas showing was our mode of acquaintance only with the transcendental (logic, ethics, aesthetics, metaphysics) for Wittgenstein, Lacan seems committed to the stronger, general thesis that "the function of language is not to inform but to evoke" (1977, 86).[4] The patient cannot *say* anything about herself, but her free associations and slips of the tongue *show* what she herself cannot say. The problem for Lacan is how the analyst can manage to say anything about what the patient's mistakes manage to evoke. It is unclear exactly how these moments of analysis when "truth grabs error by the scruff of the neck in the mistake" (1988, 265) can be reconciled with the normal misrecognition of the self. "Everyday speech," according to Lacan, "all the time runs up against failure of recognition [*méconnaissance*]" (270). But to suggest that the interpretations of the psychoanalyst somehow manage to transcend this difficulty seems like special pleading. Indeed, it looks like yet another example of epistemic neurosis: The skeptical doubts that define Lacan's views about the self seem to undermine the justification his own positive program in psychoanalysis.

Perhaps a more basic problem is that Lacan's reasoning is simply not very compelling—and not only because language has no *single* function, which might be to evoke, rather than to inform. First, from the fact that it is always possible to use words to signify something other than they say, it does not follow that one always does use words to signify something other than they say. More charitably, from the fact that for any particular use of a word it is possible that it should signify something other than it says, it does not follow that it is possible that all uses of words signify something other than they say.[5] And even if it did follow, the mere logical possibility of this fact is not sufficient grounds for doubt, unless we assume, with Descartes, that knowledge requires certainty or, with the absolute idealists, that knowing one truth requires knowing all the truths.

Indeed, Lacan's conclusion is difficult to express without the elaborate scaffolding of structuralist linguistics to support it. What words "say," I take it, is what they literally mean, which is determined, I contend, by how they are standardly used. So in the idiom I prefer, Lacan's claim comes to something like: One always uses words in a way other than they are standardly used. In a trivial sense this is right: Particular occasions of use, precisely because they are particular, will differ in some way from each other and from what they share in common. However, it does not follow from this that one's intentions in uttering a word are always other than what one takes them to be, because it does not follow that every occasional difference is *significant*.

Second, even if we grant that every use of a word drags with it a host of unacknowledged or "misrecognized" connotations and evocative effects, it does not follow that somehow only the signifier is at work here—the only dry land in a sea of changing significations, for the use of a word is not exhausted by its formal, syntactic connections with other words. As we saw in Chapter 5, there is no closed totality that constitutes the structure of a language in contrast to its empirical content. The use of a word is intimately bound up with the uses of gestures and facial expressions and with the manipulation of, and interaction with, spatio-temporal objects and events. Signification is not merely an effervescent product of the play of signifiers, but part of the use of those signifiers. The harmony between language and reality is formed in grammar—but not because "the world of words ... creates the world of things" (1977, 65).

Multiple Selves

Lacan's views have enjoyed considerable influence. Perhaps it is because his emphasis on the importance of figurative language seems to place the disciplines of the humanities on a cultural footing comparable to that enjoyed by the natural sciences. Whatever the reason, it has become overwhelmingly tempting for some scholars in the humanities to suppose that the key to interpretation lies in understanding not what is explicitly said, but what is inadvertently signified, and to say that all communication is really "misrecognized miscommunication"—or some such thing.

But the trio of Freud, Lacan, and Althusser has not provided the only source of inspiration to thinkers who contemplate the idea of a fragmented self. Recent decades have seen an increasing sensitivity to cultural and other differences within Western societies, and feminists have found efforts to build a united, international women's movement complicated by the diversity among women. If one sees the self as conditioned or constructed by social factors, it is an easy step to the idea that the self is as multiple or plural as the society of which it is part.

In accord with this further dimension of influence, not all thinkers have supposed that multiplicity should be treated in terms of a quasi-Freudian unconscious. Some have adopted a view that sees divisions of the self as more like the dissociative states of multiple personality disorder than like a Freudian or Lacanian unconscious.[6] Thus, Maria Lugones argues for an "ontological pluralism" (1990, 502) according to which "the self is not unified but plural" (503). "In giving up the unified self," she writes,

> I am guided by the experience of bicultural people who are also victims of ethnocentric racism in a society that has one of those cultures as subordinate and the other as dominant. These cases provide me with examples of people who are very familiar with experiencing themselves as more than one: having desires, character, and personality traits that are different in one reality than in the other, and acting, enacting, animating their bodies, having thoughts, feeling the emotions, etc., in ways that are different in one reality than in the other. (503)

A suggested link between oppression and self-division is not entirely new. Marx's early *Economic and Philosophic Manuscripts of 1844* uses Hegel's idea of alienation, filtered through Feuerbach's writings, to describe the worker's relation to the process and result of commodity production. Under capitalism, says Marx, the worker is alienated from the human essence, which lies in the conscious, free, social, productive activity that capitalism obstructs (Marx and Engels 1975–, 3:270–82). That alienation consists not only in the fact that the worker is denied the chance of conscious, free, social, productive activity, but in the epistemic fact that such activity does not even seem possible to the worker because "the object which labor produces—labor's product—confronts it as *something alien*, as a *power independent* of the producer." The worker's objectification of himself in his work appears as *"loss of the object and bondage to it"* (272).

Cultural subjection does not play a large role in Marx's analysis, and there is little hint that alienated labor produces multiple selves when it produces ideological self-ignorance. But interest in the divided experience of bicultural people has a history too. Writing in *The Souls of Black Folk* in 1903, W. E. B. Du Bois described his experience of the "double-consciousness" of being black in America:

> The Negro is a sort of seventh son, born with a veil, and gifted with second-sight in this American world—a world which yields him no true self-consciousness, but only lets him see himself through the revelation of the other world. It is a peculiar sensation, this double-consciousness, this sense of always looking at one's self through the eyes of others, of measuring one's soul by the tape of a world that looks on in amused contempt and pity. One ever feels his twoness,—an American, a Negro; two souls, two thoughts, two unreconciled strivings; two warring ideals in one dark body, whose dogged strength alone keeps it from being torn asunder. (1961, 16f.)[7]

This lack of "true self-consciousness," which is a "double-consciousness," is a complex phenomenon. It seems that Du Bois equates the "twoness" with a kind of self-ignorance, but it is not simply a lack of *all* and *any* self-consciousness, for the African American can still "see himself through the revelation of the other world," the world of the powerful. Nor is it a total constitution of the self by ideology, but a "twoness" of "souls" and "unreconciled strivings," threatening, but resistible. Yet, for Du Bois some kind of self-unity, "true self-consciousness," is a desirable and possible goal, though the unity seems not to be that of the "centered" subject: "The history of the American Negro is the history of this strife—this longing to attain self-conscious manhood, to merge his double self into a better and truer self. In this merging he wishes neither of the older selves to be lost" (1961, 17).[8] To Lugones, in apparent contrast to Du Bois, self-unity does not seem automatically desirable—be it possible or not. She cites, among other sources, the work of the lesbian Chicana writer Gloria Anzaldúa. Reflecting on her experience in the political and cultural "borderlands" of Texas and Mexico, Anzaldúa celebrates the consciousness of the "new *mestiza*":

> The new *mestiza* copes by developing a tolerance for contradictions, a tolerance for ambiguity. She learns to be an Indian in Mexican culture, to be Mexican from an Anglo point of view. She learns to juggle cultures. She has a plural personality, she operates in a pluralistic mode—nothing is thrust out, the good the bad and the ugly, nothing rejected, nothing abandoned. Not only does she sustain contradictions, she turns the ambivalence into something else. (1987, 79)

This "tolerance for ambiguity" and for "contradictions" is the means by which the new *mestiza* "copes" with her experience of oppression. For Anzaldúa, "Rigidity means death" (1987, 79). To deny one's plurality is to open oneself to "the enemy within" (79).

Lugones finds such remarks suggestive of her own rejection of the "unified self" (1990, 503). According to her "ontological pluralism," divisions of the self should be *preserved*, and hopes for liberation from ideology and oppression depend on this very preservation. One's cultural plurality, thinks Lugones, is crucial to overcoming one's subordination. There is a tension in radical theory between depicting the ubiquity of oppression and retaining the possibility of overcoming that oppression, and, she maintains, only an account of the self that does not treat it as essentially unified can cope with this tension. Without internal diversity oppression must seem total and inescapable, for it is "unclear how the self can be unified and contain and express both a liberatory and an oppressed consciousness" (501). What she calls "the ontological possibility of liberation" is said to "depend on embracing ontological pluralism" (502).

Phrases like "ontological pluralism" and "ontological possibility of liberation" bring to mind a problem I raised at the end of Chapter 6. If the thesis of radical incommensurability—that is, that it is in principle impossible for members of one culture to fathom the members of another culture and vice versa—were true, then the bicultural person would face an insurmountable logical barrier in trying to understand her A-communal self from the standpoint of her B-communal self. She would, it seems, be *two metaphysically distinct selves*, each unable to understand the other. Her two "souls" or "strivings" would be not just unreconciled, but *irreconcilable*.

But what barriers to the commensuration of a culturally divided self does Lugones mean to designate? Logical barriers, or pragmatic ones? Lugones's talk of "ontological" pluralism suggests the former. But then her position threatens to collapse into an internalized form of the self-defeating logical incommensurability of conceptual schemes. Rorty understands Lugones this way, criticizing her metaphysical language as a sign that she rejects the "desirability of harmonizing one's various roles, self-images, etc., in a single unifying story about oneself." To Rorty, by contrast, such a story seems "desirable" (1991a, 12 n. 22).

But some of the vocabulary that Lugones explicitly *rejects* is cast off for reasons more in tune with recognizing practical divisions of the self, not metaphysical ones. There is no "transcendental self," she says, that wears its personae as "masks" and "is distinguishable from them" (1990, 506). So it also is reasonable to expect her to deny that there are *two* or *more* "transcendental" selves, instead of one.

Other claims that she makes are reminiscent of Althusser's views on the constitutive role of ideologies in the formation of subjects. For Lugones, persons are "construct[ed] or constitute[d]" by "structures"—"patterned arrangements of role-sets, status sets and status sequences consciously recognized and regularly operative in a given society and closely bound up with legal and political norms and sanctions" (1990, 506). Maybe Lugones is suggesting that, since there are a number of distinct structures ("ideologies" in Althusser's sense), each individual is constituted as a number of distinct "subjects" by those distinct "ideologies."[9] This might seem to pose problems of just the sort that Rorty raises. As we saw in Chapter 6, Althusser's conflation of ideology in general with the ruling ideology makes it unclear how meaningful political resistance could be possible. Although Althusser raises the hope of "bad subjects" (1971, 181) who can resist the control of ideology, it is not obvious how such resistance is to proceed. His subject of ideology is constructed to be oppressed. As Benton says, "there is no basis for 'interpellations' of oppositional forms of subjectivity" (1984, 107). But if the only contrast between Lugones and Althusser is that she treats the individual as a plurality of "subjects," each constituted by a different "structure" or "ideology," then her view seems to throw up logical barriers among an individual's selves. None of an individual's "subjects" is in any position to escape from its particular constitutive ideology.

However, Lugones's position departs from Althusser's in two important ways. First, whereas "ordinary life presents structures as systematic, complete, coherent, closed socio-political-economic organizations or normative systems," she insists that "structures are not closed" (1990, 505).[10] Here is a hint of the possibility that one's different, constructed selves are not "closed" either, but pragmatically incommensurable.

Second, Lugones seems to see the possibility of agency under oppression as lying not simply in the plurality of the self, but in an *awareness* of this plurality. Thus, speaking of the different "worlds" that a bicultural person may inhabit, she says, "It is very important whether one remembers or not being another person in another reality" (504). It is to the degree that one can be made to forget one's life in another "reality" that an oppressive "reality" seems inescapable, exhaustive of *reality*. She urges us to "distinguish this dual personality"—the personality of one who cannot remember being another person—from "operating in a pluralistic mode of new mestiza" (1992, 35). Remembering one's other selves can bring to mind the possibility of an alternative to the current order: "The liberatory experience lies in this memory, on these many people one is who have intentions one understands because one is fluent in several 'cultures,' 'worlds,' realities. One understands herself in every world in which one remembers oneself. This is a strong sense of personal identity, politically and morally strong" (1990, 504f.). The very process of remembering, thinks Lugones, is an escape from the rigidity of "structures" and "into the limen," the "place in between realities" (505). Simply to remember one's other selves is to get outside one's constitution as subject by an Althusserian ideology.

But why isn't this going "into the limen"—be it sufficient to recover agency or not—itself a move in the direction of unity, not a step away from it? Why does Lugones recommend against attempts at promoting self-unity?

Agency and False Unities

One's self-descriptions and -interpretations do not spring *ex nihilo*. They arise in the context of one's dealings with others in a particular society, at a particular time in history, amid particular personal and cultural influences. One's sense of oneself, of who one is and what is possible for oneself, is affected by one's culture or cultures, by one's station in life, by how one stands with others. So if one lives in the borderlands, a product of more than one culture, then one has at one's potential disposal more than one set of vocabulary on which to draw in self-interpretation. But if one's first culture is subordinated to another, one can also come to see oneself through the eyes of that dominant culture.

What does this tell us about Lugones's views? First, if the ways of life of a bicultural person's cultures conflict practically, cultural incommensurabilities of a similarly practical nature can arise. So the vocabularies on which she can draw may also conflict. From the vantage of one of her cultures, she may have trouble understanding those parts of herself that are drawn to her other culture. This practical barrier may leave her ambivalent about her choices and behavior, about her desires and beliefs. Second, the problem will intensify if the two cultures are not just in conflict, but in a relation of domination and subordination. Among the most significant differences within a culture or between cultures are those used to justify inequitable allotments of power, and such inequities form another element of the experience on which Lugones and Anzaldúa draw.

In cases of cultural subordination, the potential to draw on several cultures in the process of self-interpretation is harder to actualize, because part of the domination of a culture by another is its devaluation. Perceived holders of the "cultural identity" of the subordinate culture may on these grounds be barred from the community of the dominant culture—from the dealings and discourse of power. Often implicit in assigning such a "cultural identity" is a mistaken idea of cultures as bounded by necessary and sufficient conditions. Intracultural differences are effectively ignored, and members of the subordinate culture are treated as essentially similar to each other, essentially different from members of the dominant community.[11] Reifying concepts into conceptual schemes, I argued in Chapter 5, leaves other schemes inscrutable from within one's own, and treating others as incomprehensible in this way threatens our ability to think of them as language users like ourselves, as *persons*. Similar conclusions apply to assigning a "cultural identity," and it is easy to see how treating cultural others as if unfathomable, even mindless in their behavior, could mesh with a devaluation and subordination of their culture.

Now, consider the effects of such devaluation on an inhabitant of the borderlands. Her dominant culture urges her to see herself as essentially different from its "essential" members and, so, not worthy of serious attention. If this control of her self-understanding succeeds, she loses sight of the richness of her subordinate culture (and of herself in that culture), for she sees it as a disqualifying "cultural identity." From the dominant culture's vantage she sees herself as less worthy, and because it is a dominant culture, it commands her attention. To get by in the dominant culture she learns to fit the interpretations that that culture would impose on her, to appear only as she is expected to appear, to maintain a certain *invisibility*. But to do this she must hide those differences in her background that make a difference. She forms a personality to fit the interpretations given her by the powerful, and she can forget her other self, interpreted in the vocabulary of the subordinate culture. So, a struggle against cultural domination is a struggle over which self-interpretations one can apply. It is a struggle over who one can be and often a struggle to know one*self*, to know what one needs and cares about.[12]

I suggested earlier that Lugones's "ontological pluralism" might be taken to treat each individual as constituted as several different "subjects" by several distinct Althusserian "ideologies." On Lugones's analysis, the oppressed person ends up in a state like (but less hopeless than) the Althusserian subject's, identifying with the conditions of her subjection. The parallel with Althusser is instructive, since for him the self-unity embodied in the subject of ideology is an illusory unity that is the condition of the individual's subjection. This clarifies why Lugones and Anzaldúa would prefer to inhabit the "borderlands," why they would want to reject a certain sort of self-unity. Their concern, I think, is that insofar as oppression effects divisions of the self, a unity of the self can be a false security—that is, it might be only an apparent unity achieved by forgetting one's other "selves," losing one's memory of "being another person in another reality." This sort of self-unity would be a full acceptance by an oppressed person of her oppressors' descriptions. It is the sort of unity that she might attain by forgetting utterly about her life in another reality and even quitting that reality entirely. The coercive nature of her social position would then be effectively hidden and that much more difficult to resist.[13] The sorts of unity that Lugones and Anzaldúa reject are specious sorts of unity—"unities" that depend on self-ignorance.

But a justified caution about false unities of the self is no threat to valuing the unity embodied in the possibility of taking one's many selves up into "one self-consciousness" (Kant 1965, B 132)—to adopt a Kantian idiom—or of articulating conflicting beliefs and desires in a way that does not occlude the conflict, but sees the conflicting attitudes as "all *mine*" (1965, B 134) and as in need of a resolution that does not consist just in embracing one set and rejecting another. This realization is implicit in Lugones's counsel that the bicultural person go "into the limen," and it hints at a plausible reading of Anzaldúa's claim that "nothing" is abandoned by the new *mestiza*. The new *mestiza*, she says,

> can be jarred out of ambivalence by an intense, and often painful, emotional event which inverts or resolves the ambivalence. I'm not sure exactly how. The work takes place underground—subconsciously. It is work that the soul performs. That focal point or fulcrum, that juncture where the mestiza stands, is where phenomena tend to collide. It is where the possibility of uniting all that is separate occurs. (1987, 79)

Lugones's stress on remembering oneself in another "reality" does not amount to embracing the self of the subordinate culture and cutting loose the self of the dominant culture, as if the former were the real, essential self, hidden by the obfuscating cloak of the ruling ideology. But to say that there is no essential self, or that the self has no essential unity, is not to say that there is neither self nor unity—any more than to say that there are no cultural essences is to say that there are no cultures. My discussion of Lugones is meant to show that in advocating a preservation of one's many selves and a going into the "limen" between "structures," Lugones tacitly advocates a kind of self-unity. Let me clarify this remark.

Unity: Its Possibility

The sort of self-unity I have in mind has Kantian roots.[14] Just as the transcendental unity of apperception grounds the fact, for Kant, that I can say of all the representations of which I can become conscious that they are "all *mine*" (1965, B 134), so the memory of one's various selves in different "realities" is linked with one's ability to say that they are all *my* selves. This "transcendental" unity should not be mistaken for the metaphysical unity that Lugones dismisses as a "transcendental self" (1990, 506). For Kant the original unity of apperception is a merely formal and general unity on which rests the possibility of the empirical unity of apperception in particular judgments. "The consciousness of myself in the representation 'I' is not an intuition, but a merely *intellectual* representation" (Kant 1965, B 278). Transcendental apperception is presupposed by the possibility of knowledge, as the grammatical subject (to use a non-Kantian term) of all my judgments. To mistake this condition for some kind of metaphysical *entity*—for example, a Cartesian substance—is to commit the error of the First Paralogism of Pure Reason (A 348/B 407).

But consider another objection. If no Cartesian substance underlies all my judgments, how can a single "grammatical subject" do so? Each judgment is distinct in time, and the series of my judgments presents only an ever growing plurality of grammatical subjects. Jacqueline Rose links this view with Lacan: "The 'I' with which we speak stands for our identity as subjects in language, but it is the least stable entity in language, since its meaning is purely a function of the moment of utterance. The 'I' can shift, and change places, because it only ever refers to whoever happens to be using it at the time" (1982, 31).[15]

The alleged instability of the "I" is, in part, an artifact of the Lacanian assumptions about saying and signifying that I criticized in the first section of this chapter. Doubts about "whether I am the same as that of which I speak" (1977, 165) get their impetus from the thesis that my utterance must always "signify *something quite other* than what it says" (1977, 155). Whatever the "I" refers to as subject of a judgment, it cannot be assumed to be any persistent thing that underlies these different judgments. As I argued, this contention rests on a modal fallacy, which confuses the possibility of using a word nonstandardly on any given occasion with the possibility of doing so on all occasions, and, in any event, it is not likely that someone who holds a view like Lugones's would want to avail herself of this sort of objection.[16]

Of course, there is more going on here. Rose emphasizes the fact that "I" is what philosophers usually call an indexical term; it "designates the subject in the sense that he is now speaking" (Lacan 1977, 298). But why should this fact entail any interesting worries about the unity of the self? It is certainly a consequence of its indexicality that "'I' is not the name of a person" (Wittgenstein 1968, §410). But that does not prevent me from teaching someone my name by saying, "I am M.H.," and it would not ordinarily make any sense for someone then to ask me, "Whom, exactly, do you mean?"[17]

If "I" refers to anything, when I use it, then it refers to *me*, and to most of my acquaintances it is no mystery who I am or where I can be found.[18] There is no more reliable way of finding me than by looking for my body, and this reliability is no merely contingent correlation. "The human body," as Wittgenstein says, "is the best picture of the human soul" (1968, 178). The concept of a person is internally related to the concept of a living human body. We learn to individuate particulars of the former kind by individuating particulars of the latter kind. But to say so is not to try to reduce personal identity to bodily identity or to answer the philosopher's question, "What conditions are necessary and sufficient to distinguish one person from another?" There is likely no answer for that query,[19] and I think that it is a mistake to try giving one. Asking what definitively distinguishes person A from person B is at least as odd as asking what definitively distinguishes two waves in a swimming pool. That the waves are distinct is clear enough when the wave crests are at opposite ends of the pool, but as they meet, there is simply no fact concerning where one ends and the other begins or to which wave a given water molecule belongs (see Haugeland 1982). Similarly, the fact that the ship of Theseus can be stripped and replanked as it crosses the ocean does not show that there is a defect in our concept of "ship" or in the notion of the "same" ship. Nor was the concept of "person" devised to do such "rigorous" work; it is not, however, therefore useless. "The sign-post is in order—if, under normal circumstances, it fulfils its purpose" (Wittgenstein 1968, §87).

The internal relation between the concept of a person and the concept of a living human body casts light on one dimension of personhood. But I began this section with the suggestion that the ideas of personal identity and self-unity are also intimately linked with what we might call the "grammatical unity of self-description." It was in response to this claim that the objection that the "I" is "shifting" and "unstable" arose, for I imagined a critic who doubted that a single "grammatical subject" could underlie all my judgments, any more than a Cartesian *res cogitans* could.

But to make such an objection would be to misunderstand the view that I am proposing. What grounds my distinct judgments (and my distinct *expressions* of my attitudes and sensations) at different times in a way that makes them judgments of one person is the possibility of my correctly judging further that they *are all my* judgments (or my expressions).[20] And if this seems merely to raise the same difficulty again, then the point can be rephrased: for me to be a competent speaker is for me to be able to say not only what I think and feel, but also what I have thought and felt.[21] Linguistic competence is itself a basic kind of self-unity, for only someone with a certain minimal ability to use language can suffer from Socratic self-ignorance, and only such a language user can be fragmented by oppression or threatened by specious self-unities.

Unity: Its Desirability

One might still want to ask whether anything but the barest version of my analogue for the unity of apperception is either possible or desirable. The perfect unity of subject and object in the *cogito*—on one interpretation—is a unity whose possibility I have already rejected. The moment we allow for self-ignorance we get rid of this ideal unity. But as long as we insist that we cannot be utterly mistaken about our own intentional attitudes, we allow for another sort of unity—the unity given in our particular self-articulations: that is, in our linguistic expressions of our intentional attitudes and sensations, and in our attempts at self-interpretation when faced with cases of Socratic self-ignorance, where the possibility of both the latter depends on the possibility of the former.

The additional question of the desirability of our self-articulations, then, must be understood in one of two ways: (1) Is it desirable that there *be* any self-articulations? (2) For a particular person in a particular context are the self-articulations at her disposal desirable? I shall return to the latter below. The former asks, at best, "Should a person try to understand herself?" and at worst, "Should there be such a thing as language, such things as knowledge and justification, such things as cultural practices, or would it be better if there were only 'mere brutes,' animals that were not language users?" I think that we should answer yes to both versions of the first question, but it is not a matter that I shall discuss here. The possibility of philosophical activity or of thinking of any sort demands a positive answer to at least the second version, and likely to the first.

Now, it is tempting to conclude from the considerations of this chapter that self-knowledge is always a good because it is agency-enhancing. My self-knowledge, my linguistic capacity to say what I think and feel, is an important element of my agency to the extent that we suppose that nonlingual creatures, prelingual persons, and some persons whose linguistic capacities have been seriously undermined do not count among those who should be held responsible for their actions. Additionally, it is the oppressed or psychically damaged person's capacity for self-interpretation, be it with or without the help of another, that holds out promise for dealing with threats to her agency.

But in particular cases, the only clear dependence relation that my discussion above need be taken to reveal is a dependence of agency on certain kinds of self-

interpretation. This suggests that some *erroneous* self-interpretations could be liberating or enabling and, conversely, that Socratic self-knowledge might sometimes even be a threat to agency.

I have to admit both possibilities, but doing so does not require that I suppose agency to have no interesting dependence on self-knowledge in many cases. This is partly due to the general dependence cited in the preceding paragraph. Although I have argued that self-knowledge claims, or first-person beliefs, can be wrong, I remain committed to the idea that I cannot be completely or mainly wrong about myself and still be a competent language user. If I am not a competent language user, then I have a diminished chance of self-interpretation and, so, a diminished capacity for agency, if any.

But I also think that often a false self-interpretation is likely to be liberating only if it tends over time to become true, or less distorted. Let me explain. In trying to cast off habits or urges that we find undesirable, we sometimes identify with certain of our desires in contrast to others. Embracing certain "self-identifying desires"[22] and viewing other desires as "not part of me," I effectively accept a self-description that is false. I *have* those desires of which I long to be rid, but they are not part of my ideal image of myself.[23] This gravitation to an ideal may be just what I need to overcome my unsavory urges. "I am not that sort of a person," I tell myself, and by so insisting I can sometimes change myself so that I no longer have the desires from which I sought relief, or at least, so that those desires no longer pull me with the same force. A false description has, partly through repeated and forceful affirmation, become a true one—or at least a less distorted one than it was. Adopting a false self-description, I have helped to liberate myself, but in the process the applicability of my self-description has also changed.

What if it had not? What if my distorted self-image did nothing to rid me of my compulsive desires? In such a case we meet with the sort of covertly coercive false unity of the self against which Lugones warns. In such a case I embrace a faulty self-description that serves to mask an underlying threat to my agency, reinforcing its efficacy by disguising its coercive nature.

Need this always be so? Maybe I wrongly believe that I can stop smoking at any time, but rationalize my smoking by saying that, all things considered, I just *prefer* to smoke. In some instances such self-deception (or mere self-ignorance) might be an advantage for my agency. Maybe I lead a stressful life without the chance to deal "properly" with my stress, and smoking helps me to cope. Trying to quit might be too much for me; it might send me into nervous collapse.

It may be appropriate to say here that a faulty self-description enhances my capacity for agency. But it does so under circumstances that present other threats to my agency. My self-ignorance helps here, because it lets me deal with other pressures in my life, pressures that might overwhelm me but for my distorted self-concept. This does not show that faulty descriptions can benefit my agency only if they stand opposed to other threats to my agency. Nor shall I try to find examples or arguments that would entail such a consequence. All that I wish to claim is that Socratic self-knowledge is very often agency-enhancing. That it is not always so can be no objection.[24]

A more interesting question in the present context, then, is whether an individual's self-articulations are desirable. Clearly, this issue must be settled in specific cases. As such, it is hard to detach from two more familiar questions: "How should I live my life?" and "What kinds of social order are desirable?" The former pertains to the kinds of self-articulations I should adopt from among those available to me. The latter pertains to what ways of articulating my attitudes *are* so available to me. If we can appeal to the desirability of a capacity for agency, then certain kinds of self-articulations do seem to be open to criticism. Certain *disunities* of the self plainly interfere with one's capacity to make rational assessments of one's situation and then to act on those assessments. And certain false unities—self-descriptions that mask debilitating self-divisions—seem likewise undesirable from this perspective.

My suggestion, then, might be summarized by saying that correct self-interpretations are often desirable, and that when they are not, some false self-predications may still be preferable to others. Perhaps we can, in turn, judge a society on the basis of the repertoire of articulations that it makes available to its citizens, especially to its least well-off. But here is not the place to examine these problems.

Notes

1. But see 1980a, §708.
2. See Szabados 1981a, 29 and 1981b, 606.
3. "Misrecognition," insists Lacan, "is not ignorance" (1988, 167), because "it cannot be conceived without correlative knowledge" (167). He continues: "There must surely be, behind this misrecognition, a kind of knowledge of what there is to misrecognize" (167).
4. Another apt comparison might be with Davidson's noncognitive account of metaphor. See Davidson 1984b, 245–64. I criticize Davidson's account in my 1998.
5. This modal fallacy is similar to the error of which Moore accused the British Idealists. See Chapter 2, note 5 and Moore 1993, 96f.
6. Multiple personality disorder, now known as dissociative identity disorder, is identified, in part, by the following diagnostic criteria: "A. The presence of two or more distinct identities or personality states (each with its own relatively enduring pattern of perceiving, relating to, and thinking about the environment and self). B. At least two of these identities or personality states recurrently take control of the person's behavior" (American Psychiatric Association 1994, 487).

Skeptics about this disorder need concern themselves only with the analogy that I am suggesting here, not with the actuality of such a disorder, on which nothing in my argument depends. For a sensitive and cautious assessment of issues surrounding the reality of multiple personality disorder, see Hacking 1986, 1991.

7. Quoted in West 1989, 142.
8. Quoted in West 1989, 143. Appiah (1985) argues that Du Bois retains a kind of racial essentialism; so if the self is conditioned by its "race" (a category which, Appiah shows, is illusory), it is unclear what sort of "merging" Du Bois has in mind. See West 1989, 138–50.

Some remarks from Du Bois's third autobiography are interesting in the present context. "Who and what is this I," he asks, "which in the last year looked on a torn world and tried to judge it?" Reflecting on his earlier autobiographies, written when he was fifty and seventy, he says: "One must . . . see these varying views as contradictions to truth, and not as final and complete authority. This book then is the Soliloquy of an old man on what he dreams his life has been as he sees it slowly drifting away; and what he would like others to believe." But despite acknowledging his fallibility and perspective he believes that he will be "near enough" the end of a full century before he dies "to speak with a certain sense of unity" (1968, 12f.).

9. Althusser would resist any such treatment, if it amounted to treating the "unconscious" as a "second consciousness," a move he classifies among "ideological misunderstandings" (1971, 208).

10. Althusser says that structures are themselves "de-centred," but, as we saw, it is doubtful that some of his other views fit with this remark.

11. I draw here on Chambers 1996.

12. It need not always be. It may be a struggle to find a better, but false, self-description or to learn what kind of person one wants to be, but is not yet. I return to these issues below.

13. I get the notion of "hidden coercion" from Campbell's account of "hidden compulsion." See Campbell 1979, 156–65.

14. See Hymers 1997a, 448–50. We might link Lugones's talk of remembering one's other selves to Locke's idea that personal identity depends on memory. Locke's mistake, and that of his critics, was to treat memory as a necessary and sufficient condition for identity, rather than as internally related to the concept of a person. See Locke 1975, bk. 2, chap. 27, §§6–26.

15. See Lacan 1977, 298.

16. It might be argued that certain versions of the liar paradox provide support for Lacan's decentered subject. When I say, "I am lying to you now," it might be contended that this involves some kind of splitting of the "I" into two subjects, "one who is lying and one who is not" (Rose 1982, 47 n. 12). But if I were to say such a thing, wouldn't the appropriate response be, "About *what*, exactly?" See my discussion of truth in Chapter 4.

17. Another can have doubts, of course, about whether I am *really* M.H., though usually only if such a person does not know me well or sees me from afar and wonders whether she mistakes me for someone else. And it would take extraordinary circumstances for *me* to have any doubts about whether I am M.H. But such pragmatic doubts are not what Rose has in mind.

18. For at least some of my self-ascriptions, it is not clear that the "I" functions as a referring term at all. This much can be argued to follow from the mitigated expressivism which I proposed in the preceding chapter. If one of the basic functions of first-person self-ascriptions is to *express* a sensation state by replacing some nonlinguistic behavior, such as a cry or a smile, then there is little reason to think of the "I" in "I am in pain" as *referring* in the way that "he" in a comparable third-person report refers to me. My cry, after all, does not refer to me, though it does draw attention to me.

Of course, expressive uses do not exhaust the field of self-ascriptions. And, as Hacker contends (1993, 221–28), it is probably an error to suppose that all nonexpressive uses of "I" can be made to fit a single model. ("I feel nauseated," uttered in answer to the query, "What's wrong with you?" is different from "I have a bump on my head," and neither is quite like, "*I* did it—it was I who broke the lamp!") So it would be hasty to insist that "I" never refers. For a discussion of these issues, see Hacker 1993, 207–28. Notice that it is consistent to claim that "I" does not refer in an expressive use and that it is *true* that I am in pain—just as it can be *true* that it is raining, even though the "it" does not refer to anything. Hacker (1993, 225) seems to waver on this point.

19. This is suggested by the puzzle cases that philosophers have created for every criterion of identity proposed: same body, same brain, same psychological profile, etc. See, e.g., Parfit 1984.

20. The *possibility* of such judgments, not any *actual* judgment, makes up this basic self-unity—though the former will not likely obtain without the latter. So the fact that I have not thought together my "consciousnesses" in a "single consciousness" does not mean that I lack self-unity. I shall not dwell on the sense of "possibility" that is relevant here.

21. The amnesiac may be unable to say what she has thought and felt, but this is not the same as *never* having been able to.

22. See Campbell 1979, 201–12. Campbell makes use of the notion of a true or real self, and one's self-identifying desires are correspondingly one's true or real desires. However, his use of these notions seems self-consciously normative, rather than metaphysical, so that there is no substantive conflict between his account and my own. As a matter of terminological preference I shall think of Campbell's "real self" as the self that I want to be, but may or may not yet be.

23. See Noddings 1984, 49–51. See also Taylor 1985a, 15–44 for a discussion that is relevant to these issues.

24. It also seems plausible that in the case of the deluded smoker a false self-description provides the means for coping, not just with preexisting threats to agency, but with preexisting false self-descriptions, incurred by those threats, but also reinforcing them. (The relation would be a dialectical one.) This would have to be established in particular cases.

Conclusion:
The Rhetoric of Neurosis

> *Disquiet in philosophy might be said to arise from looking at philosophy wrongly, from seeing it wrong, namely as if it were divided into (infinite) longitudinal strips instead of into (finite) cross strips. This inversion in our conception produces the greatest difficulty. So we try as it were to grasp the unlimited strips and complain that it cannot be done piecemeal. To be sure it cannot, if by a piece one means an infinite longitudinal strip. But it may well be done, if one means a cross-strip.—But in that case we never get to the end of our work!—Of course not, for it has no end.*
>
> —Ludwig Wittgenstein, *Zettel*

Philosophers have often thought that concepts such as "knowledge" and "truth" are appropriate objects for theoretical investigation. To ask, "What is knowledge?" or "What is truth?" it is said, is to ask a question to which we should expect a nontrivial answer, because knowledge and truth, like electromagnetism and biological speciation, are phenomena that possess hidden natures. To understand such manifest phenomena as lightning and the behavior of lodestone, or to understand how there should be such a diversity of living things in our neck of the universe, we need to formulate hypotheses whose truth would explain the occurrence of these phenomena, and we need to test those hypotheses against the available evidence, against the background of our other theoretical commitments, and against competing hypotheses that are purported to explain the same phenomena. Truth and knowledge, philosophical theoreticians assume, deserve similar treatment.

I have been concerned in this book with the negative task of showing how such philosophical theoreticism runs the permanent risk of epistemic neurosis and with the positive, "therapeutic" task of trying to redescribe some traditional problems of epistemology in a way that avoids theoreticism and its accompanying psycho-philosophical disorders. Overcoming such disorder, I have said, requires recognizing that such standard objects of philosophical inquiry as truth and knowledge are more like functional artifacts than they are like natural or metaphysical kinds.[1] Asking "What is truth?" or "What is knowledge?" is more like asking "What is a table?" than it is like asking "What is light?" or "What is an acid?" I understand what a table is by understanding its typical function, by being able to identify particular items as tables, not by having an explanatory theory that attributes certain intrinsic properties to objects in virtue of the possession of which they qualify as tables. I can investigate different acids and discover that their behavior is explained by their common possession of the property of being a proton donor. Another inquirer might propose a competing theory that leads us to disagree in certain cases about whether or not a particular compound is an acid. But someone who has frequent disagreements with co-linguists about whether or not particular objects are tables is better interpreted not as having an alternative, competing "theory" of tables, but as not understanding how the term *table* is typically used.

Truth and knowledge, I have suggested, fit the latter paradigm, not the former. Understanding what truth and knowledge are consists in understanding the functions that the terms *truth* and *knowledge* play in our epistemic practices. If *truth* and *knowledge* seem to differ from terms like *table* and *chair*, then that is because they are used in a greater variety of contexts whose salient features are more difficult to describe perspicuously. It is the complexity and variety of their functions that make truth and knowledge look like theoretical objects with hidden natures.

In Chapter 1, I drew a distinction between metaphysical realism and modest realism. The modest realist thinks that, to make sense of the objective and independent existence of the world around us, it is enough that we acknowledge that such a world existed before any of us was here to know about it and that it may well continue to exist after any of us is left to know about it. In between the primordial past and the mindless future we muddle along, making mistakes about the world around us, but not thereby falling into the delusion and ignorance that the skeptic would press on us. The metaphysical realist, on the contrary, holds that the independent reality of the world must be understood as entailing the explanatory possibility that I have always been a brain in a vat. But the metaphysical realist's responses to Putnam's argument against this view show that, although the strong objectivist's position is defined by its vulnerability to skeptical doubts, the strong objectivist must ignore those doubts or regard them as "uninteresting" in order to advance beyond his Cartesian starting point.

Throughout my discussion I have relied on a distinction between theoretical claims, or hypotheses, and nontheoretical claims. I have justified this distinction by appealing to an additional contrast between internal relations and external relations, a contrast I find employed for similar ends in Wittgenstein's later writings. For two instruments of language to be internally related, I proposed in Chapter 2, it is sufficient that an understanding of the use or role of one require an understanding of the use or role of the other. Instruments of language include not just words, but spatio-temporal objects and events that are often thought of as lying outside language. To vary the point, two objects or events are internally

Conclusion: The Rhetoric of Neurosis

related if in order to identify and describe one of them, I must also be able to identify and describe the other. I have contended that an important source of epistemic neurosis is a conflation of internal relations with external relations and a concomitant conflation of nontheoretical and theoretical claims—a conflation of statements with hypotheses, for it is a general methodological constraint on explanation that if I am to explain some given phenomenon, then I must regard it as *given*. That is, I must presuppose that I can identify and describe it independently of providing an explanation for it. I must assume that *explanandum* and *explanans* are related only externally.

To assume, then, as the metaphysical realist does, that my experience is related only externally to things in the world is to assume that I can identify and describe that experience without knowing anything about the world around me. Similarly, to assume that reference is an external relation—such as a causal one—is to assume that I can understand the use of any referring term without being able to identify and describe what it refers to.

In Chapter 3, I showed how this treatment of reference as an external relation leads to another case of epistemic neurosis. The causal theorist wants to explain how truth can be a correspondence between language and the world by reducing reference to an external, causal relation. However, by treating truth and reference as objects of theoretical explanation, the causal theorist issues an open invitation to alternative explanatory hypotheses, and the skeptic is waiting with bizarre alternatives that confer on our statements precisely the same truth-values conferred on them by a causal theory of reference—alternatives that are confirmed or disconfirmed by exactly the same evidence that confirms of disconfirms the causal theorist's story. The very activity of trying to give empirical explanations of truth and reference is epistemically neurotic, because it induces skeptical worries that undermine the goal of such explanation. This, I suggested, is the real point of Putnam's "model-theoretic" argument against the correspondence theory of truth.

To dispense with theories of truth and knowledge is to see our experience of things in the world as internally related to those things. I can neither identify nor understand my experience of the world without having some understanding of things in the world. Skeptical doubts simply do not arise for this conception of experience. Similarly, I can understand the use of a nontheoretical referring term only if I also understand what its referent is. Reference is, paradigmatically, an internal relation between word and object, even if in the case of theoretical terms like *electron* we allow this condition to lapse. Skepticism is not refuted by these considerations, but it is rendered merely optional, of interest only to those who do not resist the substantive assumption that truth and knowledge are theoretical concepts.

The general constraint that one must be able to identify and describe any phenomenon that one seeks to explain—independently of one's giving the explanation—resurfaces in the would-be relativist's attempt to justify her belief in the possibility of alternative conceptual schemes, as my examination in Chapter 5 of Davidson's argument against conceptual relativism showed. Metaphysical realism and causal theories of reference are not the only positions that are rooted in theoreticism about truth and knowledge. Contemporary relativism, no less, depends on the strong objectivist's assumptions in a number of ways: (1) by trying to offer an alternative theory of truth and knowledge; (2) by joining the substantive correspondence theorist in treating the relation between words and the world as an external relation; (3) by joining the metaphysical realist and the traditional epistemologist in thinking of our experience as related to the world only externally; and (4) by conflating metaphysical realism with modest realism, and both of these views with scientism.

The second and third ways, I argued, are the proper objects of Davidson's criticisms of the very idea of a conceptual scheme, for the conceptual relativist assumes the possibility of identifying true statements in languages that are thought not to be understandable to outsiders, and she is also committed to the existence of some scheme-neutral experiential content that could serve as undifferentiated matter for a variety of incommensurable conceptual forms and a variety of incommensurable experiences.

The fourth way, I argued in Chapter 6, mistakes historically contingent alliances of realism with scientism—in analytic philosophy and in Marxist theory—for an internal, conceptual connection.

This mistake ramifies further, for it prompts the relativist critic to develop worries about the possibility of self-knowledge. If only those claims that can pass muster with science count as knowledge, then individual experience seems to carry little weight in the epistemic balance. But here the would-be relativist is joined by critics of contemporary anti-individualism about intentional phenomena, who fear that first-person authority must evaporate in the way supposed by Ryle if we think of intentional content as individuated by aspects of a knower's natural and social environments.

In Chapter 7, I argued that Burge's attempt to alleviate these worries fails because it clings to metaphysical realism. By allowing the real possibility of the skeptic's scenarios, Burge tacitly admits the "Cartesian" view that we are authoritative about what our intentional attitudes would be in a definite range of counterfactual situations, and this admission is incompatible with his efforts to pry the skeptic's counterfactual situations apart from those relevant to assessing the counterfactual contents of our attitudes and of our "cogito-like thoughts." Abandoning strong objectivism in favor of modest realism, however, puts us in a position to make sense of non-Socratic self-knowledge as a kind of "knowing how," and to understand Socratic self-knowledge and self-ignorance as presupposing such non-Socratic self-knowledge. In Chapter 8, I extended this claim to argue that proponents of the "fragmented self" implicitly rely on a grammatical unity of self-description. The kind of self-unity that is feared by such thinkers is really a specious unity that depends crucially on self-ignorance.

My criticisms of theoreticism in philosophy invite a natural objection. What of my modest realism? Is it not a theory of a sort? And is it not, therefore, as vulnerable to the diagnosis of epistemic neurosis as metaphysical realism or relativism? Given that "modest realism" is merely the view that we can make mistakes and that the world existed before anyone was around to have knowledge of it, I do not find the charge well motivated. If one wants to say that to hold that knowledge and truth are not things of the sort about which one needs a theory is *itself* to hold a theory, then I am inclined to respond that one has again conflated statements with hypotheses. My modest realism does not see experience, or knowledge, or reference, or truth as unified phenomena whose hidden natures remain to be revealed by well-confirmed hypotheses. Could I be wrong about this? Of course, but that does not make my claim a theoretical one, any more than my belief that I have enough money for my groceries is a theoretical one. *Call* it a theory, if you want, but there is no obvious reason to do so. No relevant facts are changed by adopting a new notation.[2]

There is another sort of concern that my position may inspire. Epistemic neurosis, I have maintained, is the natural philosophical malady of those who are swept away by the urge to theorize, when what is called for is a clear overview of how our concepts function. Such compulsive theoreticism, I have claimed, leads to a confrontation with skeptical doubts that undermine the very theory whose necessity seemed so urgent. To deal with this malady I have proposed a course of philosophical therapy that tries to preserve the virtues of realism and relativism without falling back into psycho-philosophical disorder. But all this rhetoric of mental instability will, no doubt, seem *cheap* to some—not unlike J. N. Findlay's dismissal of Wittgenstein's writings as "schizoid" (1984, 21).

Let me remind readers, first, that it is not my intention to mock or belittle the views I have been criticizing here. What I am most interested in drawing attention to is the way in which certain sorts of philosophical problems and solutions can exercise an overwhelming attraction. It is an attraction that I feel as much as anyone trained in the traditions of Western philosophical thinking. Moreover, I think that my use of the term *neurosis* has been reasonable and discriminating, since I have tried in its application to criticize philosophical positions for entertaining theses—especially skeptical theses—that they cannot afford to take seriously, if their own positive proposals are to have a chance of cognitive success. I have, moreover, tried to show in some detail how these epistemic neuroses reveal themselves in the views I have examined, and I have suggested ways of avoiding the temptations that they present. That I have indulged in rhetoric and that my rhetoric is designed to persuade I do not deny. But it is part of my position that no clean break can be found between logic and rhetoric. The idea of a pristine language, appearing as an unfettered manifestation of "pure reason," is just the idea of a language whose meanings transcend our linguistic and epistemic capacities. On the other hand, I do not seek license to discard the idea of good reasoning, and I do not think that my arguments (or my rhetoric) depend on doing so.

Of course, the metaphor of neurosis that I have used invokes a classification no longer employed by psychiatrists, psychologists, and therapists.[3] Were I to search for a successor metaphor, maybe I could find something in the lexicon of psychiatric disorders that would fit the case even more suggestively than *neurosis,* or perhaps I could find a way of distinguishing a number of different epistemic disorders—or, perhaps no successor would bear the weight that I have placed on *neurosis*.

When Hume leaves his study, he tells us, his skeptical worries vanish, pushed out by the forces of habit and custom: "I dine, I play a game of back-gammon, I converse, and am merry with my friends; and when after three or four hour's amusement, I wou'd return to these speculations, they appear so cold, and strain'd, and ridiculous, that I cannot find in my heart to enter into them any farther" (1978, 269). He leads a double existence, dictated in a way by the "opinion" of the same name, which—philosophically—is "only a palliative remedy" (211). And this is not just any double existence; it is an intractable one, if we take seriously the two selves that are in conflict. The skeptical self cannot acknowledge the merrymaker, and the merrymaker cannot take the skeptic seriously. But, as I suggested in Chapter 3, the division at work here is not merely between skeptic and merrymaker; it is between skeptic and theory-building philosopher. Even while entertaining skeptical doubts, the philosopher "doesn't believe what he says, doesn't doubt when he says he's not sure" (Wisdom 1957, 174). It is almost as though the philosopher at work has two different personalities, each dependent on the other, and neither able to function entirely on its own.

In Joan Frances Casey's autobiographical account of her life with multiple personality disorder the tale told by one of her former "personalities" alternates with the journal entries of her therapist, Lynn Wilson. Wilson describes the paradoxical state of Casey's psychic affairs after a year and a half of treatment:

> I am continually struck by the essential contradiction in Jo Casey. She is both terribly fragmented and tremendously functional. When I first heard the Kendra personality (who rescues Renee when she gets in over her head) say, "We can do anything!" I considered it bravado and exaggeration. Now I see that, in comparison with most people, Kendra is right. The system of personalities can, by most criteria, do anything they attempt to do, as long as no one personality is expected to carry on for an extended period. (Casey and Wilson 1991, 125)[4]

Do philosophers suffer from an epistemic dissociative disorder? Another passage from Casey's autobiography tempts me with one last rhetorical flourish:

> Jo felt let down by her mind, by her extraordinary analytic abilities. She had always thought she was smart and had approached any intellectual challenge with glee. When presented with the philosophical hypothesis that people could be nothing more than minds in a vat, hallucinating reality, Jo wasn't perturbed or perplexed.

Amnesia and the familiar feeling of "I just got dropped in here somehow" enabled Jo to see how this improbable hypothesis served as an analogy for her life. She figured that she could be a very contented mind-in-a-vat, but Lynn had forced her to accept she wasn't alone in a vat or in her body. This was a problem that she could not puzzle. (Casey and Wilson 1991, 85)

Notes

1. Cf. Williams 1996c, 111.

2. "By a new notation no facts of geography are changed" (Wittgenstein 1958, 57).

3. Since 1980 the American Psychiatric Association has recognized a number of "dissociative disorders." This classification now includes such maladies as dissociative identity disorder (formerly multiple personality disorder), dissociative amnesia, dissociative fugue, and depersonalization disorder. These are all disorders that would once have been classified as "neuroses," since their sufferers retain some grip on reality and can be conscious of their troubles, though unable to overcome them without help. See American Psychiatric Association 1994, 477–81.

4. Let me reiterate my caution of Chapter 8 that my view does not take the reality of multiple personality disorder for granted, though I do find compelling Hacking's carefully qualified conclusion that multiple personality is "a way to be crazy, at least in an industrial/romantic, Protestant society" (1991, 844).

Credits

Excerpts from the following publications were reprinted with permission:

Davidson, Donald. 1984. *Inquiries into Truth and Interpretation.* Reprinted by permission of Oxford University Press.

Devitt, Michael. 1997. *Realism and Truth.* 2d ed. Copyright © 1984 by Princeton University Press. Reprinted by permission of Princeton University Press.

Hymers, Michael. 1997. "Realism and Self-Knowledge: A Problem for Burge." *Philosophical Studies* 86, no. 3: 303–325. Reprinted with kind permission from Kluwer Academic Publishers.

Hymers, Michael. 1996. "Internal Relations and Analyticity: Wittgenstein and Quine." *Canadian Journal of Philosophy* 26, no. 4: 591–612. Reprinted by permission of University of Calgary Press.

Lacan, Jacques. 1977. *Écrits: A Selection.* Trans. by Alan Sheridan. Copyright © 1966 by Editions du Seuil. English translation copyright © 1977 by Tavistock Publications. Reprinted in North America by permission of W. W. Norton & Company, Inc. Reprinted outside North America by permission of Editions du Seuil.

Putnam, Hillary. 1981. *Reason, Truth and History.* Reprinted by permission of Cambridge University Press.

Seller, Anne. 1988. "Realism vs. Relativism: Toward a Politically Adequate Epistemology." In *Feminist Perspectives in Philosophy.* Edited by Morwenna Griffiths and Margaret Whitford. Reprinted in North America by permission of Indiana University Press. Reprinted outside North America by permission of Macmillan Press Ltd.

Wittgenstein, Ludwig. 1981. *Zettel.* 2d ed. Edited by G. E. M. Anscombe and G. H. von Wright. Trans. by G. E. M. Anscombe. Reprinted by permission of Blackwell Publishers.

Wittgenstein, Ludwig. 1968. *Philosophical Investigations.* 3d ed. Edited by G. E. M. Anscombe and R. Rhees. Trans. by G. E. M. Anscombe. Reprinted by permission of Blackwell Publishers.

Reference List

Alcoff, Linda, and Elizabeth Potter, eds. 1993. *Feminist Epistemologies*. New York: Routledge.
Allen, Barry. 1993. *Truth in Philosophy*. Cambridge, Mass.: Harvard University Press.
Althusser, Louis. 1969. *For Marx*. Trans. Ben Brewster. New York: Pantheon Books.
_____. 1971. *Lenin and Philosophy and Other Essays*. Trans. Ben Brewster. New York: Monthly Review Press.
American Psychiatric Association. 1994. *Diagnostic and Statistical Manual of Mental Disorders*. 4th ed. Washington, D.C.: American Psychiatric Association.
Anderson, David. 1992. "What Is Realistic About Putnam's Internal Realism?" *Philosophical Topics* 20: 49–83.
Anzaldúa, Gloria. 1987. *Borderlands/La Frontera: The New Mestiza*. San Francisco: Spinsters/Aunt Lute.
Appiah, Anthony. 1985. "The Uncompleted Argument: Du Bois and the Illusion of Race." *Critical Inquiry* 12: 21–37.
Arrington, Robert L. 1996. "Ontological Commitment." In Arrington and Glock, eds. (1996), 196–211.
Arrington, Robert L., and Hans-Johann Glock, eds. 1996. *Wittgenstein and Quine*. London: Routledge.
Austin, J. L. 1964. "Truth." In Pitcher, ed. (1964), 18–31.
Ayer, A. J. 1952. *Language, Truth and Logic*. 2nd ed. New York: Dover.
_____, ed. 1959. *Logical Positivism*. Glencoe, Ill.: The Free Press.
Baier, Annette. 1986. "Trust and Antitrust." *Ethics* 96: 231–260.
Baker, G. P., and P. M. S. Hacker. 1984a. *Language, Sense and Nonsense*. Oxford: Blackwell.
_____. 1984b. *Scepticism, Rules and Language*. Oxford: Blackwell.
_____. 1985. *Wittgenstein: Rules, Grammar and Necessity*. Oxford: Blackwell.
Barnes, Barry, and David Bloor. 1982. "Relativism, Rationalism and the Sociology of Knowledge." In Hollis and Lukes, eds. (1982), 21–47.
Barwise, John, and John Perry. 1983. *Situations and Attitudes*. Cambridge, Mass.: MIT Press.
Baynes, Kenneth, James Bohman, and Thomas McCarthy, eds. 1987. *After Philosophy: End or Transformation?* Cambridge, Mass.: MIT Press.
Benton, Ted. 1984. *The Rise and Fall of Structural Marxism: Althusser and His Influence*. London: Macmillan.
Bilgrami, Akeel. 1992. "Self-Knowledge and Resentment." Department of Philosophy, Columbia University.
Bouveresse, Jacques. 1995. *Wittgenstein Reads Freud: The Myth of the Unconscious*. Trans. Carol Cosman. Princeton: Princeton University Press.

Bové, Paul A. 1990. "Discourse." In Lentricchia and McLaughlin, eds. (1990), 50–65.
Boyd, Richard N. 1973. "Realism, Underdetermination, and a Causal Theory of Evidence." *Nous* 7: 1–12.
Brandom, Robert. 1987. "Pragmatism, Phenomenalism and Truth Talk." *Midwest Studies in Philosophy* 12: 75–93.
Brittan, Gordon. 1978. *Kant's Theory of Science*. Princeton: Princeton University Press.
Brueckner, Anthony. 1986. "Brains in a Vat." *Journal of Philosophy* 83: 148–67.
Burge, Tyler. 1979. "Individualism and the Mental." *Midwest Studies in Philosophy* 4: 73–121.
_____. 1981. "Other Bodies." In *Thought and Object*, ed. A. Woodfield. Oxford: Oxford University Press, 97–120.
_____. 1982. "Two Thought Experiments Reviewed." *Notre Dame Journal of Formal Logic* 23: 284–93.
_____. 1986. "Cartesian Error and the Objectivity of Perception." In *Subject, Thought, and Context*, ed. P. Pettit and J. McDowell. Oxford: Clarendon, 117–36.
_____. 1988. "Individualism and Self-Knowledge." *Journal of Philosophy* 85: 649–63.
Callinicos, Alex. 1995. *Theories and Narratives: Reflections on the Philosophy of History*. Durham, N.C.: Duke University Press.
Campbell, Richmond. 1979. *Self-Love and Self-Respect: A Philosophical Study of Egoism*. Ottawa: Canadian Library of Philosophy.
_____. 1998. *Illusions of Paradox: A Feminist Epistemology Naturalized*. Lanham, Md.: Rowman and Littlefield.
Canfield, J. V. 1981. *Wittgenstein: Language and World*. Amherst: University of Massachusetts Press.
Carnap, Rudolf. 1956. *Meaning and Necessity*, 2d ed. Chicago: University of Chicago Press.
_____. 1959. "The Elimination of Metaphysics Through Logical Analysis of Language." In Ayer, ed. (1959), 60–81.
_____. 1963. "Intellectual Autobiography." In *The Philosophy of Rudolf Carnap*, ed. P. A. Schilpp. LaSalle, Ill.: Open Court, 3–84.
Casey, Joan Frances, and Lynn Wilson. 1991. *The Flock*. New York: Knopf.
Cavell, Stanley. 1979. *The Claim of Reason*. Oxford: Oxford University Press.
Chambers, Ross. 1991. *Room for Maneuver: Reading (the) Oppositional (in) Narrative*. Chicago: University of Chicago Press.
_____. 1996. "No Montagues Without Capulets: Some Thoughts on 'Cultural Identity.'" In *Explorations in Difference: Law, Culture, and Politics*, ed. Jonathan Hart and Richard W. Bauman. Toronto: University of Toronto Press, 25–66.
Chisholm, Roderick. 1989. *Theory of Knowledge*. 3d ed. Englewood Cliffs, N.J.: Prentice-Hall.
Chomsky, Noam. 1969. "Quine's Empirical Assumptions." In *Words and Objections: Essays on the Work of W. V. Quine*, ed. Donald Davidson and Jaako Hintikka. Dordrecht: Reidel, 53–68.
Church, Alonzo. 1956. *Introduction to Mathematical Philosophy*, Vol. 1. Princeton: Princeton University Press.
Clark, Maudmarie. 1990. *Nietzsche on Truth and Philosophy*. Cambridge: Cambridge University Press.
Code, Lorraine. 1991. *What Can She Know?* Ithaca: Cornell University Press.

Coffa, J. Alberto. 1991. *The Semantic Tradition from Kant to Carnap*, ed. L. Wessels. Cambridge: Cambridge University Press.
Cohen, G. A. 1978. *Karl Marx's Theory of History: A Defence*. Princeton: Princeton University Press.
Coppock, Paul. 1987. "Putnam's Transcendental Argument." *Pacific Philosophical Quarterly* 68: 14–28.
D'Amico, Robert. 1989. *Historicism and Knowledge*. New York: Routledge.
Davidson, Donald. 1982. "Paradoxes of Irrationality." In *Philosophical Essays on Freud*, ed. R. Wollheim and J. Hopkins. Cambridge: Cambridge University Press, 289–305.
_____. 1984a. "First Person Authority." *Dialectica* 38 (1984): 101–11.
_____. 1984b. *Inquiries into Truth and Interpretation*. Oxford: Clarendon.
_____. 1986a. "A Coherence Theory of Truth and Knowledge." In LePore, ed. (1986), 306-19.
_____. 1986b. "A Nice Derangement of Epitaphs." In LePore, ed. (1986), 433–46.
_____. 1987. "Knowing One's Own Mind." *Proceedings and Addresses of the American Philosophical Association* 60: 441–58.
_____. 1989. "The Myth of the Subjective." In *Relativism: Interpretation and Confrontation*, ed. M. Krausz. Notre Dame, Ind.: University of Notre Dame Press, 159–72.
_____. 1990. "The Structure and Content of Truth." *Journal of Philosophy* 87: 279-328.
_____. 1996. "The Folly of Trying to Define Truth." *Journal of Philosophy* 93: 263–78.
Davies, David. 1995. "Putnam's Brain-Teaser." *Canadian Journal of Philosophy* 25: 203–28.
Derrida, Jacques. 1988. "Afterword: Toward an Ethic of Discussion." Trans. S. Weber. In *Limited Inc.*, ed. G. Graff. Evanston, Ill.: Northwestern University Press, 111–60.
Descartes, René. 1984. *The Philosophical Writings of Descartes*. 2 vols. Trans. J. Cottingham, R. Stoothoff, and D. Murdoch. Cambridge: Cambridge University Press.
Devitt, Michael. 1981. *Designation*. New York: Columbia University Press.
_____. 1984. *Realism and Truth*. Oxford: Blackwell.
_____. 1997. *Realism and Truth*. 2d ed. with a new afterword. Princeton: Princeton University Press.
Devitt, Michael, and Kim Sterelny. 1987. *Language and Reality: An Introduction to the Philosophy of Language*. Oxford: Blackwell.
Dilman, Ilham. "Existence and Theory: Quine's Conception of Reality." In Arrington and Glock, eds. (1996), 173–95.
Dretske, Fred. 1970. "Epistemic Operators." *Journal of Philosophy* 67: 1007–023.
Du Bois, W. E. B. 1961. *The Souls of Black Folk*. New York: Fawcett.
_____. 1968. *The Autobiography of W. E. B. Du Bois: A Soliloquy on Viewing My Life from the Last Decade of Its First Century*, ed. Herbert Aptheker. N.p.: International Publishers.
Dummett, Michael. 1979. *Truth and Other Enigmas*. Cambridge: Cambridge University Press.
_____. 1996. "An Anti-Realist Perspective on Language, Thought, Logic and the History of Analytic Philosophy: An Interview with Michael Dummett." By Fabrice Pataut. *Philosophical Investigations* 19: 1–33.
Dwyer, Philip. 1990. *Sense and Subjectivity: A Study of Wittgenstein and Merleau-Ponty*. Leiden: Brill.
Eagleton, Terry. 1991. *Ideology: An Introduction*. London: Verso.

Ebbs, Gary. 1997. *Rule-Following and Realism*. Cambridge, Mass.: Harvard University Press.
Farrell, Frank B. 1994. *Subjectivity, Realism and Postmodernism: The Recovery of the World in Recent Philosophy*. Cambridge: Cambridge University Press.
Feyerabend, Paul K. 1987. *Farewell to Reason*. London: Verso.
———. 1988. *Against Method*. Rev. ed. London: Verso.
Field, Hartry. 1972. "Tarski's Theory of Truth." *Journal of Philosophy* 69: 347–75.
———. 1982. "Realism and Relativism." *Journal of Philosophy* 79: 553–67.
Findlay, J. N. 1984. *Wittgenstein: A Critique*. London: Routledge & Kegan Paul.
Foucault, Michel. 1980. "Truth and Power." In *Power/Knowledge*, ed. C. Gordon, trans. C. Gordon et al. New York: Pantheon.
———. 1989. *Foucault Live*. Ed. Sylvére Lotringer. Trans. J. Johnston. New York: Semiotext(e).
Frege, Gottlob. 1984. *Collected Papers on Mathematics, Logic and Philosophy*. Ed. B. McGuinness. Various trans. Oxford: Blackwell.
Freud, Sigmund. 1962. *Two Short Accounts of Psycho-Analysis*. Harmondsworth, U.K.: Penguin.
———. 1963. *The Complete Psychological Works of Sigmund Freud*. Vol. 16, *Introductory Lectures on Psycho-Analysis*. Part 3. Ed. J. Strachey. Trans. J. Strachey et al. London: Hogarth Press.
Frye, Marilyn. 1983. *The Politics of Reality: Essays in Feminist Theory*. Trumansburg, N.Y.: Crossing Press.
Gauthier, David. 1986. *Morals by Agreement*. Oxford: Clarendon.
Gettier, Edmund L. 1963. "Is Justified True Belief Knowledge?" *Analysis* 23, no. 6: 121–23.
Goldman, Alvin I. 1986. *Epistemology and Cognition*. Cambridge, Mass.: Harvard University Press.
Grandy, Richard. 1973. "Reference, Meaning and Belief." *Journal of Philosophy* 70: 439–52.
Grice, H. P., and P. F. Strawson. 1956. "In Defense of a Dogma." *Philosophical Review* 65: 141–58.
Gueroult, Martial. 1984. *Descartes' Philosophy Interpreted According to the Order of Reasons. Vol. 1: The Soul and God*. Trans. R. Ariew. Minneapolis: University of Minnesota Press.
Gutting, Gary. 1989. *Michel Foucault's Archaeology of Scientific Reason*. Cambridge: Cambridge University Press.
Habermas, Jürgen. 1970. *Toward a Rational Society*. Trans. J. J. Shapiro. Boston: Beacon.
———. 1971. *Knowledge and Human Interests*. Trans. J. J. Shapiro. Boston: Beacon.
———. 1973. "Wahrheitstheorien." In *Wirklichkeit und Reflexion*, ed. H. Fahrenbach. Pfullingen: Verlag Günther Neske, 211–66.
———. 1987a. *The Philosophical Discourse of Modernity*. Trans. F. G. Lawrence. Cambridge, Mass.: MIT Press.
———. 1987b. "Philosophy as Stand-In and Interpreter." Trans. C. Lenhardt. In Baynes, Bowman, and McCarthy, eds. (1987), 296–315.
Hacker, P. M. S. 1972. *Insight and Illusion*. Oxford: Clarendon.
———. 1993. *Wittgenstein: Meaning and Mind*, Part I. Oxford: Blackwell.
———. 1996a. On Davidson's Idea of a Conceptual Scheme." *Philosophical Quarterly* 46, no. 184: 289–307.

———. 1996b. *Wittgenstein's Place in Twentieth-Century Analytic Philosophy.* Oxford: Blackwell.
Hacking, Ian. 1982. "Language, Truth and Reason." In Hollis and Lukes, eds. (1982), 48–66.
———. 1983. *Representing and Intervening: Introductory Topics in the Philosophy of Natural Science.* Cambridge: Cambridge University Press.
———. 1986. "The Invention of Split Personalities: An Illustration of Michel Foucault's Doctrine of the Constitution of the Subject." In *Human Nature and Natural Knowledge,* ed. A. Donagan, A. N. Perovich, Jr., and M. V. Wedin. Dordrecht: Reidel, 63–85.
———. 1991. "Two Souls in One Body." *Critical Inquiry* 17: 838–67.
Hahn, Hans, Otto Neurath, and Rudolf Carnap. 1973. "The Scientific Conception of the World: The Vienna Circle." Trans. P. Foulkes and M. Neurath. In *Otto Neurath: Empiricism and Sociology,* ed. M. Neurath and R. S. Cohen. Dordrecht: Reidel, 299–318.
Harman, Gilbert. 1965. "The Inference to the Best Explanation." *Philosophical Review* 74: 88–95.
Haugeland, John. 1982. "Weak Supervenience." *American Philosophical Quarterly* 19: 93-103.
Heldke, Lisa. 1988. "Recipes for Theory Making." *Hypatia* 3, no. 2: 15–29.
Hempel, C. G. 1935. "On the Logical Positivists' Theory of Truth." *Analysis* 2, no. 4: 49–59.
———. 1965. "The Function of General Laws in History." In *Aspects of Scientific Explanation and Other Essays in the Philosophy of Science.* New York: The Free Press, 231–43.
Hockney, Donald. 1975. "The Bifurcation of Scientific Theories and Indeterminacy of Translation." *Philosophy of Science* 42: 411–27.
Hollis, Martin, and Steven Lukes, eds. 1982. *Rationality and Relativism.* Cambridge, Mass.: MIT Press.
Horkheimer, Max. 1982. *Critical Theory: Selected Essays.* New York: Continuum.
Horwich, Paul. 1990. *Truth.* Oxford: Blackwell.
Hume, David. 1978. *A Treatise of Human Nature.* 2d ed. Ed. L. A. Selby-Bigge. Oxford: Blackwell.
Hymers, Michael. 1991. "Something Less Than Paradise: The Magic of Modal Realism." *Australasian Journal of Philosophy* 69: 251–63.
———. 1996a. "Internal Relations and Analyticity: Wittgenstein and Quine." *Canadian Journal of Philosophy* 26, no. 4: 591–612.
———. 1996b. "Truth and Metaphor in Rorty's Liberalism." *International Studies in Philosophy* 28, no. 4: 1–21.
———. 1997a. "Kant's Private-Clock Argument." *Kant-Studien* 88, no. 4: 442–61.
———. 1997b. "Realism and Self-Knowledge: A Problem for Burge." *Philosophical Studies* 86: 303–25.
———. 1998. "Metaphor, Cognitivity and Meaning-Holism." *Philosophy and Rhetoric.* 31, no. 4: 266–82.
———. 1999. "Being and Being True: Does Practice Make Any Difference?" *Idealistic Studies* 29, no. 1-2: 33–51.
Jacobsen, Rockney. 1996. "Wittgenstein on Self-Knowledge and Self-Expression." *Philosophical Quarterly* 46: 12–30.
James, William. 1974. *Pragmatism.* New York: New American Library.
Joachim, H. H. 1969. *The Nature of Truth.* New York: Greenwood Press.
Kant, Immanuel. 1965. *Critique of Pure Reason.* Trans. N. Kemp Smith. New York: St. Martin's.

Kinghan, Michael. 1986. "The External World Sceptic Escapes Again." *Philosophia* 16: 161–66.
Kripke, Saul A. 1980. *Naming and Necessity.* Cambridge, Mass.: Harvard University Press.
———. 1982. *Wittgenstein on Rules and Private Language.* Cambridge, Mass.: Harvard University Press.
Kuhn, Thomas. 1970. *The Structure of Scientific Revolutions.* 2d ed. Chicago: University of Chicago Press.
Lacan, Jacques. 1977. *Écrits: A Selection.* Trans. A. Sheridan. New York: Norton.
———. 1988. *The Seminar of Jacques Lacan.* Book 1. Ed. J.-A. Miller. Trans. J. Forrester. Cambridge: Cambridge University Press.
"Lagos men fear rumor: mob attacks spurred by tales of genital thefts." *Calgary Herald*, 30 October 1990, F12.
Leibniz, G. W. 1981. *New Essays on Human Understanding.* Ed. and trans. J. Bennett and P. Remnant. Cambridge: Cambridge University Press.
Lenin, V. I. 1962. *Materialism and Empirio-Criticism.* Ed. C. Dutt. Trans. A. Fineberg. Vol. 14 of *Collected Works.* London: Lawrence and Wishart.
Lentricchia, Frank, and Thomas McLaughlin, eds. 1990. *Critical Terms for Literary Study.* Chicago: University of Chicago Press.
LePore, Ernest, ed. 1986. *Truth and Interpretation: Perspectives on the Philosophy of Donald Davidson.* Oxford: Blackwell.
LePore, Ernest, and Barry Loewer. 1988. "A Putnam's Progress." *Midwest Studies in Philosophy* 12: 459–73.
Lewis, David K. 1969. *Convention: A Philosophical Study.* Cambridge, Mass.: Harvard University Press.
———. 1983. "New Work for a Theory of Universals." *Australasian Journal of Philosophy* 61: 343–77.
———. 1984. "Putnam's Paradox." *Australasian Journal of Philosophy* 62: 221–36.
———. 1987. *On the Plurality of Worlds.* Oxford: Blackwell.
Linsky, Bernard. 1992. "A Note on the 'Carving Up Content' Principle in Frege's Theory of Sense." *Notre Dame Journal of Formal Logic* 33: 126–35.
Locke, John. 1975. *An Essay Concerning Human Understanding.* Ed. P. H. Nidditch. Oxford: Clarendon.
Lovibond, Sabina. 1983. *Realism and Imagination in Ethics.* Oxford: Blackwell.
Lugones, Maria C. 1990. "Structure/Antistructure and Agency under Oppression." *Journal of Philosophy* 87: 500–507.
———. 1992. "On *Borderlands/La Frontera*: An Interpretive Essay." *Hypatia* 7, no. 4: 31–37.
MacIntyre, Alasdair. 1987. "Relativism, Power and Philosophy." In Baynes, Bohman, and McCarthy, eds. (1987), 385–411.
Mackie, J. L. 1977. *Ethics.* Harmondsworth, U.K.: Penguin.
MacKinnon, Catharine A. 1982. "Feminism, Marxism, Method, and the State: An Agenda for Theory." *Signs* 7: 515–44.
———. 1987. *Feminism Unmodified: Discourses on Life and Law.* Cambridge, Mass.: Harvard University Press.
Malachowski, Alan. 1986. "Metaphysical Realist Semantics: Some Moral Desiderata." *Philosophia* 16: 167–74.

Malpas, J. E. 1992. *Donald Davidson and the Mirror of Meaning*. Cambridge: Cambridge University Press.

Mannheim, Karl. 1936. *Ideology and Utopia*. Trans. L. Wirth and E. Shils. New York: Harcourt Brace Jovanovich.

Marcuse, Herbert. 1964. *One-Dimensional Man*. Boston: Beacon.

Martin, Robert M. 1987. *The Meaning of Language*. Cambridge, Mass.: MIT Press.

———. 1992. *There Are Two Errors in the the Title of This Book*. Peterborough, Ontario: Broadview.

Marx, Karl. 1967. *Capital*. Vol. 1. 3d ed. Ed. Friedrich Engels. Trans. S. Moore and E. Aveling. New York: International Publishers.

Marx, Karl, and Friedrich Engels. 1975–. *Karl Marx, Friedrich Engels: Collected Works*. 47 vols. Various trans. New York: International Publishers.

McDowell, John. 1982. "Criteria, Defeasibility and Knowledge." *Proceedings of the British Academy* 68: 455–79.

———. 1994. *Mind and World*. Cambridge, Mass.: Harvard University Press.

McGeer, Victoria. 1996. "Is 'Self-Knowledge' an Empirical Problem? Renegotiating the Space of Philosophical Explanation." *Journal of Philosophy* 93: 483–515.

McGinn, Colin. 1979. "An A Priori Argument for Realism." *Journal of Philosophy* 76: 113–33.

———. 1986. "Radical Interpretation and Epistemology." In LePore, ed. (1986), 356–68.

McGrew, Timothy J. 1995. *The Foundations of Knowledge*. Lanham, Md.: Littlefield Adams Books.

McLellan, David. 1986. *Ideology*. Milton Keynes, U.K.: Open University Press.

Merquior, J. G. 1985. *Foucault*. London: Fontana.

Millikan, Ruth Garrett. 1996. "Pushmi-pullyu Representations." In *Philosophical Perspectives*. Vol. 9. Ed. J. Tomberlin. Atascadero, Calif.: Ridgeview, 185–200.

Moore, G. E. 1959. *Principia Ethica*. Cambridge: Cambridge University Press.

———. 1993. "External and Internal Relations." In *Selected Writings*, ed. T. Baldwin. London: Routledge, 79–105.

Nagel, Thomas. 1986. *The View from Nowhere*. Oxford: Oxford University Press.

Nelson, Lynn Hankinson. 1990. *Who Knows? From Quine to a Feminist Empiricism*. Philadelphia: Temple University Press.

Neurath, Otto. 1983. *Otto Neurath: Philosophical Papers, 1913–1946*. Ed. and trans. R. S. Cohen and M. Neurath. Dordrecht: Reidel.

Nietzsche, F. W. 1966. *Beyond Good and Evil*. Trans. W. A. Kaufmann. New York: Vintage.

———. 1967. *On the Genealogy of Morals*. Trans. W. A. Kaufmann and R. J. Hollingdale. New York: Vintage.

———. 1968a. *Twilight of the Idols*. Trans. R. J. Hollingdale. London: Penguin.

———. 1968b. *The Will to Power*. Ed. W. A. Kaufmann. Trans. W. A. Kaufmann and R. J. Hollingdale. New York: Vintage.

———. 1969. *Götzendämmerung*. In Part 6, Vol. 3 of *Nietzsche Werke*, ed. G. Colli and M. Montinari. Berlin: Walter de Gruyter, 49–157.

———. 1974. *The Gay Science*. Trans. W. A. Kaufmann. New York: Vintage.

"Nigerians fear dismembering as tales of genital theft grow." *Globe and Mail* (Toronto), 30 October 1990, A14.

Noddings, Nell. 1984. *Caring*. Berkeley: University of California Press.

Nozick, Robert. 1981. *Philosophical Explanations*. Cambridge, Mass.: Belknap Press.

Ogden, C. K., and I. A. Richards. 1923. *The Meaning of Meaning.* New York: Harcourt, Brace.
Papineau, David. 1987. *Reality and Representation.* Oxford: Blackwell.
Parfit, Derek. 1984. *Reasons and Persons.* Oxford: Clarendon.
Patterson, Lee. 1990. "Literary History." In Lentricchia and McLaughlin, eds. (1990), 250–62.
Pitcher, George. ed. 1964. *Truth.* Englewood Cliffs, N.J.: Prentice-Hall.
Plato. 1974. *Plato's Republic.* Trans. G. M. A. Grube. Indianapolis: Hackett.
Putnam, Hilary. 1975. *Mind, Language and Reality: Philosophical Papers.* Vol. 2. Cambridge: Cambridge University Press.
―――. 1978. *Meaning and the Moral Sciences.* London: Routledge & Kegan Paul.
―――. 1981. *Reason, Truth and History.* Cambridge: Cambridge University Press.
―――. 1983. *Realism and Reason: Philosophical Papers.* Vol. 3. Cambridge: Cambridge University Press.
―――. 1987. *The Many Faces of Realism.* LaSalle, Ill.: Open Court.
―――. 1988. *Representation and Reality.* Cambridge, Mass.: MIT Press.
―――. 1990. *Realism with a Human Face.* Cambridge, Mass.: Harvard University Press.
―――. 1992a. *Renewing Philosophy.* Cambridge, Mass.: Harvard University Press.
―――. 1992b. "Replies." *Philosophical Topics* 20: 347–408.
―――. 1992c. "Truth, Activation Vectors and Possession Conditions for Concepts." *Philosophy and Phenomenological Research* 52: 431–47.
―――. 1994a. "Sense, Nonsense and the Senses: An Inquiry into the Powers of the Human Mind." *Journal of Philosophy* 91: 445–517.
―――. 1994b. *Words and Life.* Cambridge, Mass.: Harvard University Press.
―――. 1995. *Pragmatism: An Open Question.* Oxford: Blackwell.
Quine, W. V. 1960. *Word and Object.* Cambridge, Mass.: MIT Press.
―――. 1969. *Ontological Relativity and Other Essays.* New York: Columbia University Press.
―――. 1974. *Roots of Reference.* LaSalle, Ill.: Open Court.
―――. 1980. *From a Logical Point of View.* 2d ed. Cambridge, Mass.: Harvard University Press.
―――. 1981. *Theories and Things.* Cambridge, Mass.: Belknap Press.
―――. 1990. *Pursuit of Truth.* Cambridge, Mass.: Harvard University Press.
Ramberg, Bjørn T. 1989. *Donald Davidson's Philosophy of Language: An Introduction.* Oxford: Blackwell.
―――. 1993. "Strategies for Radical Rorty ('but is it *progress?*')." In *Méta-Philosophie: Reconstructing Philosophy?* ed. J. Couture and K. Nielsen. *Canadian Journal of Philosophy*, Supplementary Vol. 19: 223–46.
Ramsey, F. P. 1990. "Facts and Propositions." In *Philosophical Papers*, ed. D. H. Mellor. Cambridge: Cambridge University Press, 34–51.
―――. 1991. *On Truth.* Ed. N. Rescher and U. Majer. Dordrecht: Kluwer.
Rawls, John. 1971. *A Theory of Justice.* Cambridge, Mass.: Belknap Press.
Rorty, Richard. 1972. "Indeterminacy of Translation and of Truth." *Synthese* 23: 443–62.
―――. 1979. *Philosophy and the Mirror of Nature.* Princeton: Princeton University Press.
―――. 1982. *Consequences of Pragmatism.* Minneapolis: University of Minnesota Press.
―――. 1989. *Contingency, Irony and Solidarity.* Cambridge: Cambridge University Press.
―――. 1991a. "Feminism and Pragmatism." *Radical Philosophy* 59 (Autumn): 3–14.

———. 1991b. *Objectivity, Relativism and Truth: Philosophical Papers.* Vol. 1. Cambridge: Cambridge University Press.
———. 1992a. "Putnam on Truth." *Philosophy and Phenomenological Research* 52: 415-18.
———. 1992b. "'We Anti-Representationalists.'" Review of *Ideology: An Introduction*, by Terry Eagleton. *Radical Philosophy* 60 (Spring): 40–42.
———. 1993. "Putnam and the Relativist Menace." *Journal of Philosophy* 90: 443–61.
———. 1998. *Truth and Progress: Philosophical Papers.* Vol. 3. Cambridge: Cambridge University Press.
Rose, Jacqueline. 1982. Introduction to *Feminine Sexuality*, by Jacques Lacan. Ed. J. Mitchell and J. Rose. Trans. J. Rose. New York: Norton, 27–57.
Rozema, David. 1992. "Conceptual Scheming." *Philosophical Investigations* 15: 293–312.
Russell, Bertrand. 1921. *The Analysis of Mind.* London: Allen & Unwin.
———. 1966. *Philosophical Essays.* Rev. ed. London: Allen & Unwin.
———. 1994. *The Collected Papers of Bertrand Russell.* Vol. 4. Ed. A. Urquhart. London: Routledge.
Ryle, Gilbert. 1963. *The Concept of Mind.* Harmondsworth, U.K.: Penguin.
Sartre, Jean-Paul. 1956. *Being and Nothingness.* Trans. H. Barnes. New York: Washington Square.
Scheman, Naomi. 1983. "Individualism and the Objects of Psychology." In *Discovering Reality: Feminist Perspectives on Epistemology, Metaphysics, Methodology, and Philosophy of Science*, ed. S. Harding and M. B. Hintikka. Dordrecht: Reidel, 225–44.
———. 1996. "Forms of Life: Mapping the Rough Ground." In *The Cambridge Companion to Wittgenstein*, ed. H. Sluga and D. G. Stern. Cambridge: Cambridge University Press.
Schiffer, Stephen. 1989. *Remnants of Meaning.* Cambridge, Mass.: MIT Press.
Schlick, Moritz. 1959. "The Foundations of Knowledge." Trans. D. Rynin. In Ayer, ed. (1959), 209–27.
Schmitt, Frederick F. 1995. *Truth: A Primer.* Boulder: Westview Press.
Schouls, P. A. 1980. *The Imposition of Method: A Study of Descartes and Locke.* Oxford: Clarendon.
Seller, Anne. 1988. "Realism vs. Relativism: Toward a Politically Adequate Epistemology." In *Feminist Perspectives in Philosophy*, ed. M. Griffiths and M. Whitford. Bloomington: Indiana University Press, 169–86.
———. 1990. "Sex organ scare touches off rioting." *Edmonton Journal*, 13 November 1990, B4.
Shiner, R. A. 1977/78. "Wittgenstein and the Foundations of Knowledge." *Proceedings of the Aristotelian Society*, 78: 103–24.
Sperber, Dan. 1982. "Apparently Irrational Beliefs." In Hollis and Lukes, eds. (1982), 149–80.
Skorupski, John. 1994. Review of *Unnatural Doubts*, by Michael Williams. *Mind* 103: 400–404.
Smith, Barbara Herrnstein. 1988. *Contingencies of Value: Alternative Perspectives for Critical Theory.* Cambridge, Mass.: Harvard University Press.
———. 1997. *Belief and Resistance: Dynamics of Contemporary Intellectual Controversy.* Cambridge, Mass.: Harvard University Press.
Steinitz, Yuval. 1994. "Brains in a Vat: Different Perspectives." *Philosophical Quarterly* 44: 213–22.

Stevenson, C. L. 1959. "The Emotive Meaning of Ethical Terms." In Ayer, ed. (1959), 264–81.
Strawson, P. F. 1949. "Truth." *Analysis* 9, no. 6: 83–97.
———. 1959. *Individuals: An Essay in Descriptive Metaphysics*. London: Methuen.
———. 1964. "Truth." In Pitcher, ed. (1964), 32–53.
Stroud, Barry. 1984. *The Significance of Philosophical Scepticism*. Oxford: Clarendon.
———. 1996. "Epistemological Reflection on Knowledge of the External World." *Philosophy and Phenomenological Research* 56: 345–58.
Sturgeon, Nicholas. 1985. "Moral Explanations." In *Morality, Reason and Truth*, ed. D. Copp and D. Zimmerman. Totowa, N.J.: Rowman and Allanheld, 49–78.
———. 1986. "Harman on Moral Explanations of Natural Facts." In *Spindel Conference 1986: Moral Realism*, ed. N. Gillespie. *Southern Journal of Philosophy*. Supplementary Vol. 24: 69–78.
Szabados, Béla. 1981a. "Wittgenstein on Belief." *Philosophical Papers* 10: 24–34.
———. 1981b. "Wittgenstein on 'Mistrusting One's Own Belief.'" *Canadian Journal of Philosophy* 11: 603–12.
Tarski, Alfred. 1949. "The Semantic Conception of Truth." In *Readings in Philosophical Analysis*, ed. H. Feigl and W. Sellars. New York: Appleton-Century-Crofts, 52–84.
Taylor, Charles. 1985a. *Human Agency and Language: Philosophical Papers*. Vol. 1. Cambridge: Cambridge University Press.
———. 1985b. *Philosophy and the Human Sciences: Philosophical Papers*. Vol. 2. Cambridge: Cambridge University Press.
———. 1989. *Sources of the Self: The Making of the Modern Identity*. Cambridge, Mass.: Harvard University Press.
Tichy, Pavel. 1986. "Putnam on Brains in a Vat." *Philosophia* 16: 137–46.
Trebilcot, Joyce. 1988. "Dyke Methods *or* Principles for the Discovery/Creation of the Withstanding." *Hypatia* 3, no. 2: 1–13.
———. 1990. "More Dyke Methods." *Hypatia* 5, no. 1: 140–44.
———. 1992. "Relativism—There Is No Given—On Liberation." *Hypatia* 7, no. 1: 97–99.
"Vanishing organs spark mob attacks." *Montreal Gazette*, 4 November 1990, B4.
"Vanishing penises." *Edmonton Journal*, 19 January 1997, A2.
West, Cornel. 1989. *The American Evasion of Philosophy: A Genealogy of Pragmatism*. London: Macmillan.
White, Alan R. 1971. *Truth*. London: Macmillan.
White, Morton. 1950. "The Analytic and the Synthetic: An Untenable Dualism." In *John Dewey Philosopher of Science and Freedom*, ed. S. Hook. New York: Dial Press, 316–30.
Williams, Bernard. 1978. *Descartes: The Project of Pure Inquiry*. Harmondsworth, U.K.: Penguin.
Williams, Michael. 1980. "Coherence, Justification, and Truth." *Review of Metaphysics* 34: 243–72.
———. 1996a. "Exorcism and Enchantment." Critical Study of *Mind and World*, by John McDowell. *Philosophical Quarterly* 46: 99–109.
———. 1996b. "Understanding Human Knowledge Philosophically." *Philosophy and Phenomenological Research* 56: 359–78.
———. 1996c. *Unnatural Doubts*. Princeton: Princeton University Press.
Wilson, E. O. 1998. *Consilience: The Unity of Knowledge*. New York: Knopf.

Wisdom, John. 1957. "Philosophy and Psycho-Analysis." In *Philosophy and Psycho-Analysis*. Oxford: Blackwell, 169–81.

Wittgenstein, Ludwig. 1922. *Tractatus Logico-Philosophicus*. Trans. C. K. Ogden. London: Routledge & Kegan Paul.

———. 1958. *The Blue and the Brown Books*. New York: Harper.

———. 1968. *Philosophical Investigations*. 3d ed. Ed. G. E. M. Anscombe and R. Rhees. Trans. G. E. M. Anscombe. Oxford: Blackwell.

———. 1972. *On Certainty*. Ed. G. E. M. Anscombe and G. H. von Wright. Trans. D. Paul and G. E. M. Anscombe. New York: Harper.

———. 1974. *Philosophical Grammar*. Ed. R. Rhees. Trans. A. Kenny. Oxford: Blackwell.

———. 1975. *Philosophical Remarks*. Ed. R. Rhees. Trans. R. Hargreaves and R. White. Chicago: University of Chicago Press.

———. 1976. *Wittgenstein's Lectures on the Foundations of Mathematics—Cambridge, 1939*. Ed. C. Diamond. Chicago: University of Chicago Press.

———. 1978. *Remarks on the Foundations of Mathematics*. Rev. ed. Ed. G. H. von Wright, R. Rhees, and G. E. M. Anscombe. Trans. G. E. M. Anscombe. Cambridge, Mass.: MIT Press.

———. 1980a. *Remarks on the Philosophy of Psychology*. Vol. 1. Ed. G. E. M. Anscombe and G. H. von Wright. Trans. G. E. M. Anscombe. Oxford: Blackwell.

———. 1980b. *Remarks on the Philosophy of Psychology*. Vol. 2. Ed. G. H. von Wright and H. Nyman. Trans. C. G. Luckhardt and M. A. E. Aue. Oxford: Blackwell.

———. 1981. *Zettel*. 2d. ed. Ed. G. E. M. Anscombe and G. H. von Wright. Trans. G. E. M. Anscombe. Oxford: Blackwell.

———. 1992. *Last Writings on the Philosophy of Psychology*. Vol. 2. Ed. G. H. von Wright and H. Nyman. Trans. C. G. Luckhardt and Maximilian A. E. Aue. Oxford: Blackwell.

———. 1994. *The Wittgenstein Reader*. Ed. A. J. P. Kenny. Oxford: Blackwell.

Woolf, Leonard. 1970. "Hunting the Highbrow." In *Hogarth Essays*, ed. L. Woolf and V. Woolf. Freeport, N.Y.: Books for Libraries, 135–59.

Wright, Crispin. 1992. *Truth and Objectivity*. Cambridge, Mass.: Harvard University Press.

Index

Abductive argument, 142
Abductive inference, 34(n18), 140–141
Agency, 132, 146–147, 173, 183, 188–190
Agreement, 119, 122
Alienation, 175, 180
Allen, Barry, 102(n19), 131
Althusser, Louis, 10, 143, 144–145, 146–148, 175–176, 180, 182–183, 185
Analytic, the, 6, 37, 41, 42, 46, 49, 79(n26), 109, 111. *See also* Analyticity; Analytic propositions; Analytic sentences; Analytic statements; Analytic-synthetic distinction; Analytic truths
Analyticity, 37, 42, 45–50, 54(n15), 111
  stimulus, 48
  See also Analytic, the
Analytic propositions, 6, 37, 42, 43, 47. *See also* Analytic, the
Analytic sentences, 48, 49. *See also* Analytic, the
Analytic statements, 45–46, 49, 111. *See also* Analytic, the
Analytic-synthetic distinction, 6, 42, 45, 49, 111, 112, 125(n16), 141. *See also* Analytic, the; Synthetic, the
Analytic truths, 36, 37, 42, 45–47, 49, 50, 55(nn 15, 17), 78(n14), 89, 110. *See also* Analytic, the
Anderson, David, 28
Anti-individualism, 9, 11(n6), 152, 154–159, 170(n11), 196
  as distinct from externalism. *See* Externalism, as distinct from anti-individualism
Antirealism, 13–14, 18
Antirealist, 16, 72, 119
Anzaldúa, Gloria, 181, 184–185
Appearances, 34(n16), 131, 137, 138, 142, 170(n11). *See also* Experience
Appiah, Anthony, 190(n8)
A priori, the, 46, 55–56(n23), 163
Artifacts, 3, 11(n1), 130, 193. *See also* Essences; Natural kinds; Natures
Assent, 50, 116–117, 119, 120
Assertibility, 87, 100(n8)
  right, 105
  warranted, 87, 112: idealized, 86. *See also* Warrant, idealized
  See also Justification; Rational acceptability; Warrant
Assertibility-conditions, 13, 86
Austin, J. L, 77(n2)
Authority. *See* First-person authority
Avowals. *See* Expressions; Expressivism
Awareness of self, 147. *See also* Self-awareness
Ayer, A. J., 138–139, 160

Baier, Annette, 171(n14)
Baker, G. P., 11(n3), 42, 54(n13)
Barnes, Barry, 8, 106–107, 148(n1)
Barwise, John, 61
Becoming, 131
Bedeutung, 64, 77(n4)
Behavior, 43, 50, 96, 102(n20), 115, 117, 119, 120, 125(nn 21, 26), 165, 174, 191(n18)
  expression, 42, 168
  expressive, 10, 163, 168
  functional explanation of. *See* Explanation, functional
  linguistic, 8, 125(nn 21, 26), 165
  pain, 42–44, 49, 55(n17), 163, 168
  speech, 91, 115, 120
  verbal, 48
Behavior cycle, 39, 93
Behaviorism, 48–49, 54(n8), 56(n25), 140
Being, 115, 131, 144, 149(n15), 166, 176
Beliefs, 29–30, 34(n16), 39, 45, 49–50, 51, 54(n6), 60, 87, 89, 91, 92, 95–96, 97, 98–99, 100(n8), 101(n18), 105, 106, 114, 116–117, 119, 122, 124(n7), 130, 140, 141, 145, 148(n10), 152, 155- 156, 158, 160, 168–169
  and coherence, 71–72, 85, 102(n27), 130
  content of. *See* Beliefs, individuation of; Content, intentional
  expression of. *See* Expressions, of belief
  functional explanation of. *See* Explanation, functional
  individuation of, 61, 117, 151 153–154, 158. *See also* Anti-individualism; Content, intentional

213

and interpretation, 117, 119, 122, 125(n29), 126(nn 29, 33), 161–162
and knowledge, 19, 29, 30–31, 34(n11), 98–99, 157, 163
and realism, 14–17, 18, 81, 82, 95, 99, 135, 139
and relativism, 103, 106, 108–109, 115, 129, 143
and self-knowledge, 160, 163–164, 169, 189
theoretical, 29, 197. *See also* Claims, theoretical
Benton, Ted, 147, 183
Berkeley, George, 144
Bloomsbury group, 137–138
Bloor, David, 8, 106–107, 148(n1)
Body, 25, 164, 166, 174, 181, 187, 199
Bohr, Niels, 112
Bové, Paul, 129–130
Boyd, Richard N., 84
Brains in a vat, 5, 19, 21, 22–24, 26–28, 31, 32, 34(n18), 35(n29), 58, 80–81, 94, 100(n3), 114, 126(n29), 137, 151, 155, 157, 171(n11), 199. *See also* Minds in a vat; Skepticism, external world
Brandom, Robert, 89
Brittan, Gordon, 20
Burge, Tyler, 9, 152–159, 169(nn 4, 5, 6), 170(nn 7, 8, 10, 11), 196

Callinicos, Alex, 77(n2), 78(n7)
Campbell, Richmond, 191(n13), 192(n22)
Capitalism, 145, 147, 180
Carnap, Rudolf, 45, 49, 52, 110, 111, 120, 124(n15), 125(nn 15, 16), 138–139, 141
Cartesianism, 16, 92, 149(n15), 157, 178, 194. *See also* Cartesian substance; Certainty; *Cogito*; Descartes, René; Doubts, Cartesian; Epistemic priority, Cartesian; First-person authority, Cartesian conception of; *Res cogitans*; Self, Cartesian; Skeptic, Cartesian; Skepticism, Cartesian; Subjectivity, Cartesian; Subjects, Cartesian
Cartesian substance, 102(n23), 186. *See also Res cogitans*; Self, Cartesian; Subjectivity, Cartesian; Subjects, Cartesian
Casey, Joan Frances, 198–199
Causal theories of reference. *See* Reference, causal theories of
Cavell, Stanley, 4
Certainty, 16, 18, 83–84, 99, 134, 166, 175–176, 179
Chambers, Ross, 129, 191(n11). *See also* Identity, cultural
Charity. *See* Principle of charity
Claims
  counterfactual, 28, 101(n19), 157. *See also* Statements, counterfactual
  knowledge, 5, 15, 140, 142, 159, 160

moral, 141–142
nontheoretical, 72, 194–195. *See also* Concepts, nontheoretical; Discourse, nontheoretical; Notions, nontheoretical; Statements, nontheoretical; Terms, nontheoretical
subjunctive conditional, 30
theoretical, 71–72, 194–195. *See also* Beliefs, theoretical; Concepts, theoretical; Discourse, theoretical; Notions, theoretical; Statements, theoretical; Terms, theoretical
See also Statements
Clark, Maudmarie, 33(n4), 131
Cogito, 146, 154, 166–167, 175–176, 178, 188. *See also* Cartesianism
Cogito-like thoughts, 154–155, 159, 196. *See also* First-person authority
Cohen, G. A., 145
Coherence, 72
  explanatory, 71, 140–141, 142
  ideal, 85
Coherence theories of knowledge. *See* Knowledge, coherence theories of
Coherence theory of truth. *See* Truth, and coherence
Coherentism, 2, 102(n27). *See also* Coherence
Commensurability, 109. *See also* Incommensurability
Communication, 52, 110, 112–113, 123–124, 124(n7), 180
Community, 103, 143, 184
  linguistic, 64
Concepts, 6, 8–9, 14, 35(n31), 37, 41, 42, 43–45, 47–48, 52–53, 93, 94, 109, 113–115, 121–122, 123, 130, 177, 184, 197
  explanatory, 106, 140–141. *See also* Notions, explanatory
  functional, 92
  mathematical, 48
  nontheoretical, 95. *See also* Claims, nontheoretical; Notions, nontheoretical
  normative, 132, 141. *See also* Notions, normative
  theoretical, 100(n2), 195. *See also* Claims, theoretical; Notions, theoretical
  See also Conceptual schemes; Notions; Relativism, conceptual
Conceptual schemes, 8, 51, 85, 92–93, 100(n2), 104, 108, 109–115, 119, 120–121, 123, 143, 182, 184, 196. *See also* Relativism, conceptual
Confirmation, 45–46, 78(n14), 110, 112, 134, 139, 142
Connotation, 60–61, 62, 64 *See also* Sense (*Sinn*); *Sinn*
Consciousness, 52, 102(n23), 146, 166–167, 171(n21), 181–182, 186, 191(nn 9, 20)

double, 181
false, 143, 145. *See also* Ideology
of self, 166, 175. *See also* Self-consciousness
self-. *See* Self-consciousness
technocratic, 145
Consciousness-raising, 134–135, 143
Content, 76, 77(n6), 93, 104, 120, 156, 170–171(n11), 196
　conceptual, 53(n1)
　empirical, 8, 108, 109–110, 111, 112, 114–115, 129, 179
　intentional, 9, 11(n6), 155, 159, 196
　narrow, 153, 169(n4)
　semantic, 11(n6)
Contextualism, 35(n40), 71–72
Correspondence theories of truth. *See* Truth, and correspondence
Counterfactual situations, 9, 154–155, 158, 196
Counterfactual statements. *See* Statements, counterfactual
Criteria, 42, 55(n19)
Critical theory, 4, 145, 147. *See also* Frankfurt school; Habermas, Jürgen; Horkheimer, Max; Marcuse, Herbert
Culture, 1, 5, 8, 103, 104, 105, 107, 114, 115, 120, 121, 123, 125(n29), 128, 136, 139, 151, 169(n1), 181, 182, 183–185, 186
　dominant, 180, 184, 185, 186
　subordinate, 180, 184–186
See also Conceptual schemes; Relativism

Darwin, Charles, 144, 175
Davidson, Donald, 8, 10, 33(n6), 35(n29), 50, 53(n1), 56(n27), 61, 62, 77(n2), 78(n7), 84, 89–91, 93, 109–110, 111–112, 113–114, 115–117, 118–119, 121–122, 156, 160–161, 163, 165, 171(n13), 173, 174, 190(n4), 196
Davies, David, 22, 27, 35(n33)
Decentered subject. *See* Subjects, decentered
Deconstruction, 105, 132. *See also* Derrida, Jacques
Demonstrative representation. *See* Representations, demonstrative
Denotation, 60, 62, 64, 75. *See also* Extension; Reference
Derrida, Jacques, 132–133. *See also* Deconstruction
Descartes, René, 16, 18–19, 34(n11), 98, 102(n23), 133, 134, 149(nn 15, 16), 150(nn 16, 26), 154, 165, 166, 175–176, 179. *See also* Cartesianism
Desires, 26, 39, 45, 73, 93, 96, 117, 122, 143, 146, 148, 161, 184, 185, 189
　and ideology, 145
　self-identifying, 189, 192(n22)
　and self-knowledge, 159, 160, 169
　unconscious, 93

Devitt, Michael, 13–15, 28–29, 33(n3), 63, 65–66, 73–75, 76, 79(nn 29, 30), 92, 119, 125(n28)
Diagnosis, 1, 8, 11, 12, 36, 57, 75, 197
　theoretical, 2
　therapeutic, 2–3
Disconfirmation. *See* Confirmation
Discourse, 105, 129, 147–148, 149(n11), 175, 176–177, 178
　criticism, 129
　material object, 71
　moral, 71
　nontheoretical, 73. *See also* Claims, nontheoretical; Statements, nontheoretical
　theoretical, 73, 111. *See also* Claims, theoretical; Statements, theoretical
Disorder, 2, 8, 11, 31, 36, 58, 165, 190(n6), 198
　dissociative, 198, 199(n3)
　dissociative identity. *See* Multiple personality disorder (dissociative identity disorder)
　multiple personality. *See* Multiple personality disorder (dissociative identity disorder)
　psycho-philosophical, 1, 36, 57, 80, 99, 193, 197
Doubts, 1, 4, 21, 24, 27, 35(n27), 52, 57, 80, 82, 101(n10), 102(n20), 111, 123, 136, 138, 162, 167, 176, 191(n17), 198
　Cartesian, 18, 136, 138, 149(n14). *See also* Cartesianism; Skeptic, Cartesian; Skepticism, Cartesian
　and self-knowledge, 145, 163–166, 167, 186, 191(n17)
　skeptical, 1–3, 5, 6, 7, 15, 16, 17, 18–19, 28, 31, 67, 70, 75, 77, 81, 83, 84, 92–94, 97, 99, 145, 149(nn 14, 15), 151, 157, 159, 179, 194, 195, 197, 198. *See also* Skeptic, the; Skeptical scenarios; Skepticism
Du Bois, W. E. B., 181, 190–191(n8)
Dühring, Eugen, 144
Dummett, Michael, 4, 11(n3), 13–14, 72
Dwyer, Philip, 55–56(n23)

Eagleton, Terry, 176
Ebbs, Gary, 126(n34)
Ego, 146–147, 150(n27), 175. *See also* 'I'
Emotions, 96–97
Empiricism, 15, 45, 51, 109, 110–111
　logical, 37, 110–111, 139–140. *See also* Positivism, logical; Vienna Circle
See also Positivism
Engels, Friedrich, 143–144, 145, 180
Enlightenment, 133
Entities, 63, 101(n18), 110, 113, 141, 186
　linguistic, 105
　physical, 33(n3), 157
　posited, 56(n31), 83, 149(n12). *See also* Objects, as posits; Posits

theoretical, 13, 83
unobservable, 13, 56(n31), 140
See also Objects
Epistemic closure, 35(n40)
Epistemic priority, 7, 33(n9), 34(nn 15, 16), 99, 102(n27), 151, 158, 159
  Cartesian, 34(n15)
  See also Epistemic privilege; Evidence
Epistemic privilege, 84. *See also* Epistemic priority; Evidence
Epistemology, 2, 3, 7, 8, 34(n11), 49, 89, 97–99, 106, 114, 128, 133, 143, 193, 196
  naturalized, 29. *See also* Devitt, Michael; Nozick, Robert; Quine, W. V.
  See also Knowledge, theories of
Essences, 43, 51, 88–89, 96–97
  cultural, 186
  hidden, 4, 88, 92
  human, 180
  See also Artifacts; Natural kinds; Natures
Essentialism, 4, 184, 186, 190(n8)
Ethical-political argument for relativism, 9, 104, 108, 127–128, 133
Ethics, 140, 178
Evidence, 7, 14, 21, 28, 29, 34(n18), 84, 86, 99, 114, 115, 117, 126(n29), 138, 160–161, 162, 164, 167, 193, 195. *See also* Epistemic priority; Epistemic privilege
Evil demon, 19, 157. *See also* Cartesianism; Skepticism, external world
Exemplars, 44, 52, 168. *See also* Paradigms; Samples
Expectation, 39–40, 45, 54(n11), 63. *See also* Intentional attitudes
Experience, 2, 5, 7–8, 16, 21–22, 24, 27, 28, 29–30, 33(n9), 34(nn 15, 18), 35(n27), 46, 51, 75, 82, 85, 94–99, 102(nn 22, 23, 24), 110, 111, 114–115, 120, 134, 136, 138, 143, 145, 151–152, 153, 157–159, 170–171(n11), 180–181, 183, 184, 195–197. *See also* Appearance
Explanation, 3, 7–8, 19, 20–21, 24, 28, 30, 34(n18), 52, 69, 76–77, 81–85, 87, 92, 93, 95, 96, 97, 98, 99, 104, 106, 107, 114, 128, 140, 141, 142, 156, 158, 195
  functional, 143, 145, 148, 151–152
Explanationism, 140
Explanatory coherence. *See* Coherence, explanatory
Explanatory hypotheses. *See* Hypotheses, explanatory
Explanatory relation, 6, 7, 50, 94
Explanatory scenario, 19, 22
Expression behavior. *See* Behavior, expression
Expressions, 43, 89, 140–141, 162, 163, 164, 166, 167, 168, 169, 187–188

behavioral, 44
of belief, 49, 160, 162, 174
characteristic, 43, 44, 96, 168
facial, 6, 37, 44, 179
linguistic (syntactic), 4, 40, 47, 48, 60–62, 70, 83, 87, 94, 101(n16)
Expressivism, 10, 133, 163, 167–168, 171(n23), 173–174, 191(n18)
pure, 163, 171(n16)
See also Behavior, expressive; Use (linguistic), expressive
Extension, 60–62, 63, 78(n8), 153. *See also* Beliefs, individuation of; Denotation; Facts, individuation of; Reference
Externalism, 58, 73, 74–77, 80–81, 82, 99
as distinct from anti-individualism, 11(n6). *See also* Anti-individualism
See also External relations; Internalism
Externalist perspective (Putnam), 27
External questions (Carnap), 110
External relations, 6–7, 11(n6), 36–37, 39, 52, 67, 70, 94, 104, 115, 194–195
and beliefs, 152
and concepts, 8, 104: of meaning, 104; of realism, 128; of reference, 8, 25, 104, 120; of scientism, 128; of understanding, 126(n30); of use, 8, 120, 126(n30)
and correspondence, 44, 59, 141
and desire, 45, 93
between experience and world, 94, 114, 120, 151, 158, 170(n11), 195–196
between intentional attitudes and the world, 152
between knower and known, 7, 94
between mind and world, 7, 9
to objects, 6, 54(n8), 39, 75, 93. *See also* External relations, and reference; External relations, to referents
and reference, 6–7, 45, 58, 67, 70, 72, 73, 74, 76, 78(n8), 80, 82, 83, 94, 195. *See also* External relations, to objects; External relations, to referents
to referents, 25, 49, 81, 94. *See also* External relations, to objects; External relations, and reference
between scheme and content, 108, 115. *See also* External relations, and concepts
and truth, 84, 141
See also Externalism; Internal relations
External world. *See* World, external

Fact
questions of, 110
statement of, 138
See also Facts

Index

Facts, 6, 39–40, 45, 54(n11), 59–60, 63, 66, 77(n5), 78(n7), 107, 130, 159
  atomic, 38, 54(n12), 60
  individuation of, 54(n11), 60–62
  negative, 63
  See also States of affairs
Fallibilism, 19, 28, 34(nn 11, 15), 157
False consciousness. *See* Consciousness, false
Feminism, 11(n5), 133–134, 139, 143, 149(n11), 150(n22), 180
Feuerbach, Ludwig, 180
Feyerabend, Paul, 8, 106–107, 123, 129, 136–137
Field, Hartry, 65–66, 73, 101(n10)
Findlay, J. N., 197
First-person authority, 9, 152, 154–155, 156, 157, 158–159, 167, 169, 170(n11), 196
  and asymmetry, 10, 152, 159–161, 167
  Cartesian conception of, 152, 154, 156, 158, 159, 175. *See also* Introspection; Observations, inner; Privileged access
  See also Self-knowledge
Fitting, 39–40, 44. *See also* Truth, and correspondence
Force (illocutionary), 172(n23)
Foucault, Michel, 132, 133, 148(nn 8, 9)
Foundationalism, 2, 18, 33(n9), 34(n15), 78(n14), 102(n27)
Fragmentation, 10, 173–174. *See also* Pluralism, ontological; Plurality; Self, divisions of the; Self, fragmented; Self-divisions; Self-fragmentation; Subjects, decentered; Subjects, fragmented
Fragmented subject. *See* Subjects, fragmented
Frameworks. *See* Linguistic frameworks
Frankfurt school, 145–146. *See also* Critical theory; Habermas, Jürgen; Horkheimer, Max; Marcuse, Herbert
Freedom, 146, 147, 150(n28), 180. *See also* Liberation
Frege, Gottlob, 60, 64, 77(n4)
Freud, Sigmund, 54(n8), 146, 174–175, 178, 180. *See also* Psychoanalysis
Fundamentalism, 137–138, 149–150(n16)

Games, 41, 92, 102(n20)
  language, 43–44, 87, 168–169, 173
Gauthier, David, 150(n21)
Genital theft, 108, 115, 124(n12)
Gestures, 6, 37, 44, 179
Gettier, Edmund L., 34(n11)
Grammar, 41, 44, 47, 179
Grammatical investigation, 88
Grammatical subject. *See* Subjects, grammatical
Grammatical system, 40

Grammatical unity. *See* Self, unity of the; Self-descriptions, unity of; Self-unity
Grice, H. P., 48, 53
Grounding thought. *See* Thoughts, grounding
Gueroult, Martial, 166, 175–176
Gutting, Gary, 132, 148(n8)

Habermas, Jürgen, 4, 11(n4), 132, 145
Hacker, P. M. S., 11(n3), 42, 54(n13), 55(n19), 56(n25), 91, 125(n20), 126(n34), 191(n18), 192(n18)
Hacking, Ian, 25, 69, 78(n18), 190(n6), 199(n4)
Hahn, Hans, 139
Harman, Gilbert, 140
Haugeland, John, 187
Hegel, G. W. F., 143, 150(n22), 175, 181
Hempel, C. G., 100(n4), 140
Holding true. *See* Assent
Holism, 40, 45–46, 49, 177
Hope, 60, 160–161, 164, 169. *See also* Anti-individualism; Content, intentional
Horkheimer, Max, 4
Horwich, Paul, 101(n14)
Hume, David, 2, 57, 76, 198
Hypotheses, 7, 19, 27, 29–30, 36, 53, 56(n31), 65, 71, 72–73, 76, 140, 174, 193, 194–195, 197, 198–199
  explanatory, 21, 28, 111, 151, 161, 195
  external-world, 19, 21, 95, 97, 156. *See also* World, external
  and interpretation, 116, 118, 125(n21), 161
  justification (testing) of, 19, 29, 84, 193
  scientific, 110–111, 139, 142
  skeptical, 19, 21–22, 24, 28, 30, 76–77, 81, 94, 95, 126(n29), 155–156, 170(n11)
  See also Explanation; Explanatory relation; Explanatory scenario

'I', 146, 169(n3), 186–187, 191(nn 8, 18), 192(n18). *See also* Ego
Idealism, 13, 14, 15, 16, 86, 128, 129, 133, 143, 148, 149(n14)
  absolute, 176. *See also* Idealists, absolute
  British, 37, 42. *See also* Idealists, British
  linguistic, 72, 105, 130, 132
  transcendental, 35(n27), 72, 129
  See also Berkeley, George; Hegel, G. W. F.; Idealists; Joachim, H. H.; Kant, Immanuel
Idealists, 38, 53(n3), 89, 144, 149(nn 12, 14)
  absolute, 37, 130, 177, 179. *See also* Idealism, absolute
  British, 190(n5). *See also* Idealism, British
  subjective, 131
  See also Berkeley, George; Hegel, G. W. F.; Idealism; Joachim, H. H.; Kant, Immanuel

Identity, 133, 146, 176, 183, 186, 187, 190(n6), 191(n14), 192(n19)
  cultural, 184–185. *See also* Chambers, Ross
Ideology, 10, 143, 144–148, 150(n23), 175–176, 181, 182, 183, 185, 186. *See also* Consciousness, false
Impressions, 96–97
Incommensurability, 8, 104, 109, 113, 115, 119, 125–126(n29), 143, 182, 196
  practical, 123, 183–184
  See also Commensurability; Conceptual schemes
Independence. *See* World, independence of
Indeterminacy, 45
  of intentional objects, 39, 93
  of reference, 49, 70, 73–75, 82
  of translation, 50
Individualism, 11(n6), 100(n2), 152–153, 169(n4), 171(n11)
  as distinct from internalism. *See* Internalism, as distinct from individualism
  See also Anti-individualism
Induction, 114, 140–141, 160, 161
Inductivism, 7, 34(n18), 84, 99
Instrumentalism, 13, 56(n31), 83, 140
Instruments of language, 6, 37, 41, 44, 54(n14), 94, 194. *See also* Linguistic instruments
Intentional attitudes, 9, 39, 39, 51, 93, 100(n2), 125(n26), 152, 153, 155, 162, 164, 165–166, 167, 168, 173, 188, 196
  unconscious, 54(n8)
  See also Beliefs; Desires; Expectation; Hope; Intentional phenomena; Intentional states; Intentions; Properties, intentional; Wishes
Intentional phenomena, 9, 19, 21, 33(n5), 151–153, 154, 156, 157, 158, 159, 165, 196. *See also* Intentional attitudes
Intentional states, 100(n2). *See also* Intentional attitudes
Intentions, 11, 56(n30), 64, 77(n1), 179, 183
  picture conception of, 38. *See also* Meaning, picture theory of
  unconscious, 54(n8), 56(n30), 177–178. *See also* Intentional attitudes
Interests, 4, 121, 123, 135, 143, 145, 149(n11)
Internalism, 78(n14), 94
  as distinct from individualism, 11(n6). *See also* Individualism
  See also Externalism; Internal relations
Internal properties. *See* Properties, internal
Internal relations, 6–7, 11(n6), 13, 36–45, 46, 49–50, 51, 52–53, 53(nn 4, 11, 14), 57, 79(n26), 87, 93–94, 101(n13), 104, 112, 125(n20), 141, 194–195

and analyticity, 36–37, 42–43, 46, 47, 49, 50–51, 55(n17), 89, 111
and concepts, 41, 42, 43–44, 47, 94, 114: of assertibility, 87; of belief, 50, 87, 117; of a human body, 187; of interpretation, 114; of justification, 13, 49, 87, 89; of meaning, 50, 52, 117; of memory, 191(n14); of pain, 42, 43, 44, 55(n17), 168; of a person, 187, 191(n14); of realism, 128, 197; of reference, 52, 126(n30); of scientism, 128, 197; of truth, 13, 49–50, 87, 88, 89, 114, 117, 121; of understanding, 114, 121, 126(n30); of use, 126(n30)
and correspondence, 59
between experience and world, 94, 152, 158–159, 170(n11), 195–196
between facts and statements, 54(n11), 59–60
between instruments of language, 37, 41, 44, 47, 53, 54(n15), 94, 194
between meanings, 42
between mind and world, 7, 9, 94, 152
to objects, 5–6, 53, 54(n8), 81, 152, 195. *See also* Internal relations, and reference; Internal relations, to referents
between order and execution, 40
and reference, 7, 56(n31), 59, 71, 75, 80–81. *See also* Internal relations, to objects; Internal relations, to referents
to referents, 22, 25, 52, 58, 72–73. *See also* Internal relations, to objects; Internal relations, and reference
between rule and instance, 40, 52, 54(n13)
between terms in use, 54(n15)
See also External relations; Internalism
Interpretation, 8, 10, 49, 90, 109, 114–119, 122–123, 125(n26), 126(n33), 161–162, 171(nn 13, 14), 165, 194
  of our thoughts, 155, 170(n8)
  and psychoanalysis, 178–180
  and Putnam's model-theoretic argument, 67–69, 74, 76, 77, 79(n30)
  radical, 115, 117, 118. *See also* Interpreter, radical
  self-. *See* Self-interpretations
  of a text, 132
  and translation, 118–119, 123, 125(n27). *See also* Translation
  See also Interpreter
Interpreter, 117
  radical, 51, 117, 123
  See also Interpretation
Intersubjectivity, 124(n15), 134
Introspection, 160, 164, 172. *See also* First-person authority, Cartesian conception of;

Observations, inner; Privileged access;
Self-knowledge
Intuition, 56(n23), 142, 166–167, 186
Irrationalism, 132

Jacobsen, Rockney, 171–172(n23)
James, William, 89
Janet, Pierre, 174
Joachim, H. H., 130
Justification, 19, 21, 29, 34(n11), 84, 98–99, 106–107, 113, 132, 134, 136, 140–141, 142, 156, 159, 188
  and coherence, 71–72, 102(n27)
  and contextualism, 71–72
  ideal, 86–87, 101(n10). *See also* Justification, idealized; Rational acceptability, ideal; Warrant, ideal
  idealized, 86. *See also* Justification, ideal; Rational acceptability, idealized; Warrant, idealized
  and self-knowledge, 9–10, 152, 159. *See also* First-person authority
  and trust, 282(n14)
  and truth, 13, 17, 49, 89, 95, 106–107, 132. *See also* Justification, ideal; Justification, idealized
  See also Abductive inference; Assertibility; Fallibilism; First-person authority; Foundationalism; Rational acceptability; Warrant

Kant, Immanuel, 14, 20, 34(nn 15, 17), 35(n27), 42, 56(n23), 72, 102(nn 22, 23), 109, 115, 129, 149(n14), 185–186
Kinghan, Michael, 35(n32)
Knowledge, 1–5, 7–10, 11(n1), 13–22, 24, 29–30, 32, 33(n9), 34(n11), 73, 75, 81, 83–84, 92, 94, 95, 97–99, 103–105, 106, 107, 112, 117, 119, 124(n5), 128, 129, 130, 131, 133, 134, 135, 137- 138, 139, 141–142, 146, 148, 149(nn 12, 15), 150(n23), 154, 156, 157–158, 159, 163, 166, 167, 171(n14), 176, 177, 179, 186, 188, 190(n3), 193–197
  Absolute, 175
  claims. *See* Claims, knowledge
  coherence theories of, 102(n27)
  empirical, 95, 155
  of experience, 7, 94
  mathematical, 47
  of other cultures, 1, 5, 8, 151
  of others, 10, 159–161. *See also* Other-knowledge
  of ourselves, 5, 166. *See also* Self-knowledge
  perceptual, 157

  and possibility of doubt, 163
  propositional, 102(n20), 166
  of reference, 6, 70, 75–76, 80, 82–84, 94
  self-. *See* Self-knowledge
  theoretical, 102(n20)
  theories of, 2, 7, 8, 100, 104, 105, 106, 107, 120, 128, 129, 133, 135, 140, 195. *See also* Epistemology
  as "truth-tracking," 30, 155
Kripke, Saul A., 54(n13), 64–66, 78(n12)
Kuhn, Thomas, 112–113, 125(n18), 149(n12)

Lacan, Jacques, 10, 102(n21), 130, 131, 146, 150(n27), 164, 166, 175–180, 186–187, 190(n3)
Language, 4, 10, 14, 22, 23–24, 25, 26, 35(n31), 36, 40–41, 42, 43–44, 45, 47, 48, 49, 50, 51, 52, 54(nn 14, 15), 56(n25), 58, 62, 67–69, 71, 74, 75, 76, 77, 77(n1), 79(n28), 80, 83, 88, 90, 91, 92, 94, 100(n2), 105, 109–110, 111–112, 113, 115, 116–120, 121, 122, 123–124, 125(n27), 126(n29) 129, 140, 160, 161–162, 164, 168, 170(n8), 174, 177–178, 186, 188, 194, 195, 196, 197
  artificial, 116
  as a calculus, 40–41
  contingently private, 162
  figurative, 180. *See also* Metaphor; Metonymy; Use (linguistic), figurative
  formalized, 90, 101(n16), 116
  games. *See* Games, language
  harmony between, and reality, 179
  instruments of. *See* Instruments of language
  intertranslatable, 109, 119. *See also* Translatability; Translation
  logical, 4
  natural, 13, 23, 33(n6), 60, 63, 70, 90, 116, 118, 119
  observation, 110
  ordinary, 86
  private, 16
Language users, 18, 24, 120, 121, 160, 184, 188
  competent, 10, 189. *See also* Linguistic competence; Speakers, competent;
Learning, 43–44, 48–49, 52, 82, 87–88, 91, 95, 96, 102(n20), 118, 162, 163, 167–168, 187
  of concepts, 7, 43, 53, 55(n17)
  of language, 43, 118, 162
  See also Teaching
Leibniz, G. W., 174
Lenin, V. I., 143, 144
Lewis, David, 73, 74–75, 79(nn 27, 28), 100(n2)
Liar paradox, 90, 191(n16). *See also* Truth, paradoxes of

Liberation, 149(n12), 173, 182. *See also* Freedom
Linguistic abilities, 24, 166
   and self-knowledge, 163, 167
   See also Linguistic competence
Linguistic articulation, 173. *See also* Expressions
Linguistic behavior. *See* Behavior, linguistic
Linguistic capacities, 164–165, 188, 197
   and self-knowledge, 164, 167
   See also Linguistic competence
Linguistic community. *See* Community, linguistic
Linguistic competence, 118, 125(n25), 161, 162, 165, 188
   and First-person authority, 152
   and self-knowledge, 161, 165
   See also Language users, competent; Linguistic abilities; Linguistic capacities; Speakers, competent
Linguistic expressions. *See* Expressions, linguistic (syntactic)
Linguistic frameworks, 110, 138, 140
Linguistic instruments, 41, 44, 47, 53. *See also* Instruments of language
Linguistic phenomena, 83, 118
Linguistics, structuralist, 177, 179. *See also* Saussure, Ferdinand de
Linsky, Bernard, 77(n6)
Literary theorists, 10, 129–130, 175
Locke, John, 133, 191(n14)
Logic, 2, 22, 36, 41, 42, 50–51, 70, 78(n18), 85, 132–133, 170(n7), 178, 197
Logical atomism, 40
Logical empiricism. *See* Empiricism, logical
Logical form, 38
Logical positivism. *See* Positivism, logical
Logical possibility. *See* Possibility, logical
Logical truths. *See* Truths, logical
Lugones, Maria C., 10, 147, 180, 181–184, 185–187, 189, 191(n14)
Lukács, Georg, 150(n22)
Lying, 162, 171(n17), 191(n16). *See also* Liar paradox

McDowell, John, 11(n4), 82, 102(n22)
McGeer, Victoria, 171(n15)
McGinn, Colin, 16, 33(n6)
Mach, Ernst, 144
MacIntyre, Alasdair, 5, 121–122
Mackie, J. L., 141–142, 150(n21)
MacKinnon, Catharine A., 134, 135–136, 138, 139, 143, 144, 149(nn 12, 13, 14)
Mannheim, Karl, 150(n23)
Marcuse, Herbert, 4, 145, 147, 150(n28)
Marx, Karl, 143–145, 146, 150(n24), 175, 180–181.
   See also Marxism

Marxism, 139, 143, 144–145, 146, 147, 150(nn 22, 23), 151, 171(n12)
   structuralist, 145
   See also Althusser, Louis; Engels, Friedrich; Frankfurt school; Horkheimer, Max; Lenin, V. I.; Marcuse, Herbert; Marx, Karl; Marxists; Marxist theory; Marxist tradition; Radical theory
Marxists, 135, 150(n23). *See also* Marxism
Marxist theory, 9, 128, 143, 144, 196. *See also* Marxism
Marxist tradition, 143–144, 148. *See also* Marxism
Materialism, 13, 144
   eliminative, 124(n5)
   historical, 143. *See also* Engels, Friedrich; Marx, Karl; Marxism
Mathematicians, 47, 51
Mathematics, 47, 50–51, 55–56(n23)
   knowledge of. *See* Knowledge, mathematical
Meaning, 2, 3, 4, 11(n4), 13, 14, 26, 37, 39, 40, 41–42, 43, 45, 47, 49, 50, 52, 53, 77(n4), 84, 92, 93–94, 104, 109–111, 113, 116–117, 119, 120, 132, 152, 153, 160, 162, 168, 170(n8), 171(n23), 174, 197
   hidden, 178
   picture theory of, 38
   theories of, 4, 52, 56(n27), 77, 78(n8), 84, 120, 172(n12)
   and use, 42, 71, 91, 126(n30), 162, 172(n23)
   and verification. *See* Verifiability, and meaning; Verification, and meaning; Verificationism
   See also Signification; Use (linguistic)
Meaningfulness, 2–3, 51–52, 71, 94, 100(n3), 124(n15), 140
Memory, 183, 185, 186, 191(n14)
Metaphor, 31, 80, 81, 178, 190(n4), 198
   and paraphrase, 47–48
   See also Language, figurative; Rhetoric; Use (linguistic), figurative
Metaphysics, 38, 137, 139–140, 178
Method, 134–136, 140, 144
   of feminist theory, 134
   philosophical, 3
   scientific, 135–136
   unity of, 134–135. *See also* Unity, topical; Unity, of science
Metonymy, 178. *See also* Language, figurative; Rhetoric; Use (linguistic), figurative
Millikan, Ruth Garrett, 172(n23)
Mind, 1, 7, 9, 14, 16, 27, 32, 33(n5), 58, 66, 94, 129, 151, 152, 154, 158–160, 164, 165, 166, 174–175
   Absolute, 131
   philosophy of, 124(n5), 151
Minds, other. *See* Other minds

Minds in a vat, 198–199. *See also* Brains in a vat
Model-theoretic argument (Putnam), 6, 45, 67–68, 70, 78(n24), 87, 92, 93, 94, 195
Moore, G. E. 36–38, 42, 53(n4), 92, 137–138, 174, 190(n5)
Moore's Paradox, 174
Moral constructivism, 150(n21)
Morality, 139
Moral value. *See* Value, moral
Multiple personality disorder (dissociative identity disorder), 174, 180, 190(n6), 198, 199(nn 3, 4)
Multiplicity, 10, 180

Nagel, Thomas, 16–17, 32
Names. *See Proper names*
Naturalism, 7, 30–31, 58
  moral, 141–142
  See also Epistemology, naturalized
Natural kinds, 3, 130. *See also* Artifacts; Essences; Natures
Natures, 88, 97, 105, 106, 116, 141
  hidden, 7, 84, 92, 96, 106, 142, 193, 194, 197
  simple, 166, 171(n20)
  See also Artifacts; Essences; Natural kinds
Necessity, 35(n32), 37, 48, 69, 127, 146, 176, 177.
  See also Possibility; Truths, necessary
Needs, 26, 122, 144, 145–146, 150(n28), 185
  false, 147
Neurath, Otto, 100(n4), 139, 140, 150(n19)
Neuroses, 2, 3, 4, 11, 12, 32, 80, 81, 197–198, 199(n3)
  epistemic, 1–2, 5–6, 8, 10, 13, 22, 31, 36, 56, 57, 75, 77, 80, 103, 121, 173, 179, 193, 195, 197.
  See also Disorder, psycho-philosophical
  See also Disorder
Neurotic, the, 1, 12, 31–32. *See also* Disorder; Neuroses
New *mestiza* (Anzaldúa), 181, 183, 185
Nietzsche, Friedrich, 131–133, 148(n3), 174
Noncontradiction, 34(n17), 51, 75, 177
Nonnaturalism, 137–138
Non-realism, 72
Normal circumstances, 91, 167 187. *See also* Ordinary circumstances
Normativity, 56(n25)
Notions
  explanatory, 6, 84, 141. *See also* Concepts, explanatory
  intentional, 24, 45, 58, 77(n1)
  nontheoretical, 8. *See also* Claims, nontheoretical; Concepts, nontheoretical
  normative, 2. *See also* Concepts, normative
  theoretical, 70, 74, 83, 85, 135. *See also* Claims, theoretical; Concepts, theoretical

See also Concepts
Nozick, Robert, 30–31, 35(n40), 155

Objectification, 137, 181
Objectivism, 8, 127
  strong, 8, 16, 18, 31–32, 71, 73, 81, 82, 99, 103, 113, 115, 136, 142, 150(n21), 159, 196. *See also* Objectivists, strong; Realism, metaphysical
  See also Objectivists; Realism
Objectivists, 107, 124(n5), 129
  strong, 8, 28, 32, 81, 99, 120, 124(n5), 149(n15), 194, 196. *See also* Objectivism, strong; Realists, metaphysical
  See also Realists
Objectivity, 2, 3, 4, 7, 8, 9, 14, 16, 17, 31, 33(nn 3, 9), 63, 66, 74, 80–81, 123, 128–129, 130, 131, 132, 133–136, 137–139, 143, 148(n8), 151, 170(n8)
  of the world, 2, 13, 14, 16, 32, 135, 138. *See also* World, independence of; World, objective
  See also Objectivism; Realism
Objects, 5, 6, 13, 14, 16, 24–25, 29, 35(n27), 36, 37, 38, 43, 44, 51–52, 53, 63, 66, 67–68, 71, 74, 75, 78(n16), 79(n24), 85, 86, 94, 110, 111, 117, 119, 122, 123, 124(n15), 138, 141, 152, 157, 158, 159, 160, 161, 162, 167, 170(n11), 171(n13), 177, 179, 180–181, 194, 195
  "Platonic", 42, 43
  as posits, 52, 56(nn 30, 31), 92, 141. *See also* Entities, posited; Posits
  private, 159, 167
  simple, 38, 77(n5)
  See also Entities
Observables, 83, 110, 124(n15), 140, 142. *See also* Entities, unobservable
Observations, 68, 96, 110, 138
  inner, 159, 164. *See also* First-person authority, Cartesian conception of; Introspection; Privileged access; Self-knowledge
Observation sentences, 50, 67, 70, 111
Observation statements, 68, 110, 124(n15)
Ogden, C. K., 39
Oppression, 8, 9, 10, 129, 134, 135, 145–146, 147, 149(n11), 180, 181–182, 183, 185, 188
Order (command), 40, 168. *See also* Rules
Ordinary circumstances, 111. *See also* Normal circumstances
Ordinary language. *See* Language, ordinary
Ostensive definition, 177
Ostensive teaching. *See* Teaching, ostensive
Other-knowledge, 10, 159, 160, 165. *See also* Knowledge, of others
Other minds, 33(n5), 52, 160, 169(n1), 171(n21)

Pain, 42–43, 44, 49, 55(n17), 96, 97, 163–164, 167–168, 191–192(n18)
Pain behavior. *See* Behavior, pain
Papineau, David, 16, 34(n16)
Paradigms, 6, 37, 44, 50–51, 52
  and Kuhn, 112–113, 125(n18)
  See also Exemplars; Samples
Patterson, Lee, 130
Peirce, C. S., 71–72, 78(nn 23, 24)
Perry, John, 61
Philosophers, 1–2, 3, 4, 5, 7, 12, 31, 57, 128, 153, 187, 193, 198
  analytic, 18–19, 25, 140, 167. *See also* Philosophy, analytic
  Anglophone, 34(n11), 166. *See also* Philosophy, Anglophone
  environmental, 138
  French, 175
  radical, 10. *See also* Radical theory
  theoretical, 10. *See also* Philosophy, theoretical
  therapeutic, 2, 9. *See also* Philosophy, therapeutic
  See also Philosophy
Philosophical method. *See* Method, philosophical
Philosophical problems, 3, 4, 17, 18, 57, 124, 197. *See also* Philosophy
Philosophical puzzlement, 107, 127. *See also* Philosophy
Philosophical questions, 4, 57–58. *See also* Philosophy
Philosophical writing, 132
Philosophy, 1–2, 3–4, 11(n4), 5, 10, 12, 41, 127, 193, 197
  analytic, 11(n3), 9, 37, 128, 139, 175, 196. *See also* Philosophers, analytic
  Anglophone, 109, 140. *See also* Philosophers, Anglophone
  theoretical, 105. *See also* Philosophers, theoretical; Theoreticians, philosophical; Theoreticism, philosophical; Theory, philosophical
  therapeutic, 4. *See also* Philosophers, therapeutic; Therapists, philosophical; Therapy, philosophical
  See also Method, philosophical; Philosophers; Philosophical problems; Philosophical puzzlement; Philosophical questions; Philosophical writing; Theory, philosophical
Physicalism, 13, 33(n3), 65, 73, 105, 111, 124–125(n15), 140
Picture theory of meaning. *See* Meaning, picture theory of
Plato, 138, 149(nn 15, 16), 150(n16)
Pluralism, 72, 181, 183
  ontological, 180, 182, 185
  See also Fragmentation

Plurality, 173, 182–183, 186. *See also* Fragmentation
Positivism, 135, 139, 140, 141, 142, 144
  logical, 111, 125(n17), 138–141. *See also* Empiricism, logical; Vienna Circle
  See also Empiricism
Posits, 29, 51–52, 92, 142, 171(n13)
  cultural, 56(n30), 171(n13)
  explanatory, 52, 141
  theoretical, 56(n31), 140
  See also Entities, posited; Objects, as posits
Possible worlds, 20–21, 30–31, 68–69, 78(n17), 155, 158, 170(n8)
  logically, 20. *See also* Possibility, logical
  physically, 20–21, 23. *See also* Possibility, physical
  really, 20–21, 24, 35(n34). *See also* Possibility, real
  See also Possibility
Possibility, 19, 20, 27–28, 32, 34(nn 17, 18), 38, 157, 179, 191(n20)
  epistemic, 19, 170(n10)
  explanatory, 19, 33(n9), 157, 194. *See also* Possibility, real
  inductive, 34(n18)
  logical, 5, 19, 24, 27, 28, 34(n17), 149(n15), 157, 179. *See also* Possible worlds, logically
  ontological, 182
  physical, 20–21, 24. *See also* Possible worlds, physically
  real, 5, 7, 9, 19–21, 22, 23–24, 28, 29, 31, 34(n17), 57, 75, 80, 81, 82, 83–84, 95, 99, 115, 119, 120, 125(nn 21, 29), 137, 156, 157–158, 160, 196. *See also* Possibility, explanatory; Possible worlds, really
  See also Necessity; Possible worlds
Power, 8, 9, 123, 148(n1), 132, 136, 145–146, 181, 184
  causal, 79(n28)
  of discourse, 129
  explanatory, 21, 141, 156
  predictive, 67
  synthesizing, 14, 115
  will to, 131
Practices, 4, 16, 41–42, 48, 52, 118, 122–123, 126(n33), 129, 130, 131, 140, 147–148, 188
  cognitive, 47. *See also* Practices, epistemic
  discursive, 29. *See also* Practices, linguistic
  epistemic, 2, 17, 82, 106, 132, 135. *See also* Practices, cognitive
  linguistic, 44, 53, 58, 94, 95, 106, 122. *See also* Practices, discursive
Pragmatics, 53, 90, 91, 118, 122, 172(n23), 174
Pragmatism, 11(n5), 6, 37, 49, 72, 78(nn 23, 24), 81, 84, 85, 89, 90, 105, 110, 111–112, 138
Principle of charity, 119–120, 125(n28), 121–122

Privileged access, 159. *See also* First-person authority, Cartesian conception of; Introspection; Observations, inner; Self-knowledge
Proof (mathematical), 47–48, 55(nn 18, 19), 56(n23)
Properties, 36, 53(n4), 63, 74, 78(n7), 125(n16), 141, 194
  intentional, 170(n11)
  internal, 38, 39, 41, 43, 170–171(n11)
  moral, 141–142
  natural, 75, 79(n28)
  phenomenal, 154
  See also Truth, as a property
Propositions, 28, 36, 38, 40–41, 51, 54(n11), 63, 101(n18), 110
  analytic. *See* Analytic propositions
  atomic, 60
  empirical, 36, 41
  of logic, 36
  of mathematics, 47, 55–56(n23)
Protagoras, 107
Psychoanalysis, 93, 102(n21), 127, 174, 177, 178–179. *See also* Freud, Sigmund; Lacan, Jacques; Psychoanalytic theory
Psychoanalytic theory, 93, 130, 146. *See also* Freud, Sigmund; Lacan, Jacques; Psychoanalysis
Psychological anti-individualism. *See* Anti-individualism
Psychological disorder. *See* Disorder
Psychological individualism. *See* Individualism
Psychological states, 100(n2), 153
  narrow, 153
  See also Intentional attitudes
Psycho-philosophical disorder. *See* Disorder, psycho-philosophical
Psychoses, 12, 165
Psychotic, the, 12, 31
Putnam, Hilary, 1, 11(n3), 5–6, 7, 11, 14, 17, 22–28, 32, 34(n17), 35(nn 28, 29, 32, 35), 36, 44–45, 49, 58, 64, 66–67, 68–77, 77(n3), 78(nn 18, 23, 24), 79(nn 26, 28), 80, 82–83, 84–87, 89, 92, 93, 94, 100(n2), 101(nn 9, 10, 16), 105, 128, 132, 153–154, 169(nn 3, 4), 171(n12), 194, 195

Quietism, 4, 11(n4)
Quine, W. V., 6, 28–29, 37, 42, 45–46, 48–52, 53, 56(nn 25, 27, 30), 71, 92, 101(n18), 109, 110–112, 117, 119, 120

Radical theorists, 139, 144. *See also* Philosophers, radical
Radical theory, 5, 143, 147–148, 150(n23) 151, 158, 182. *See also* Critical theory; Feminism; Marxism; Philosophers, radical; Radical theorists
Ramberg, Bjørn T., 122, 125(n22)
Ramsey, F. P., 101(n14)
Rational acceptability, 86
  ideal, 86. *See also* Justification, ideal; Rational acceptability, idealized; Warrant, ideal
  idealized, 71–72, 86. *See also* Justification, idealized; Rational acceptability, ideal; Warrant, idealized
  See also Justification
Rawls, John, 150(n21)
Realism, 5, 9, 13–14, 15, 16, 27, 29, 33(nn 3, 6, 8), 78(n24), 104, 119, 127–128, 129, 133–139, 142–145, 148, 158, 196, 197
  metaphysical, 5, 8, 9, 14, 15–19, 22, 26–28, 31–32, 33(n6), 35(n28), 36, 40, 57, 58, 59, 66–67, 71, 72–73, 75, 77(n2), 78(nn 23, 24), 80–82, 84, 94, 98–99, 103, 104, 127–128, 133–134, 135, 138, 142, 148, 149(n16), 150(nn 16, 21), 156, 158, 170(n11), 194, 196, 197. *See also* Realists, metaphysical
  modest, 5, 8, 9, 15, 16–18, 22, 27–28, 37, 40, 66, 71, 73, 77(n2), 80, 81–82, 89, 106, 124(n5), 128, 129, 131, 133–134, 135, 139, 145, 158–159, 194, 196, 197. *See also* Realists, modest
  scientific, 56(n31)
  See also Objectivism; Objectivity; Realists; World, independence of
Realists, 14–15, 16, 18, 33(n5), 57, 59, 68, 105, 128, 133, 135, 138, 143
  metaphysical, 5–6, 7, 13, 15, 17, 18, 20, 21–22, 26–28, 31–33, 33(n9), 34(n18), 35(n28), 57–59, 63, 67–68, 77, 80–82, 87, 95, 98–99, 103, 105, 114, 115, 119, 126(n29), 120, 123, 128, 130, 131, 135, 137, 138, 141, 142, 149(n15), 151, 156, 157, 158, 170(nn 8, 11), 194–196. *See also* Realism, metaphysical
  modal, 20
  modest, 5, 9, 15–17, 20, 21, 33(nn 5, 8), 34(n18), 54(n12), 73, 80, 95, 99, 104, 105, 106, 107, 119, 135, 139, 152, 156, 158–159. *See also* Realism, modest
  transcendental, 149(n14)
  See also Objectivism; Objectivity; Realism; World, independence of
Reality, 8, 14, 16, 28, 44, 52, 59, 62, 66–67, 83, 89, 93, 106–107, 108, 114, 119, 131, 136, 143, 145, 147, 150(n21), 176, 179, 180, 183, 198
  absolute conception of, 16
  independent, 16, 66–67, 115, 135–136, 194
  social, 5, 135, 145
  See also World
Reason, 18, 81, 107, 129, 132–133, 136–137, 198
Reductionism, 109, 111, 140–141

Reference, 2, 3, 5–8, 24–27, 32, 36, 45, 49, 52, 58, 63–67, 70–71, 73–76, 77(nn 1, 4), 79(nn 28, 30), 80–83, 84–85, 92, 94–95, 99, 100(n2), 104, 113, 116, 120, 120, 122, 126(n30), 129, 130, 132, 141, 153, 160, 168, 186–187, 191–192(n18), 195, 197
    causal theories of, 6, 8, 35(n35), 59–60, 63, 65, 66–67, 70, 72, 73–74, 75–77, 83, 85, 103, 104, 120, 140, 141, 195, 196
    as an external relation. *See* Externalism; External relations, to objects or referents; External relations, and reference
    indeterminacy of. *See* Indeterminacy, of reference
    interactive conception of, 5, 6, 24–26, 35(n49), 36, 53, 58–59, 65, 71
    as an internal relation. *See* Internalism; Internal relations, to objects or referents; Internal relations, and reference
    metalinguistic, 70, 82–84
    theories of, 2, 6, 7, 8, 52, 65, 78(n8), 83, 84, 121
    Turing Test for, 25–26, 44
Relativism, 8, 9, 18, 89, 103–107, 108, 113, 115, 123, 124(n6), 127–129, 131–132, 133, 135, 136–137, 139, 143, 145, 148, 148(nn 1, 8), 169(n1), 158, 196, 197
    conceptual, 8, 104, 109, 113, 119, 120, 123, 124(n12), 127, 129, 196. *See also* Relativists, conceptual
    epistemic, 103–104, 105–106, 108, 120, 124(n6), 129, 149(n11). *See also* Relativists, epistemic; Truth, and consensus
Relativists, 8–9, 89, 103–104, 105–107, 113–114, 115, 120, 122, 124(nn 3, 5), 126(n30), 127–129, 132, 139, 142–143, 148(n1), 149(n12), 158, 159, 195–196
    conceptual, 8, 104, 115, 119–120, 125(n21), 196. *See also* Relativism, conceptual
    epistemic, 8–9, 120. *See also* Relativism, epistemic; Truth, and consensus
Representation, 32, 76, 89, 129, 146, 177, 186
    demonstrative, 66
    perspicuous, 82, 88, 92
Repression, 174
Res cogitans, 102(n23), 146, 187. *See also* Self, Cartesian; Subjectivity, Cartesian; Subjects, Cartesian
Rhetoric, 12, 107, 124(n6), 132–133, 197
Richards, I. A., 39
Rorty, Richard, 4, 11(nn 3, 5), 17, 26, 33(n8), 35(n29), 37, 47, 49, 53(n1), 62, 71, 76, 77(nn 2, 3), 81, 84, 85, 88, 89–90, 91, 100(n8), 101(nn 10, 14), 103, 104, 105–107, 109, 123, 124(n3), 130, 171(n12), 182–183
Rose, Jacqueline, 146, 186–187, 191(nn 16, 17)
Rozema, David, 100(n2)

Rules, 3, 40–41, 52, 54(nn 13, 14), 102(n20), 110, 116, 123, 132
    semantical, 45, 48, 112
Russell, Bertrand, 36–37, 38–39, 42, 45, 53(n3), 54(n8), 64, 73, 93
Ryle, Gilbert, 159–160, 196

Samples, 54(n14), 44. *See also* Exemplars; Paradigms
Sartre, Jean-Paul, 17, 27, 63, 166–167, 171(n21)
Satisfaction (Tarski), 65, 116
Saussure, Ferdinand de, 130, 177. *See also* Linguistics, structuralist
Scheme-content distinction, 112. *See also* Conceptual schemes; Content
Schiffer, Stephen, 101(n18), 125(n25)
Schlick, Moritz, 78(n14), 100(n4)
Schmitt, Frederick F., 102(n19)
Science, 4, 29, 46, 51, 85, 86, 92, 97, 104, 106, 111, 112–113, 128, 129, 130, 133, 135–137, 139–140, 141–142, 148(nn 1, 8), 149(n11), 150(nn 19, 23), 144, 146, 147–148, 196
    natural, 29, 56(n31), 84, 97, 112, 140, 142, 144, 180
    normal, 113
    social, 104, 140
Scientism, 4, 6, 7, 8, 9, 37, 50, 87, 124(n6), 128, 133–140, 142–143, 148, 149(n11), 150(nn 21, 24), 158, 196
Self, 95, 143, 146, 166–167, 173, 174–176, 179, 180–181, 182, 183, 185–186, 190, 190(nn 6, 8) 192(n22)
    Cartesian, 29. *See also Res cogitans*
    divisions of the, 180, 182, 185. *See also* Fragmentation
    fragmented, 175, 180. *See also* Fragmentation
    unified, 173, 180, 182. *See also* Self-unity
    unity of the, 10, 173, 185, 187, 189. *See also* Self-unity
    See also Subjectivity; Subjects
Self-articulations, 174, 188, 190
Self-ascriptions, 191(n18)
Self-awareness, 166. *See also* Awareness of self
Self-consciousness, 166–167, 181, 185. *See also* Consciousness, of self
Self-deception, 189
Self-descriptions, 10, 143, 145, 151, 184, 189–190, 191(nn 12, 24)
    unity of, 10, 187, 196. *See also* Self-unity
Self-divisions, 10, 173, 175, 180, 190. *See also* Fragmentation
Self-fragmentation, 173. *See also* Fragmentation
Self-ignorance, 10, 147, 152, 164–166, 169, 171(n14), 173, 174–175, 176, 181, 185, 188, 189, 196

Index

Socratic, 165, 167, 188, 196
Self-interpretations, 145, 184, 185, 188–189, 190
Self-knowledge, 9, 10, 143, 145, 148, 151, 159, 160, 161–165, 166–167, 173, 176–177, 178, 188, 196
    authoritative, 154, 157, 170(n7)
    basic, 154, 155, 159, 165–166
    claims, 10, 175, 189
    as epistemic achievement, 152, 161, 164, 165
    as knowing how, 160, 164, 169, 196
    non-Socratic, 159, 160, 164, 169, 173, 196
    Socratic, 10, 152, 165, 167, 169, 173, 189, 190, 196
    See also First-person authority; Introspection; Observations, inner; Privileged access
Self-understanding, 32, 80, 184
Self-unity, 10, 146, 173–174, 183, 185–186, 187–188, 192(n20), 196
    desirability of, 173–174, 181, 188
    possibility of, 173, 181, 192(n20)
    See also Self, unified; Self, unity of the; Self-descriptions, unity of; Subjects, grammatical unity of; Subjects, unified; Unity, of apperception
Sellars, Wilfrid, 16
Seller, Anne, 107, 114, 124(n6), 128, 133–135, 137, 139, 143, 149(n11)
Semantic content. *See* Content, semantic
Semantics, 13–14, 65, 72, 90, 91, 172(n23)
    formal, 33(n2)
Sensations, 94, 146, 151, 154, 162, 164, 167–168, 173, 181, 187, 188, 191(n18)
Sense (*Sinn*), 44, 77(n4), 78(n10), 172(n23). *See also* Connotation; *Sinn*
Sense data, 14, 111, 124(n15), 140, 151
Sense experience. *See* Experience
Senses, the, 2, 5, 19, 21, 25, 29, 34(n18), 95, 98–99, 100(n3), 114, 137, 157
Sentences, 40, 44, 49, 54(n14), 85, 87, 90–91, 101(nn 16, 18), 116–118
    observation. *See* Observation sentences
    theory. *See* Theory, sentences
Sentence-tokens, 90–91
Sign, 40, 177
Signification, 177–179, 186. *See also* Meaning
Signified, 176–177
Signifier, 176–178, 179
Signifying chain, 177–178
Sinn, 64, 77(n4). *See also* Connotation; Sense (*Sinn*)
Skeptic, the, 1, 2–3, 5–6, 15, 17–18, 19, 21–22, 24, 26–27, 28–32, 33(n9), 34(n18), 35(nn 29, 31), 57–58, 68, 75, 76–77, 80, 81, 94, 95, 97, 104, 126(n29), 128, 130, 131, 136, 138, 149(n14), 155–156, 157–158, 170(nn 10, 11), 194, 195, 196, 198
    Cartesian, 34(n15), 138. *See also* Doubts, Cartesian; Skepticism, Cartesian
    external-world, 2, 7, 13, 15, 18, 19, 21, 57, 76, 81, 95, 98, 114, 138, 151, 155. *See also* Skepticism, external-world
    logical, 75
    See also Skepticism
Skeptical doubts. *See* Doubts, skeptical
Skeptical scenarios, 19, 21, 28, 31, 34(n18), 35(n29), 75, 80, 99, 119, 155, 156, 158, 170(n11). *See also* Skepticism
Skepticism, 5, 15–17, 18, 27, 28, 29, 31–32, 33(nn 6, 9, 10), 34(nn 10, 15, 18), 54(n12), 57, 75, 80, 82, 84, 99, 130, 132, 149(n14), 157, 195
    about truth, 129, 132, 133
    Cartesian, 34(n15). *See also* Doubts, Cartesian; Skeptic, Cartesian
    external-world, 5, 9, 19, 22, 26, 28, 31, 77, 119, 120, 156, 158, 159. *See also* Skeptic, external-world
    possible ways of responding to, 21, 157
    rule, 54(n13)
    See also Doubts, skeptical; Skeptical scenarios; Skeptic, the
Skolem-Löwenheim theorem, 67, 69–70
"Slingshot", 61
Smith, Barbara Herrnstein, 8, 106, 107, 124(n5), 129
Socialism, 145
Sociology of knowledge, 150(n23). *See also* Barnes, Barry; Bloor, David
Socrates, 175. *See also* Self-knowledge, Socratic
Solipsism, 105
Speakers, 5, 10, 35(n31), 43, 49, 52, 56(n25), 62–66, 76, 77(n1), 90–91, 100(n8), 115, 116–119, 123, 125(nn 25, 26), 153, 160–161, 163, 164, 168, 171(n14), 178
    competent, 5, 10, 25, 75, 91–92, 125(n26), 188. *See also* Language users, competent; Linguistic competence
Sperber, Dan, 108
Statements, 13–14, 36, 54(n11), 71, 83, 89, 90–91, 94, 111, 120, 126(n29), 139, 140, 174, 195, 196, 197
    counterfactual, 30, 155. *See also* Claims, counterfactual
    moral, 141
    nontheoretical, 141. *See also* Claims, nontheoretical; Discourse, nontheoretical
    observation. *See* Observation statements
    pseudo, 139
    theoretical, 84, 100(n3), 141. *See also* Claims, theoretical; Discourse, theoretical
    theory. *See* Theory, statements
States of affairs, 6, 38, 63, 66. *See also* Facts
Strawson, P. F., 48, 53, 77(n2), 88–89, 171(n23)

Stroud, Barry, 16–18, 81, 97, 130
Structuralism. *See* Althusser, Louis; Lacan, Jacques; Linguistics, structuralist; Marxism, structuralist; Saussure, Ferdinand de
Subjectivism, 142, 143, 150(n21), 169(n1)
Subjectivity, 95–96, 98, 135, 142, 143, 183
 Cartesian, 52. *See also Res Cogitans*
 See also Self; Subjects
Subjects, 145, 146–147 153, 166, 175–176, 178, 181, 182–183, 185, 186–187, 188, 191(n16)
 Cartesian, 173–174, 176. *See also Res cogitans*
 decentered, 175, 191(n16). *See also* Fragmentation
 fragmented, 10. *See also* Fragmentation
 grammatical, 186, 187
 grammatical unity of, 174. *See also* Self-unity
 unified, 173–174. *See also* Self-unity
Subjunctive conditional claims. *See* Claims, subjunctive conditional
Synonymy, 45–46, 47, 48, 50, 109, 110–111, 125(n16)
 stimulus, 48
Synthetic, the, 6, 37, 41–42, 46, 79(n26), 109, 111. *See also* Analytic-synthetic distinction; Synthetic *a priori*, the; Synthetic sentences
Synthetic *a priori*, the, 20, 55–56(n23). *See also A priori*, the; Synthetic, the
Synthetic sentences, 49. *See also* Synthetic, the

Tarski, Alfred, 48, 65–66, 90–91, 100(n4), 101(n16), 115–116, 118–119
Tautologies, 41
Taylor, Charles, 123, 127, 133
Teaching, 43–44, 49, 53, 55(n17), 87, 168, 187
 ostensive, 177
 See also Learning
Terms
 general, 49, 63–64
 indexical, 44, 90, 169(n3), 187
 moral, 142
 natural-kind, 64
 nonreferring, 11(n1)
 nontheoretical, 92, 94, 195. *See also* Claims, nontheoretical
 psychological, 171(n23)
 referring, 5–6, 7, 8, 22, 25, 35(n36), 45, 52, 58, 59, 63–64, 72–73, 76, 167, 191(n18), 195. *See also* Reference
 theoretical, 11(n1), 35(n36), 195. *See also* Claims, theoretical
Theoretical claims. *See* Claims, theoretical
Theoretical concepts. *See* Concepts, theoretical
Theoretical diagnosis. *See* Diagnosis, theoretical
Theoretical discourse. *See* Discourse, theoretical
Theoretical entities. *See* Entities, theoretical
Theoretical notions. *See* Notions, theoretical
Theoretical statements. *See* Statements, theoretical
Theoretical terms. *See* Terms, theoretical
Theoreticians, philosophical, 103, 193. *See also* Philosophy, theoretical
Theoreticism, philosophical, 102(n22), 193. *See also* Philosophy, theoretical
Theories, 7, 14, 56(n31), 84–85, 87, 92, 93, 102(n20), 112, 124(n5), 194, 197
 explanatory, 2, 3, 4, 6–7, 9, 83, 84, 92, 107, 128, 148, 194
 folk, 29–30, 70, 92, 171(n15)
 ideal, 67–68, 70–71, 72–73, 78(n24), 82
 of knowledge. *See* Knowledge, theories of
 of meaning. *See* Meaning, theories of
 metaphysical, 7, 104
 naturalistic, 7, 58
 of reference. *See* Reference, theories of
 scientific, 9, 104, 140–141, 142
 of truth. *See* Truth, theories of
 See also Theory
Theory, 85, 87, 111–112
 burden of, 17
 change, 112–113
 critical. *See* Critical theory
 ethical, 150(n21)
 Marxist. *See* Marxist theory
 moral, 150(n21)
 -neutrality, 110, 111
 philosophical, 103. *See also* Philosophy, theoretical
 psychoanalytic. *See* Psychoanalytic theory
 radical. *See* Radical theory
 sentences, 111
 statements, 68, 140
 See also Theories
Therapists, 198
 philosophical, 2, 4, 6, 8, 103. *See also* Philosophy, therapeutic
Therapy, 1–4, 11
 philosophical, 3, 197. *See also* Philosophy, therapeutic
 See also Diagnosis
Thomson, J. J., 112, 113
Thought, 3, 16, 27, 66, 127, 146, 176
 harmony between, and reality, 44, 52
Thoughts, 36, 53, 96, 97, 155, 157, 159, 170(nn 8, 11), 171(n11)
 cogito-like. *See* Cogito-like thoughts
 grounding, 66, 78(n14)
 unconscious, 93
Tools, 44, 52, 54(n14)
Translatability, 109, 115. *See also* Language, intertranslatable

Translation, 23, 50, 62, 103, 104, 109, 110, 115, 117, 118–119, 121, 123, 125(n27)
  indeterminacy of. *See* Indeterminacy, of translation
  radical, 125(n16), 161
  as a syntactic notion, 119
  See also Interpretation; Language, intertranslatable
Trebilcot, Joyce, 108, 124(n6), 124(n7), 129, 130
True, 82, 88–90, 91, 116, 131
  cautionary use of, 88, 89
  disquotational use of, 88, 90, 91
  endorsing use of, 88–89, 101(n14)
  redundant use of, 91, 101(nn 14, 19)
  See also Truth
Trust, 171(n14)
Truth, 2–3, 4, 7, 8, 9, 11(n2), 13, 14, 17, 33(n2), 37, 48, 49–50, 58, 65, 67, 68, 71, 72, 80, 81, 82, 83, 84–87, 88–92, 95, 99, 100(n8), 101(nn 14, 18, 19), 103–105, 106, 107, 110, 113–114, 115–117, 120, 124(nn 5, 6), 128, 129–132, 133–134, 138, 139, 141, 142, 143, 145, 148, 148(nn 3, 8, 9, 10), 150(n16), 170(n8), 176–177, 178–179, 193–194, 195
  and coherence, 72, 85, 89, 100(n4). *See also* Hegel, G. W. F.; Idealism, absolute; Idealists, absolute; Joachim, H. H.
  and consensus, 103. *See also* Relativism, epistemic; Relativists, epistemic
  and correspondence, 6, 7, 22, 33(n4), 40, 45, 58–60, 62–63, 66–68, 69, 72, 73, 78(n14), 80, 83, 84, 127, 129–130, 131, 140, 141, 142, 195, 196. *See also* Fitting
  and deflation, 87, 102(n19). *See also True*, redundant use of
  and disquotation, 48. *See also True*, disquotational use of
  as epistemic, 13, 89. *See also* Justification, and truth; *True*, endorsing use of
  nihilism about, 105
  paradoxes of, 90. *See also* Liar paradox
  as pragmatic, 90, 118
  as a property, 85, 87, 90, 101(nn 9, 18), 105, 118, 132
  semantic conception of, 90
  skepticism about, 129, 132
  theories of, 2, 4, 7, 8, 56(n27), 82, 84, 86, 87, 92, 100, 104, 105, 106–107, 116, 120, 128, 129, 133, 135, 140, 195, 196, 197
  value of, 131
  will to, 131
  See also True; Truths
Truth-aptness, 10
Truth-assessability, 171(n23)
Truth-conditions, 13, 33(n6), 69, 90, 116, 118
Truth definition, 90, 116

Truth-functions, 50
Truths
  analytic. *See* Analytic truths
  contingent, 46
  logical, 45–46, 50, 110
  mathematical, 50, 55(n23)
  necessary, 46
  synthetic. *See* Synthetic propositions
  See also True; Truth
Truth theory, for a language, 90, 116–117, 118–119
Truth-tracking. *See* Knowledge, as "truth-tracking"
Turing Test for Reference. *See* Reference, Turing Test for
Twin Earth, 100(n2), 153–154

Underdetermination, 29
Understanding, 5–6, 7, 8, 9, 10, 22, 25, 34(n17), 38, 40–41, 44–45, 47–48, 49, 50, 51, 52, 53, 56(n23), 58, 59–60, 73, 76, 83, 87, 89, 91, 93–94, 102(n20), 106, 110, 111, 113, 114, 115, 116–117, 118–119, 120, 121, 122, 123–124, 125(nn 16, 25), 126(nn 29, 30, 34), 135, 143, 152, 161, 162, 167, 168, 180, 182, 183, 184, 188, 194, 195
  self-. *See* Self-understanding
Unity, 102(n23), 96, 97–98
  of apperception, 102(n23), 186, 188. *See also* Self-unity
  epistemological, 98
  grammatical. *See* Self-descriptions, unity of; Subjects, grammatical unity of
  of method. *See* Method, unity of
  of science, 97, 140, 150(n19). *See also* Method, unity of; Unity, topical
  self-. *See* Self-unity
  topical, 97–98. *See also* Method, unity of; Unity, of science
Universals, 13, 64, 101(n18)
Unthinkability, 38, 39
Use (linguistic), 3, 5–6, 7, 8, 10, 13, 22, 25–26, 35(n36), 41–42, 43–44, 47–48, 49, 52, 53, 58, 54(nn 14, 15), 56(nn 25, 31), 59, 64–65, 73, 76–77, 77(n1), 82–84, 87–89, 90–92, 94, 95, 107, 113, 116, 117, 118, 120, 126(n30), 152, 163, 164–165, 167–168, 177–178, 179, 187, 188, 194–195
  expressive, 10, 168, 171(n23), 191, 192(n18)
  figurative, 177. *See also* Language, figurative; Metaphor; Metonymy
  first-person, 10, 168, 173
  and meaning. *See* Meaning, and use
  standard, 5, 25, 43, 48, 49, 58, 91, 162–163, 179
  of *true*. *See True*, cautionary use of; *True*, disquotational use of; *True*, endorsing use of; *True*, redundant use of

Value, 142, 150(n21)
   aesthetic, 137
   judgments, 140
   moral, 137
   objective, 141–142
Verifiability, 138, 139–140
   and meaning, 45. *See also* Verification, and meaning; Verificationism
Verification, 54(n6), 78(n14), 89, 140, 144
   and meaning, 111. *See also* Verifiability, and meaning; Verificationism
Verificationism, 72. *See also* Verifiability, and meaning; Verification, and meaning
Vienna Circle, 55(n17), 78(n14), 100(n4), 139, 140. *See also* Carnap, Rudolf; Empiricism, logical; Hempel, C. G.; Neurath, Otto; Positivism, logical; Schlick, Moritz; Verificationism

Warrant, 4, 13, 86–87, 89, 132
   ideal, 87, 101(n10). *See also* Justification, ideal; Rational acceptability, ideal
   idealized, 87, 105. *See also* Assertibility, warranted: idealized; Justification, idealized; Rational acceptability, idealized
   See also Justification
Williams, Bernard, 16
Williams, Michael, 2–3, 7, 11(nn 1, 2), 17, 29, 31, 33(nn 8, 9), 34(n15), 35(n40), 70–71, 72, 73, 97–99, 102(nn 22, 26, 27)
Wilson, Lynn, 198–199
Wisdom, John, 1, 4, 12–13, 31–32, 57, 198
Wishes, 39, 93, 160–161, 163. *See also* Intentional attitudes
Wittgenstein, Ludwig, 2, 3–4, 6, 7, 11(nn 4, 5), 16, 22, 34(n26), 36, 37, 38–44, 45, 46–47, 49–53, 54(nn 9, 11, 12, 13, 14), 55(nn 19, 22, 23), 59, 60, 64, 71, 72, 73, 77(n5), 78(nn 12, 14), 80, 85, 87–88, 93, 95, 96–97, 102(n24), 125(n20), 121–122, 151, 160, 161, 163, 167–168, 171(nn 17, 23), 172(n23), 173–174, 178, 187, 193, 194, 199(n2), 197
Woolf, Leonard, 150(n17)
World, the, 5, 7–9, 14–18, 19, 22, 24, 25–26, 28–29, 31–32, 34(n18), 40, 44, 49–50, 54(n12), 56(n31), 59, 62–63, 66–67, 68, 69, 73, 74, 76, 78(n7), 79(n28), 81, 84, 92, 94–95, 97, 98–99, 107, 109, 111, 113–115, 117, 119, 120, 122, 126(n33), 129–130, 131, 135–139, 141–142, 149(n15), 151–153, 155, 156, 158–159, 161, 163, 167, 169, 179, 194–195, 197
   external, 1, 3, 5, 7, 13, 15, 17, 18, 19, 21, 29–30, 32, 35(n27), 46, 76, 82, 92, 94, 95, 97–99, 104, 114, 120, 123, 128, 135, 138, 144, 149(n14), 156, 157, 170(n11). *See also* Skeptic, external-world; Skepticism, external-world
   independence of, 5, 14–18, 28, 31, 32, 40, 130, 131, 133, 135, 136, 137, 138, 139, 194. *See also* Objectivity, of the world; World, independent; World, objective
   independent, 130
   objective, 17–18, 81, 130, 131, 142
   objectivity of. *See* Objectivity, of the world; World, objective
   true, 131
   See also Reality
Worlds
   different, 109, 113, 115, 183
   of meaning, 120
   possible. *See* Possible worlds
Wright, Crispin, 11(n4)

For Product Safety Concerns and Information please contact our EU representative GPSR@taylorandfrancis.com
Taylor & Francis Verlag GmbH, Kaufingerstraße 24, 80331 München, Germany

www.ingramcontent.com/pod-product-compliance
Lightning Source LLC
Chambersburg PA
CBHW062214300426
44115CB00012BA/2052